高等学校交通运输与工程类专业教材建设委员会规划教材

English in Traffic Engineering
交通工程专业英语

（第2版）

裴玉龙　**主编**
孙小端　于　雷　**主审**

人民交通出版社股份有限公司
北京

内 容 提 要

本书系统介绍了交通调查、交通规划与设计、公共交通、智能交通等方面的基本概念、相关理论和方法，吸收了包括大数据、车联网、无人驾驶、停车换乘等交通工程新技术研究成果，选取了 48 篇英语文章，根据文章内容将其归纳整理为 24 个单元（Unit），每一单元包含两篇文章及其参考译文，附有单词表（Vocabulary）、习题（Excises）和主题讨论（Topics for Discussion）等模块，以帮助读者对文章进行理解。单元结尾处安排了知识拓展（Knowledge Link）模块，对单元内出现的或与单元内容相关的知识点进行讲解。书后附有英文文献翻译技巧和英语论文写作技巧模块，使学生做到从能读到能写，全面提升专业英语应用能力。

本书可作为交通工程、交通运输、交通设备与控制工程、道路桥梁及渡河工程等专业的本科生教材，也可作为交通工程等相关领域技术人员和管理人员的参考用书。

图书在版编目（CIP）数据

交通工程专业英语/裴玉龙主编. — 2 版. — 北京：人民交通出版社股份有限公司，2020.8
ISBN 978-7-114-16568-9

Ⅰ.①交… Ⅱ.①裴… Ⅲ.①交通工程—英语—高等学校—教材 Ⅳ.①U491

中国版本图书馆 CIP 数据核字（2020）第 084369 号

高等学校交通运输与工程类专业教材建设委员会规划教材
Jiaotong Gongcheng Zhuanye Yingyu

书　　名：	交通工程专业英语（第 2 版）
著 作 者：	裴玉龙
责任编辑：	李　晴　钱　堃
责任校对：	孙国靖　扈　婕
责任印制：	刘高彤
出版发行：	人民交通出版社股份有限公司
地　　址：	(100011)北京市朝阳区安定门外外馆斜街 3 号
网　　址：	http://www.ccpcl.com.cn
销售电话：	(010)59757973
总 经 销：	人民交通出版社股份有限公司发行部
经　　销：	各地新华书店
印　　刷：	北京市密东印刷有限公司
开　　本：	787×1092　1/16
印　　张：	21.25
字　　数：	575 千
版　　次：	2002 年 12 月　第 1 版 2020 年 8 月　第 2 版
印　　次：	2024 年 2 月　第 2 版　第 2 次印刷　总第 16 次印刷
书　　号：	ISBN 978-7-114-16568-9
定　　价：	49.00 元

（有印刷、装订质量问题的图书由本公司负责调换）

高等学校交通运输与工程类专业(道路、桥梁、隧道与交通工程)教材建设委员会

主 任 委 员:沙爱民 (长安大学)

副主任委员:梁乃兴 (重庆交通大学)
陈艾荣 (同济大学)
徐 岳 (长安大学)
黄晓明 (东南大学)
韩 敏 (人民交通出版社股份有限公司)

委 员:(按姓氏笔画排序)

马松林	(哈尔滨工业大学)	王云鹏	(北京航空航天大学)
石 京	(清华大学)	申爱琴	(长安大学)
朱合华	(同济大学)	任伟新	(合肥工业大学)
向中富	(重庆交通大学)	刘 扬	(长沙理工大学)
刘朝晖	(长沙理工大学)	刘寒冰	(吉林大学)
关宏志	(北京工业大学)	李亚东	(西南交通大学)
杨晓光	(同济大学)	吴瑞麟	(华中科技大学)
何 民	(昆明理工大学)	何东坡	(东北林业大学)
张顶立	(北京交通大学)	张金喜	(北京工业大学)
陈 红	(长安大学)	陈 峻	(东南大学)
陈宝春	(福州大学)	陈静云	(大连理工大学)
邵旭东	(湖南大学)	项贻强	(浙江大学)
胡志坚	(武汉理工大学)	郭忠印	(同济大学)
黄 侨	(东南大学)	黄立葵	(湖南大学)
黄亚新	(解放军理工大学)	符锌砂	(华南理工大学)
葛耀君	(同济大学)	裴玉龙	(东北林业大学)
戴公连	(中南大学)		

秘 书 长:孙 玺 (人民交通出版社股份有限公司)

第2版前言

　　交通工程专业英语(English in Traffic Engineering)是为了满足高等院校交通运输类专业英语课程教学的需要,根据高等院校培养目标的要求而编写的。希望通过对本书的学习,学生能够掌握必要的专业词汇,具备专业英语阅读能力、专业英语文献翻译和专业论文英语写作的初步能力,使英语学习与专业知识学习有机地结合在一起。本书使用对象为已完成基础英语课程学习的交通运输类专业本科、专科学生和研究生,也可供有关专业技术人员参考使用。本书按48学时编写,教师在教学安排上可根据实际情况灵活掌握,选择全部或部分内容进行教学。

　　本书题材选自国外正式出版物,如专业学术著作、期刊等,选题广泛,相较于第1版有如下改动:(1) 在篇幅上,从25个单元调整为24个单元,保留了第1版50篇文章中的31篇文章(课文14篇、阅读材料17篇),并添加了17篇新文章;(2) 在内容上,新增大数据、车联网、无人驾驶、停车换乘等方面的内容;(3) 在结构上,考虑到学生反映的需求,新增了课文(Text)参考译文、知识拓展(Knowledge Link),以及翻译技巧(Translation Skills)、写作技巧(Writing Skills)等模块,删减了第1版中的注释(Notes)模块。本书在编写中吸取了我国相近学科专业英语教材的优点和基础英语课程教学的经验。本书在符合专业英语教学需要的同时,试图使读者在有限的篇幅内尽可能多地了解现代交通工程专业技术的主要内容。

　　本书由东北林业大学裴玉龙教授担任主编,美国路易斯安那大学孙小端教授和德克萨斯南方大学于雷教授担任主审。全书由东北林业大学裴玉龙、胡宝雨、马丹编写,具体分工为:裴玉龙(1~6单元、Translation Skills、Writing Skills)、胡宝雨

(17~24单元、Vocabulary)、马丹(9~16单元、Key to Exercises)。曹永臣、钟晓斌、于舰、王乃卉参加了资料搜集整理、参考译文翻译、练习题试做、插图绘制与文字校核工作,具体分工为:曹永臣(1~6单元)、钟晓斌(7~12单元)、于舰(13~18单元)、王乃卉(19~24单元)。

  本书在编写过程中得到了各兄弟院校及有关单位的帮助和支持,同时引用了所列参考文献中的部分内容,在此向各兄弟院校、有关单位、参考文献作者一并致以衷心的感谢。

  由于水平所限,加之时间较为仓促,本书难免存在不少缺点和错误,恳请读者提出宝贵的批评意见。

裴玉龙

2020年2月于哈尔滨

目录

Unit 1　Traffic and Transport ··· 1
　　Text ··· 1
　　Reading Material　Traffic Engineering ································· 5
　　Knowledge Link ·· 9
Unit 2　Traffic Surveys ··· 10
　　Text ·· 10
　　Reading Material　Theoretical Relationship between Speed, Flow and Density ············· 15
　　Knowledge Link ··· 22
Unit 3　Four-step Planning Procedure ····································· 23
　　Text ·· 23
　　Reading Material　Traffic Assignment ································ 29
　　Knowledge Link ··· 32
Unit 4　One-way Traffic ··· 34
　　Text ·· 34
　　Reading Material　Multimodal Freight Transportation Planning ············· 40
　　Knowledge Link ··· 43
Unit 5　Traffic Management ··· 45
　　Text ·· 45
　　Reading Material　Traffic Surveillance ······························ 50
　　Knowledge Link ··· 54
Unit 6　Traffic Signal Timing ··· 55
　　Text ·· 55

Reading Material　Traffic Signal System Timing for Arterial Routes ………… 59
　Knowledge Link ………………………………………………………………… 64
Unit 7　Urban Transit Mode …………………………………………………… 65
　Text …………………………………………………………………………… 65
　Reading Material　Rail Transit ……………………………………………… 70
　Knowledge Link ………………………………………………………………… 74
Unit 8　Parking ………………………………………………………………… 76
　Text …………………………………………………………………………… 76
　Reading Material　Parking：Design and Control ………………………… 81
　Knowledge Link ………………………………………………………………… 86
Unit 9　Park and Ride ………………………………………………………… 88
　Text …………………………………………………………………………… 88
　Reading Material　Transit-Oriented Development ………………………… 92
　Knowledge Link ………………………………………………………………… 96
Unit 10　Bikeways ……………………………………………………………… 97
　Text …………………………………………………………………………… 97
　Reading Material　Levels of Service for Pedestrians …………………… 101
　Knowledge Link ………………………………………………………………… 106
Unit 11　Freeways ……………………………………………………………… 108
　Text …………………………………………………………………………… 108
　Reading Material　Basic Freeway Segments ……………………………… 113
　Knowledge Link ………………………………………………………………… 119
Unit 12　Intersections ………………………………………………………… 120
　Text …………………………………………………………………………… 120
　Reading Material　Grade-separated Junctions and Interchanges ………… 125
　Knowledge Link ………………………………………………………………… 130
Unit 13　Geometric Design Controls and Criteria ………………………… 132
　Text …………………………………………………………………………… 132
　Reading Material　Horizontal and Vertical Alignment …………………… 138
　Knowledge Link ………………………………………………………………… 141
Unit 14　Sight Distance ………………………………………………………… 143
　Text …………………………………………………………………………… 143
　Reading Material　Capacity of Signalized Intersections ………………… 149
　Knowledge Link ………………………………………………………………… 153

Unit 15　Highway Capacity	154
Text	154
Reading Material　Level of Service	161
Knowledge Link	165
Unit 16　Reinforcement in Concrete Road Slabs	166
Text	166
Reading Material　Flexible Pavement	170
Knowledge Link	172
Unit 17　Road Traffic Safety	173
Text	173
Reading Material　Roadside Safety	178
Knowledge Link	183
Unit 18　The Environmental Effects of Highway Traffic Noise	184
Text	184
Reading Material　The Environmental Effects of Highway Traffic Pollution	190
Knowledge Link	194
Unit 19　Economics and Transportation Engineering	196
Text	196
Reading Material　Problems of Benefit-cost Analysis	200
Knowledge Link	204
Unit 20　Transport Telematic	205
Text	205
Reading Material　Electronic Toll Collection	210
Knowledge Link	214
Unit 21　ITS Offers A New Approach	216
Text	216
Reading Material　GIS and GPS in ITS	221
Knowledge Link	224
Unit 22　Big Data in Traffic	225
Text	225
Reading Material　Application of Big Data	230
Knowledge Link	234
Unit 23　Internet of Vehicles	235
Text	235

Reading Material The IoV Technology ········· 240
  Knowledge Link ········· 245
Unit 24 Unmanned Ground Vehicle ········· 246
  Text ········· 246
  Reading Material The Technologies of Unmanned Driving ········· 250
  Knowledge Linkage ········· 253
Key to Exercises ········· 255
Vocabulary ········· 284
Translation Skills ········· 303
Writing Skills ········· 315
References ········· 326

Unit 1

Traffic and Transport

Text

1. Traffic

Traffic on roads consists of road users who use the public road for purposes of travel at the same time, either singly or together, including pedestrians, ridden or herded arimals, cars, streetcars, buses and other conveyances. Traffic laws are the laws which govern the traffic and regulate vehicles, while rules of the road are both the laws and the informal rules that may develop over time to facilitate the orderly and timely flow of traffic.

Organized traffic generally has well-established priorities, lanes, right-of-way, and the traffic control at intersections.

Traffic is formally organized in many jurisdictions, with marked lanes, junctions, intersections, interchanges, traffic signals or signs. Traffic is often classified by types as heavy motor vehicles (e. g. , cars, trucks), other vehicles (e. g. , mopeds, bicycles), and pedestrians. Different classes can have the same or different speed limits and easement. Some jurisdictions may have very detailed and complex rules of the road while others rely more on drivers' common sense and willingness to cooperate.

Organization typically produces a better combination of travel safety and efficiency. Events, which disrupt the flow and may cause traffic to degenerate into a disorganized mess, include road construction, collisions, and debris in the roadway. A complete breakdown of organization may result in traffic congestion and gridlock. Simulators of organized traffic frequently involve queuing theory, stochastic processes and equations of mathematical physics applied to traffic flow.

2. Transport

Transport is the movement of humans, animals and goods from one location to another. In other words, the action of transport is defined as a particular movement of an organism or thing from the point A to point B. Modes of transportation include air, land (rail and road), water, cable, pipeline and space. The fields can be divided into infrastructures, vehicles and operations. Transport is important because it enables trade between people, which is essential for the development of civilizations.

Transport infrastructure consists of the fixed installations, including roads, railways, airways, waterways, canals; and pipelines and terminals such as airports, railway stations, bus stations, warehouses, trucking terminals, refueling depots and seaports. Terminals may be used both for interchanges of passengers and cargoes and for maintenance.

Vehicles traveling in these networks include automobiles, bicycles, buses, trains, trucks, helicopters, watercraft, spacecraft and aircraft.

Operations deal with the way the vehicles are operated and the procedures set for this purpose, including financial, legal and policy aspects. In the transport industry, operation rights and ownership of infrastructures can be either public or private, depending on the country policies and manners in which the infastuctures are operated.

Passenger transport may be public, as operators provide scheduled services, or private. Transport plays an important part in economic growth and globalization, but most types cause air pollution and use large amounts of lands. While it is heavily subsidized by governments, good planning of transport is essential to make orderly traffic flow and restrain urban sprawl.

New Words and Expressions

pedestrian [pəˈdestrɪənz]	n. 步行者;行人　adj. 徒步的
streetcar [striːtkɑː(r)]	n. 有轨电车
conveyance [kənˈveɪəns]	n. 运输;运输工具;财产让与
facilitate [fəˈsɪlɪteɪt]	vt. 促进;帮助;使容易
well-established	既定的;固定下来的;久负盛名的
lane [leɪn]	n. 小路;车道
right-of-way	通行权;优先权;先行权;路权
jurisdiction [ˌdʒʊərɪsˈdɪkʃn]	n. 司法权;管辖权;管辖区域
truck [trʌk]	n. (铁路上运送货物或动物的)敞篷车,无盖货车;卡车　v. 用卡车装运
moped [ˈməʊped]	n. 机器脚踏车;摩托自行车
easement [ˈiːzmənt]	n. 地役权;缓和;减轻
common sense	常识

debris [ˈdebriː]	n. 残骸;碎片;残渣;垃圾;废弃物
congestion [kənˈdʒestʃən]	n. (交通)拥挤
gridlock [ˈgrɪdlɔk]	n. 交通堵塞
simulator [ˈsɪmjuleɪtə(r)]	n. 模拟器;仿真器
queuing theory	排队论
stochastic processes	随机过程
organism [ˈɔːgənɪzəm]	n. 有机体;生物体;有机组织;有机体系
pipeline [ˈpaɪplaɪn]	n. 输油管道;输气管道;输送管线
infrastructure [ˈɪnfrəstrʌktʃə(r)]	n. 基础建设;基础设施
installation [ˌɪnstəˈleɪʃn]	n. 安装的设备;装置;安装
canal [kəˈnæl]	n. 运河;灌溉渠
railway station	火车站
warehouse [ˈweəhaus]	n. 仓库;货栈;货仓
refueling depot	加油站
cable [ˈkeɪbl]	n. 缆绳;钢索;电缆
trucking [trʌkɪŋ]	n. 货车运输;货车运输业
depot [ˈdepəu]	n. 仓库;停车场;航空站
seaport [ˈsiːpɔːt]	n. 海港;港口都市
cargo [ˈkaːgəu]	n. (船或飞机装载的)货物
helicopter [ˈhelɪkɒptə(r)]	n. 直升机
watercraft [ˈwɔːtəkraːft]	n. 船只;水运工具;驾船技术
financial [faɪˈnænʃl]	adj. 财政的;财务的;金融的
legal [ˈliːgl]	adj. 法律的;法律允许的;合法的
schedule [ˈʃedjuːl]	n. 工作计划;日程安排;清单 v. 安排;预定;将……列入计划表
subsidize [ˈsʌbsɪdaɪz]	vt. 以津贴补助;资助
globalization [ˌgləubəlaɪˈzeɪʃn]	n. 全球化
urban sprawl	城市扩张

Exercises

I True or false.

(　　)(1) Organized traffic generally has well-established priorities, lanes, right-of-way, and the traffic control at intersections.

(　　)(2) Every jurisdiction has very detailed and complex rules of the road.

(　　)(3) A complete breakdown of organization may result in traffic congestion and gridlock.

(　　)(4) Transport enables trade between people, which is essential for the development of civilizations.

(　　)(5) In the transport industry, operation rights and ownership of infrastructures can be always public.

(　　)(6)Good planning of transport is essential to make orderly traffic flow and restrain urban sprawl.

II Complete the following sentences.

(1)Traffic is often classified by types as _____, other vehicles (e.g., mopeds, bicycles), and _____.

(2)Terminals may be used both for _____ and for maintenance.

(3)Operations deal with _____ and _____, including financial, legal and policy aspects.

(4)Transport plays an important part in economic growth and globalization, but most types cause _____ and _____.

(5)Organization typically produces a better combination of _____ and _____.

III Answer the following questions.

(1)What are the definitions of traffic laws and rules of the road?

(2)What does organized traffic generally have?

(3)What do simulations of organized traffic frequently involve?

(4)Why is transport important?

(5)What does the operation rights and ownership of infrastructures in the transport industry depend on?

Topics for Discussion

(1)What is the difference between traffic and transport?

(2)Why a complete breakdown of organization may result in traffic congestion and gridlock?

(3)Why does transport play an important part in economic growth and globalization? And how does transport cause air pollution and use large amounts of lands?

参 考 译 文

交通和运输

1. 交通

道路交通由同一时间使用公共道路出行的一种或几种道路"使用者"组成,包括行人、放牧或用于骑乘的动物、汽车、有轨电车、公共汽车和其他交通工具。交通法是指用来管理交通和车辆的法律,而道路的规则包含法律和非正式规定,并随时间的推移而发展,以促进交通流的有序及适时调整。

交通组织通常具有既定的优先权、车道划分、通行权以及交叉路口控制方式。

在多数辖区内都有正式交通组织,包含车道标线、道路节点、平面交叉路口、互通式立交、交通信号或交通标志。道路交通通常按其"使用者"类型不同,分为重型机动车辆(如汽车、卡车)、其他车辆(如电动自行车、自行车)和行人。"使用者"根据不同的类型可以有相同或不同的速度限制和通行权。有些辖区会有非常详细和复杂的道路规则,而其他辖区则更加依赖驾驶人的常识积累和自觉。

交通组织通常会将出行安全和出行效率更好地结合起来。扰乱交通流并可能导致交通混乱的事件包括道路施工、碰撞和道路上出现废弃物。交通组织的彻底崩溃可能会导致拥挤和堵塞。对交通组织的模拟通常涉及排队理论、随机过程和应用于交通流的数理公式。

2. 运输

运输是指人类、动物和货物等从一个地方转移到另一个地方。换言之,运输为生物或物体从 A 点到 B 点的特定移动。运输方式包括空运、陆运(铁路和公路)、水运、电缆运输、管道运输和太空运输。运输领域可划分为基础设施、交通工具和营运三部分。运输之所以重要,是因为它能促进人与人之间的贸易,这对于文明的发展至关重要。

交通基础设施由道路、铁路、航线、航道、运河、管道等固定设施,以及机场、火车站、公共汽车站、仓库、货运站、加油站和海港等枢纽组成。枢纽可用于乘客和货物的交换以及交通工具的维护。

在这些运输网中运行的交通工具包括小汽车、自行车、公共汽车、火车、卡车、直升机、船舶、宇宙飞船和航天器。

运营部门管理车辆的运营方式,并为管理车辆而设定规程,包括经济、法律和政策等方面的规程。在运输业中,基础设施的运营权和所有权可以是政府的,也可以是私人的,这取决于基础设施所在国家的政策及设施的运营方式。

客运可以是公用的,像运营商提供预订服务那样,也可以是私人的。运输在经济增长和经济全球化中起着重要作用,但大多数运输都会造成空气污染,并占用大量土地。虽然政府已经在这些方面提供了大量补贴,但良好的交通规划对有序交通流的产生和城市土地扩张的抑制至关重要。

Reading Material

Traffic Engineering

1. Definition

Traffic engineering uses engineering techniques to achieve the safe and efficient movement of people and goods on roadways. It focuses mainly on research for safe and efficient traffic flow, such as road geometry characteristics, sidewalks and crosswalks, cycling infrastructure, traffic signs, road surface markings and traffic lights. Traffic engineering deals with the functional part of transportation system, except the infrastructures provided.

2. Disciplines associated with traffic engineering

(1) Transport engineering

Transport engineering is the application of technology and scientific principles to the planning, functional design, operation and management of facilities for any mode of transport in order to provide for the safe, efficient, rapid, comfortable, convenient, economical, and environmentally compatible movement of people and goods transport.

(2) Pavement engineering

Pavement engineering is a branch of civil engineering that uses engineering techniques to design and maintain flexible (asphalt) and rigid (concrete) pavements. It includes streets and highways and involves knowledge of agrology, hydraulics, and material properties. Pavement engineering involves new construction as well as rehabilitation and maintenance of existing pavements. Maintenance often involves using engineering judgment to make maintenance repairs with the highest long-term benefit and lowest cost. The Pavement Condition Index (PCI) is an example of an engineering approach applied to existing pavements maintenance. Another example is the use of a Falling Weight Deflectometer (FWD) to non-destructively test existing pavements. Calculation of pavement layer strengths can be performed from the resulting deflection data. The two methods—empirical or mechanistic—are used to determine pavement layer thicknesses.

(3) Bicycle transportation planning engineering

Bicycle transportation planning engineering is a discipline related to transportation engineering and transportation planning concerning bicycles as a mode of transport and the concomitant study, design and implementation of cycling infrastructure. It includes the study and design of dedicated transport facilities for cyclists (e.g. cyclist-only paths) as well as mixed-mode environments, where cyclists share roads and paths with vehicular and foot traffic, and the study of how both of these examples can be made to work safely. In jurisdictions such as the United States, it is often practiced in conjunction with planning for pedestrians as a part of active transportation planning.

(4) Highway engineering

Highway engineering is an engineering discipline branching from civil engineering that involves the planning, design, construction, operation, and maintenance of roads, bridges, and tunnels to ensure safe and effective transportation of people and goods. Highway engineering became prominent towards the latter half of the 20th Century after World War II. Standards of highway engineering are continuously being improved. Highway engineers must take into account future traffic flow, design of highway intersections/interchanges, geometric alignment and design, highway pavement materials and design, structural design of pavement thickness, and pavement maintenance.

(5) Transportation planning

Transportation planning is the process of defining future policies, goals, investments and designs to prepare for future needs to move people and goods to destinations. As practiced today, it is a collaborative process that incorporates the inputs of many stakeholders including various government agencies, the public and private businesses. Transportation planners apply amulti-modal and/or a comprehensive approaches to analyzing the wide range of alternatives and impacts on the transportation system to influence beneficial outcomes.

(6) Urban planning

Urban planning is a technical and political process concerned with the development and design of land use and the environment construction, including air, water and the infrastructure passing into and out of urban areas, such as transportation, communications, and distribution networks. Urban planning deals with physical layout of human settlements. The primary concern is the public welfare, which includes considerations of efficiency, sanitation, protection and use of the environment as well as effects on social and economic activities. Urban planning is considered an interdisciplinary field that includes social, engineering and design sciences. It is closely related to the field of urban design, and some urban planners provide designs for streets, parks, buildings and other urban areas. In various areas worldwide urban planning is also referred to as regional planning, town planning, city planning, rural planning, urban development or a combination of the above.

(7) Human factors engineering

Human factors and ergonomics (commonly referred to as human factors) is the application of psychological and physiological principles to the design of products, processes and systems. The goal of human factors is to reduce human error, increase productivities and enhance safety and comfort with a specific focus on the interaction between human and things of interest.

Exercises

I True or false.

(   ) (1) Traffic engineering deals with the functional part of transportation system, and the infrastructures provided.

(   ) (2) Highway engineers do not need to take into account future traffic flow, design of highway intersections/interchanges, geometric alignment and design.

(   ) (3) Transportation planning is a collaborative process that incorporates the inputs of many stakeholders including various government agencies, the public and private businesses.

(   ) (4) Urban planning is only a technical and process concerned with the development and design of land use and the environment construction, including air, water, and the infrastructure passing into and out of urban areas.

(   ) (5) Urban planning deals with physical layout of human settlements.

II Complete the following sentences.

(1) Traffic engineering uses engineering techniques to achieve _____.

(2) Bicycle transportation engineering includes the study and design of _____ as well as _____ and how both of these examples can be made to work safely.

(3) The goal of human factors is _____, _____ and _____ with a specific focus on the interaction between the humans and the things of interest.

(4) Pavement engineering is a branch of civil engineering that uses engineering techniques to _____.

(5) Bicycle transportation planning engineering is a discipline related to _____ and transportation planning _____ and the concomitant study, design and implementation of cycling infrastructure.

Ⅲ Answer the following questions.

(1) What is the definition of traffic engineering?
(2) What disciplines are associated with traffic engineering?
(3) What is highway engineers must take into account?
(4) What is the definition of transportation planning?
(5) What is the goal of human factors?

参 考 译 文

交 通 工 程

1. 定义

交通工程使用工程技术实现人和货物在道路上安全及高效的运输。交通工程的研究目的主要是为了实现安全和高效的交通流,研究的内容包括道路几何特征、人行道和人行横道、自行车基础设施、交通标志、路面标线以及交通信号灯。交通工程研究交通运输系统的功能部分,但不包括系统提供的基础设施。

2. 交通工程相关学科

(1)运输工程

运输工程是将技术和科学原理应用于运输设施的规划、功能设计、运营和管理中,以实现人及货物安全、高效、快速、舒适、方便、经济和环保的运输。

(2)路面工程

路面工程是土木工程的一个分支,它利用工程技术来设计和保养柔性(沥青)路面及刚性(混凝土)路面,包括城市道路和公路,并涉及土壤学、水力学和材料特性的知识。路面工程包括新路面的建设以及现有路面的修复和保养。路面的保养通常需要利用工程判断方法,并以长期效益最高和成本最低为目标。路面状况指数(PCI)就是工程方法应用于现有路面维修的例子。另一个例子是使用落锤式弯沉仪(FWD)对现有路面进行无损检测,可根据产生的挠度数据计算路面层的强度。这两种方法(经验法和机械法)都用于确定路面层的厚度。

(3)自行车交通规划工程

自行车交通规划工程是指在交通工程和交通规划中与自行车有关的一门学科,内容包括自行车基础设施的研究、设计和建设,包括研究和设计自行车专用设施(如自行车专用道)和混合交通环境(自行车与车辆和行人共享道路和路线的情况)以及研究如何在以上情况下安全地运行。美国等辖区的交通规划中,自行车规划通常作为主动交通规划的一部分,与步行规划协同实施。

(4)公路工程

公路工程是土木工程的一个分支学科,它涉及道路、桥梁和隧道的规划、设计、施工、运营和保养,以确保人和货物安全、高效的运输。在第二次世界大战后的20世纪后半叶,公路工程的地位变得尤为重要。公路工程标准不断提高。公路工程师必须考虑未来的交通流、公路平面交叉口/互通式立交的设计、几何线形设计、公路路面材料设计、路面厚度结构设计和路面保养等问题。

(5) 运输规划

运输规划是明确未来政策、目标、投资和设计的过程,为满足未来人和货物向目的地移动的需求做准备。运输规划是一个合作的过程,它融合许多利益相关者的投入。这些利益相关者包括各种政府机构、公共企业和私营企业,正如当今的实践结果。运输规划者采用多模式和(或)综合方法,分析各种备选方案及其对运输系统和最终效益的影响。

(6) 城市规划

城市规划是一个包含技术和政治的过程,涉及土地利用和环境建设(包括空气、水,以及将物资传递进出市区的基础设施,如运输、通信和配电网)的开发和设计。城市规划研究人类居住区的物理布局,首要关注的是公共福利,包括效率、卫生、保护和利用环境,以及对社会活动和经济活动的影响。城市规划是一个跨学科的领域,包括社会科学、工程科学和设计科学。它与城市设计领域密切相关,一些城市规划者为街道、公园、建筑和其他城市内的区域提供设计。在世界各地,城市规划又称区域规划、城镇规划、市区规划、乡村规划、城市开发,或以上几种规划的组合。

(7) 人因工程

人的因素和人体工程学(通常指人的因素方面)是指将心理学和生理学原理应用于产品、工序和系统的设计中。人因工程的目标是减少人为错误,提高生产力,提高安全性和舒适性,特别关注人与感兴趣的事物之间的交互作用。

Knowledge Link

Institute of Transportation Engineers

The Transport Engineer Association is an international educational and scientific association of transport professionals, responsible for meeting traffic and safety needs, working to improve mobility and safety for all users of transport systems, and helping to build intelligent and livable communities. Established in 1930, Institute of Transportation Engineers (ITE) is a professional transportation group composed of traffic engineers, traffic planners, consultants, educators, technicians and researchers. Through meetings, seminars, publications and networks of more than 15000 members working in more than 90 countries, ITE is a source of expertise, knowledge and idea.

ITE helps to apply technology and scientific principles to the research, planning, functional design, implementation, operation, policy formulation and management of any ground transportation mode. Through its products and services, ITE promotes the professional development of its members, supports and encourages education, promotes research, develops public awareness projects and serves as a channel for exchanging professional information.

Although it is a worldwide organization, its members are mainly concentrated in North America, especially in the United States. ITE is also a standard-setting organization designated by the U. S. Department of Transportation (U. S. DOT). ITE is also known for publishing articles on parking generation and parking demand.

Unit 2
Traffic Surveys

Text

Traffic engineering is used to either improve an existing situation or, in the case of a new facility, to ensure that the facility is correctly and safely designed and adequate for the demands that will be placed on it.

We have to know the present day demands and patterns of movement, so that the new measures can be designed adequately. With a new road or facility, there is obviously not existing demands to base the design on; therefore, we have to estimate the expected demands.

If a new facility, for example, a bypass or a new cycle track, replaces or relieves existing roads, we can estimate the proportion of traffic that could be expected to transfer by using a traffic assignment.

If the facility is completely new, for example a road in a new development, then the expected traffic and the scale of the construction needed has to be estimated in another way. This is usually done by a transport impact analysis, which will seek to assess the likely level of traffic by referring to the traffic generated by similar developments elsewhere.

In either case the starting point should be a traffic survey.

The main purpose for undertaking a traffic survey is to provide an objective measure of an existing situation. A survey provides a measure of conditions within the survey period. A survey does not give a definitive description of a situation for a period of time or a day, and if the results are to be used as representative of "normal" traffic conditions, the survey must be designed and used with caution.

Traffic volume also tends to vary by day of the week. On a typical urban road, traffic volume tends to build during the weekdays and to a peak on Friday. Flow is lower at the weekend, when fewer people work, and lowest on Sunday; although the introduction of Sunday trading has affected the balance of traveling at the weekend.

The variation in pattern of travel over the year depends a great deal upon location. In urban areas, which are employment centers, flow drops during the summer period when schools are closed and workers tend to take annual holidays. This is balanced by a reverse trend in holiday areas, where traffic volume increases dramatically in July and August, and roads, which are adequate most of the year, become heavily congested. The effect can be less dramatic on interurban roads, other than those providing access to holiday areas, as to an extent, the decline in interurban business travel during the summer is offset by tourism.

The information above shows that the pattern of flow on any road can be highly variable, and in deciding when and where to undertake a traffic survey, it is important to ensure that the survey provides a fair measure of the traffic conditions that are being studied. To take the example of the roads in a tourist area, a traffic survey on August public holiday would measure peak traffic conditions. As these levels occur only one or two days a year, there would be little point in using this data as a basis for design, as the scheme should be for traffic conditions of most of the time.

Generally, traffic surveys should not be planned to measure the peak of the peak but to measure the "normal" peak conditions. Trunk road surveys may require a full year's survey of traffic.

The starting point in defining a traffic survey is to decide what question has to be answered and choose the type of survey accordingly. If the survey is not adequately planned, there is a danger that the wrong data will be collected and the traffic situation will not be correctly understood.

The only exception to this rule occurs when one is faced with a complex situation where it may not be possible, at first, to adequately understand what is going on, in terms of traffic volume and circulation.

Some surveys are adequate for measuring traffic volume and direction of movement at a single point or a single junction. However, if we wish to understand movement over a wider area, then other methods have to be used. Three techniques are described below.

(1) Number plate survey

We may wish to understand how traffic is circulating in a limited area. This could be, for example, a residential area, or even a town center ring road where we wish to understand if traffic uses the ring road or passes through the town center.

The technique used is to record the registration mark of each vehicle as it enters and leaves the system being studied and then to match the registration marks, to establish how a vehicle traveled through the road system being studied. It is not normally necessary to record the full registration mark.

(2) Origin and destination survey

The alternative way to establish where drivers are traveling is to ask them, using an Origin and Destination (OD) survey. Various types of OD surveys are used as a part of the transport planning process. However, this is beyond the scope of this paper and is not explored here. The standard techniques are roadside interview survey and self-completion questionnaire.

In most cases it will be impossible to carry out a 100% survey of drivers. Therefore, we must rely on a response from a sample of drivers in the traffic flow. Clearly, if the survey results are to be relied on, the sample should be unbiased with all types of vehicles and movements represented. The screen line of the OD surveys is shown in Figure 2-1.

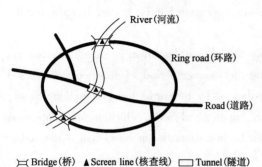

Figure 2-1　The screenline of the OD surveys
（OD 调查的核查线）

(3) Roadside interview survey

At a roadside interview survey, samples of drivers are stopped at the side of the road and asked their origin and destination, plus any other data, which could be of relevance, such as journey purpose.

New Words and Expressions

survey [ˈsɜːveɪ]	vt. 调查;测量　vi. 测量土地　n. 测量;调查
in the case of	在……的情况下;假如;如果发生
facility [fəˈsɪlətɪ]	n. 便利;条件;设备;设施工具
relieve [rɪˈliːv]	vt. 减轻;解除;缓解
bypass [ˈbaɪpɑːs]	n. 旁路;旁道;支路
cycle track	自行车道
proportion [prəˈpɔːʃn]	n. 部分;份额;比例
assignment [əˈsaɪnmənt]	n. 分配;委派;任务;(课外)作业
seek [siːk]	vt. 寻找;探索;寻求
assess [əˈses]	vt. 估定;评定
generate [ˈdʒenəreɪt]	vt. 产生;引起;造成
undertake [ˌʌndəˈteɪk]	vt. 承担;许诺;保证
representative [ˌreprɪˈzentətɪv]	adj. 典型的;具有代表性的
traffic flow	交通流
variation [ˌveərɪˈeɪʃn]	n. 变化;变动;变量;变异
reverse [rɪˈvɜːs]	n. 相反;背面;反面;倒退　adj. 相反的;颠倒的 vt. (使)颠倒;(使)倒转
dramatically [drəˈmætɪklɪ]	adv. 戏剧性地;引人注目地
congest [kənˈdʒest]	vt. 充满;拥挤
decline [dɪˈklaɪn]	vi. 下倾;下降　vi. 谢绝;婉拒　n. 下倾;下降;衰退
offset [ˈɒfset]	n. 抵销　vt. 弥补;抵销;用平版印刷　vi. 偏移;形成分支

to an extent	在某种程度上
tourism [ˈtuərɪzəm]	n. 旅游业;观光业
variable [ˈveərɪəbl]	adj. 可变的;变化的;[生]变异的 n. 可变情况;变量;可变因素
scheme [skiːm]	n. 计划;方案 v. 计划;设计
trunk road	干道
accordingly [əˈkɔːdɪŋlɪ]	adv. 因此;于是;相应地
in terms of	根据;按照
junction [ˈdʒʌŋkʃn]	n. 交叉口
circulation [ˌsɜːkjəˈleɪʃn]	n. 循环;运行;传播;流通(量)
number plate survey	车牌号调查
residential [ˌrezɪˈdenʃl]	adj. 适合居住的;住宅的
registration [ˌredʒɪˈstreɪʃn]	n. 注册;登记
origin and destination survey	起讫点调查
alternative [ɔːˈltɜːnətɪv]	n. 可供选择的事物 adj. 可供替代的;备选的
transport planning process	交通规划程序
roadside interview survey	路边访问调查
unbiased [ʌnˈbaɪəst]	adj. 没有偏见的
screenline [ˈskriːnlaɪn]	n. 核查线

Exercises

I True or false.

(　　)(1) If the facility is completely new, for example a road in a new development, then the expected traffic and the scale of the construction needed has to be estimated by a traffic survey.

(　　)(2) If the results are to be used as representative of "normal" traffic conditions, the survey must be defined with care and the information used with caution.

(　　)(3) It is in urban areas that traffic volume increases dramatically in July and August, and roads, which are adequate most of the year, become heavily congested.

(　　)(4) Generally, traffic surveys should not be planned to measure the normal peak conditions but to measure the peak of the peak.

(　　)(5) Number plate survey is to record the registration mark of each vehicle as it enters and leaves the system being studied and then to match the registration marks, to establish how a vehicle traveled through the road system being studied.

II Complete the following sentences.

(1) The main reason for undertaking a traffic survey is to _____.

(2) In urban areas, which are employment centers, flow drops during _____.

(3) In deciding when and where to undertake a traffic survey, it is important to _____.

(4) The starting point in defining a traffic survey is to _____.

(5) Three techniques are described in this paper, they are: _____, _____ and _____.

Ⅲ Answer the following questions.

(1) What is the use of traffic engineering?

(2) When the facility is completely new, how to estimate the expected traffic and the scale of the construction?

(3) What is the characteristic of traffic flows?

(4) What should we do in deciding when and where to undertake a traffic survey?

(5) What is the starting point in defining a traffic survey?

Topics for Discussion

(1) What are the basic requirements of a traffic survey?

(2) What should be included in the traffic survey plan?

(3) How to convert different types of vehicles into passenger car unit in a traffic survey?

参 考 译 文

交 通 调 查

交通工程既可用于优化已有设施,也可用于新建交通设施,以确保设施设计的正确和安全,满足未来的交通需求。

我们必须了解现在的交通需求和出行方式,以便能够全面设计新方案。对于新的道路和设施,显然不能使用现在的交通需求作为设计基础,因此,我们必须预估交通需求。

如果新设施消除或减轻了已有道路的交通压力,例如修建支路或新的自行车道,那么我们可以使用交通分配来估计可能转移的交通量比例。

如果设施是全新的,例如新建道路,那么必须以另一种方式预估交通量及所需的建设规模。一般是通过交通影响分析来完成估算。该分析通过参考其他地方类似情况下产生的交通量来估算建设后可能出现的交通量。

以上两种情况无论哪一个,预估交通需求的出发点都是交通调查。

进行交通调查的主要目的是提供对现有情况的客观测量。交通调查提供了调查时段内的交通状况。交通调查不可能准确描述一段时间或一天内的交通状况,如果要用调查结果代表一般交通状况,则交通调查必须谨慎设计,并且在使用信息时也必须慎重。

一周内交通流量每天都在变化。在典型的城市道路上,交通流量往往会在工作日增长,并在周五达到峰值。尽管周日购物影响了周末的出行平衡,但因周日上班的人较少,因而周末交通量较低且周日交通量最低。

一年当中出行方式的变化很大程度取决于所在地区。在夏季学校未开放和职员休年假期间,作为就职中心的市区交通量下降,这与度假区的反向趋势相平衡。7月和8月交通流量急剧增加,使一年中流量较大的道路形成严重拥堵。与通向度假区的道路不同,城际道路所受的影响可能不那么明显,因为在某种程度上,在夏季城际商务出行交通量下降会被旅游出行交通量抵消。

上述信息表明,任何道路上的流量都会有很大变化。因此,在决定何时何地进行交通调查时,重要的是确保调查能够客观反映所研究的交通状况。以旅游区道路为例,在8月公共假日进行的交通调查将得到高峰时期的交通状况。这种交通状况每年仅出现一两天,使用这些数据作为设计基础意义不大,因为设计方案应当适应大部分交通状况。

通常,交通调查不应测量高峰时期的峰值,而应测量"通常"时期的峰值。主干道的交通调查可能需要持续一整年。

交通调查的出发点是确定需要解决的问题,并相应地选择调查类型。如果调查计划不完备,则存在收集到错误数据和无法准确掌握交通状况的风险。

这一准则的唯一例外是面临不太可能出现的复杂情况时,无法第一时间充分获取交通流量和交通运行状况信息。

有的调查足以测量一个位置或一个节点的交通流量和交通流向。但是,如果我们希望了解更大区域的交通流状况,则必须使用其他方法。下文描述了三种方法。

(1)车牌号调查

我们希望掌握固定区域内的交通流状况。例如,这个区域可能是一个被认为有小巷的住宅区,甚至是市中心的环路,而我们希望了解车辆是否在环路上行驶或穿过市中心。

调查方法是,记录每一辆进出所研究道路系统车辆的车牌号,然后匹配车牌号,以确定车辆如何穿过所研究道路系统。通常,调查不需要记录完整的车牌号。

(2)起讫点调查

确定驾驶人出行路线的另一种方法是询问他们,进行起讫点(OD)调查。不同类型的OD调查是交通规划过程的一部分,但是,这超出本文的研究范围,因此不在此进行探讨。路边访问调查和自主问卷是OD调查的标准方法。

在大多数情况下,不可能对所有驾驶人进行调查,因此我们必须依靠交通流中样本驾驶人的反映。显然,如果要使调查结果可靠,样本必须代表所有类型的车辆和出行行为。OD调查的核查线如图2-1所示。

(3)路边访问调查

在路边访问调查中,可在路边拦下一些车辆的驾驶人进行抽样调查,询问他们起讫点以及其他可能相关的信息,例如出行目的。

Reading Material

Theoretical Relationship between Speed, Flow and Density

When considering the flow of traffic along a highway three descriptors are of considerable significance. They are: the speed; the density or concentration, which describes the qualities of service

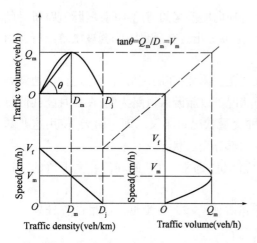

Figure 2-2 Basic relationship among traffic volume, speed and density(流量、速度和密度间的基本关系)

experienced by the stream; and the volume, which measures the quantities of the stream and the demand on the highway facility. Basic relationship among traffic volume, speed and density has been shown in Figure 2-2.

The speed is space mean speed. The density or concentration is the number of vehicles per unit length of highway. The volume is the number of vehicles passing a given point on the highway per unit time.

The relationship between these parameters of the flow may be derived as follows. Consider a short section of highway of length L in which N vehicles passing a point in the section during a time interval T, all the vehicles traveling in the same direction.

$$\text{The traffic volume} \quad Q = N/T \tag{2-1}$$

$$\text{The density } D = \frac{\text{average vehicles travelling over } L}{L} \tag{2-2}$$

The average number of vehicles traveling over $L(a)$ is given by

$$a = \frac{\sum_{i=1}^{N} t_i}{T} \tag{2-3}$$

Where, t_i—— time of travel of the i th vehicle over the length L. Then

$$D = \frac{\frac{\sum_{i=1}^{N} t_i}{T}}{L} = \frac{\frac{N}{T}}{\frac{L}{\frac{1}{N}\sum_{i=1}^{N} t_i}} \tag{2-4}$$

or

$$\text{density} = \frac{\text{the traffic volume}}{\text{space mean speed}} \tag{2-5}$$

Numerous observations have been carried out to determine the relationship between any two of these parameters, because with one relationship established, the relationship between the three parameters is determined. Usually the experimenters have been interested in the relationship between speed and flow because of a desire to estimate the optimum speed for maximum flow.

Greenshields is one of the earliest reported researchers in this field, and in a study of rural roads in Ohio he found a linear relationship between speed and density of the form.

$$\overline{V}_s = \overline{V}_f - \left(\frac{\overline{V}_f}{D_j}\right) D \tag{2-6}$$

Where, $\bar{V}_s$ —— space mean speed;

$\bar{V}_f$ —— space mean speed for free flow conditions;

D_j —— jam density.

With this relationship determined, the flow density relationship can be obtained by substitution of equation (2-5) in equation (2-6) to give

$$Q = \bar{V}_f D - \frac{\bar{V}_f}{D_j} D^2 \qquad (2\text{-}7)$$

and similarly the relationship between flow and speed may be obtained as

$$Q = D_j \bar{V}_s - \frac{D_j}{\bar{V}_f} \bar{V}_s^2 \qquad (2\text{-}8)$$

The density and speed at which flow is a maximum can be obtained by differentiating equations (2-7) and (2-8) with respect to density and speed. The density when flow is a maximum can be obtained from equation (2-7)

$$\frac{dQ}{dD} = \bar{V}_f - \left(2 \times \frac{\bar{V}_f}{D_j} D\right) = 0 \qquad (2\text{-}9)$$

for a maximum value

$$D = D_{max} = \frac{D_j}{2} \qquad (2\text{-}10)$$

The speed when flow is a maximum can be obtained from equation (2-8)

$$\frac{dQ}{d\bar{V}_s} = D_j - \left(2 \times \frac{D_j}{\bar{V}_f} \bar{V}_s\right) = 0 \qquad (2\text{-}11)$$

$$\bar{V}_s = \bar{V}_{max} = \frac{\bar{V}_f}{2} \qquad (2\text{-}12)$$

Substituting these maximum values in equation (2-5) gives

$$\bar{Q}_{max} = D_{max} \bar{V}_{max} = \frac{D_j \bar{V}_f}{4} \qquad (2\text{-}13)$$

Observations obtained by Greenshields gave the following values

$$\bar{V}_f = 74 \text{km/h}$$
$$D_j = 120 \text{veh/km}$$

from equation (2-9) $\quad D_{max} = 60 \text{veh/km}$

from equation (2-10) $\quad \bar{V}_{max} = 37 \text{km/h}$

from equation (2-11) $\quad Q_{max} = 2220 \text{veh/h}$

A considerable number of relationships have been proposed between speed and density and the fit of some these hypotheses to observed data had been investigated by Drake, Schofer and Mary. Each hypothesis then affected the relationship between speed and volume and also between density and volume.

Greenberg observed traffic volume in the north tube of the Lincoln Tunnel in New York City. He assumed that high density traffic behaved in a similar manner to a continuous fluid for which the equation of motion is

$$\frac{d\bar{V}_s}{dT} = -\frac{C^2}{D} \times \frac{\partial D}{\partial L} \qquad (2\text{-}14)$$

Where, C——a constant and the remaining symbols are as previously defined.

From the equation of continuity of flow

$$Q = CD\ln\frac{D_j}{D} \qquad (2\text{-}15)$$

and

$$D = \frac{CD}{\bar{V}_s}\ln\frac{D_j}{D} \qquad (2\text{-}16)$$

It is interesting to note that the Greenberg model does not give $\bar{V}_s = \bar{V}_f$. When $D = 0$ the boundary conditions are:

When, $Q = 0, D = 0$ or $D = D_j$;

When, $D = D_j, V_s = 0$.

The volume is obviously zero when the density is zero, and at the jam density the volume may also be assumed to be zero. Between these limits the volume must rise to at least one maximum, often referred to as maximum capacity.

Lighthill and Whitham using a fluid-volume analogy had shown that the speed of waves causing continuous changes of volume through vehicular volume is given by dQ/dD, that is

$$V_w = \frac{dQ}{dD} \qquad (2\text{-}17)$$

Where, V_w—— the speed of the wave. From equation (2-4)

$$V_w = \frac{d(\bar{V}_s D)}{dD} = \bar{V}_s + D\frac{d\bar{V}_s}{dD} \qquad (2\text{-}18)$$

The space mean speed decreases with increasing density so that $d\bar{V}_s/dD$ is negative. Hence wave speed is less than that of the traffic stream.

Exercises

I True or false.

(　　)(1)The volume is the number of vehicles per unit length of highway. The density is the number of vehicles passing a given point on the highway per unit time.

(　　)(2)Numerous observations have been carried out to determine the relationship between any two of these parameters, because with one relationship established, the relationship between the three parameters is determined.

(   )(3) The space mean speed increases with increasing density so that $d\bar{V}_s/dD$ is positive.

(   )(4) According to Drake, Schofer and Mary's investigation, each hypothesis affected the relationship between speed and volume and also between density and volume.

(   )(5) A linear relationship between speed and density was found by Greenberg.

II Complete the following sentences.

(1) When considering the volume of traffic along a highway three descriptors are of considerable significance. They are _____, _____, _____.

(2) Greenshields is one of the earliest reported researchers in this field, and in a study of rural roads in Ohio he found a linear relationship between speed and density of the form. It is _____.

(3) Greenberg observed traffic volume in the north tube of the Lincoln Tunnel, New York City. He assumed that high density traffic behaved in a similar manner to a continuous fluid for which the equation of motion is _____.

(4) According to Lighthill and Whitham's analogy, the speed of waves can be expressed in _____.

(5) The speed and density describes _____.

III Answer the following questions.

(1) What is the specific definition of three descriptors?

(2) Why had experimenters been interested in the relationship between speed and volume?

(3) Where did Greenshields find a linear relationship between speed and density of the flow?

(4) What did Greenberg assume after observing traffic volume in the north tube of the Lincoln Tunnel?

(5) What does the fluid-flow analogy show?

参 考 译 文

车速、交通量和车流密度的理论关系

在分析公路上的交通流时,有3个参数具有很重要的意义,它们分别是车速、车流密度和交通量。其中车速和车流密度(或称为交通密集程度)描述交通流得到的服务质量,交通量则用来衡量道路上交通流或交通需求的数量,交通量、车速和密度之间的基本关系如图2-2所示。

车速是指区间平均车速,车流密度是指单位道路长度上的车辆数目,交通量是指单位时间内通过道路某一给定地点的车辆数目。

这些交通流参数之间的关系可推导如下。考虑道路的某一段长度为L,在时间间隔T内有N辆车通过该段道路的一点,并且所有车辆的行驶方向相同,则

$$交通量: Q = N/T \tag{2-1}$$

$$车流密度: D = 长度为L的路段上驶过的车辆平均数/L \tag{2-2}$$

其中,驶过长度为L的路段上的车辆数(a)按下式计算:

$$a = \frac{\sum_{i=1}^{N} t_i}{T} \tag{2-3}$$

式中：t_i——驶过长度 L 第 i 辆车的行驶时间。则

$$D = \frac{\frac{\sum_{i=1}^{N} t_i}{T}}{L} = \frac{\frac{N}{T}}{\frac{1}{N}\sum_{i=1}^{N} t_i} \tag{2-4}$$

或

$$车流密度 = 交通量/空间平均车速 \tag{2-5}$$

任意两个参数的关系确定之后，三参数之间的相互关系就会相应确定，因此为了确定任意两个参数之间的关系，人们进行了大量的观测。人们所期望得到的是交通量达到最大值时的最佳车速，故测试人员感兴趣的通常是车速与交通量的关系。

格林希尔茨是该领域最早的研究者之一，他在对俄亥俄州一条乡村公路的研究中，提出了车速与车流密度之间的线性关系：

$$\overline{V}_s = \overline{V}_f - \left(\frac{\overline{V}_f}{D_j}\right)D \tag{2-6}$$

式中：$\overline{V}_s$——空间平均车速；

$\overline{V}_f$——自由流条件下的区间平均车速；

D_j——阻塞密度。

此关系确定后，将式(2-5)代入式(2-6)可得：

$$Q = \overline{V}_f D - \frac{\overline{V}_f}{D_j}D^2 \tag{2-7}$$

同样，交通量与车速的关系式也可为：

$$Q = D_j \overline{V}_s - \frac{D_j}{\overline{V}_f}\overline{V}_s^2 \tag{2-8}$$

交通量最大时的车流密度和车速，可通过式(2-7)和式(2-8)分别对车流密度和车速求导获得。由式(2-7)可得交通量最大时的车流密度：

$$\frac{dQ}{dD} = \overline{V}_f - \left(2 \times \frac{\overline{V}_f}{D_j}D\right) = 0 \tag{2-9}$$

$$D = D_{max} = \frac{D_j}{2} \tag{2-10}$$

由式(2-8)可得交通量最大时的车速：

$$\frac{dQ}{d\overline{V}_s} = D_j - \left(2 \times \frac{D_j}{\overline{V}_f}\overline{V}_s\right) = 0 \tag{2-11}$$

$$\overline{V}_s = \overline{V}_{max} = \frac{\overline{V}_f}{2} \tag{2-12}$$

将上述两个最大值代入式(2-5)可得交通量的最大值：

$$\overline{Q}_{max} = D_{max}\overline{V}_{max} = \frac{D_j\overline{V}_f}{4} \tag{2-13}$$

格林希尔茨得到的观测结果给出如下数值：

$$\overline{V}_f = 74 \text{km/h}$$
$$D_j = 121 \text{veh/km}$$

由式(2-5)得
$$D_{max} = 60 \text{veh/km}$$

由式(2-6)得
$$\overline{V}_{max} = 37 \text{km/h}$$

由式(2-7)得
$$Q_{max} = 2220 \text{veh/h}$$

人们提出过许多关于车速与车流密度之间的关系式，瑞克、斯高佛和玛丽曾对一些假设与观测数据相吻合的情况进行了调查，得知每种假设都会对车速与交通量及车流密度与交通量之间的关系产生影响。

格林伯格对纽约市林肯隧道北段的交通量进行了观测。他假定高密度车流与连续的流体运动方式相似，其运动方程为：

$$\frac{d\overline{V}_s}{dT} = -\frac{C^2}{D} \times \frac{\partial D}{\partial L} \tag{2-14}$$

式中：C——一个常数；
其他符号含义同上。

由流体的连续性方程可得：

$$Q = CD\ln\frac{D_j}{D} \tag{2-15}$$

和

$$D = \frac{CD}{\overline{V}_s}\ln\frac{D_j}{D} \tag{2-16}$$

有趣的是，根据格林伯格的模型并不能得到 $\overline{V}_s = \overline{V}_f$。当 $D = 0$ 时，其边界条件为：

当 $Q = 0$ 时，$D = 0$ 或 $D = D_j$；

当 $D = D_j$ 时，$\overline{V}_s = 0$。

当车流密度为零时，交通量显然为零，而车流密度达到阻塞密度时，交通量也可以假设为零。在这些极值之间，交通量应达到一个最大值，即通常所说的通行能力。

莱特赫和惠特汉利用液体流的模拟表明，引起车流量连续变化的波速为 dQ/dD，即：

$$V_w = \frac{dQ}{dD} \tag{2-17}$$

式中：V_w——波速。

由式(2-4)可得：

$$V_w = \frac{d(\overline{V}_s D)}{dD} = \overline{V}_s + D\frac{d\overline{V}_s}{dD} \tag{2-18}$$

空间平均车速随着车流密度的增大而减小，故 $d\overline{V}_s/dD$ 为负值，因此波速小于交通流的速度。

Knowledge Link

Classification of Traffic Surveys

Taking traffic survey aims to know about the current situation of traffic on the roads, clarify the causes and natures of traffic problems, and seek solutions. It can also be used to analyze the laws of traffic changes, determine the corresponding parameters, and provide basic information for the development of traffic forecasting models. According to the survey contents, traffic surveys can be divided into traffic volume surveys, speed surveys, density surveys, and delay surveys. Different methods can be adopted depending on the contents of the survey.

(1) Traffic volume survey

Usual methods for traffic volume surveys include manual counting, floating car method, photography method and automatic counting. Traffic volume data can provide a basis for determining road classification, road geometric design and traffic management facility design, and provide a good foundation for road construction plans, traffic operation plans, and traffic control measures.

(2) Speed survey

The speed survey includes spot speed survey and overall speed survey. The spot speed can be obtained by detectors, radars, photocell, aerial photography, etc. The overall speed can be obtained by number plate survey, floating car method, vehicle-following method. The spot speed parameter and overall speed parameter are important parameters to measure the economics of vehicle operation on the roads. They can be used as the main indicators to evaluate the level of service and the grounds for traffic management measures such as road reconstruction.

(3) Density survey

Traffic density survey methods include photography method and so on. Traffic density is very useful in dividing levels of services, and research on road capacity.

(4) Delay survey

Delay survey includes traffic delay survey and intersection delay survey. Traffic delay survey methods include vehicle-following method, while intersection survey methods include number plate survey, point sample method, and measurement method in the US *Highway Capacity Manual* (*HCM*). Delay data has important applications in transportation planning, transportation facility design, traffic management, etc. It can be used to evaluate the levels of congestion and service quality of roads.

Unit 3

Four-step Planning Procedure

Text

Urban transportation planning calls for more than just providing for the safe and efficient movement of people and goods. It involves the planning of transportation facilities or operations responsive to the goals of the community being served.

Identifying goals and seeing that plans are responsive to them can be difficult. One way to bridge gaps between community viewpoints and the planner's technical processes is to set up an interlocking set of guiders that proceed from the general to the particular. A hierarchy of values, goals, objectives, criteria and standards has been suggested, in which:

(1) Values are basic social drive that governs human behavior. They include the desire to survive, the need to belong, the need for order, and the need for security.

(2) Goals define conditions to be achieved, as environments favorable to maximizing values. They can be stated, although the degree of their achievement may not be definable. "Equal opportunity," for example, is a goal based on the values of security and belonging.

(3) Objectives are specific, attainable, and measurable. In relation to the goal of equal opportunity, a transportation objective might be equal public transportation costs for all citizens regardless of location within the city.

(4) Criteria are the measures or tests to show whether or not objectives are attained. For exam-

ple, the ratio of transit fare to personal income may be the criterion for determining whether or not the foregoing equal-transportation-cost objective has been met.

(5) Standards establish a performance level that must be equaled or surpassed. For example, transit service within 0.4km of every residence would be a standard.

To explain and develop land use/travel relationship, four steps of trip generation, trip distribution, modal split, and traffic assignment are typically followed. Figure 3-1 is the diagram of the four steps planning procedure.

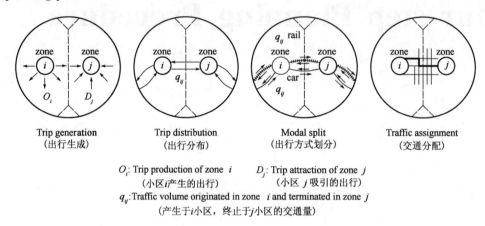

Figure 3-1　Four-step planning procedure(四阶段规划法)

1. Trip generation

In major urban studies, trip generation mathematically relates survey-reported trip making to household characteristics and other land-use types, using statistical procedures to establish trip rates, such as person-trips per household. The trip-distribution procedure usually determines the necessary level of detail. In some studies, trip generation expressed as auto driver trips per 1000ft (300m) of floor space. Reported trip rates published in trip generation or other sources may be applied to a land-use data base.

2. Trip distribution

The preceding step of trip generation typically develops a tabulation of trip origins or trip attractions by small areas. Trip distribution links trip origins to destinations in order to produce estimates of network travel. Several models may be used: the Fratar method, the intervening opportunities model and the gravity model. In the latter technique, which is most commonly used, trip flow from zone A to zone B is calculated as a direct function of the product of trip-end quantities in both zones and as an inverse function of the time or distance separating them. Typically, trips will be stratified into groups by trip purpose, and the distribution for each group will be determined independently. Groupings might include:

(1) Home-based trips to work, shopping, social-recreation, schools, and all other purposes.

(2) Nonhome-based trips (neither origin nor destination at home).

(3) Truck trips.

(4) Taxi trips.

The model's performance is first verified by using the network and traffic assignment techniques to see if model-produced OD patterns and network loadings are comparable to those obtained from trip surveys and their assignment to the network. Once calibrated, the model is then ready to develop travel patterns based on forecast data for the target planning year.

3. Modal split

The trip-generation and trip-distribution steps may be concerned with the problem of converting person-trips into automobile trips or transit passenger trips. Where mode choice is essential, several procedures are available to determine the split either before or after the trip-distribution step. Trip diversion based on travel-time differences between modes is the basis for some methods, but it is being supplanted by techniques relying heavily on trip-maker or household characteristics. The choice of the mode of transportation depends on objective and subjective ones. Modeling the modal split requires the knowledge of the relationship between many variables and the choice of the person traveling. The modal split of traffic models most common in the literature is mostly based on the logit model.

4. Traffic assignment

The fourth step brings the outputs from preceding tasks to a coded transportation network. The estimates from the trip-generation step are loaded on the network from zone-level "loading nodes". They are then routed over those links giving the shortest time paths to zonal destinations as determined by the trip-distribution model. If certain links become overloaded as a result of assignments, the model may use "capacity-restraint" procedure to limit the flow, usually by increasing link travel times or reassigning subsequent trips to alternative paths. When the process is done, the results can be produced as tabulations of link loadings or plotted graphically. Depending on available subroutines, other results, such as link and area volume/capacity ratios, vehicle-miles, and vehiclehours of travel, or tabulations of OD matrix using selected links, may also be derived. Similar procedures apply to person-trips assigned to transit networks.

New Words and Expressions

urban transportation planning	城市运输规划
transportation facility	运输设施
responsive [rɪˈspɒnsɪv]	adj. 响应的;响应的
identify [aɪˈdentɪfaɪ]	vt. 识别;认出　vi. 确定;认同
gap [gæp]	n. 间隙;差距,隔阂
community [kəˈmjuːnətɪ]	n. 社会;团体;社区;(政治)共同体
interlocking [ˌɪntəˈlɒkɪŋ]	adj. 连锁的
security [sɪˈkjuərətɪ]	n. 安全

favorable	[ˈfeɪvərəbl]	adj. 赞成的；有利的；起促进作用的
attainable	[əˈteɪnəbl]	adj. 可到达的；可得到的
foregoing	[ˈfɔːgəʊɪŋ]	adj. 在前的；前述的
residence	[ˈrezɪdəns]	n. 住宅；住处
household	[ˈhaʊshəʊld]	n. 家庭 adj. 家庭的
data base		数据库
statistical	[stəˈtɪstɪkl]	adj. 统计的；统计学的
tabulation	[ˌtæbjuˈleɪʃn]	n. 作表；表格
network	[ˈnetwɜːk]	n. 网络；网状系统；路网 v. 将……连接成网络
intervene	[ˌɪntəˈviːn]	v. 干涉；干预；插入；介入
gravity	[ˈgrævətɪ]	n. 地心引力；重力
zone	[zəʊn]	n. 地区；(规划的)区域 v. 将……划作特殊区域；将……分成区
inverse	[ˌɪnˈvɜːs]	adj. 倒转的；反转的；逆向的
stratify	[ˈstrætɪfaɪ]	v. 分层；划分
home-based trip		基于家的出行
nonhome-based trip		非基于家的出行
performance	[pəˈfɔːməns]	n. 性能
verify	[ˈverɪfaɪ]	vt. 检验；核实；证明
calibrate	[ˈkælɪbreɪt]	v. 标定；校准(刻度，以使测量准确)
zonal	[ˈzəʊnl]	adj. 带状的
code	[kəʊd]	n. 密码；暗码；电码；准则 v. 为……编码；编码
route	[ruːt]	n. 路线；路途；常规路线 v. 按某路线发送；给……规定路线
subroutine	[ˈsʌbruːtiːn]	n. 子程序
plot	[plɒt]	n. (专用的)小块土地 v. 绘制(图表)
matrix	[ˈmeɪtrɪks]	n. [数]矩阵

Exercises

I True or false.

(   )(1) Urban transportation planning calls for just providing for the safe and efficient movement of people and goods.

(   )(2) Criteria are the measures or tests to show whether or not objectives are attained.

(   )(3) Objectives establish a performance level that must be equaled or surpassed.

(   )(4) In major urban studies, trip generation mathematically relates survey-reported trip making to household characteristics and other land-use types.

(　　)(5) Trip distribution links origins to destinations in order to produce estimates of network travel.

II Complete the following sentences.

(1) Four-step planning procedure includes _____, _____, _____ and _____.

(2) The preceding step of trip generation typically develops _____.

(3) In trip distribution, several models may be used, these are the _____, _____ and _____.

(4) The trip-generation and trip-distribution steps may be concerned with the problem of _____.

(5) The traffic-assignment step brings _____.

III Answer the following questions.

(1) What does the urban transportation planning involve?
(2) How to bridge gaps between community viewpoints and the planner's technical processes?
(3) How to determine the modal split?
(4) How to verify the model's performance of trip distribution?
(5) What does the trip-generation and trip-distribution steps concern with?

Topics for Discussion

(1) What are the forecasting methods of traffic generation?
(2) What are the main influencing factors of traffic production and attraction?
(3) What are the advantages and disadvantages of the gravity model?

参 考 译 文

四阶段规划法

城市交通规划不仅要求对人员和货物提供安全和高效的运输,还包括对所在社区的服务目标、交通设施、计划运营方式的规划。

确定目标并确保依照目标做出规划可能很困难。一种将公众观点与规划者技术相衔接的方法是建立一套紧密联系的由一般到特殊的指导方针。一般来说,价值观、目的、目标、标准和准则的层次如下:

(1) 价值观是管理人类行为的基本社会动力,包括生存的欲望、归属的需求、秩序的需求以及安全的需求。

(2) 目的是把有利于价值最大化的环境作为要达成的条件。虽然目的达成程度可能无法被确定,但可以被表述,例如,"机会平等"是一个基于安全和归属价值的目的。

(3) 目标是具体的、可实现的和可衡量的。对机会平等的目的而言,交通运输的阶段目标是,无论处于城市的哪个位置,所有市民的公共交通成本均等。

(4) 标准是指是否达成目标的度量或检验。例如,公交票价与个人收入的比率可以作为确定是否达成均等运费成本目标的标准。

(5)准则是必须达到或超过的性能水平。例如,可以将距住宅 0.4 千米范围内都要有公交服务作为一项准则。

为了解释和研究土地利用与出行之间的关系,通常的做法是遵循出行生成、出行分布、出行方式划分和交通分配这 4 个步骤。四阶段规划法的示意图如图 3-1 所示。

1. 出行生成

在大多数城市研究中,出行生成使用统计学方法得到出行率,在数学上将调查报告中的出行与家庭特征及其他土地利用类型建立联系,例如每个家庭个人出行率。出行分布程序通常确定了所需要的详细程度。在一些研究中,出行生成被定义为每 1000 英尺(300 米)占地面积上汽车驾驶人的行程。在出行生成或其他来源中得到的出行率会应用于土地利用数据库。

2. 出行分布

在出行生成的前一步通常会得到区域出行发生和吸引的列表。出行分布将出行的起始点与目的地连接起来,以便估计交通网络内的出行交通量。可以使用这几种模型:Fratar 法、介入机会模型和重力模型。最后一种模型,也即最常用的方法中,从小区 A 到小区 B 的出行交通量是两个小区间出行交通量的正函数,也是它们之间的行程时间或距离的反函数。通常,按出行目的将出行分组,每组的分布将独立确定。分组包括:

(1)基于家庭的工作、购物、社交娱乐、上学和所有其他目的的出行。

(2)非基于家庭的出行(家既不是出发地也不是目的地)。

(3)货运出行。

(4)出租车出行。

首先通过使用网络和交通分配技术来验证模型的性能,以确定模型产生起讫点(OD)的方式是否与出行调查得到的相吻合、模型的路网荷载与实际分配到路网上的情况是否相吻合。一旦校准,模型就可以根据目标规划年度的预测数据得到出行分布模式。

3. 出行方式划分

出行生成和出行分布有可能涉及将人的出行转换成汽车出行或公交出行的问题,因此出行方式的选择不可或缺。在交通分布前后,有几种程序可用于出行方式划分。基于不同出行方式间出行时间差异的出行转移是一些方法的基础,但是它逐渐被基于出行者特征或家庭特征的方法所取代。出行方式的选择取决于客观因素和主观因素。对出行方式划分进行建模需要了解许多变量之间的关系及出行者的选择。文献中最常见的出行方式划分模型大多基于 logit 模型。

4. 交通分配

第 4 步是将前面任务所得的结果输入编制好的交通网络中。将来自出行生成的估计值输入由区域级"质心"组成的网络中。然后将节点连接起来,通过出行分布模型得到到达目的地时间最短的路径。如果某些线路交通分配的流量过大,模型可以使用"容量限制法"程序,通过增加路段出行时间或将相关行程重新分配到备选路径上来限制流量。完成该过程后,结果可以以路线荷载的列表或图形表示。还可以根据可用的子程序和其他结果,如线路或区域交通量与通行能力的比值,得到出行车辆行驶里程、车辆行驶时间以及所选路线的 OD 矩阵。类似程序适用于公交网络的个人出行分配。

Reading Material

Traffic Assignment

Previously the estimation of generated trip ends has been discussed together with the distribution of trips between the traffic zones. Modal split methods also have been reviewed in which the proportion of trips by the varying travel modes are determined. At this stage the number of trips and their origins and destinations are known but the actual routes through the transportation system is unknown. This process of determining the links of the transportation system on which trips will be loaded is known as traffic assignment.

Apart from the very largest transportation survey, traffic assignment tends to deal with highway traffic. This is because it is usually not difficult to estimate the routes taken by public transport users, and also because the loading trips on the public transport network does not materially affect the journey time.

Trip ends where there is no choice of travel mode, which is from non-car-owing households, are accumulated as public transport trip ends. Choice trips where a car is available are separated by the modal choice procedure into car trips and public transport trips, the public users and also because the loading of trips on the public transport trips being accumulated and the car trips assigned to the network.

Usually it will then be found that proposed road network is overloaded and some car trips will need to be restrained. If a car cannot be used then some trips will not be made at all, while other trips will be transferred to public transport and accumulated.

As the basis of assignment is usually travel times, the travel times on the network links will vary the imposed loading. In addition as travel times are used in the trip distribution process, it is necessary to carry out an iterative procedure between distribution, modal choice and assignment.

The change in speed with flow on a highway link is carried out using speed flow relationships for the varying highway types and it is interesting to consider just what the effects of a speed change are. Firstly, it affects the choice of route because assignment is made on the basis of travel times through the network. Secondly, it affects the destinations of trips because trips are distributed to varying destinations on the basis of travel times when a gravity model is used. Thirdly, it may affect the choice of travel mode because modal choice is often made by a comparison of travel times.

There are many problems associated with speed flow relationships, considerable variations being observed between differing highways even of the same type. There is also an additional problem that most transportation studies are based on 24h flow so that it is necessary to know the hourly variation and the directional distribution of volume.

In assignment it is first necessary to describe the transport network to which trips are being assigned. The network is described as a series of nodes and connecting links. In a highway network, the nodes would be the junctions, and the links the connecting highways. Centroids of traffic zones, at which it is assumed that all zonal trips are generated and to which they are attracted, are either at nodes or connected to them by additional links. The cost of using a link and a junction, usually in the form of travel times and delays, is given on the basis of the review of transport facilities carried out during the initial stages of the transportation survey.

Three methods by which the assignment may be made, they are:

(1) All-or-nothing assignment.

(2) Capacity restrained assignment.

(3) Multipath proportional assignment.

In all-or-nothing assignment method, an algorithm is used to compute the route of least cost, usually based on travel time between all the zonecentriods. For each zone centriod selected as origin, a set of shortest routes from the origin to all the other zone centroids are referred to as a minimum tree. When the trips between two zones are assigned to the minimum path between the two zones, then the assignment is said to take place on an all-or-nothing basis.

There are obvious difficulties with such a simplified approach, some of which are inherent in the other assignment methods. It is obviously incorrect to assume that all trips commence and terminate at a zonecentriod. If the length of the links within the zones is small compared with the length of remainder of the minimum link path, then the errors may not be so serious. Because of its simplicity, travel times are usually employed as a measure of link impedance, but travel times may not be precisely estimated by a traveler. The use of a cost function, which reflects the perceived cost of travel, is desirable. The loading on a link in this method is extremely sensitive to estimated link and node costs, if these have been incorrectly estimated, then the resulting assignment is open to question. There is also a problem that links with small travel cost will attract trips without any adjustment in link cost.

Exercises

I True or false.

(　　)(1) The traffic assignment plays an important role in highway traffic because we can easily predict the routes of trips.

(　　)(2) The change in the speed of the cars is decided by the speed, flow and direction of the different types of roads.

(　　)(3) Three methods by which the assignment may be made, they are:

① All-but-nothing or nothing-but-all assignment;

② Capacity restricted assignment;

③ Multipath proportional assignment.

(　　)(4) Minimum tree refers to a series routes, which are the shortest ones from one to other centroids.

(　　)(5) We need to adjust the link cost so that the least expensive links would attract more trips.

II Complete the following sentences.

(1) _____ is referred to the transportation system on which trips will be loaded.

(2) Beside the large-scale transportation survey, traffic assignment aims to _____.

(3) Since the basis of assignment is mostly travel times, the travel times on the network links _____ the imposed loading.

(4) It is not right to suppose that all trips start and _____.

(5) The main idea of the passage is _____.

III Answer the following questions.

(1) What is known and what is unknown in traffic-assignment stage?

(2) Why does traffic assignment tend to deal with highway traffic?

(3) What is the first necessary in assignment?

(4) What is a set of shortest routes from the origin to all the other zone centroids referred to?

(5) Why are travel times usually employed as a measure of link impedance?

参 考 译 文

交 通 分 配

此前,我们曾讨论过对生成的出行端点的预测和交通区域之间的出行分布问题,也评述过确定不同交通方式之间的出行比例的交通方式划分方法。在现阶段,出行次数及其起终点虽已知,但是在交通系统中出行者所经过的实际路线还不明确就把出行分配到交通系统路线上的过程叫作交通分配。

除了大规模的综合交通调查以外,交通分配主要针对道路交通而言。这是因为,估计公共交通乘客所走的路线并不困难,以及公共交通网交通出行分配对行程时间的影响不大。

不能选择交通方式的出行端点,也就是没有小汽车的家庭应列入公共交通的出行端点中。当家庭有小汽车时,则出行选择可根据选择过程区分为小汽车出行和公共交通出行,同时对公共交通出行进行累加,并将小汽车出行分配在道路交通网上。

这时通常会发现规划的道路网呈超负荷状态,这就需要对小汽车出行加以限制。如果不使用小汽车,一些出行根本不会产生,而其他可以不采用小汽车的出行将会转移到公共交通上去,并且积累起来。

由于交通分配通常以行程时间为依据,道路网路段上的行程时间将改变所分配的交通负荷。再者,由于行程时间在出行分布过程中也要采用,因此应在出行分布、交通方式选择和交通分配之间进行必要的迭代计算。

道路路段上的车速随交通量的变化而改变,而且这种车速的变化可以根据不同类型道路的速度—流量关系求得。车速变化产生的影响是值得注意的事情。第一,它将影响路线的选择,因为交通分配工作是以经过该道路网所需的行程时间为根据的;第二,它将影响出行的终点,因为当采用重力模型时,出行是依据行程时间来分布到不同终点的;第三,它将影响交通方式的选择,因为交通方式的选择通常是对出行所需时间进行比较之后决定的。

与速度—流量有关的问题很多,即使同一类型的道路,在不同路线之间也会有很大的差别。还有一个问题就是大多数交通调查是以 24 小时的交通量为根据的,因此还需要知道每小时的交通量变化,以及交通量的方向分布情况。

在进行交通分配时,首先要表示出将要进行分配的交通网。交通网络通常由一系列的节点以及节点之间的连线组成。在一个道路网络中,假设节点是交叉路口,那么连线就是相连接的道路。假定一个交通小区内所有的出行都是从该小区的形心产生的或吸引到该点上去的,这些形心可位于节点上或由另外的连线与路网相接。通过连线和交叉点的费用,常常以行程时间和延误的形式表示。在交通调查开始阶段,通过评价各种交通设施运行效果得到相关计算依据。

交通分配方法有三种:
(1)全有全无分配法。
(2)交通容量限制分配法。
(3)多路径概率分配法。

全有全无分配法采用一种算术方法来计算路线最小费用,它通常以各交通小区形心之间的所有行程时间为依据。对每一个交通小区,选择形心作为起点,从这个起点到所有其他交通小区形心的一组最短路线称为"最小树"。把两个交通小区之间的出行分配到该两区之间最短路径上,这一方法叫做全有全无分配法。

用这样一种简化的方法分配交通有不少明显的缺陷,其中一些也存在于其他分配法中。假定所有的出行都是起始于和终止于一个交通小区的形心,显然是不正确的。如果在交通小区内的联络线长度与其余区间最短路径相比小很多,则误差可能不太大。由于这种简化,人们常常把行程时间作为路线的阻滞指标,但是,出行者无法精确估计出行时间。因此,人们希望采用一种能够反映感知出行成本的费用函数。在该方法中,一条路线的交通分配情况对所估计的路线和节点费用特别敏感。如果对这些费用的估计有错误,则所获得的分配结果就有问题。还有一个问题是,费用小的路段不需要调整其出行费用就会吸引较多的出行。

Knowledge Link

Division of traffic zones

In the process of traffic demand forecasting, in order to facilitate investigation and forecast social and economic indicators, traffic generation and traffic distribution, it is necessary to divide the target area into appropriate number of traffic zones according to certain rules. Generally, the division of traffic zones follows the following principles:

(1)Convenience of collecting available statistics

Social and economic indicators are generally counted and forecasted according to administrative regions. The division of traffic zones should make full use of administrative division to improve the accuracy of investigation and reduce work.

(2)Homogeneity and size of non-target area

Population, traffic production and traffic attraction should be homogeneous in the traffic zones. For the traffic zones outside the target area, the size of the traffic zones should be gradually increased as the distance from the target area becomes farther.

(3) Making full use of natural obstacles

Make the best use of natural obstacles such as mountains, rivers and so on in the region as the boundary of the zones. The bridge is frequently regarded as a screenline. Normally, natural obstacles such as mountains and rivers are used as administrative division, so this is not inconsistent with the first rule.

(4) Including freeway ramps, stations and hubs

The ramp, station and hub should be completely included in the traffic zones in the area containing expressway, rail transit so as to make the analysis of the flow of these traffic facilities easier and avoid the split of ramp into two parts by the traffic zones.

(5) Consideration of land use

It is important to avoid dividing area with the same use into different traffic zones, so that the statistical analyses of land utilization can be carried out.

As for the methods of dividing traffic zones, there is no uniform way and relevant standard at present. The method of division of traffic zones in European countries is based on population. For example, regulations in Russian are: cities with population of 100 to 250 thousand are divided into 5 to 10 zones; cities with population of 250 to 500 thousand are divided into 8 to 20 traffic zones; cities with population of 0.5 to 1 million are divided into 15 to 20 traffic zones; In cities with a population of 1 million to 2 million, the number of traffic zones should be more than 50.

Unit 4
One-way Traffic

Text

Although most streets and highways are designed for use by two-way traffic, increasing traffic volume, conflicts among vehicular flow and between pedestrians and vehicles, and the resulting congestion and accidents often lead to consideration of one-way traffic regulation. In major activity centers, such as the central business districts of cities with a large number of high traffic, and the closely spaced intersections, one-way traffic regulation is frequently used because of traffic signal timing consideration and to improve street capacity. In the development of new activity centers, such as shopping centers, sports arenas, industrial parks, and so on, one-way regulation is frequently incorporated into original street and traffic plans.

One-way traffic is generally operated in one of three ways as below.

(1) A street on which traffic moves in one direction at all times.

(2) A street that is normally one-way but at certain times may be operated in the reverse direction to provide additional capacity in the predominant direction of flow.

(3) A street that normally carries two-way traffic but which during peak traffic hours may be operated as one-way traffic, usually in the heavier direction of flow. Such a street may be operated in one direction during the morning peak hours and in the opposite direction during the evening peak hours, with two-way traffic during all other hours.

Operational status of one-way traffic intersections is shown in Figure 4-1.

Advantages and disadvantages of one-way traffic are as below.

One-way regulation is generally used to reduce congestion and to increase the capacity of astreet network. One-way traffic also inproves the safety and utilization of adjacent land.

(1) Effect on capacity

Traffic conflicts and delays at intersections are principal causes of congestion and reduced travel times on two-way urban streets. On one-way traffic, left-turning movements are not delayed by opposing traffic. In addition, full use may be made of street pavements of unusual width. The capacity of a street may be increased by as much as 50% by use of one-way regulation.

The increased capacity afforded by one-way regulation may also make it feasible to permit parking either part or full time on streets that, if operated as two-way traffic, could not be used for parking. More efficient signal timing can also increase traffic capacity.

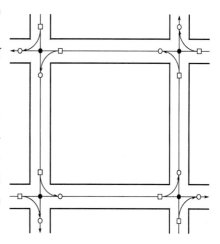

Figure 4-1 Operational status of one-way traffic intersections(单向交通交叉口运行状况)

(2) Effect on safety

One-way traffic with traffic signal controls at major intersections provide gaps in traffic for safer crossing movements by pedestrians and vehicles at other cross streets and driveways. In addition, drivers and pedestrians crossing one-way traffic needs look in only one direction to observe traffic.

Numerous studies have shown that the conversion of two-way traffic to one-way operation reduces the total number of accidents by 10% to 50%. In some cases, the number of specific kinds of accidents are reduced even more. Minor traffic collisions may increase as a result of improper weaving by drivers to position themselves for an available parking space or to get in the proper lane for a turn. However, transition areas between one-way and two-way operations are frequently hazardous and require special traffic control treatment.

(3) Effect on traffic flow

A primary reason for use of one-way traffic is to improve traffic operations and to reduce congestion. The degree of improvement in operating conditions, travel speed, and safety depends, of course, on the previous situations. Generally, travel times can be reduced from 10% to 50% and the number of accidents from 10% to 40% even with a slight increase in total traffic volumes. Such general improvement in traffic operations must be balanced against the following negative aspects:

① Some motorists must travel extra distances to reach their destinations. This wastes times and fuel.

② Strangers may become confused with the one-way traffic pattern, especially if network geometry is irregular, and particularly if clear markings and signal indications are not provided.

③ Transit operations may be adversely affected if routes are forced to operate on two-way traffic instead of one.

④ Emergency vehicles, such as fire trucks, may need to take a more circuitous route to reach their destination. This may be alleviated somewhat, however, by providing signal control that will allow emergency vehicles to move against the flow of traffic on one-way traffic before the emergency vehicles will enter the one-way system.

(4) Effect on area economic conditions

Improved traffic movement and increased safety generally produce broad economic benefits both to adjacent land users and to the general public. Nevertheless, when planning the one-way system, especially one involving commercial streets, traffic engineers should expect objections from affected business owners who may contend that one-way traffic will adversely affect their trade.

Yet studies made in various parts of the United States have generally tended to disprove such claims. Moreover, where one-way systems have once been implemented, many businessmen formerly opposed to the one-way traffic plan have become its staunchest supports. One-way traffic is rarely changed back to two-way operation unless the construction of major new highway facilities makes the continued operation of the one-way traffic system unnecessary.

Although the economic and environmental impact of converting to a one-way traffic system will undoubtedly vary from one place to another, the results of an in-depth study by the Michigan Department of State Highways reveals some interesting results.

① The greatest degree of environmental dissatisfaction existed with the residents who resided adjacent to the one-way traffic.

② This attitude or feeling diminished in the study area, where at least one residential lot removed from the one-way traffic.

③ Residents felt that the one-way conversions would cause a loss in property value, and would make the area less desirable from an environmental viewpoint. However, results of the market analysis showed that the greatest residential property value increase occurred on the low-traffic-flow converted residential streets.

④ There was no indication of adverse economic influence on business activities within the one-way corridors. The number of business failures was reduced substantially after one-way conversion.

New Words and Expressions

one-way traffic	单向交通
sports arena	运动场;体育场
original [əˈrɪdʒənl]	adj. 起初的;最早的;首创的;独创的 n. 原件;正本;原稿;原作
at all times	始终;一直
predominant [prɪˈdɒmɪnənt]	adj. 有影响力的;卓越的;占主要地位的
afford [əˈfɔːd]	vt. 提供;给予
opposing traffic	对向交通;双向通行
slight [slaɪt]	adj. 轻微的;少量的;不重要的 vt. 轻视;忽略;怠慢 n. 轻蔑;忽视;冷落

numerous ['nju:mərəs]	adj. 很多的;许多的
conversion [kən'vɜ:ʃn]	n. 转变;转换;转化
hazardous ['hæzədəs]	adj. 危险的;冒险的
negative ['negətɪv]	n. 否定;负数 adj. 否定的;消极的;负的 vt. 否定;拒绝(接受)
indication [ˌɪndɪ'keɪʃn]	n. 指出;指示;迹象;暗示
emergency [ɪ'mɜ:dʒənsɪ]	n. 紧急情况;突然事件;非常时刻
fire truck	救火车;消防车
circuitous [sə'kju:ɪtəs]	adj. 迂回的;绕道的;曲折的
alleviate [ə'li:vɪeɪt]	vt. 减轻;缓和
somewhat ['sʌmwɒt]	adv. 有点;稍微
disprove [ˌdɪs'pru:v]	vt. 反驳;驳斥;证明……是虚假的
residential lot	居民区
formerly ['fɔ:məlɪ]	adv. 以前;从前;原来;原先
staunch [stɔ:ntʃ]	adj. 忠实的;坚定的
dissatisfaction [ˌdɪsˌsætɪs'fækʃn]	n. 不快;不悦;不满
vary from	不同于;不等于
in-depth	彻底的;深入的
diminish [dɪ'mɪnɪʃ]	vt. (使)减少;(使)变小
desirable [dɪ'zaɪərəbl]	adj. 可取的;值得拥有的;值得拥有的
property value	属性值;产权价值;物业价值
adverse ['ædvɜ:s]	adj. 不利的;有害的
corridor ['kɒrɪdɔ:(r)]	n. 通道;走廊
substantially [səb'stænʃəlɪ]	adv. 充分地;本质上;实质上

Exercises

I True or false.

(　　)(1) One-way regulation can solve all of the problems, such as congestion, safety, and so on.

(　　)(2) On one-way traffic, traffic conflicts are no less than those on two-way traffic.

(　　)(3) There is a primary reason for use of one-way traffic. It is to improve traffic operation and to reduce congestion.

(　　)(4) When planning the one-way system, there is no necessary for engineers to consider the disadvantages brought to business.

(　　)(5) The greatest degree of environmental dissatisfaction existed with the residents who resided adjacent to the one-way traffic.

II Complete the following sentences.

(1) In the development of new activity centers, _____ is frequently incorporated into o-

riginal street and traffic plans.

(2) Four aspects: _____, _____, _____ and _____ are concluded to interpret the advantages and disadvantages when converting one street into one-way traffic.

(3) A street that normally carries two-way traffic but which during peak traffic hours may be operated as a one-way traffic, usually in the _____ of flow.

(4) Traffic _____ and _____ at intersections are principal causes of congestion and reduced travel time on two-way urban traffic.

(5) Strangers may become confused with the one-way traffic pattern, especially if network geometry is irregular, and particularly if _____ and _____ are not provided.

Ⅲ Answer the following questions.

(1) One-way traffic is generally operated in three ways. What are they?
(2) Which aspects do the advantages of one-way traffic exist in?
(3) What is the reason for use of one-way traffic?
(4) What is the principal cause of congestion and reduced travel time on two-way urban streets?
(5) What does improved traffic movement and increased safety generally produce?

Topics for Discussion

(1) What do you think of one-way traffic?
(2) What others can the one-way traffic do effect on area economic conditions?
(3) Which aspects does the disadvantages of one-way traffic exist in?

参 考 译 文

单 向 交 通

虽然大多数城市道路和公路在设计时都采用双向交通管制(简称双向交通),但交通量的增加、车辆之间、行人和车辆之间的冲突以及由此产生的拥堵和事故往往会使人们将目光转向单向交通管制(简称单向交通)。在主要活动中心,例如有着长期高流量、高密度交通流交叉口的城市中央商务区,出于交通信号配时的考虑和提高道路通行能力的原因,经常使用单向交通。在新开发的活动中心,如购物中心、体育场馆、工业园区等,单向交通经常被纳入已有道路的交通规划。

单向交通常以下面三种方式之一在道路上运行,采用单向交通的道路一般被称为单行道。

(1)交通流一直朝着一个方向流动。

(2)交通流通常按一个方向行驶,但有时可以反向行驶,为主要流向提供额外通行能力。

(3)单行道通常承担双向交通,但在高峰时段以单向交通运行,交通流早高峰时段向一个方向行驶,并且在晚高峰时段向相反的方向行驶,在其他时段则双向行驶。

单向交通交叉口运行状况如图 4-1 所示。

单向交通的优点和缺点如下。

实施单向交通将会减少拥堵并提高道路网通行能力,也会提高邻近土地的安全性和利用率。

（1）对通行能力的影响

交叉口的交通冲突和延误是导致城市双向交通拥堵和畅行时间减少的主要原因。在单向交通中，左转车流不会因对向车流而产生延误。此外，不常用的道路路面得到了充分的利用。通过实施单向交通管理，道路的通行能力可增加50%。

实施单向交通后提高了道路通行能力，同时实现了双向交通不允许的临时的或全天的路内停车。更高效的信号配时也可以提高道路通行能力。

（2）对安全的影响

在信号控制的主要交叉口，单行道提供了交通流空档，以便其他相交道路和车道上的行人和车辆能够更安全地通过。此外，横穿单行道的驾驶人和行人只需朝一个方向看就能观察交通状况。

大量研究表明，将双行道改为单行道可将总事故量减少10%~50%。在某些情况下，特定种类的事故数量甚至会减少更多。驾驶人为了找到空隙停车或为了转向而进入相应车道时，采取不适当的穿行可能会增加道路上的轻微交通冲突数量。但是，单向交通和双向交通之间的过渡区域往往是危险的，需要使用特殊的交通控制来处理。

（3）对交通流的影响

采用单向交通的主要原因是改善交通运行状况并减少拥堵。当然，运行条件、行驶速度和安全性的改善程度取决于之前的状况。一般来说，即使总交通流量略有增加，行程时间也可以减少10%~50%，事故数量可以减少10%~40%。交通运行的整体改善必须平衡以下负面因素：

① 有些驾驶人需要行驶额外的距离才能到达目的地，这会浪费时间和燃料。

② 外地人可能会不适应单行道模式，尤其是在路网几何结构不规则、没有提供明确标志和信号指示的情况下。

③ 如果路线被迫在两条道路上而非一条道路上运行，则可能对公共交通的运营产生不利影响。

④ 紧急车辆（如消防车）可能需要采取更迂回的路线才能到达目的地。然而，在应急车辆进入单向交通系统之前，通过提供信号控制，允许应急车辆在单行道上逆向行驶，会使这种情况有所缓解。

（4）对区域经济条件的影响

改善交通流和增强安全性通常会对邻近土地使用者和公众产生广泛的经济效益。然而，规划单向交通系统时，特别是涉及商业街时，商家可能认为实施单行道对他们的生意会产生不利影响，因而交通工程师们应该预想到他们会提出反对意见。

然而在美国各地进行的研究通常不支持这种说法。而且一旦实施了单向交通系统，许多原来反对实施单向交通的商家反而成为最忠实的拥护者。除非建设新的道路设施使得单向交通系统的持续运行变得没有必要，否则单行道很少会改回双行道。

虽然向单向交通系统的转换对经济和环境的影响因地而异，但密歇根州高速公路局进行的深入研究却揭示了一些有趣的结果。

① 居住在单行道附近的居民对环境的不满程度最大。

② 这种态度在所研究的区域有所减弱，该区域至少有一个住宅区居民对单行道的态度发生改变。

③ 居民认为,向单向交通转换会导致物业价值的损失,从环境的角度来看,会使这个区域的环境变得不理想。然而,市场分析的结果表明,住宅物业价值最大的增长发生在交通量较小、转换为单向交通后的住宅街道上。

④ 单向交通通道内没有对经济活动产生不利影响的迹象。转换为单向交通后,交易失败的数量实质上反而大幅减少。

Reading Material

Multimodal Freight Transportation Planning

Freight transportation is a key supply chain component to ensure the efficient movement and timely availability of raw materials and finished products. Demand for freight transportation results from producers and consumers who are geographically apart from each other. Following trade globalization, the conventional road mode is no longer an all-time feasible solution, necessitating other means of transportation (and their combinations).

The freight transportation market has witnessed several trends. In many parts of the world, new markets are rising and the customer base is growing. Furthermore, several trade regulations encourage easier and smoother international trade. Following the economic crisis in 2008, many industries had browsed their business processes in order to decrease their costs and increase performance. As a consequence, shippers, carriers and Logistics Service Providers (LSP) were urged to work at lower cost, while still maintaining high quality. Companies found the solution in more cooperation and integration, as such utilizing resources more efficiently.

Besides economic factors, environmental concerns are high on the agenda. New regulations and taxes were raised to encourage companies to shift to more sustainable solutions. Clearly, in this context, efficient and effective transportation is needed, as the transportation cost share in the supply chain is significant.

A transportation chain is basically partitioned in three segments: pre-haul (or first mile for the pickup process), long-haul (or door-to-door transit of containers), and end-haul (or last mile for the delivery process). In most cases, the pre-haul and end-haul transportation are carried out via road, but for the long-haul transportation, road, rail, air and water modes can be considered. As pointed out, long-haul transportation usually involves combining different modes, but also in pre-haul and end-haul transportation, more and more multimodal systems are also observed (using a combination of trucks and bicycles in city logistics, for instance).

Most of multi-modal freight transportation is containerized (growing around 15% annually). Key reasons for containerization are an increase in the safety of cargo and accessibility to multiple modes of transportation, and a reduction of handling costs and standardization. There are four different terminologies: multimodal, intermodal, co-modal and synchro modal transportation.

(1) Multimodal transportation

Multimodal transportation is defined as the transportation of goods by a sequence of at least two different modes of transportation. The unit of transportation can be a box, a container, a road/rail vehicle, or a vessel. The regular and express delivery system on a regional or national scale, and long-distance pickup and delivery services are also examples of multimodal transportation.

(2) Intermodal transportation

Intermodal transportation is defined as a particular type of multimodal transportation where the load is transported from an origin to a destination in one and the same intermodal transportation unit without handling of the goods themselves when changing modes. Intermodal terminals around the globe give companies the flexibility and the economies of scale of using multiple modes.

(3) Co-modal transportation

This type of transportation focuses on the efficient use of different modes on their own and in combination. Co-modality is defined by the Commission of the European Communities as the use of two or more modes of transportation, but with two particular differences from multimodality: it is used by a group or consortium of shippers in the chain; transportation modes are used in a smarter way to maximize the benefits of all modes, in terms of overall sustainability.

(4) Synchro modal transportation

Synchro modal transportation is positioned as the next step after intermodal and co-modal transportation, and involves a structured, efficient and synchronized combination of two or more transportation modes. Through synchro modal transportation, the carriers or customers select independently at any time the best mode based on the operational circumstances and/or customer requirements.

It is striking to see the common aspects in all definitions: the use of more than one transportation mode. Of course, some definitions put more emphasis on certain aspects of the transportation process. Synchro modal emphasizes the (real-time) flexibility aspect, intermodal focuses on the same loading unit, and co-modal adds resource utilization.

Exercises

I True or false.

(　　)(1) Demand for freight transportation results from producers and consumers who are geographically apart from each other.

(　　)(2) Key reasons for containerization are an increase in the safety of cargo, reduction of handling costs, standardization, and accessibility to multiple modes of transportation.

(　　)(3) In most cases, the pre-haul and end-haul transportation is carried out via road, but for the long-haul transportation, road, rail, air and water modes can be considered.

(　　)(4) Multimodal freight transportation is defined as a particular type of multimodal transportation where the load is transported from an origin to a destination in one and the same intermodal transportation unit without handling of the goods themselves when changing modes.

(　　)(5) Through synchro modal transportation, the carriers or customers select independently at any time the best mode based on the operational circumstances and/or customer requirements.

Ⅱ Complete the following sentences.

(1) A transportation chain is basically partitioned in three segments: _____ (or first mile for the pickup process), _____ (door-to-door transit of containers), and _____ (or last mile for the delivery process).

(2) Most of multi-modal freight transportation is _____ (growing around 15% annually).

(3) Thereare four different terminologies: _____, _____, _____, and _____ transportation.

(4) _____ is defined as the transportation of goods by a sequence of at least two different modes of transportation.

(5) _____ is positioned as the next step after intermodal and co-modal transportation, and involves a structured, efficient and synchronized combination of two or more transportation modes.

Ⅲ Answer the following questions.

(1) How does the demand for freight transportation come into being?

(2) What are the three main parts of the transportation chain?

(3) What are the main reasons for containerization?

(4) What is intermodal transportation?

(5) What is synchro modal freight transportation?

参 考 译 文

多模式货运规划

货物运输是供应链的一个重要组成部分，它保证了原材料和成品的高效流动和及时供应。货物运输需求是由于生产者和消费者地理位置不同而产生的。在贸易全球化之后，传统的道路运输模式已不再是一劳永逸的解决方案，需要其他运输工具的参与（及配合）。

货运市场出现了以下几个发展趋势。在世界许多地方，新市场正在崛起，客户群也在增长。此外，一些贸易法规鼓励更便利和更通畅的国际贸易。在2008年经济危机之后，许多行业梳理了他们的业务流程，以降低成本和提高绩效。因此，要求托运人、承运人和物流服务提供商（LSP）以较低的成本工作，同时仍保持高的运输质量。公司在更多的合作和整合中找到了解决方案，比如更有效地利用资源。

除经济因素外，环境问题也被提上议事日程。提出了新的法规和提高税收的想法，以鼓励公司采取更具可持续性的解决方案。显然，在这种情况下，需要更高效的运输，因为供应链中的运输成本份额很大。

运输链基本上分为3个部分：预运输（提货过程的第一英里）、长途运输（集装箱的门到门运输）和终运输（交货过程的最后一英里）。在大多数情况下，预运输和终运输是通过公路进行的,但对于长途运输,可以考虑公路、铁路、航空和水运方式。正如所指出的那样,长途运输通常涉及不同运输方式的组合,但在预运输和终运输中,也会有越来越多的多式联运系统(例如在城市物流中使用货车和自行车的组合)。

大多数多式联运采用集装箱运输(每年增长15%左右)。集装箱化的主要原因是它提高了货物的安全性、多种运输方式的可达性,降低了装卸成本、标准化要求。有4种不同的运输方式:多式联运、联合运输、综合运输和同步运输。

(1)多式联运

多式联运是指至少两种不同的运输方式运输货物。运输单元可以是箱子、集装箱、公路或铁路车辆以及船舶。区域或国家规模的定期快递系统以及长途集送货服务也是多式联运的例子。

(2)联合运输

联合运输是指货物在一个多式联运单元内从起点运输到终点,在改变运输方式时不需要对货物本身进行处理的一种特殊的多式联运方式。全球的多式联运终端通过多种运输方式为企业提供了使用的灵活性和成规模的经济效益。

(3)综合运输

这种运输方式主要是单独或组合使用不同运输方式。欧洲共同体委员会将综合运输定义为使用两种或更多种运输方式,但其与多式联运有两个特殊差别:它被运输链中的多个或一组托运人所使用;从整体可持续性方面看,它使用更智能的运输方式,最大化所有运输方式的优势。

(4)同步运输

同步运输是继多式联运和综合运输之后的又一发展方向,是两种或两种以上运输方式结构化、高效率的同步结合。通过同步运输,承运商或客户可根据经营情况和客户要求,随时自主选择最佳运输方式。

令人吃惊的是,我们看到了所有运输种类的共同点:使用多种运输方式。当然,一些种类更加强调运输过程的某些方面。同步运输强调运输的灵活性(实时),联合运输关注相同的承载单元,综合运输提高了资源利用率。

Knowledge Link

Diverging Traffic

Diverging traffic is traffic that changes the directions or types of traffic on certain lanes at different times. Diverging traffic is also called "tidal traffic."

According to its function, diverging traffic can be divided into two categories: directional traffic and non-directional traffic. Traffic that changes the directions of some lanes in different time periods is called directional traffic. This kind of traffic can alleviate the uneven distribution of traffic flow directions and improve the utilization rate of the roads. Non-directional traffic refers to the traffic changing the driving types on some lanes in different time periods. It can be divided into vehicles and pedestrians, motor vehicles and non-motor vehicles between the mutual transformations of the use of the lane change. This kind of diverging traffic has good effect on alleviating the inhomogeneity of time distribution of all kinds of traffic. For example, in the morning peak bicycle time, change the outer vehicle lane to bicycle lane, and in the peak vehicle time, change the bicycle lane to vehicle lane. In addition, measures like in the central business district changing the car lane for sidewalks and setting timing pedestrian streets, etc., are non-directional change of traffic.

The advantage of diverging traffic is to use the roads reasonably, to improve the utilization rate of the roads sufficiently, so as to improve the traffic capacity of the roads, which has a good effect on solving the contradiction between the traffic flow direction and the uneven time distribution of various types of traffic.

The disadvantage of diverging traffic is that it increases the workloads of traffic control and corresponding facilities, and requires the drivers to have better quality and focus, especially in the transition areas.

Unit 5

Traffic Management

Text

1. Objectives

Traffic management arose from the need to maximize the capacity of existing highway networks within finite budget and, therefore, with a minimum of new construction. Methods, which were often seen as a quick fix, required innovation solutions and new technical developments. Many of the techniques devised affected traditional highway engineering and launched imaginative junction designs. Introduction of signal-controlled pedestrian crossings not only improved the safety of pedestrians on busy roads but improved the traffic capacity of roads by not allowing pedestrians to dominate the crossing points.

More recently the emphasis has moved away from simple capacity improvements to accident reduction, demand restraint, public transport priority, environmental improvement, and restoring the ability to move around safely and freely on foot and by pedal cycle.

2. Demand management

There has been a significant shift in attitudes away from supporting unrestricted growth in highway capacity. The potential destruction of towns and cities and the environmental damage to rural areas is not acceptable to a large proportion of the population. Traffic management has, largely, maximized the capacity of the highway network, yet demand and congestion continues to increase.

Highway authorities accept that they do not have a mandate to provide funds for large amounts of new construction. It is clear that, for the foreseeable future, resources will not be available to provide for unrestricted growth in private vehicular traffic. Traffic engineering alone cannot provide for sufficient highway capacity even with limited amount of new construction.

One method of demand management that has received considerable interest and study is congestion charging. This is where vehicles are surcharged for their use of road space depending on the prevailing levels of congestion. New technologies in the form of smart cards and vehicle identification are needed to ensure that the system is practical and fair. Measures to accommodate foreign or non-local vehicles are also needed. Video image analysis has reached a level of sophistication that can be used for this purpose.

3. Engineering measures

The traffic engineers have a vast array of measures which can be applied to achieve their objectives. These objectives include capacity enhancements, accident reduction, environmental protection and enhancement, servicing of premises and providing access, providing assistance to pedestrians and cyclists, assisting bus or tram operators, providing facilities for persons with disabilities, regulating on-street and off-street parking.

The majority of capacity problems occur at road junctions. In urban areas road junctions are important focal points for pedestrians and cycling activities and are often the site of public transport interchanges. Due to the various conflicting demands it is not surprising that two-thirds of urban traffic accidents occur at road junctions. Selection of an appropriate junction design for a particular site can be very difficult. Some designs, such as roundabouts, can significantly reduce the severity of vehicle-vehicle accidents but can prove hazardous for cyclists. In some instances, installation of traffic signals with full pedestrians and cycle facilities and bus priority measures might also reduce the overall traffic-handling capacity.

Careful allocation of road space to separate traffic flow into designated traffic lanes can reduce confusion and limit accidents. Designation of traffic lanes might include special vehicle lanes, such as cycle and bus lanes and dedicated left-turn or right-turn lanes.

Introduction of banned turns and one-way traffic can reduce potential conflicts and accident. These measures can be used to implement protected pedestrian or cycle crossings and simplify junction layouts generally. Great care must be exercised when one-way traffic schemes are being considered as they can result in speeding by drivers who are confident that they will not be opposed by other vehicles.

Point road closures are used to simplify junction and highway layouts and eliminate turning conflicts. The resulting continuous footway can also improve pedestrian safety and provide space for bus stops, cycle racks, pedestrian crossings, and hard and soft landscaping.

Closure of long sections of road to general traffic can produce pedestrianized shopping streets. Such scheme can be very complex to design and introduce, because facilities for buses, emergency services vehicles, residents/proprietors and service vehicles must be considered.

Carriageway narrowing can be used to limit capacity or vehicle speeds and reduce parking and pedestrian crossing distances.

The key to all successful traffic engineering schemes is that the visual cues provided by the road must give a clear indication to users who have priority.

4. Road markings

It is not possible to overestimate the importance of road markings as part of the road system. In a few instances road markings merely emphasize the layout of the highway and guide road users to a safe course of action. In many cases the whole of the success of a scheme relies upon the visual messages emanating from the road markings.

5. Traffic signs

Traffic signs fall into four categories: warning signs, regulatory signs, directional informatory signs and other informatory signs.

Warning signs provide information to road users about hazards such as junctions, changes of direction, carriageway width, gradient or humped back bridges, roadworks, etc.

Regulatory signs provide a message that must be obeyed, such as stop, give way, banned turns, compulsory turns, no entry, one-way traffic, prohibited vehicle types, weight and width restrictions, waiting and loading restrictions, speed restriction, etc.

Directional informatory signs provide information about routing and important places of interest, such as railway stations, airports, etc.

Other informatory signs provide information about footway and other parking schemes, heritage sites, census points, etc. Traffic signs are often installed in association with road markings.

New Words and Expressions

traffic management	交通管理
highway networks	公路网
finite [ˈfaɪnaɪt]	adj. 有限的
innovation solutions	革新方案
signal-controlled	信号控制的
pedestrian crossing	人行横道
traffic capacity of road	道路通行能力
demand management	需求管理
congestion charging	拥堵收费
surcharge [ˈsɜːtʃɑːdʒ]	n. 超载;追加罚款;额外费用 vt. 使装载过多;追加罚款
nonlocal [ˌnɒnˈləʊkəl]	adj. 非局部的;非本地的
vehicular [vəˈhɪkjələ(r)]	adj. 车的;用车辆运载的
enhancement [ɪnˈhɑːnsmənt]	n. 增进,增加

traffic signs	交通标志
warning signs	警告标志
regulatory signs	禁令标志
directional informatory signs	指示指路标志
pedal ['pedl]	n. (自行车等的)脚蹬子;踏板　vt. 骑自行车
overestimate [ˌəuvər'estɪmeɪt]	n. 过高的评估　vt. 对……估计过高
	vi. 高估
census points	人口普查点
footway ['futweɪ]	n. 人行道;小路
eliminate [ɪ'lɪmɪneɪt]	vt. 排除;消除;清除;淘汰
carriageway ['kærɪdʒweɪ]	n. 车道;马路

Exercises

I True or false.

(　　)(1) Introduction of signal-controlled pedestrian crossing only improved the safety of pedestrians on busy roads.

(　　)(2) Traffic management has, largely, maximized the capacity of the highway network, yet demand and congestion continues to increase.

(　　)(3) Traffic engineering alone can provide for sufficient highway capacity.

(　　)(4) Careful allocation of road space to separate traffic flow into designated traffic lanes can reduce confusion and limit accidents.

(　　)(5) It is impossible to overestimate the importance of road markings as part of the road system.

II Complete the following sentences.

(1) The majority of capacity problems occur at _____.

(2) _____ road junctions are important focal points for pedestrians and cycling activities and are often the site of public transport interchanges.

(3) Traffic signs fall into four categories: _____, _____, _____ and _____.

(4) Warning signs provide information to road users about _____ such as junctions, changes of direction, carriageway width, gradient, low, opening or humped back bridges, roadworks, etc.

III Answer the following questions.

(1) What does traffic management arise from?

(2) What is the emphasis of traffic management?

(3) What technologies are needed to ensure that the congestion charging system is practical and fair?

(4) What are the traffic engineers' objectives in engineering measures?

Topics for Discussion

(1) What is the connection between traffic system management and traffic demand management?

(2) How to implement traffic system management and traffic demand management?

(3) How to evaluate traffic management measures?

参 考 译 文

交 通 管 理

1. 目标

交通管理源于在有限预算内最大限度地提高现有道路网通行能力的需要。交通管理被视为快速解决问题的方法，需要创新的解决方案和新技术的发展。许多交通管理中发明的技术影响了传统的道路工程，并发明了创新性的和节约成本的交叉口设计方法。信号控制人行横道的引入不仅提高了大流量道路上的行人安全，而且通过限制行人的过街位置来提高道路通行能力。

最近，交通管理的重点已从单纯提升通行能力转向减少事故、限制需求、公交优先、改善环境以及保障行人和骑车人安全畅通通行等方面。

2. 需求管理

人们支持道路通行能力无限制增长的态度发生了重大转变。大多数人都无法接受交通对城镇的潜在破坏和对乡村地区环境的破坏。交通管理在很大程度上提高了道路网的容量，但交通需求和交通拥堵程度还在继续增加。

道路管理部门认为他们不能为大量新建工程项目过多地提供资金。很明显，在可预见的未来，道路资源将无法满足私人车辆交通的无限制增长。单靠交通工程无法提供足够的道路通行能力，更何况新建工程项目的数量有限。

拥堵收费是需求管理中一种受到广泛关注和研究的方法。即对车辆使用道路空间收取附加费的方法。收费的多少取决于当前的拥堵程度，需要采用智能卡和车辆识别的新技术来确保系统的实用性和公平性。还需要采取措施来顾及国外的或非本地的车辆。视频图像分析精度已经可以达到这个目的。

3. 工程措施

交通工程师有很多措施可以用来实现他们的目标，包括提高通行能力，减少事故，保护和改善环境，提供营业场所和路径，为行人和骑行者提供帮助，支持公交车和电车运营，为残疾人提供便利，以及规范路内和路外停车。

大多数通行能力问题都发生在道路交叉口。在市区，道路交叉口是步行和骑行活动的集中地，通常也是公共交通交汇的地点。由于不同交通需求间相互冲突，2/3 的城市交通事故发生在道路交叉口便不足为奇。为特定地点选择合适的交叉口设计非常困难。有些设计(如环形交叉口)可以显著降低车辆间交通事故的严重程度,但对骑车人来说可能是危险的。在某些情况下,设置行人和自行车交通信号以及公交车优先措施也可能降低整体的通行能力。

谨慎分配道路空间,按指定的车道分隔交通流,可以减少混乱和事故。指定车道包括专用车道,例如自行车车道和公交车车道以及专用的左转和右转车道。

禁止转弯和单向交通的引入可以减少潜在冲突和事故隐患。这些措施可用于保证人行横道和自行车道上的安全,并在整体上简化交叉口布局。须谨慎考虑单向交通方案,因为这些方案可能导致驾驶人确信自己不会遇到对向车辆而超速驾驶。

封闭关键道路可简化交叉口和道路布局,并消除转弯冲突。由此产生的连续人行道还可以提升行人安全,并为公交车站、自行车停放区、人行横道以及软质和硬质景观提供空间。

从整个道路网中封闭一大段路可以形成步行商业街。由于必须为公交车、抢险车辆、居民(业主)和服务车辆提供便利,因此这种方案的设计和实施会非常复杂。

缩窄行车道可限制通行能力,降低车速,减少停车并缩短行人过街距离。

所有交通工程方案成功的关键是,在道路上提供的视觉提示必须明确指出哪类道路使用者具有优先通行权。

4. 道路标线

将道路标线作为交通系统的一部分非常重要。在少数情况下,道路标线只强调道路布局并引导道路使用者采取安全的行动方案。在多数情况下,方案能否成功完全取决于道路标线传递的视觉信息。

5. 交通标志

交通标志分为4类:警告标志、禁令标志、指路标志及其他标志。

警告标志向道路使用者提供与危险有关的信息,例如交叉口、方向变化、行车道、斜坡和拱形桥、道路施工等。

禁令标志提供一些必须遵守的信息,如停车、让路、禁止转弯、强制转弯、禁入、单行道、车种限制、车重和车宽限制、停留及装载限制以及速度限制等。

指路标志提供有关路线和重要景点的信息,例如火车站、机场等。

其他标志提供有关人行道和其他停车方案、历史遗址、人口普查地点等信息。交通标志有时须结合道路标线进行设置。

Reading Material

Traffic Surveillance

Traffic surveillance is an integral and essential part of freeway traffic management systems. Surveillance entails the status monitoring of traffic conditions and of control system operation as well as the collecting of information for implementing controls and for incident detection. The surveillance system provides data on the system operating conditions, upon which appropriate decisions and control actions are taken, whose effects on the system operations are then monitored by the surveillance system. There is thus a closed loop of information, decision, control and impact.

These aspects of surveillance are common to both urban street and freeway traffic control systems, whose effectiveness is clearly dependent on the reliability and accuracy of the surveillance system, especially in the case of traffic responsive control. For freeways, however, perhaps the most important aspect of surveillance is the detection and servicing of incidents, which principally contribute to nonrecurring freeway congestion. In addition, problems caused by incidents on urban streets are generally less severe than those on freeways, since emergency and repair services, along with alternative routes, are usually more readily available. Thus, the provision of surveillance for incident detection and servicing on urban streets is less common than on freeways.

1. Incident detection

The earliest traffic surveillance techniques used for incident detection were field observations, periodic studies, police reports and citizen calls. Today, surveillance for incident detection is carried out through the deployment of a wide variety of methods as below:

(1) Electronic surveillance.
(2) Closed-circuit television.
(3) Aerial surveillance.
(4) Emergency motorist call systems.
(5) Citizen-band radio.
(6) Police and service patrols.

2. Electronic surveillance

Electronic surveillance for incident detection is accomplished by the real-time computer monitoring of traffic data collected by detectors installed at critical locations. The measurement of traffic performance and control effectiveness, for urban streets as well as for freeways, can also be carried out by such an installed system. It remains, therefore, to describe how incident detection is accomplished through electronic surveillance.

When a delay-causing incident occurs on a freeway, the capability of the freeway is reduced at the point of occurrence and, if it is reduced to a value less than the prevailing demand, the traffic flow upstream of the incident is also affected. Most freeway incident detection algorithms involve the determination of changes in certain traffic flow variables which are believed to be caused by, or correlated with, the occurrence of incidents. If detected changes in the traffic flow variables are greater than some predetermined values, the occurrence of an incident is indicated. Thus, incidents are detected by logically evaluating the variations in traffic flow characteristics.

An operational system in which this concept has been effectively used is the Los Angeles Freeway Surveillance and Control Project. In this system, changes in lane occupancy between adjacent detectors are used to sense congestion and indicate the occurrence of an incident. At the end of each sampling period, a computer calculates the percent difference in occupancy between adjacent detectors stations spaced at 1/2mi (800m) intervals. When the relative percent change between the present occupancy and the occupancy of the preceding sample for the downstream detector exceeds a predetermined value, the computer automatically signals an alert. Additional information on traffic conditions immediately upstream of the incident can then be obtained, and judgment decisions are made with regard to what response is needed.

The principal advantages of electronic surveillance for incident detection are: it is the only system that provides a continuous network wide monitoring capability at relatively low costs; the installed systems can be used for many other tasks, such as the establishment of metering rates for traffic-responsive, ramp-metering systems. The main disadvantage is that the nature of the incident cannot be determined by the system, so that some follow-up surveillance is required to determine the response needed. Also, electronic surveillance for incident detection is yet to be tested for a large network, and general incident-detection strategies have not been perfected.

Exercises

I True or false.

(　　)(1) Problems caused by incidents on urban streets are more severe than those on freeways.

(　　)(2) When a delay-causing incident occurs on a freeway, the capability of the freeway is reduced at the point of occurrence, but the traffic flow upstream of the incident isn't affected.

(　　)(3) If detected changes in the traffic flow variables are greater than some predetermined values, the occurrence of an incident is indicated.

(　　)(4) An operational system in which this concept has been effectively used is the Los Angeles Freeway Surveillance and Control Project.

(　　)(5) Electronic surveillance for incident detection has been used for a large network, and general incident-detection strategies have been perfected for this purpose.

II Complete the following sentences.

(1) Traffic surveillance is an integral and essential part of _____.

(2) For freeways, perhaps the most important aspect of surveillance is _____.

(3) The various methods of _____ presented in this section are most typically applied to freeways for incident detection and servicing.

(4) The earliest traffic surveillance techniques used for incident detection were _____, _____, _____ and _____.

(5) _____ for incident detection is accomplished by the real-time computer monitoring of traffic data collected by detectors installed at critical locations.

III Answer the following questions.

(1) What does traffic surveillance entail?

(2) What is the most important aspect of surveillance for freeways?

(3) What is the earliest traffic surveillance techniques used for incident detection?

(4) What is electronic surveillance for incident detection accomplished by?
(5) What does freeway incident detection algorithms involve?

参 考 译 文

交 通 监 测

　　交通监测是高速公路交通管理系统的重要组成部分。监测包括对交通状况和控制系统运行的状态进行监控,以及为实施控制和事故检测收集信息。监测系统提供与系统运行条件有关的数据,根据这些数据人们可以做出正确的决策并采取相应的控制措施,它们对系统的影响也将被监测系统监视到。因此,形成了一个信息、决策、控制和影响的闭环。

　　对于城市道路与高速公路的交通控制系统来说,两者的监测系统是相同的,它们的工作效率显然取决于监测系统的可靠性与精确度,尤其是在交通感应控制的情况下。然而,对于高速公路而言,监测可能是对事故的检测和处理。大多数情况下事故会导致高速公路的非经常性拥堵。另外,城市道路上的事故造成的问题通常比高速公路上的问题要轻,因为通常更容易获得应急和维修服务以及替代路线。因此,在城市道路上提供事故检测和处理的监测不如在高速公路上常见。

1. 事件检测

　　最早用于事件检测的交通监测技术是实地观察、定期研究、警察报告和市民电话。目前,可通过部署各种方法,对事件检测进行监测。这些方法如下:

　　(1)电子监测。
　　(2)闭路电视。
　　(3)空中监测。
　　(4)紧急驾驶人呼叫系统。
　　(5)市民波段收音机。
　　(6)警察和服务巡逻。

2. 电子监测

　　用于事故检测的电子监测由实时电脑监测系统来完成,所需的交通数据由安装在关键位置的检测器采集。城市道路和高速公路的交通运行情况和控制效果的检测也可以通过上述系统进行,因此,仍然需要描述如何通过电子监测完成事件检测。

　　当高速公路上发生由延误引起的事故时,高速公路在事故发生点的通行能力会降低,如果下降到低于通行需求的值,事故发生位置上游的交通流也会受到影响。大多数高速公路事故检测运算方法都涉及确定某些交通流变量的变化,这些变化被认为是由事故造成的,或与事故有关。如果检测到交通流变量的变化大于某些预定值,则表示发生了事故。因此,可以通过合理评估交通流特性的变化来检测事故。

　　洛杉矶高速公路监测项目是一个有效利用这一概念的操作系统。系统通过相邻检测器之间车道占用率的变化来检测拥堵并指明事件的发生。在每个采样周期结束时,计算机计算间隔为1/2英里(800米)的相邻检测站之间的占用率差异百分比。当下游探测器当前占用率和前一样本占用率之间的相对百分比变化超过预定值时,计算机自动发出警报。然后,可以获得事故发生位置上游交通状况的附加信息,并根据需要做出判断决定。

用于事故检测的电子监测的主要优点是：它是唯一一个成本相对较低，具有提供全网络连续监视能力的系统；安装的系统可用于许多其他任务，例如建立交通响应比率计量和匝道计量系统。主要缺点是系统无法确定事件的性质，因此需要一些后续监测来确定所需的响应。此外，用于事故检测的电子监测还没有在大型网络中进行测试，一般的事故检测部署还没有完善。

Knowledge Link

Transportation Organization

Traffic organization refers to the comprehensive use of transportation planning, traffic restriction and management measures to reasonably assign traffic on the basis of time, type of vehicles and flow direction, so that keeping the traffic in an orderly and efficient operation state.

Traffic organization optimization is a systematic work. it can be divided into three levels: macro traffic organization optimization, regional traffic organization optimization and micro traffic organization optimization. For macro traffic organization optimization, it mainly contains cutting peak and filling valley in time, controlling density in space according to the principle of space-time equalization. For micro traffic organization optimization, it considers the signal timing and traffic channelization, which reflects the full use of time and road space. In other words, macro traffic organization optimization needs to solve the problem of traffic equalization, while micro traffic organization optimization needs to solve the problem of conflict separation.

Measures of macro-traffic organization optimization include controlling traffic origination, improving traffic service and transforming road traffic into other modes. Regional traffic organization optimization includes separation and assignment of traffic flow. The micro traffic organization optimization includes the optimization of traffic at intersections and road sections. Specific methods include one-way traffic organization, tidal traffic organization, channelized traffic organization at signalized intersections, flow restriction at intersections, public transportation organization, etc.

Unit 6
Traffic Signal Timing

Text

The increasing flow of traffic in cities has a significant effect on the road traffic congestion as does the time required for road users to reach their destinations. Widening roads and increasing their capacity are not sufficient by itself, as the intersections then become bottlenecks. Bottlenecks cannot be prevented. However, the way intersections are controlled has room for improvement.

Since the 1960s, different methods have been presented to manage intersections and for controlling traffic signals' timing, as one of the first traffic signal controllers, fixed-time or pre-timed controllers applied historical data to determine appropriate time for traffic signals. Fixed-time control method is not based on current traffic demands and cannot handle unexpected conditions in traffic. Based on the historical traffic flow, the cycle time is divided to several phases. A fixed amount of time is required for clearing the intersections and starting the next phase after each phase, called the safety time. The safety time increases per hour for the case of shorter cycle time. Therefore, there is a lower overall capacity for intersections with shorter cycle times. In addition, longer waiting times and longer queues are the consequences of longer cycle times. As fixed-time control methods cannot predict traffic demand accurately, they are not appropriate for situations such as accidents, and other disturbances that may disrupt traffic conditions.

The next step for improving the control method was actuated or real-time controllers. This type of controller emerged in the 1970s. Traffic-actuated control methods utilize inductive detectors to observe the actual traffic situations. The traffic-actuated controller must have the ability to determine whether the last vehicle of the queue formed at the stop line during the red phase has passed. This detection is useful for having efficient extension or termination of green time, and it is performed by measuring the gap between vehicles. The green time is terminated when the gap between vehicles is larger than the threshold maximum gap.

The optimal placement of detectors at an intersection impacts the performance of actuated control method. In addition, by increasing the number of detectors, the accuracy of the system is improved. In actuated control methods, a pre-specified block period time is considered for extending the green time of a phase. Therefore, detection of sparse traffic can have a considerable influence on delay time.

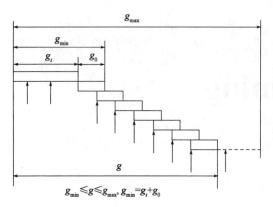

Figure 6-1　The working principle of induction signal(感应式信号工作原理)

The working principle of induction signal is shown in Figure 6-1.

Where, g_0——unit extension time;
　　　g_i——initial green time;
　　　g_{min}——minimum green time;
　　　g_{max}——limit extension time;
　　　g——actual green time.

Parameters like time, day, season, weather, and some unpredictable situations such as accidents and special events are highly influential on traffic load. Traffic-adaptive control systems were created to take these elements in account in order to more efficiently predict green times. Fixed-time and actuated control method do not use a control policy or a parameterized value function. Furthermore, these systems do not utilize accumulative information for improving their performances. In adaptive traffic control systems, the traffic conditions are sensed and monitored continuously and the timing of traffic signals is adjusted accordingly. It is useful to note that adaptive controllers and real-time ones are two different concepts; however, it is possible to have a system with both abilities. The controllers with real-time ability in response to sensory inputs are real-time systems, in which the parameters of the controllers and internal logic remain unchanged. Alternatively, one of the special features of adaptive systems is their characteristic in adjusting their parameters and internal logic in response to the significant change of the environment.

Both SCATS and SCOOTS are famous adaptive systems that gather data of the traffic volume in real time at each intersection to control timing of traffic lights. To obtain traffic information, SCATS counts vehicles at each stop line, and SCOOTS applies a set of advanced detectors placed upstream of the stop line. Using these detectors, SCOOTS gives a higher resolution of the traffic condition such as traffic volume and number of cars in the queue before they reach the stop line. SCATS and SCOOTS both use centralized control. The use of artificial intelligence methods to control traffic signals started in 1990s. Multiple optimization and estimation methods have been applied for adaptive control. Machine learning techniques are beneficial to create adaptive controllers with the ability to address unpredictable traffic condition issues.

New Words and Expressions

destination [ˌdestɪˈneɪʃn]	n. 目的地；终点
bottleneck [ˈbɒtlnek]	n. 瓶颈路段；瓶颈；阻碍；障碍
intersection [ˌɪntəˈsekʃn]	n. 十字路口；交叉路口；交点；交叉；相交
queue [kjuː]	n.（人、汽车等的）队；行列；队列 vt.（人、车等）排队等候 vi.（使）排队
fixed-time	固定周期
pre-timed	预设周期
fixed amount	定额；固定金额
actuate [ˈæktʃueɪt]	vt. 开动；激励；驱使
threshold [ˈθreʃhəuld]	n. [物]阈值
accuracy [ˈækjərəsɪ]	n. 准确(性)；精确(性)
accumulative [əˈkjuːmjələtɪv]	adj. 积聚的；累积的
sensory [ˈsensərɪ]	adj. 感觉的；感官的
real-time	实时
parameter [pəˈræmɪtə(r)]	n. 限制因素；决定因素；参数
sparse traffic	稀疏的交通
in response to	响应；回答；对……有反应
upstream [ˌʌpˈstriːm]	adv. 向(在)上游；逆流 n. 上游
centralized control	集中控制，中心控制
artificial intelligence	人工智能
adaptive control	自适应控制
continuously [kənˈtɪnjuəslɪ]	adv. 连续不断地
optimal [ˈɒptɪməl]	adj. 最优的；最佳的
monitor [ˈmɒnɪtə(r)]	n. 显示屏，监视器 vi. 监视 vt. 监听
initial [ɪˈnɪʃl]	adj. 最初的；开始的

Exercises

I True or false.

(　　)(1) A fixed amount of time is required for clearing the intersections and starting the next phase after each phase, called the safety time.

(　　)(2) The green time is initiated when the gap between vehicles is larger than the threshold maximum gap.

(　　)(3) Parameters like time, day, season, weather, and some unpredictable situations such as accidents and special events are highly influential on traffic load.

(　　)(4) One of the special features of adaptive systems is their characteristic in adjusting their parameters and internal logic in response to the significant change of the environment.

(　　)(5) SCATS and SCOOTS both use decentralized control.

Ⅱ Complete the following sentences.

(1) Traffic-actuated control methods utilize _____ to observe the actual traffic situation.

(2) The controllers with real-time ability in response to sensory inputs are _____, in which the parameters of the _____ and _____ remain unchanged.

(3) A fixed amount of time is required for clearing the intersection and starting the next phase after each phase, called the _____.

(4) One of the special features of adaptive systems is their characteristic in adjusting their _____ and _____ in response to the significant change of the environment.

(5) Both _____ and _____ are famous adaptive systems that gather data of the traffic volume in real-time at each intersection to control timing of traffic lights.

Ⅲ Answer the following questions.

(1) Which kind of controllers applied historical data to determine appropriate time for traffic signals?

(2) What is called the safety time?

(3) What are the consequences of longer cycle times?

(4) What has a great impact on traffic load?

(5) When did the use of artificial intelligence methods to control traffic signals start?

Topics for Discussion

(1) Please propose several different methods for managing intersections and controlling traffic signals' timing.

(2) Please resume the working principle of actuated or real-time controllers.

(3) What are the differences between SCATS and SCOOTS?

参 考 译 文

交通信号配时

城市交通量的增加对道路交通拥堵产生了显著的影响,因此道路使用者到达目的地所需的时间也会受到影响。仅通过拓宽道路来提高通行能力是不够的,因为之后交叉口会成为瓶颈。瓶颈是无法避免的,但是,交叉口控制的设计方式还有改进的余地。

自20世纪60年代以来,人们提出了不同的方法来管理交叉口和控制交通信号的配时。固定周期或预设周期交通信号控制器是第一批交通信号控制器之一,利用历史数据来确定交通信号的合理配时。固定周期控制方法不是基于即时的交通需求,因此不能处理意外的交通情况。根据历史交通量,周期时间分为几个相位。清空交叉口的车辆和一个相位结束到下一个相位开始所需的固定时间,称为安全时间。周期时间越短,安全时间越长。因此,对于周期较短的交叉口,其总通行能力较低。此外,周期较长会导致较长的等待时间和较长的排队长度。由于固定周期控制方法无法准确预测交通需求,因此不适用于出现事故等可能干扰交通的情况。

改进控制方法的下一步是使用感应或实时控制器。这种控制器出现在20世纪70年代。交通感应控制方法利用感应探测器来观测实际交通状况。交通感应控制器必须能够确定红灯阶段在停车线形成的最后一队排队车辆是否已通过。这种检测能够有效延长或终止绿灯时间,它通过测量车辆之间的间隙来实施。当车辆间隙大于最大间隙阈值时,绿灯时间终止。

交叉口检测器的最优配置影响了感应控制方法的性能。此外,通过增加探测器的数量,提高了系统的精度。在感应控制方法中,为了延长相位的绿灯时间,考虑预留一小段时间。因此,对较小交通流的检测会对延误时间产生相当大的影响。

感应式信号工作原理如图6-1所示。其中,g_0表示单位绿灯延长时间,g_i表示初期绿灯时间,g_{min}表示最短绿灯时间,g_{max}表示绿灯限制延长时间,g表示实际绿灯时间。

时间、日期、季节、天气以及一些不可预测的情况(如事故和特殊事件)等参数对交通负荷有很大影响。在考虑这些因素的情况下,人们为了更有效地预测绿灯时间,建立了交通自适应控制系统。固定周期和感应控制方法没有使用控制策略或参数化的价值函数。此外,这些系统没有利用累积信息来提高性能。自适应交通控制系统对交通状况进行连续的感知和监视,并相应地调整交通信号配时。需要注意的是,自适应控制器和实时控制器是两个不同的概念,但是,可能存在同时拥有这两种能力的系统。对传感器输入具有实时响应能力的控制器是实时系统,其中控制器的参数和内部逻辑保持不变。相对地,自适应系统的一个特殊特征是,它们具有根据环境的重大变化调整参数和内部逻辑的特性。

SCATS和SCOOTS都是著名的自适应系统,它们实时收集每个交叉口的交通量数据,以控制交通灯的时间。为了获取交通信息,SCATS会计算每条停车线前排队的车辆数量。而SCOOTS会在停车线上游应用一组先进的检测器。使用这些检测器,SCOOTS可以具备更高的交通状况分辨能力,可检测如交通量和到达停车线前排队的车辆数量。SCATS和SCOOTS都使用集中化控制。人工智能方法在交通信号控制中的应用始于20世纪90年代。在自适应控制中采用了多种优化和估计方法。机器学习技术有助于创造能够处理不可预测交通状况的自适应控制器。

Reading Material

Traffic Signal System Timing for Arterial Routes

A signal system is defined as having two or more individual signal installations which are linked together for coordination purpose. To obtain system coordination, all signals must operate with the same (common) cycle length, although in rare instances some intersections within the system may operate at double or one-half the cycle length of the system. Although at individual intersections, the intervals (red, green and yellow) may vary according to traffic conditions, it is desirable that the arterial routs for which coordination is being provided have a green plus yellow interval equivalent to at least 50% of the cycle length.

In a discussion of the two-way and one-way traffic applications of system timing, the following terms are frequently used:

①Through-band: the space between a pair of parallel speed lines which delineates a progressive movement on a time-space chart.

②Band speed: the slope of the through-band representing the progression speed of traffic moving along the arterial routs.

③Bandwidth: the width of the through-band expressed in seconds, indicating the period of time available for traffic to flow within the band.

1. One-way traffic

The simplest form of coordinating signals is along a one-way traffic, or to favor one direction of traffic on a two-way traffic that contains highly directional traffic flow. Essentially, the mathematical relationship between the band speed S and the offset L can be described as

$$S(\text{mph}) = \frac{D(\text{ft})}{1.47L} \tag{6-1}$$

or

$$S(\text{km/h}) = \frac{D(\text{m})}{0.278L} \tag{6-2}$$

Where, S——speed of progression;
D——spacing of signals;
L——offset in seconds.

2. Two-way street

For a two-way movement, four general progressive signal systems are possible: simultaneous, alternate, limited (simple) progressive and flexible progressive. The relative efficiency of any of these systems is dependent on the distances between signalized intersections, the speeds of traffic, the cycle length, the roadway capacities, and the amount of friction caused by turning vehicles, parking and parking maneuvers, improper or illegal parking or loading, and pedestrians. In general, a two-way progression with maximum bandwidth can be achieved only if the signal spacing is such that vehicular travel times between signals are a multiple of one-half the common cycle length; otherwise, inevitable compromises have to be made in the progression design. A discussion of the four general progressive signal systems follows.

(1) Simultaneous System

All signals along a given street operate with the same cycle length and display the green indication at the same time. Under this system, all traffic moves at one time, and a short time later all traffic stops at the nearest signalized intersections to allow cross-street traffic to move.

The mathematical relationship between the band speed (in both directions) and signal spacing in a simultaneous system can be described as follows:

$$S(\text{mph}) = \frac{D(\text{ft})}{1.47C} \tag{6-3}$$

or
$$S(\text{km/h}) = \frac{D(\text{m})}{0.278C} \tag{6-4}$$

Where, S ——speed of progression;
D ——spacing of signals;
C ——cycle length in seconds.

(2) Alternate System

Each successive signal or group of signals shows opposite indications to that of the next signal or group. If each signal alternates with those immediately adjacent, the system is called single-alternate system. If pairs of signals alternate with adjacent pairs, the system is termed double-alternate system, and so on.

The band speed in a single alternate system is

$$S(\text{mph}) = \frac{D(\text{ft})}{0.735C} \tag{6-5}$$

or
$$S(\text{km/h}) = \frac{D(\text{m})}{0.139C} \tag{6-6}$$

(3) Limited (or Simple) Progressive System

This system uses a common cycle length, and the various signal faces controlling a given street provide green indications in accordance with a time schedule to permit continuous operation of platoons along the street at a designed rate of speed, which may vary within different parts of the system.

(4) Flexible Progressive System

This is a refinement of the limited progressive system where the signal offsets, splits, and/or cycle length of the common cycle are changed to suit the needs of traffic throughout the day. For example, an inbound progression toward the central business district during the morning peak can be changed to an outbound progression during the remainder of the day merely by adjusting the signal offsets, or a longer cycle length can be used during the morning and evening peak hours in order to provide a greater capacity than during the off-peak period.

Exercises

I True or false.

(　　)(1) At single intersections, the time proportion of red, green or yellow maybe change with the traffic conditions.

(　　)(2) Band speed is the speed of vehicles to cross the band.

(　　)(3) The mathematical relations between band speed and offset L is $L = \frac{D(\text{ft})}{S(\text{mph})} \times 1.47$.

(　　)(4) Only when the vehicular travel time between signals is one second times the common cycle length, could the two-way progression obtain the maximum bandwidth.

(　　)(5) Every adjacent group of signals indicates the adverse information to the next one.

Ⅱ Complete the following sentences.

(1) Although at individual intersections, the intervals (red, green and yellow) may vary according to traffic conditions, it is desirable that the arterial routes for which coordination is being provided have a green plus yellow interval equivalent to at least _____ of the cycle length.

(2) _____: the space between a pair of parallel speed lines which delineates a progressive movement on a time-space chart.

(3) For a two-way movement, four general progressive signal systems are possible: _____, _____, _____, and _____.

(4) Each successive signal or group of signals shows opposite indications to that of the next signal or group. If each signal alternates with those immediately adjacent, the system is called _____.

(5) Each successive signal or group of signals shows opposite indications to that of the next signal or group. If pairs of signals alternate with adjacent pairs, the system is termed _____.

Ⅲ Answer the following questions.

(1) In what conditions could the traffic conditions be ideal?

(2) What is the bandwidth in a discussion of the two-way and one way street applications of system timing?

(3) When does the bandwidth get its biggest volume?

(4) How does the simultaneous system work?

(5) From flexible progressive system we could know, when we want to offer a greater capacity during the peak hours than off-peak hours, what shall we do?

参 考 译 文

干线道路交通信号系统配时

信号系统是指需要相互协调联系在一起的拥有两个或两个以上单个信号设备的系统。虽然在少数情况下有些交叉口信号运行周期可能是整个系统运行周期的两倍或二分之一,为了获得系统的协调性,所有的信号必须以相同的周期运行。虽然在一个单独的交叉口,信号间隔(红灯、绿灯和黄灯)可能根据交通环境发生变化,但主干路上的信号协调最好能够达到绿灯加黄灯控制时间至少是周期长的50%的水平。

在讨论双向道路和单向道路系统配时应用时,经常应用以下术语:

(1)绿波带:两条描绘时空图上连续活动的平行速度线之间的空间。

(2)带速:绿波带的倾斜度,用来表示主干路上车辆运行的速度。

(3)带宽:绿波带的宽度,单位为秒,表示交通流通过穿越带的可用时间。

1. 单向交通

形式最简单的协调信号存在于单向交通,或者存在于一个有高度方向性交通流的双向交通的一个交通方向。从本质上说,带速 S 和绿时差 L 的数学关系如下:

$$S(英里/小时) = \frac{D(英尺)}{1.47L} \tag{6-1}$$

或

$$S(公里/小时) = \frac{D(米)}{0.278L} \tag{6-2}$$

式中:S——运行速度;

D——信号间隔;

L——绿时差,以秒计。

2. 双向交通

对于双向交通的交通流,一般的续进式信号系统有 4 种:同步式、交互式、限制(或简单)续进式和灵活续进式。这些系统中任何一个系统的相对效率取决于两个相邻信号交叉口之间的距离、交通流的速度、控制信号的周期长、道路的容量、转弯车辆所产生的摩擦量、停车和非停车的机动性、不适当的或非法的停车和装载以及行人的影响。一般来说,对于双向交通,仅仅当信号间隔能达到下述情况时,即当车辆在两个信号之间的运行时间是半个共同周期长的倍数时,双向交通才能达到最大的带宽,否则就必须在续进式设计中做一些必不可少的折中处理。下面逐一讨论 4 种一般续进式信号系统。

(1)同步式系统

在一条道路上,所有的信号用相同长度的周期运行,并同时显示绿灯。在这样的系统中,所有的交通在同一时刻流动,过一段时间后,所有车辆在最近的信号交叉口停止,让相交道路的车辆通过。

在同步式协调控制系统中,带速(在两个方向)和信号间隔之间的数学关系式如下:

$$S(英里/小时) = \frac{D(英尺)}{1.47C} \tag{6-3}$$

或

$$S(公里/小时) = \frac{D(米)}{0.278C} \tag{6-4}$$

式中:S——运行速度;

D——信号间隔;

C——以秒为单位的周期长度。

(2)交互式系统

每个连续的信号或信号组所作出的指示都与相邻的信号或信号组作出的指示相反。如果每个信号都跟着最相邻的信号变化,那么这个系统就叫作单变化系统。如果每两个信号都随着最相邻的成对信号变化,那么这个系统就叫作双变化系统。以此类推。

单变化系统中的带速为

$$S(英里/小时) = \frac{D(英尺)}{0.735C} \tag{6-5}$$

或

$$S(公里/小时) = \frac{D(米)}{0.139C} \tag{6-6}$$

（3）受限（或简单）的续进式系统

这个系统使用一个共同的周期长，并且为了让一条道路上的每一队车辆都能够保持在一个设计好的速率（这在系统的不同部分也可能不同）上连续不断的行驶，这条道路上不同方向的信号控制都按时间表为它们提供绿灯。

（4）灵活的续进式系统

这个系统是限制续进系统的一个改进形式，在这个系统中，信号的绿时差、绿信比和（或）公共信号周期长度都在一整天内根据交通的需要来变化。举例来说，仅仅通过调节信号时差便可以将在早高峰流向中心商业区的交通量转变成在其他时间流出中心商业区的交通量，或者在早高峰和晚高峰时可以使用一个更长的信号周期来提供比非高峰时间更大的通行能力。

Knowledge Link

Auxiliary Facilities for Improving the Benefit of Line Control System

In order to improve the efficiency of the line control system, thepre-signal and variable speed indicator can be set on the main road.

1. Pre-signal

A traffic signal is set a few tens of meters in front of the main intersection, so that the traffic flow can be concentrated at the signal and pass continuously at the intersection, so that the green time at the intersection can be effectively used and the traffic capacity of the intersection can be improved.

2. Variable speed indicator

Set up speed signs at one or more places in front of the intersection, and instruct the driver to drive at the indicated speed through the intersection. The value of the speed indicator on the variable speed indicator is related to the time and is controlled by the signal control machine at the intersection.

Unit 7

Urban Transit Mode

Text

1. Overview

Transit plays two major roles in North America. First, it accommodates choice riders — those who choose transit for their mode of travel even though they have other means available. These riders choose transit to avoid congestion, save money on fuel and parking, use their travel time productively for other activities, and reduce the impact of automobile driving on the environment. Transit is essential for mobility in the central business districts (CBDs) of some major cities, which could not survive without it.

The other major role of transit is to provide basic mobility for segments of the population that are unable to drive for age, physical, mental or financial reasons. About 11% of the adult population in the United States does not have a driver's license and must depend on others to transport them in automobiles, on transit, or via other modes, including walking, bicycling, and taxis. These transit users have been termed captive passengers.

2. Human factors

Transit passengers frequently rely on other modes to gain access to transit. Transit use is greater where population densities are higher and pedestrian access is good. Typical transit users do not have transit service available at the door and must walk, bicycle, or drive to a transit stops and walk or bicycle from the transit discharge points to their destinations. In contrast, suburban areas are mainly automobile-oriented, with employment and residences dispersed, often without sidewalks or direct access to transit stops. If potential passengers cannot access service at both ends of their trip, transit is not an option for that trip.

Unlike the other modes addressed in the *Highway Capacity Manual*(*HCM*), transit is primarily focused on a service rather than a facility. Roadways, bicycle lanes, and sidewalks, once constructed, are generally available at all times to users. Transit service, in contrast, is only available at designated times and places. Another important difference is that transit users are passengers, rather than drivers, and not in direct control of their travel. Thus, the frequency and reliability of service are important quality-of-service factors for transit users. Travel speed and comfort while making a trip are also important to transit users.

Transit is about moving people rather than vehicles. Transit operations at their most efficient level involve relatively few vehicles, each carrying a large number of passengers. In contrast, roadway capacity analysis typically involves relatively large numbers of vehicles, most carrying only a single occupant. In evaluating priority measures for transit and automobile users, the number of people affected is often more relevant than the number of vehicles.

3. On-street transit characteristics

The *HCM* addresses only those major transit modes (in terms of passengers carried) that operate on streets and interact with other users of streets and highways. These modes are bus, streetcar, and light rail described briefly in the following sections.

(1) Bus

The bus mode is operated by rubber-tired vehicles that follow fixed routes and schedules along roadways. Although the electric trolleybus (a bus receiving its power from overhead wires) is classified as a separate mode by the Federal Transit Administration (FTA), for the purposes of the *HCM*, it is also considered a bus. In 2007, more than 53% of all transit passenger traveling in the United States occurred on buses.

The bus mode offers considerable operational flexibility. Service can range from local buses stopping every two to three blocks along a street, to limited-stop service stopping every 1/2 to 1mi (0.8 to 1km), to express service that travels along a roadway without stopping. Buses may stop in the travel lane (on-line) or in a parking lane or pullout (off-line). On-line stops reduce bus delay but may increase vehicle and bicycle delay. Because buses frequently carry more people than the vehicles stopped behind them, on-line stops may help reduce overall person delay.

(2) Streetcar

The streetcar mode is operated by vehicles that receive power from overhead wires and run on tracks. For FTA reporting purposes, streetcars are considered to be a form of light rail.

Streetcars make on-line stops, which minimize their delay of entering and leaving a station, but may increase delay to vehicles and bicycles stopped behind the streetcars.

(3) Light rail

As is streetcar, light rail is a mode operated by vehicles that receive power from overhead wires and that run on tracks. Trains typically consist of multiple cars; fares are typically paid before passengers boarding the trains (thus allowing passengers to board through all doors, reducing dwell time); station spacing tends to be relatively long, particularly outside downtown areas; and traffic signal preemption or priority is frequently employed.

When light rail operates along a roadway, it typically does so in an exclusive lane or in a segregated right-of-way in the street median or along the side of the street. Most light rail routes include lengthy sections where tracks are located in a separate, potentially grade-separated right-of-way and any interaction with traffic occurs at gate-controlled grade crossings.

New Words and Expressions

transit [ˈtrænsɪt]	n. 轨道交通;经过;通行;运输
available [əˈveɪləbl]	adj. 可获得的;可找到的;有空的
fuel [fjuəl]	vt. 供以燃料;给……加燃料 n. 燃料;刺激因素
flexibility [ˌfleksəˈbɪləti]	n. 灵活性;弹性;适应性
Central Business District (CBD)	中央商务区
mobility [məʊˈbɪləti]	n. 移动性;机动性
sidewalk [ˈsaɪdwɔːk]	n. 人行道
driver's license	驾驶执照
light rail	轻轨
trolleybus [ˈtrɒlɪbʌs]	无轨电车
block [blɒk]	n. 块;街区;大厦;障碍物
bicycle lane	自行车道
fare [feə]	n. 票价;费用;旅客
platform [ˈplætfɔːm]	n. 平台;月台;站台
dwell time	停顿(留)时间
preemption [prɪˈempʃən]	n. 优先权;先占
gate-controlled	闸门控制的
on-line stop	路内停车
in contrast	相反
density [ˈdensɪtɪ]	n. 密度
suburban [səˈbɜːbən]	adj. 郊区的;城郊的 n. 郊区居民
automobile [ˈɔːtəməliːl]	n. 小汽车

Exercises

I True or false.

(　　)(1) Transit is essential for mobility in the central business districts (CBDs) of some major cities, which could not survive without it.

(　　)(2) Typical transit users can have transit service available at the door.

(　　)(3) If potential passengers cannot access service at both ends of their trip, transit is still an option for that trip.

(　　)(4) Roadways, bicycle lanes, and sidewalks, once constructed, are generally available at all times to users. Transit service, in contrast, is only available at designated times and places.

(　　)(5) In evaluating priority measures for transit and automobile users, the number of people affected is often more relevant than the number of vehicles.

(　　)(6) Streetcars make on-line stops, which minimize their delay of entering and leaving a station, and will not increase delay to vehicles and bicycles stopped behind the streetcars.

II Complete the following sentences.

(1) Transit use is greater where _____ and _____.

(2) Suburban areas are mainly automobile-oriented, with _____ and _____, often without _____.

(3) Transit operations at their most efficient level involve relatively _____.

(4) The bus mode is operated by rubber-tired vehicles that _____ and _____.

(5) Because buses frequently carry more people than the vehicles stopped behind them, _____.

III Answer the following questions.

(1) Choice riders are those who choose transit for their mode of travel even though they have other means available. Why do these riders choose transit?

(2) What are the two major roles that transit plays in North America?

(3) Typical transit users do not have transit service available at the door, so how do they get transit service?

(4) What are the important factors for transit users?

(5) What is the range of the bus mode service?

Topics for Discussion

(1) What is the difference between bus, streetcar and light rail in function?

(2) Transit is unlike the other modes addressed in the *HCM*. Then why is transit primarily focused on a service rather than a facility?

(3) Why don't typical transit users have transit service available at the door?

参考译文

城市公共交通模式

1. 概述

在北美地区，公共交通（简称公交）有两个主要作用。首先，它可以运载那些具有选择权的乘客，即那些可以使用其他交通工具，却依然选择公交出行的乘客。这些乘客选择乘坐公共交通工具（简称公交工具）来避免拥堵、节省燃料和停车费用，有效地利用出行时间进行其他活动，并减少驾驶小汽车对环境的影响。公共交通在一些城市的中央商务区是必不可少的，否则这些小城市便无法正常运行。

公共交通的另一个主要作用是为那些由于年龄、身体、心理或经济原因不能进行驾驶的人提供基本的乘车出行服务。在美国，大约11%的成年人没有驾驶执照，必须搭乘别人的小汽车、公交工具或使用其他交通方式（包括步行、自行车和出租车）出行。这些公交用户被称为没有选择权的乘客。

2. 人的因素

公交乘客通常使用其他交通方式以达到乘坐公交工具的目的。人口密度越高、步行越方便的地方，公交使用率越高。一般的公交用户不能在家门口乘坐公交工具，必须步行、骑自行车或开车到公交停靠站搭乘公交工具，并在下车后从公交的下车地点步行或骑自行车到目的地。相比之下，郊区的工作区与住宅区较分散，往往没有直达公交站点的人行道或车行道，因此人们以小汽车出行为主。如果潜在乘客不能在行程的两端乘坐公交，则不会选择公交作为该次行程的交通方式。

与《道路通行能力手册》中讨论的其他交通方式不同，公交的重中之重在于服务而不是设施。通常，车行道、自行车道和人行道一旦建成，便随时可供用户使用。相比之下，公共交通只在指定的时间和地点提供服务。另一个重要的区别是，公共交通的用户是乘客，而不是驾驶人，乘客不能直接掌控自己的出行路线。因此，对于公交用户，公共交通的频率和可靠性是其服务质量的重要因素，出行中的行驶速度和舒适度也很重要。

公共交通是关于人的移动，而不是车辆的移动。公共交通运营效率最高时涉及的车辆反而较少，且每个车辆携带大量乘客。相比之下，道路通行能力分析通常涉及相对较多的车辆，且大多数车辆仅搭载一个乘员。在评估公交用户和小汽车用户的优先程度时，受影响的人数通常比受影响的车辆数更重要。

3. 城市道路公交特征

《道路通行能力手册》仅讨论在城市道路上运行，并与城市道路和公路上其他交通方式的用户相交互的主要公共交通模式（就载客而言）。这些公共交通模式是公交车、有轨电车和轻轨，将在下文作简要介绍。

（1）公交车

公交车的运营方式，即装有橡胶轮胎的车辆沿着固定的路线和特定的时刻表在道路上行驶。尽管电动无轨电车（从架空电线接收电力的公交车）被美国联邦公共交通管理局单独归类为一种公交模式，但就《道路通行能力手册》而言，它依然被视为公交车。2007年，在美国超过53%的公共交通乘客搭乘公交车。

公交车的操作灵活性相当大。服务范围包括:沿城市道路每2~3个街区就有一辆当地的公交车停靠,每1/2~1英里(0.8~1公里)就有限停服务以及不停车的快速路沿线服务。公交车可以停在行车道上(路内),也可以停在停车道上或行车道以外(路外)。路内停车减少了公交车的延误,但可能会增加其他机动车和非机动车的延误。因为公交车的载客量通常要多于停在他们后面的车辆,因此公交车路内停车可能有助于减少整体延误。

(2) 有轨电车

有轨电车从架空的电线接收电力并在轨道上移动。美国联邦公共交通运输局的报告将有轨电车视为轻轨的一种形式。

有轨电车在路内停车,最大限度地减少了其进出停靠站时的延误,但可能会增加停在有轨电车后面机动车和非机动车的延误。

(3) 轻轨

与有轨电车一样,轻轨从架空的电线接收电力并在轨道上移动。轻轨通常由多节车厢组成;乘客在上车前购买车票(因此允许乘客从所有车门上车,以减少滞留时间);车站间距往往较长,尤其是在市区外;通常拥有交通信号的抢占权和优先通行权。

当轻轨沿道路运行时,它通常处于专用车道上,或在道路的中央分隔带和两侧的隔离带中运行。大多数轻轨路线包含较长的路段,这些路段中的轨道有着单独的、潜在的互通式通行权,并且与其他交通流的交织都发生在闸门控制的平面交叉口处。

Reading Material

Rail Transit

1. Light railtransit

The right-of-way for light rail transit routes includes sections of shared, semi-exclusive, and exclusive facilities. The last of these becomes similar to heavy rail transit design, except that power distribution systems and station platform lengths differ.

Shared, on-street track alignment is primarily determined by the geometry of the streets available for the routes. Turning radii can be quite short, but track spacing at sharp curves must be increased so that front and rear overhangs of one vehicle do not collide with the center portion of a vehicle on the adjacent track. This may preclude simultaneous 90° turns at intersections of two narrow streets, and dictate single-track, alternate movement or other design solutions.

Semi-exclusive route sections can be placed in the median strip of wide arterial routes with crossings at grade. In this case, tracks are usually laid on open ballast between intersections, both for a low-cost comfortable profile and to prevent motor vehicles from encroaching on the tracks. Curve geometrics are usually designed for somewhat higher speeds (larger radius), but clearances of vehicles at curves can still be a problem.

Methods of priority treatment for buses aresometimes applicable to streetcar operation. This applies particularly to signal priority measures and exclusive use of streets in downtown areas.

Light Rail Transit(LRT) can offer platform speeds and track capacities that are only moderately lower than heavy rail transit. More direct service with branch or parallel lines can often be provided: stops may be located more accessible and spaced more closely to reduce walking distances. Thus, overall door-to-door travel times for urban trips up to perhaps 10mi (16km) may be in the same range as those provided on fully grade-separated urban rapid transit facilities. Attractive linear park treatments, such as those along St. Charles and Carrollton Avenues in New Orleans and Beacon Street in Boston-Brookline, can provide additional amenities to the streetcars located in street medians.

2. Heavy rail transit

Because of the enormous investment required for the infrastructure of fully separated rail transit, such routes are only built in corridors with very large traffic demand. This technology offers very fast, high-capacity service, but the network extent is necessarily limited by available funds, and feeder services are required to serve the rail routes.

Heavy rail transit alignments are based on very detailed studies of demand, station locations and relative costs.

The decision on vertical alignment is made primarily so that the sum of land, construction and environmental costs is minimized, although irregular topography also plays a role. Construction costs are least at grade, but this requires permanent occupancy of a strip of land and building of grade separations for all crossings. It is therefore generally feasible only in outlying areas where land is inexpensive, or in freeway medians where the cost of land and grade separations can be shared with the highway project. Elevated construction costs are perhaps twice as much as for facilities at grade, but the land below can be used for a street, for parking or industrial uses, or even for linear parks; Bay Area Rapid Transit(BART) in Albany and El Cerrito, California, is an example of the latter. In densely built up areas, including CBDs, the adverse impacts of noise and reduction of daylight militate against the building under elevated construction. A doubling, or even tripling, of costs occurs if underground alignments are considered.

An operational analysis determines the need for crossovers and storage tracks. The former are needed primarily for track maintenance purposes, while the latter provide opportunity for turning trains back short of the end of the line, or for storing disabled vehicles.

3. Commuter railroads

In some large metropolitan areas, such as New York, London, Paris and Tokyo, a large burden of urban transportation is borne by intercity railroads. Many of the lines involved were located for intercity travel and found themselves serving increasing numbers of local trips in generating urban land uses along their corridors. Up to about 1920 some railroads added routes in the suburbs where they found sufficient demand. However, since that time many routes have been abandoned because of the high costs of railroad operation and the reluctance by management to allow long-distance passengers and freight customers to subsidize urban transportation.

Originally, railroads were usually laid out at grade with level highway crossings. In some cities, such crossings were eliminated later by changing the grade of the railroad, thereby providing it with a fully exclusive right-of-way. Passenger operation was, however, still sharing this facility with freight movements.

A major problem of urban railroad services is the location of the central terminals. There is almost always only one downtown access point per corridor, and this is often located at the edge of or outside the CBD. Typically, it is a stub terminal with inherent limitations to the number of train movements that can be handled per hour. In some cities with extensive electrified suburban lines, such as Brussels, Munich, Hamburg and Philadelphia, these drawbacks have been overcome by connecting terminals located on opposite sides of the CBD with underground tracks and one or more intermediate stations for direct access to the city center. Capacity is increased because trains no longer need to be reversed at crowded terminals. In Paris, suburban rail lines were diverted before reaching their old terminals into a new network of lines across the inner city. The resulting operations in these cities are a mixture of heavy rail transit in the center and commuter railroad outside it.

Exercises

I True or false.

(　　)(1) Shared, on-street track alignment is primarily determined by the geometry of the streets available for the route.

(　　)(2) LRT can offer platform speeds and track capacities that are higher than heavy rail transit.

(　　)(3) Because of the enormous investment required for the infrastructure of fully separated rail transit, such routes are only built in corridors with very large traffic demand.

(　　)(4) Up to about 1920 some railroads cut routes in the suburbs where they found few demand.

(　　)(5) In some large metropolitan areas, such as New York, London, Paris and Tokyo, a large burden of urban transportation is borne by intercity railroads.

II Complete the following sentences.

(1) The right-of-way for light rail transit routes includes _____.

(2) Semi-exclusive route section can be placed _____.

(3) _____ offers very fast, high-capacity service, but the network extent is necessarily limited by _____, and feeder service is required to _____.

(4) Heavy rail transit alignments are based on _____.

(5) A major problem of urban railroad services is _____.

III Answer the following questions.

(1) What is on-street track alignment primarily determined by?

(2) Where are semi-exclusive route sections placed?

(3) Which direct service with branch or parallel lines can often be provided?

(4) What are the disadvantages of heavy rail transit?
(5) What are heavy rail transit alignments based on?

参 考 译 文

轨 道 交 通

1. 轻轨交通

轻轨交通根据其通行权可分为共用设施、半专用设施和专用设施三类。这三类中的最后一项即专用设施与重轨运输的设计相似，只是其动力分布系统和车站站台长度有所不同。

共用设施的城市轨道路线定位主要取决于其路线所经过城市道路的几何线形。其转弯半径可以很小，但是在急转弯处，轨道之间的间隔必须增大，以避免车辆的前后外伸部分与相邻轨道上车辆的中部相撞。这项要求不允许轻轨在两条狭窄街道相交的十字交叉口上同时进行90°转弯，但允许单轨、交替通行轨道和其他类型轨道的此类设计方案。

半专用的轨道设施可以设置在宽的干线道路的中央分隔带上，轨道之间的交叉采用平交形式。在这种情况下，交叉口之间的轨道通常被铺设在裸露的碎石上，目的是使造价低、乘坐舒适，并防止机动车辆驶入轨道。曲线的几何线形设计通常采用较高的车速（较大的半径），但是车辆在转弯处的横向净空仍然是一个问题。

公共汽车优先的方法有时被应用到有轨电车的运行上，尤其是信号优先的管理措施和设立中心区的专用街道的方法。

轻轨交通的站台车速和轨道通行能力仅比重轨交通略低。由于轻轨路线有分支或平行路线，因此它可以提供更多的便捷服务。行人更容易进入站点，站点间距变小，从而减少了人们的步行距离。因此，对于10英里（16公里）长的城市出行距离，所要花费的门到门出行时间与那些全部设置互通式立交的城市快速运输设施所要用的时间大致相同。建设对出行者有吸引力的带状公园，可为处于街道中央的有轨电车提供额外的便利设施，例如新奥尔良的查尔斯街、卡尔顿大街以及波士顿的比肯街沿线。

2. 重轨交通

由于修建完全立交的轨道运输基础设施需要大量的投资，所以这种线路只修建在交通需求很大的运输通道内。虽然这种建设方法可以提供快捷、大容量的服务，但是其网络的拓展不可避免地受到可用资金的限制，并且需要支线列车运行来为铁路线路提供服务。

重轨运输路线的设计需要以非常详细的交通需求、站点位置和相关费用研究为基础。

虽然确定路线的纵断面一定程度上受不规则地形的影响，但主要还是为了尽量减少总的土地、建筑和环境成本。地面线路的结构造价若要最小，则需要永久地占用一定量的土地，而且所有的交叉口必须采用立交形式。因此通常只有在地价便宜的外围地区或在高速公路的中央分隔带上修建才可行，因为这里的土地和立交的成本可以分摊到公路工程项目中。高架结构的造价大约是地面设施的两倍，但高架结构的下部空间可以用作城市道路、停车或工业用途，甚至可以作为带状公园。美国奥尔巴尼市和加利福尼亚州埃尔塞利托镇的海湾地区快速运输系统便是后者的一个例子。在建筑密度大的地区，包括中心商业区在内，噪声以及日照减少的不利因素会对高架结构下的建筑产生不利影响。如果考虑采用地下方案，造价将会是立交方案的两倍甚至三倍。

运营分析将决定是否有必要修建天桥和备用轨道。其中前者主要是供检修轨道使用,后者则供车辆在路线终点倒车或停放不能行驶的车辆用。

3. 市郊列车

在一些国际大都市,如纽约、伦敦、巴黎和东京,城市交通的大部分是由城际轨道运输来承担的。许多为城际通行而设置的轨道路线,在其沿线的土地上兴起了新的城市,致使利用轨道运输进行地方旅行的数量也日益增加。到大约1920年,为了满足大量的交通需求,一些铁路线路持续增加市郊线路。然而,从那时开始,由于铁路运营费用过高以及不愿通过管理手段向长途乘客和货运客户征收城市交通建设费等原因,许多线路已经停止运行。

起初,铁路通常铺设在地面上,与公路平面交叉。后来,通过调整轨道的坡度,这种形式的交叉在一些城市被取消。因此,轨道运输就具有了专用通行权。但是,客运仍然与货运共同使用这种运输设施。

确定中央枢纽的位置是城市轨道交通系统的一个主要问题。每条交通走廊通常只有一个进入中心区的站点,它一般设置在中心商业区的边缘或以外的地区。通常,一个终端枢纽每小时可以处理的列车数量有限。在一些拥有广泛电气化郊区线路的城市,如布鲁塞尔、慕尼黑、汉堡和目前的费城,通过将位于中心商业区两侧的枢纽与地下轨道和一个或多个中间站相连接,直接进入市中心,可以克服这些缺点。由于车辆不需要在拥挤的终点站调头,轨道的通行能力得到了提高。在巴黎,郊区的铁路路线在到达旧终点站前改道,接入穿过市中心的新线路网。在这些城市中,由此产生的运营模式将中心的重轨运输和外部的通勤铁路结合起来。

Knowledge Link

The Characteristics of Urban Rail Transit

Urban rapid rail transit system (subway, light rail) is a multi-disciplinary in a complex system. The development experience of many major cities in the world over the past century tells us that only adopting rapid rail transit system as the backbone of public transport network can we effectively address urban transport problems.

(1) Urban rail transit provides a way of high-capacity transport services. Urban rail transit provides intensive use of resources, environmental protection, and comfortable, safe and efficient way of high-capacity transport services, which has no interference with other modes of transport of the city. With strong transport capacities, higher service levels, significant resources to environment benefits, it is the fundamental way to solve the problem of large urban transport and sustainable development.

(2) Rail transport provides an intensive mode of transport. Rail transport not only provides efficient and quality bus travel services, but also is an intensive mode of transport, saving energies and land resources. Use and develop valuable resources of underground space to provide new transport supply, to ease the tension in the ground space resources and to support the sustainable development of cities.

(3) Urban rail transit is a huge complex system of comprehensive.

① Large building scale. A city rail transit network generally has hundreds of kilometers.

② High technically demand. Involving almost to the modern civil engineering, mechanical and electrical equipment works with high-tech fields.

③ Great project investment. The cost is 3 to 4 billion per kilometer.

④ Long construction period. In-line construction period is 4 to 5 years, while network-building generally needs 30 to 50 years.

⑤ Many participating units. There are hundreds of ones.

Unit 8
Parking

Text

The rapid growth in population has led to substantial traffic bottlenecks in recent transportation systems. This not only causes significant air pollution, and waste in time and energy, but also signifies the issue of parking. Parking is a commodity that is subject to the basic laws of economics. Thus, for example, if a parking policy is developed which results in a reduction in the number of long-stay parking spaces in a town centre, then a new equilibrium point will be established which will result in a higher price to the consumers for parking. This higher price, in turn, will make it less attractive to make the journey-to-work trip to the town centre by car. Thus parking policy affects how people would travel and good parking management and control can lead to some or all of the following: higher car occupancies, decreasing person-trips, faster travel times and less travel delays, greater public transport usage, decreasing congestion, and reduced air and noise pollution.

1. Traffic and parking: some associated effects

(1) Aesthetics

An environmental "disamenity" which receives more attention is the aesthetic deterioration often associated with the parking of vehicles.

(2) Business, accessibility and parking

Commercial interests consider that they are directly affected by the parking situation and, even in this day, many merchants and business people in city center tend to regard packed kerb a necessary visual evidence of trade prosperities.

2. Accidents

Although vehicles parked at, or manoeuvring into or out of, kerb parking can be an important cause of accidents, the number of studies which have been carried out in order to produce an understandable and accurate description of the role of parking in accident occurrence is relatively few.

3. Surveys

Parking surveys are carried out in order to obtain the information necessary to provide an assessment of the parking problem in the area(s) being studied. The objective of any such study is to determine facts which will provide the logical points of departure in relation to indicating parking needs. Common to all types of parking studies, whatever their scale, are parking supply and parking usage surveys.

(1) Parking supply survey

A parking supply survey is concerned with obtaining detailed information regarding those on-street and off-street features which influence the provision of parking space, the existing situation with regard to parking space, and how it is controlled. A typical survey would require an inventory of the on-street accommodation, and of all off-street car parks and parking garages serving the traffic area being studied. Whether the survey area involves the central area of a town (which may be broadly define as the area in which all streets have business frontage), or a suburban shopping area, or a hospital or university, it should also include the surrounding fringe area where vehicles are parked by persons with destinations within the survey area.

(2) Parking usage survey

The parking phenomenon is very much based on the law of supply and demand, whereby supply is the total number of spaces available within a designated area, and demand is the desire to park based solely on the location of the trip destination. However, unlike the true supply and demand situation, there is a third variable-usage-associated with parking which reflects the desire to park close to the destination, but within the limitations imposed by the available supply, as well as the desire to park at a reasonable cost. In other words, demand is a constant, reflecting the desire to park at the trip destination, whereas usage is a variable that depends upon the conditions at the terminal area and upon the characteristics of the trip as well as of the trip-maker.

If the parking supply is in excess of the parking demand, then the true demand can be determined by means of a parking concentration survey — usually carried out in conjunction with a parking duration survey. If the parking supply is less than the demand, then an indication of the demand may be obtained by means of a direct-interview parking survey. However, the true demand, which might include "suppressed" vehicles not able or willing to find parking within the survey area, can only be properly estimated from comprehensive land use/transport surveys of the nature.

(3) Concentration survey

The purpose of a concentration survey is to determine not only where vehicles do park, but also the actual number parked at any given instant at all locations (on-street and off-street) within the survey area. The street phase of the survey is usually carried out by dividing the survey area into "small zones" each short enough to be toured on foot or by car within a predetermined time interval. Information regarding the numbers of vehicles parked (legally and illegally) at each street and alleyway location is then noted on prepared forms or spoken into a tape recorder for transcribing at the end of the day. Each zone normally forms a closed circuit so that no time is lost by the observer(s) in returning to the starting point for successive inspections.

(4) Duration survey

The primary purpose of a duration survey is to determine the lengths of time that vehicles are stored within the survey area. In so doing, data normally collected during a concentration survey can also be collected (in essentially the same way, in the case of the on-street survey) during the duration survey.

(5) Parker interview survey

This, the most expensive and comprehensive of the parking surveys, normally involves interviewing motorists at their places of parking and questioning them regarding the origins of the trips just completed, the primary destinations, and the purposes of the trip. Particulars regarding parking duration and concentration may also be gathered during this survey and, if required, information may be obtained regarding the number, sex and age of each vehicle's occupants.

New Words and Expressions

equilibrium [ˌiːkwɪˈlɪbrɪəm]	n. 平衡;平静;均衡
merchant [ˈmɜːtʃənt]	n. 商人;批发商;贸易商;店主 adj. 商业的;商人的
scale [skeɪl]	n. 规模;比例;数值范围;等级
disamenity [ˌdɪsəˈmiːnɪtɪ]	n. 不舒适;不愉快
prosperity [prɒˈsperətɪ]	n. 繁荣
inventory [ˈɪnvəntrɪ]	n. 详细目录;财产清册
accommodation [əˌkɒməˈdeɪʃn]	n. 住处;住宿
phenomenon [fəˈnɒmɪnən]	n. 现象
terminal [ˈtɜːmɪnl]	n. 终点站;终端 adj. 末期的;晚期的;定期的
comprehensive [ˌkɒmprɪˈhensɪv]	adj. 全面的;广泛的;综合的
predetermine [ˌpriːdɪˈtɜːmɪn]	v. 预定,预先确定
transcribe [trænˈskraɪb]	v. 转录
inspection [ɪnˈspekʃn]	n. 检查;视察;查看;审视
concentration [ˌkɒnsnˈtreɪʃn]	n. 集中;集合;专心;专注
duration [djuˈreɪʃn]	n. 持续;持续时间
conjunction [kənˈdʒʌŋkʃn]	n. 联合;关联;连接
alleyway [ˈælɪweɪ]	n. 小巷;胡同;窄道;通道
kerb [kɜːb]	n. (由条石砌成的)路缘;道牙

suppress [sə'pres]　　　　　　　　　v. 镇压;压制;忍住;止住
designate ['dezɪgneɪt]　　　　　　　 v. 指定;指明
occupant ['ɒkjəpənt]　　　　　　　　n. 占有者;居住者

Exercises

I True or false.

(　　)(1) The number of studies, which have been carried out in order to produce an understandable and accurate description of the role of parking in accident occurrence is relatively few.

(　　)(2) A typical survey would require an inventory of the on-street accommodation, and of all off-street car parks and parking garages serving the traffic area being studied.

(　　)(3) If the parking supply is less than the demand, then the true demand can be determined by means of a parking concentration survey — usually carried out in conjunction with a parking duration survey.

(　　)(4) Data normally collected during a duration survey can also be collected (in essentially the same way, in the case of the on-street survey) during the concentration survey.

(　　)(5) Particulars regarding parking duration and concentration may be gathered during the parking interview survey and, if required, information may be obtained regarding the number, sex and ages of each vehicle's occupants.

II Complete the following sentences.

(1) Although vehicles parked at, or manoeuvring into or out of, _____ can be an important cause of accidents.

(2) _____ are carried out in order to obtain the information necessary to provide an assessment of the parking problem in the area(s) being studied.

(3) The parking phenomenon is very much based on the law of _____, whereby _____ is the total number of spaces available within a designated area, and _____ is the desire to park based solely on the location of the trip destination.

(4) If the _____ is in excess of the _____, then the true demand can be determined by means of a parking concentration survey — usually carried out in conjunction with a parking duration survey.

(5) The primary purpose of a _____ is to determine the lengths of time that vehicles are stored within the survey area.

III Answer the following questions.

(1) What can good parking management and control lead to?
(2) What is the objective of parking study?
(3) What is a parking supply survey concerned with?
(4) What is the purpose of a concentration survey?

(5) What does the parker interview survey normally involve?

Topics for Discussion

(1) What is the relationship between parking and accidents?
(2) Please outline how to conduct parking supply survey.
(3) What are the benefits of good parking management and control?

参 考 译 文

停 车

近年来,人口的快速增长导致交通系统产生了严重的交通瓶颈。这不仅会造成严重的空气污染以及时间和能源的浪费,而且也揭示了停车问题。停车是一种符合经济学基本规律的行为。一项导致市中心长期停车位减少的停车政策颁布后,消费者停车费用将会随之提高,这就会使停车供需达到一个新的平衡点。相对地,停车费用的提高会降低驾车去市中心上班的吸引力。因此,停车政策会影响人们如何出行。合理的停车管理和控制策略能够带来下列部分或全部效果:提高客车实载率,减少人们的出行量,减少出行时间和延误,增加市区公共交通使用率,减少拥堵,降低空气、噪声污染。

1. 交通和停车:一些相关的影响

(1)美学

由于车辆停放对美感的破坏,一些环境"不和谐"问题也开始受到更多关注。

(2)商业、可达性和停车

商业的利益相关者认为他们直接受到停车状况的影响,即使在现在,市中心的许多商人和商务人员往往认为挤满车辆的路是贸易繁荣的必要体现。

2. 事故

尽管停放在路边停车位或进出路边停车位的车辆可能是造成事故的一个重要原因,但对停车行为在事故发生中的作用进行了易于理解和准确描述的研究相对较少。

3. 调查

进行停车调查是为了获得相关必要信息,以评估所研究区域的停车问题。此类研究的目的是确定一些实际情况,提供与停车需求指示相关的逻辑出发点。无论规模多大,所有停车研究的共同点都是对停车位供给和使用情况的调查。

(1)停车位供应调查

停车位供应调查的目的是获取与路内路外特征相关的详细信息,这些特征影响停车位的规定和现存状况以及管理它们的方法。一般的调查包括路内停车位数量以及在研究区域内服务交通的所有路外停车场和停车库。调查区域包括城市中心区域(大致定义为所有道路都有邻街商业区的区域)、郊区购物区域、医院或大学,以及有着出行目的的人停放车辆的周围边缘区域。

(2)停车位使用情况调查

停车现象与供需规律的关系密切,其中供应是指定区域内可用停车位的总数,需求是仅与出行目的地位置有关的停车位期望数。然而,与实际供需情况不同的是,存在着第三个与停车位使用相关的变量。这个变量反映了在目的地附近的停车期望,但是变量的取值受到可用停车位供应的限制以及人们对停车费用合理期望的影响。换句话说,需求量是一个常量,反映了出行者在出行目的地停车的期望,而使用量是一个变量,它取决于终点区域的条件以及出行行为和出行者的特征。

如果停车供应超过停车需求,则可以通过停车集中调查确定实际需求——通常与停车持续时间调查同时进行。如果停车供应量小于需求量,则可以通过直接访问的停车调查方法获得需求量的指标。然而,真正的需求,包括无法或不愿意在调查区域内寻找停车位的"被排挤"的车辆,只能通过自然的综合土地利用调查或交通性质调查来适当估计。

（3）集中调查

集中调查的目的不仅是确定车辆停放的位置,还要确定在调查区域内所有停车位(路内和路外)在任一特定时刻实际的停车数量。在道路调查阶段,将调查区域划分为小分区,每个分区足够小,以便能在预定时间段内以步行或乘车方式完成巡视。然后,在准备好的表格上记录每条街道和小巷(包括合法的和不合法的)停车的车辆数量信息,或在录像机中记录,以便在当天结束时进行转录。每个分区通常形成一个闭合路线,使得观察者回到起始点进行连续检查时不会浪费时间。

（4）持续时间调查

持续时间调查的主要目的是确定调查区域内车辆持续停放的时间。通过持续时间调查可以得到集中调查所需要的数据(路内调查基本以相同的方式进行)。

（5）停车访问调查

这是成本最高、最全面的停车调查,包括在停车场采访驾驶人并询问他们刚刚完成出行的起点、主要目的地以及出行目的。在调查期间,也可以收集有关停车持续时间调查和集中调查的内容。如果有需要,可以获取每辆车乘车人员的数量、性别和年龄信息。

Reading Material

Parking: Design and Control

1. Introduction

The traffic engineers need to know how to provide parking spaces best, and how to control parking facilities, both on the highway and off-street, both in surface site and structures. However, several design aspects should be well investigated and analyzed before implementing such solutions. This paper describes the key factors that need to be considered.

Parking provision on the highway in England, Scotland and Wales is constrained by legislation. Government rules and guidelines determine where parking can be provided, the methods of control and the design standards to be used. Separate legislation applies in Northern Ireland.

Off-street car parks are provided to meet a variety of needs and the type of needs can affect the design of the car parks. For example, an office car park could be designed to a lower standard than would be considered necessary for a public car park, as most of the users will be familiar with the geometry of the car park. If, for example, cars are parked too close together, the work colleague can usually be found and asked to move his vehicle.

Although off-street car park design is not governed by legislation in the same way as parking on the highway, the operation of a public car park can be subject to regulation using statutory powers.

Car parking control equipment is becoming increasingly more sophisticated, and the advent of microprocessor-based systems has allowed parking control systems to become more flexible, to meet the varied demands of users more closely. However, as the availability of increasingly sophisticated control systems has affected the way parking is controlled off-street, on-street parking controls have seen a different kind of revolution. This has allowed more flexibility, to better meet users' needs, through the use of both high-tech and very low-tech control equipment.

2. On-street parking

Most roads, in most places, are not subject to any form of parking control. It is widely believed that there is a right to park where no controls are present. This is not true. There is a right to pass along (travel) on a highway but no absolute right to stop.

(1) Road markings

The design and marking of parking bays on the highway is governed by legislation, these show a variety of markings for cars, buses and taxis, etc.. Echelon parking is seldom used because, although it may allow additional parking spaces to be accommodated in a wide street, drivers tend to have difficulty manoeuvring in and, particularly, out of the space.

The current regulations specify a standard bay width, of between 1.8m and 2.7m, although a bay width of 2.7 to 3.6m is specified for parking bays for the disabled. In reality, these widths may not be achievable in narrow streets, and it may be necessary to make a pragmatic trade off between the need to provide parking and the need to ensure road width for moving traffic. Prior to the 1994 regulations, government guidance allowed bays as narrow as 1.6m. Below this, the width of the average of modern car would mean that many vehicles would protrude outside the bay. "Code for setting of on-street parking spaces" has already specified three forms of arrangements: Figure 8-1 is parallel, Figure 8-2 is inclined and Figure 8-3 is vertical.

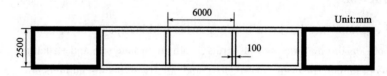

Figure 8-1 Parallel(平行式停车泊位)

Where parking is provided with restrictions then signs are used to show what type of vehicle can park and how. The signs either specify the type of vehicle allowed to use the parking place, or specify the conditions and restrictions attached to the use of the parking place. If the parking is available for a particular class of vehicle to use, without other constraint, the signing will identify the class of vehicle that can use the parking. Alternatively, the signing may display information about the limits and conditions of use for parking.

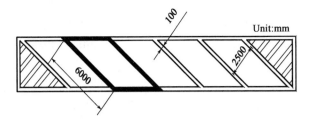 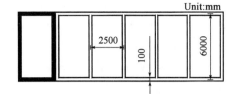

Figure 8-2 Inclined(倾斜式停车泊位)　　　　Figure 8-3 Vertical(垂直式停车泊位)

(2) Regulations

In U. K. , parking on the highway can be provided using a number of different methods of regulation. The principal legislation is *The Road Traffic Regulation Act 1988* (hereinafter referred to Act), as modified by later legislation.

Part I of the *Act* provides general powers to allow traffic regulation. Using powers in this part of the *Act*, a highway authority can make regulations restrict parking or, within the wording of the legislation, "waiting and loading". This legislation also allows for exemptions to be made to any order and so some parking provision made be made by exception. This means that, in a street where parking is otherwise banned, a parking place may be provided in this way, for example for motorcycles. Thus if any other vehicle parks in a motorcycle bay, it is in breach of the order of banning parking. Great care has to be taken in using the law in this way. If a street had a waiting restriction, without a ban on loading, for example, a motorcycle parking bay, then any other vehicle parking in the bay would be committing an offence. However, if the vehicle were loading goods, then no offence would be committed! This is clearly confusing and unsatisfactory.

The design of a car park structure is a complex exercise requiring a detailed understanding of many factors.

The layout of a surface car park will be greatly influenced by the shape and form of the land over which it is constructed. Obviously, a flat, square site offers an easier design problem than a steeply sloping irregularly shaped one. As a rule of thumb, to estimate the number of cars that can be accommodated on a site, each car space requires about 20 to $25m^2$ of space.

(3) Disabled drivers

Parking facilities designed specifically for disabled drivers should be fully accessible throughout for wheelchair users. Parking bays should be 1.5 times the width of a normal bay with access by ramps with a maximum gradient of 7%. Where lifts are provided they should have controls at wheelchair level, which is at about 1.2 to 1.4m.

(4) Servicing bays and lorry parking

Shops and factories require service bays, to accommodate commercial vehicles delivering and collecting goods. The demand for service bays should be determined as part of a traffic/transport impact study, undertaken to assess the transport needs of a new development.

A loading bay would typically be 3.3m wide with a length determined by the scale of vehicle expected to use the bay, which could be up to 15.5m long. The access route to the loading bay should be sufficient to allow the commercial vehicle to access the bay and manoeuvre into and out of the bay with ease. A 15m articulated lorry, typically has a 13m radius outer and a 5.3m inner turning circle and the design of the manoeuvring area for service vehicles should ensure that this swept path is clear of obstructions.

This must be approached with common sense. Lorries are driven by human beings and allowance must be made for the variability that this will introduce to the path that a lorry follows when manoeuvring. Thus it is not good practice, having determined the path of the vehicle, to place an obstruction within a few centimeters of the path. It is surprising how often other "wise sensible" architects and engineers do just this.

Exercises

I True or false.

(　　)(1) In the U.K., parking provision on the highway is constrained by the common legislation.

(　　)(2) It is true that we can not park in the place where parking is banned, but we could park where no controls are present.

(　　)(3) Echelon parking is not often used because it makes the drivers have difficulty in manoeuvring in and out of the spaces.

(　　)(4) The layout of the park is influenced most by the geometry of the land on which park is to be built.

(　　)(5) We can not understand why many architects and engineers always place an obstruction in the swept path.

II Complete the following sentences.

(1) Although off-street car park design is not governed by legislation in the same way as parking on the highway, the operation of a _____ car park can be subject to regulation using statutory powers.

(2) Car parking control equipment is becoming increasingly more sophisticated, and the advent of _____ has allowed parking control systems to become more flexible, to meet the varied demands of users more closely.

(3) The current regulations specify a standard bay width, of between _____ and _____ m, although a bay width of _____ m is specified for parking bays for the disabled.

(4) As a rule of thumb, to estimate the number of cars that can be accommodated on a site, each car space requires about _____ m^2 of space.

(5) A loading bay would typically be _____ m wide with a length determined by the scale of vehicle expected to use the bay, which could be up to _____ m long.

III Answer the following questions.

(1) Why is the design standard of office parking lower than that of the public car parking?
(2) What are the designing rules of parking bays?
(3) What are the designing rules of parking bays for disabled drivers?
(4) Why the echelon parking is not often used?
(5) How much is the space that is taken up by every vehicle averagely?

参 考 译 文

停车设计和控制

1. 引言

交通工程师需要知道如何在路内和路外以及在地面上和结构物内提供最佳停车泊位和建设停车设施。然而,在实施这些方案之前,应该对几个设计因素进行充分的调查和分析。本文将论述一些需要考虑的重要因素。

在英格兰、苏格兰和威尔士,路内停车泊位的设置是受法律约束的。停车泊位设置地点、控制方法和采用的设计标准由政府的法规和细则决定,北爱尔兰则有其单独的法律规定。

为了满足各种需求我们需要设置路外停车场,而需求类型将会影响到停车场的设计。例如,办公用停车场的设计标准有可能比公共停车场要求的设计标准低一些。因为大多数办公用停车场的使用者都熟悉停车场的情况,如果车辆停放在一起导致过于密集,找到同事让他把车稍微移动一下位置就好了。

虽然路外停车场的设计不像路内停车场那样有法可依,但公共停车场的使用还是要服从具有法律效力的相关规章制度。

停车场的控制设备越来越精密复杂,微处理器系统的出现使停车控制系统越来越灵活,从而能更好地满足使用者的各种需求。然而,当日益复杂的控制系统的实用性影响到路外停车控制方式时,路内停车控制有了不同的改进。该系统通过将高科技和低科技的控制设备结合从而更具灵活性,能够更好地满足用户的需求。

2. 路内停车

大多数地方的绝大部分道路并不受任何形式的停车控制设施限制。人们普遍认为没有停车控制的地方就有权停车。这样的认知是不对的。实际上人们虽然有在路内通行的权利,却没有在路内随便停车的绝对权利。

(1) 道路标线

路内停车泊位的设计及其标线已经有明文规定,对于小汽车、公共汽车、出租车等应采用不同的标线。阶梯式停车场很少被使用,因为尽管它可以在宽阔的道路上提供额外的停车泊位,但驾驶人进出泊位,特别是驶出泊位时有一定的困难。

现行规则规定了泊位的标准宽度为1.8~2.7米,而专门为残疾人设置的停车泊位宽度则规定为2.7~3.6米。实际上,在狭窄的道路上并不能提供这样宽的空间,因此有必要在停车需求和确保车流行驶的道路宽度之间进行一些实际的调整。在1994年的规则制定前,政府允许停车泊位只有1.6米宽。对比现代汽车的一般宽度,如果低于此数,将意味着有许多车辆将凸出停车泊位。《城市道路路内停车泊位设置规范》已经规定了三种停车泊位的排列形式：平行式，如图8-1所示；倾斜式，如图8-2所示；垂直式，如图8-3所示。

在有停车限制的地方，停车标志将用来表明何种车辆可以停放以及如何停放、允许使用停车场的车辆类型或规定使用停车场的条件和限制。如果停车场允许某一种特殊类型的车辆使用，而且没有其他限制，则停车标志将表明可以使用该停车场的车辆类型。此外，停车标志会显示使用停车场的条件和限制等信息。

（2）停车管理规则

在英国，路内停车可以采用各种不同的管理方法。但主要的立法还是《1988年道路交通管理条例》（以下简称《条例》），此条例后来曾被依法修订过。

《条例》中第一部分规定了交通管理的基本权力。通过使用该条例的这部分权力，道路管理机构可以制定条例来限制停车，或采用条文中的措辞，即"短时停车和装载"。该条例也允许有例外的情况出现，因此制定了一些特殊的停车条款。这意味着在禁停的道路上只有规定的车辆可以停放，比如摩托车。因此如果其他车辆停放在本该由摩托车停放的位置，则违反了限制停车的规定。在道路上必须慎重地使用该法令。如果一条道路有停车限制，而不限制装载货物，例如在摩托车停车泊位上，其他车辆在此处停放都是违法的，但是如果车辆停下来装载货物就不违法，会使人们感到疑惑和不满。

停车场结构设计是复杂的，需要详细地了解很多因素。

地面停车场的布局受地址地形的影响很大。显而易见，表面平坦规则的地形比不规则的陡坡地形更容易设计。为了估计某一场地的停车位容量，通常按照经验将每辆车所占用的空间定为20~25平方米。

（3）残疾驾驶人停车

专门为残疾驾驶人设计的停车设施应该让轮椅可以自由进出，停车泊位的宽度应为标准宽度的1.5倍，入口匝道的最大坡度为7%，有电梯的地方应控制在轮椅能够到达的标准，为1.2~1.4米宽。

（4）服务停车泊位和货车停车泊位

商店和工厂需要服务停车泊位以方便商业车辆装卸货物。服务停车泊位需求的确定应作为交通影响研究的一部分，可以用来评估新发展的交通需求。

装货泊位的尺寸一般为宽3.3米，长度则由预计使用该泊位的车辆大小确定，其长可达15.5m，装货泊位的引道路线应该足以让商业车辆自由进出泊位。一辆15米长的铰接货车，外侧转弯半径一般为13米，内侧转弯半径为5.3米，服务性车辆运行场地的设计应确保在行驶路线范围内无障碍。

由常识可知，车辆是由人来驾驶的，因此必须考虑人的变通性，这种变通使得驾驶人能够灵活选择行车路线。因此，确定了行车路线后，在该行驶路线范围外几厘米处，设置障碍物的做法理论上可行但并不可取。但令人惊讶的是，"明智"的建筑师和工程师们却往往这么做。

Knowledge Link

Parking Guidance Information System

Parking Guidance Information System (PGIS), also known as parking guidance system, provides drivers with parking locations, usages, guidance lines, traffic control and traffic congestion conditions around parking lot by means of traffic information display boards and wireless communication equipment.

PGIS consists of information collection, information processing, information transmission and information release. Its working principle is to collect all the remaining empty parking spaces and traffic information around the parking lot through certain equipment, calculate and process the information through the control center, and then make it easy for drivers to use. It is released to roadside dynamic display board or internet database through data transmission equipment for users to receive or query.

PGIS can improve the convenience of parkers, promote smooth traffic, ensure traffic safety, improve parking efficiency, and increase the economic vitality of commercial areas.

Unit 9
Park and Ride

Text

1. Park and ride development

U. S. citizens have high degrees of car dependency, and densely developed areas usually face serious parking shortages because limited land spaces can be devoted to parking. To mitigate congestion in central city areas, where land is most constrained, Park and ride program has been implemented in many cities.

Park and ride program was originated in the 1930 as ad hoc parking along public transport routes in the rural areas of large cities. With years of development, this program has been gradually improved and applied in many western and US cities due to its competitive advantages, such as low user cost, low energy consumption, less travel time, relatively high travel comfort, etc. The core idea of Park and ride scheme is to encourage more private car users to use public transport services, especially in city center, by providing transfer facilities. The expected outcome is to increase the mode shift rate from lower occupancy modes to higher occupancy modes.

2. Definition

Park and ride facilities are parking lot with public transport connections that allow commuters and other people heading to city centers to leave their vehicles and transfer to a bus, rail system (rapid transit, light rail or commuter rail), or carpool for the remainder of the journey. The vehicles are left in the parking lot during the day and retrieved when the owners return. Park and ride facilities are generally located in the suburbs of metropolitan areas or on the outer edges of large cities. A park and ride that only offers parking for meeting a carpool and not connections to public transport may be called a park and pool. Park and ride is abbreviated as 'P + R' on road signs in the UK, and is often styled as 'Park & Ride' in marketing.

3. Advantage

Park and ride facilities allow commuters to avoid a stressful drive along congested roads and a search for scarce, expensive city-center parking. They may well reduce congestion by assisting the use of public transport in congested urban areas.

There are not many researches on the pros and cons of park and ride program. It has been suggested that there is 'a lack of clear-cut evidence for park and ride's widely assumed impact in reducing congestion'.

Park and ride facilities help commuters who live beyond practical walking distance from the railway station or bus stop. They may also suit commuters with alternative vehicles, which often have reduced range, when the facility is closer to home than the ultimate destination. They also are useful as a fixed meeting place for those car-sharing or car pooling. Also, some transit operators use park and ride facilities to encourage more efficient driving practices by reserving parking spaces for low emission designs, high-occupancy vehicles, or car-sharing.

Many park and rides have passenger waiting areas and/or toilets. Travel information, such as leaflets and posters, may be provided. At larger facilities, extra services such as a travel office, food shop, car wash or cafeteria may be provided. These are often encouraged by municipal operators to encourage use of park and rides.

4. Adoption

In Sweden, a tax has been introduced on the benefit of free or cheap parking paid by an employer, if workers would otherwise have to pay. The tax has reduced the number of workers driving into the inner city, and increased the usage of park and ride areas, especially in Stockholm. The introduction of a congestion tax in Stockholm has further increased the usage of park and ride.

In Prague, park and ride facilities are established near some metro and railway stations (about 17 parks near 12 metro stations and 3 train stations, in 2011). The parking lot offers low prices and all-day and return tickets including the public transport fare.

New Words and Expressions

park and ride	停车换乘体系;转乘停车场
commuter [kəˈmjuːtə(r)]	n. (远距离)上下班往返的人;通勤者
carpool [ˈkɑːpuːl]	v. 合伙用车;拼车
parking lot	停车场
retrieve [rɪˈtriːv]	vt. 取回;索回

public transport	公共交通;公交车辆
rapid transit	高速交通系统;地铁
abbreviate [əˈbriːvieɪt]	v. 缩略;把(词语、名称)缩写(成……)
clear-cut [ˌklɪəˈkʌt]	adj. 明确的;明显的;鲜明的
walking distance	步行距离
emission [ɪˈmɪʃn]	n. (光、热、气等的)发出;射出;排放;散发物
meeting place	聚集的地方;会场
leaflet [ˈliːflət]	n. 散页印刷品;传单;(宣传或广告)小册子 v. (向……)散发传单(或小册子)
may be	多半
car wash	洗车处;洗车场
usage [ˈjuːsɪdʒ]	n. 利用率
cafeteria [ˌkæfəˈtɪəriə]	n. 自助餐厅;自助食堂
inner city	内城区
municipal [mjuːˈnɪsɪpl]	adj. 市政的;地方政府的
ultimate [ˈʌltɪmət]	adj. 最后的;最终的;终极的;极端的 n. 最好的事物,极品,精华
scarce [skeəs]	adj. 缺乏的;不足的;稀少的;罕见的 adv. 勉强;仅仅;几乎不;简直不
poster [ˈpəʊstə(r)]	n. 招贴画;海报
adoption [əˈdɒpʃn]	n. 采用;(候选人的)选定
assume [əˈsjuːm]	v. 假定;认为

Exercises

I True or false.

(　　)(1) Park and ride facilities are generally located in the suburbs of metropolitan areas or on the outer edges of large cities.

(　　)(2) Park and ride facilities can't well reduce congestion by assisting the use of public transport in congested urban areas.

(　　)(3) A lack of clear-cut evidence for park and ride's widely assumed impact in reducing congestion.

(　　)(4) Park and ride facilities help commuters who live beyond practical walking distance from the railway station or bus stop. They may also suit commuters with alternative vehicles, which often have reduced range, when the facility is closer to home than the ultimate destination.

(　　)(5) In Sweden, park and ride facilities are established near some metro and railway stations. The parking lot offers low prices and all-day and return tickets including the public transport fare.

II Complete the following sentences.

(1) _____ facilities allow commuters to avoid a stressful drive along congested roads and a search for scarce, expensive city-center parking.

(2) Park and ride facilities are generally located in the _____ or on the _____ of large cities.

(3) They may well reduce congestion by assisting the use of _____ in congested urban areas.

(4) In _____, a tax has been introduced on the benefit of free or cheap parking paid by an employer, if workers would otherwise have to pay.

(5) The introduction of a _____ in Stockholm has further increased the usage of park and ride.

III Answer the following questions.

(1) What are the park and ride facilities?
(2) What supporting facilities do the park and ride facilities have?
(3) What kind of people do the park and ride facilities often help?
(4) What are the advantages of park and rides?
(5) What policies does Sweden have to support park and ride facilities?

Topics for Discussion

(1) What are the disadvantages of park and rides?
(2) What can be done to alleviate congestion?
(3) What kind of people would like to use park and ride facilities?

参 考 译 文

停 车 换 乘

1. 停车换乘的发展

美国公民对汽车的依赖程度很高,人口密集的发达地区通常面临严重的停车位短缺问题,因为可用于停车的土地空间是有限的。为了缓解城市中心区的交通拥堵,在土地利用紧张的地区,许多城市都实施了停车换乘计划。

停车换乘计划起源于 1930 年,起初是在大城市的郊区,作为公共交通线路的临时停车场。经过多年的发展,该方案以其用户成本低、能耗低、出行时间短、出行舒适度高等竞争优势,在欧美许多城市逐步得到完善和应用。其核心思想是通过提供换乘设施,鼓励更多的私家车用户使用公共交通服务,特别是在城市中心区域。预期结果是提高从低载客方式到高载客方式的转换率。

2. 定义

停车换乘设施是与公共交通连接的停车场,允许通勤者和其他前往市中心的人下车,换乘公交车、轨道系统(快速公交、轻轨和通勤铁路)或拼车。车主白天把车辆停放在停车场,归来时将车辆取走。停车换乘设施通常位于大都市的郊区或大城市的外围。仅满足拼车出行需求而提供停车位且不与公共交通连接的停车换乘设施,可称为停车场。在英国,"停车换乘"在路标上的缩写为"P+R",它在市场营销中通常被称为"Park & Ride"。

3. 优点

停车换乘设施使通勤者不必在拥挤的道路上紧张地开车,也不用在市中心寻找稀缺且昂贵的停车位。在拥挤的市区,停车换乘设施通过提高公共交通利用率来减少拥堵。

关于停车换乘计划利弊的研究不多,有人指出"对于停车换乘能够减少拥堵这一假设,尚缺乏明确的证据来证明"。

停车换乘设施能够帮助住处与火车站或公交车站之间的距离较远的通勤者。当停车换乘设施离家距离比离出行最终目的地更近时,也可以减少通勤者驾驶其他车辆的里程。对于那些想共享车辆和拼车的人来说,停车换乘设施也是一个固定的会面场所。此外,一些公共交通运营商利用停车换乘设施,为低排放设计、高实载率的车辆或拼车行为预留停车位,以鼓励更高效率的出行。

许多停车换乘设施都有乘客等候区和厕所,可通过传单或海报提供出行信息。在规模较大的停车换乘设施中,还会有旅行社、食品商店、洗车间或自助餐厅等其他服务。市政管理者鼓励人们使用停车换乘设施。

4. 应用

在瑞典,对免付或仅支付较低停车费的雇主进行征税,如果职员们不使用停车换乘设施,就必须缴纳更高的停车费。这种税收政策减少了开车进入市内的职员数量,从而增加了停车换乘的使用,尤其在斯德哥尔摩地区表现得更为明显。斯德哥尔摩在引入拥堵税后,进一步提高了停车换乘的利用率。

在布拉格,一些地铁站和火车站附近建有停车换乘设施(2011年,在12个地铁站和3个火车站附近大约有17处停车场),这些停车场提供包含公共交通费用在内的低价位的全天往返票。

Reading Material

Transit-Oriented Development

In urban planning, Transit-Oriented Development (TOD) is a type of urban development that maximizes the amount of residential, business and leisure space within walking distance of public transport. In doing so, TOD aims to increase public transport ridership by reducing the use of private cars and by promoting sustainable urban growth.

A TOD typically includes a central transit stop (such as a train station, or light rails or bus stops) surrounded by a high-density mixed-use area, with lower-density areas spreading out from this center. A TOD is also typically designed to be more walkable than other built-up areas, through using smaller block sizes and reducing the land area dedicated to automobiles.

The densest areas of a TOD are normally located within a radius of 1/4 to 1/2 mile (400 to

800m) around the central transit stop, as this is considered to be an appropriate scale for pedestrians, thus solving the last mile problem.

Many of the new towns created after World War II in Japan, Sweden, and France have many of the characteristics of TOD communities. In a sense, nearly all communities built on reclaimed land in the Netherlands or as exurban developments in Denmark have had the local equivalent of TOD principles integrated in their planning, including the promotion of bicycles for local use.

In the United States, a half-mile-radius circle has become the common standard for rail-transit catchment areas for TOD. A half mile (800m) corresponds to the distance someone can walk in 10 minutes at 3mph (4.8km/h) and is a common estimate for the distance people will walk to get to a rail station. The half-mile ring is a little more than 500 acres ($2.0km^2$) in size.

TOD is sometimes distinguished by some planning officials from 'transit-proximate development', because it contains specific features that are designed to encourage public transport use and differentiate the development from urban sprawl. A few examples of these features include mixed-use development that will use transit at all times of day, excellent pedestrian facilities such as high quality pedestrian crossings, narrow streets, and tapering of buildings as they become more distant from the public transport node.

Opponents of compact or TOD typically argue that Americans, and persons throughout the world, prefer low-density living, and that any policies that encourage compact development will result in substantial utility decreases and large social welfare costs. Proponents of compact development argue that there are large, often unmeasured benefits of compact development, or that the American preference for low-density living is a misinterpretation made possible in part by substantial local government interference in the land market.

Factors driving the trend toward TOD

(1) Rapidly growing, mind-numbing traffic congestion nation-wide.
(2) Growing distaste for suburbia development.
(3) Growing desire for quality urban lifestyle.
(4) Growing desire for more walkable lifestyles away from traffic.
(5) Changes in family structures: more singles, empty-nesters, etc.
(6) Growing national support for Smart Growth.
(7) New focus of Federal policy.

"Traffic congestion has increased so much in virtually every metropolitan area that two-hour commutes now are routine. Attempts to alleviate the problem by constructing more highways almost always have led to more city sprawl and, eventually, more congestion." — Jim Miara.

TOD is regional planning, city revitalization, suburban renewal, and walkable neighborhoods combined. TOD is rapidly sweeping the nation with the creation of exciting people places in city after city. The public has embraced the concept across the nation as the most desirable places to live, work and play. Real estate developers have quickly followed to meet the high demand for quality urban places served by rail systems.

TOD is also a major solution to the serious and growing problems of climate change and global energy security by creating dense, walkable communities that greatly reduce the need for driving and energy consumption. This type of living arrangement can reduce driving by up to 85%.

Exercises

I True or false.

(　　)(1) TOD aims to increase public transport ridership by reducing the use of private cars and promoting sustainable urban growth.

(　　)(2) A TOD is also typically designed to be more walkable than other built-up areas, through using smaller block sizes and reducing the land area dedicated to automobiles.

(　　)(3) Many of the new towns created after World War II in Japan, China and France have many of the characteristics of TOD communities.

(　　)(4) TOD is sometimes distinguished by some planning officials from 'transit-proximate development', because it contains specific features that are designed to encourage public transport use and differentiate the development from urban sprawl.

(　　)(5) Proponents of compact development argue that there are large, often unmeasured benefits of compact development, or that the American preference for low-density living is a misinterpretation made possible in part by substantial local government interference in the land market.

II Complete the following sentences.

(1) _____ is a type of urban development that maximizes the amount of residential, business and leisure space within walking distance of public transport.

(2) The densest areas of a TOD are normally located within a radius of _____ to _____ mile (400 to 800m) around the central transit stop.

(3) In the United States, a _____ circle has become the common standard for rail-transit catchment areas for TOD.

(4) Another key feature of transit-oriented development that differentiates it from 'transit-proximate development' is _____.

(5) _____, or _____ argue that Americans, and persons throughout the world, prefer low-density living, and that any policies that encourage compact development will result in substantial utility decreases and hence large social welfare costs.

III Answer the following questions.

(1) What is TOD?
(2) Where does the TOD often sit?
(3) Which countries have the characteristics of TOD communities after World War II?
(4) What do the opponents of compact or TOD typically think?

参 考 译 文

以公共交通为导向的发展

在城市规划中,以公共交通为导向的发展(TOD)是指在能步行搭乘公共交通工具的距离内,使住宅、商业和休闲空间利用最大化的一种城市开发类型。因此,TOD 的目标是通过降低私家车使用率来增加公共交通的客流量,从而促进城市的可持续发展。

TOD 通常包括被高行人密度的混合使用区域包围的中心公交站(如地铁站、轻轨或公共汽车站),而低密度区域则从该中心向外扩展。TOD 区域使用的街区面积很小,用于汽车出行的土地面积很小,因此在设计上比已经建成的区域更适合步行。

TOD 行人密度最高的区域通常位于中央公交站周围以 1/4 至 1/2 英里(400~800 米)为半径的范围内,因为这被认为是最合适的步行距离,从而解决了最后一英里的出行问题。

第二次世界大战后在日本、瑞典和法国新建的许多城镇都具有 TOD 社区的特征。从某种程度上说,几乎所有在荷兰填海土地上建造的社区或丹麦远郊开发的社区,都在规划中纳入了包括推广当地自行车使用等与 TOD 相适应的地方性原则。

在美国,以半英里(800 米)为半径的范围已经成为 TOD 区域的通用标准。半英里相当于人们以每小时 3 英里(4.8 公里/小时)的速度在 10 分钟内步行的距离,这是对人们步行到火车站距离的一般估计。半英里长环形公路的占地略大于 500 英亩(2 平方公里)。

一些规划者有时将 TOD 与"近距离公交开发"区分开来,因为它包含一些具体特征,旨在鼓励公共交通使用和将城市发展与城市扩张区分开来。符合这些特点的例子包括:对公共交通全天混合使用的开发,优质的人行横道,狭窄的街道,以及建筑物离公共交通站点越远而逐渐减少。

紧凑型发展或 TOD 的反对者认为,美国人和世界各地的人更倾向低密度的生活,任何鼓励紧凑型发展的政策都会导致实际效用的下降与社会福利成本的加大。紧凑型发展的支持者认为,紧凑型发展带来的好处是巨大的,往往是无法衡量的。或许人们认为美国人对低密度生活有偏好是一种误解,其一定程度上是因为地方政府对土地市场的大量干预。

推动 TOD 发展趋势的因素
(1)全国范围内迅速增长的、人们习以为常的交通拥堵。
(2)越来越令人反感的郊区开发。
(3)人们越来越渴望优质的城市生活方式。
(4)人们渴望更多适合步行的生活方式并远离乘车出行。
(5)家庭结构的变化:有更多的单身人士、空巢老人等。
(6)国家不断加大对科学发展的支持力度。
(7)联邦政策的新焦点。

"几乎每个大都市市区都出现了很多交通拥堵现象,现在两小时通勤都很普遍。人们试图通过建造更多公路来缓解这个问题,但几乎总是导致更大的城市扩张,并最终导致更多的拥堵。"——吉姆·米拉。

TOD 是由区域规划、城市复兴、郊区革新和步行社区相结合的。TOD 正在迅速席卷全美国,在一个又一个城市中创造出令人十分满意的场所。全国范围内的公众已经接受了最理想的生活、工作和娱乐场所等概念。房地产开发商已迅速跟进,以满足铁路系统对优质城市场所的高需求。

TOD 也是气候变化和全球能源安全问题日益严重的主要解决方案,通过建立高密度的、可用于步行的社区,大大减少对驾车和能源消耗的需求。这种居住安排可以减少高达 85% 的驾车出行行为。

Knowledge Link

The Origin of the TOD Pattern

In the 1950s, many urban residents in the United States moved to the suburbs, and the center showed a declining trend and a phenomenon of reverse urbanization. Portland made the old city prosperous again and realized the re-urbanization by building trams. This line was a regional circular public transportation system, which had reduced residents' dependence on cars by 35% through the TOD development mode, which was also one of the earliest successful cases of the TOD development mode. At the same time, urban planning academia had recognized that one of the best cases of TOD development in the United States was a county around Washington, building bus systems and rail transit corridors throughout the region. The channel was not only a trunk line, other traffic could be accessed. The development of the highest density on both sides of the channel made the two-way buses very effective, and the utilization rate of the whole channel facilities reached the maximum, which not only restrained the tidal traffic flow, but also effectively reduced the per capita car mileage.

At the beginning of the 20th century, a TOD-like land development plan emerged in Japan, which was one of the earliest countries to develop this model. Especially in Tokyo, Osaka and other metropolitan areas, the railways were regarded as the axis of urban land development through the implementation of 'commercial focus' in several transportation hubs (such as the construction of department stores), as the construction of residential communities or the development of new towns along the railway. Its characteristics are dominated by private iron operators, such as Tokyo, Osaka and other large-scale private iron.

Unit 10

Bikeways

Text

1. Bikeway options

Several options should be considered in planning and implementing a bikeway system. The first option is to do nothing, and where it is adequate and safe permit bicyclists to use the existing street system. At present city, streets are typically used by bicyclists, and perhaps as much as 70% of our total urban street system may be fairly safe for bicyclists without significant improvement.

Bicyclists are more sensitive than motorists to street-surface irregularities. Thus, depressions and bumps should be minimized. Shoulders where bicyclists are expected should be smooth. Adequate conditions for bicycle use include proper curb and gutters as well as sewer grates that have slits, which are oriented perpendicular to the lane.

The use of the sidewalk as a bikeway is an option that has very limited application but may be developed in unusual circumstances by either letting the bicycle share the sidewalk with pedestrians or by designating a selected portion of the sidewalk for bicycles. This option may present problems because of the potential conflict between pedestrians and bicyclists.

2. Design speed

It is possible to attain speeds approaching 30mph (48km/h) or more on a bicycle, but normal speeds range from 7 to 20mph (10 to 32km/h). A desirable working design speed is 20mph (32km/h).

Where rolling terrain and significant downgrades greater than 4% are prevalent, a design speed of 30mph (48km/h) may be used.

3. Bikeway widths

The actual bikeway pavement width depends on bicycle width, maneuvering allowance, clearance between oncoming and passing bicycles, and edge conditions.

A two-way off-street bike path should have a minimum paved width of 8ft (2.4m) and a desirable width of 12ft (3.6m) plus a 2ft (0.6m) graded width on each side. A width of at least 10ft (3m) will allow maintenance and emergency vehicles to utilize the path.

When a bikeway is shared with normal pedestrian traffic, there must be at least a 2.5ft (0.75m) horizontal separation between bicycles and pedestrians (preferably more). This means the sidewalk must be 11 to 15ft (3.3 to 4.5m) wide to accommodate both pedestrians and bicyclists.

A one-way bike lane at the curb requires a minimum width of 4ft (1.2m), measured from the face of the curb. A one-way bike lane next to a parking lane requires a total width of parking and bike lane of 13ft (3.9m), with 15ft (4.5m) desirable, between the curb and the edge of the motor vehicle lane. This dimension will allow for parked cars with an open door extending out 3.5ft (1.05m) plus the bike lane. Where there is no curb or gutter the bike lane should be a minimum 4ft (1.2m) wide outside the motor vehicle lane.

A combined walkway and bikeway on a bridge, tunnel, or similar facility, which is physically separated from vehicular traffic, may be allowed with limited width for economic reasons. Where there are low pedestrian and bicycle volumes on such a facility, a width of 8ft (2.4m) can be utilized. Desirable additional width should be provided if moderate to heavy pedestrian and bicycle volumes existed.

4. Grades

Grades are important because bicyclists are sensitive to topographical variation. Acceptable grades for bicyclists depend on variable conditions such as the characteristics of the rider (age, weight, condition), the bicycle (type, gear ratio, tires), the traveling surface, wind velocity, and length of grade.

Bicyclists are capable of negotiating 10% grades over short distances. However, grades of 4% to 5% represent maximum desirable grades.

5. Intersection treatment

Accident statistics indicate that about two-thirds of bicycle/motor vehicle accidents occur at intersections. Two movements are particularly dangerous to the bicyclist. The first is the conflict with a right-turning motorist. The second is the left-turning bicyclist in conflict with through vehicular traffic. Consideration should be given to the minimization of these conflicts.

New Words and Expressions

do nothing	无所作为
implement [ˈɪmplɪmənt]	v. 贯彻;执行;实施
curb [kɜːb]	vt. 控制;抑制;限定;约束(不好的事物) n. 路边;路缘
gutter [ˈɡʌtə(r)]	n. 檐沟;天沟;路旁排水沟,阴沟 vi. 忽明忽暗;摇曳不定
sewer [ˈsuːə(r)]	n. 污水管,下水道,阴沟
slit [slɪt]	n. 狭长的切口;狭缝,裂缝 vt. 在……上开狭长口子;切开;划破
perpendicular [ˌpɜːpənˈdɪkjələ(r)]	adj. 垂直的;成直角的;垂直式的 n. 垂直线
bikeway	自行车道,自行车专用道
motor vehicle	机动车
rolling terrain	起伏地形
design speed	设计速度
maneuver [məˈnuːvə]	vi. 移动 vt. 操纵
clearance [ˈklɪərəns]	n. 清除;排除间隙;空隙
pavement width	路面宽度
edge condition	边界条件
dimension [daɪˈmenʃn]	n. 尺寸
gear ratio	齿轮比;传动比
topographical [ˌtɒpəˈɡræfɪkl]	adj. 地形的,地貌的
wind velocity	风速
capable of	可以……的;能……的;易……的;敢于……的
accident statistic	事故统计
be given to	有……癖好;倾向于……

Exercises

I True or false.

(　　)(1) We can ride most of the way in the urban street system, which doesn't need dramatic improvement.

(　　)(2) Most of the bikeways today are bicycle path.

(　　)(3) When the bicyclists and pedestrians are using the same walkway, they are apt at disturbing each other.

(　　)(4) The width of a two-way off-street bike path ranges from 2.4m to 3.6m.

(　　)(5) The accidents concerning the bicycles happen everywhere, especially at crossings.

Ⅱ Complete the following sentences.

(1) Adequate conditions for bicycle use include _____ and _____ as well as _____ that have slits, which are oriented perpendicular to the lane.

(2) The use of the sidewalk as a bikeway is an option that has very limited application but may be developed in _____ by either letting the bicycle share the sidewalk with pedestrians or by designating _____.

(3) Another option is the bicycle lane, which is established within the roadway directly adjacent to the outside motor vehicle lane or on the shoulder. Bicycle lanes are designated by _____ and _____.

(4) A two-way off-street bike path should have a minimum paved width of _____ and a desirable width of _____ plus a _____ graded width on each side. A width of at least _____ will allow maintenance and emergency vehicles to utilize the path.

(5) The actual bikeway pavement width depends on _____, _____, _____, and _____.

Ⅲ Answer the following questions.

(1) What does the actual bikeway pavement width depend on?
(2) How can we use sidewalk as a bikeway?
(3) When can the speed of the bike be designed at the level of 48km/h?
(4) What is the dimension of a sidewalk if we want it to attain both pedestrians and bicyclist?
(5) Where do the accidents of bikes / vehicles most likely to happen?

Topics for Discussion

(1) Why do the bikeways must be one-way instead of bidirectional ways?
(2) What do you think of bikeways?
(3) What are the advantages of cycling?

参 考 译 文
自行车专用道

1. 自行车专用道的选择

在规划和实施自行车专用道系统时，应对几种选择进行考虑。第一种选择就是什么都不做，在保证足够的空间和安全的前提下，允许骑车人使用现有的城市道路系统。目前城市道路普遍可以用作自行车道，并且可能多达70%的城市道路对骑车人来说都是相当安全的，不需要做大的改善。

骑车人对路面的不平整性比机动车驾驶人更加敏感，因此，应该尽量减少路面的凹陷和凸起，路肩应如骑车人所期望的那样是平整的。自行车道的理想条件包括路缘石和排水沟要设置合理，而且雨水口的格栅缝也要垂直于行车道方向。

人行道作自行车道使用也是自行车专用道设置的一种选择，尽管这种选择的应用有一定的局限性，但它可在特殊情况下使用。仅存在两种方式：一种是自行车与行人共用同一条人行道;另一种是在人行道上留出一部分给自行车行驶。以上两种选择方式会给行人和骑车人之间带来潜在冲突,因此还存在一些问题。

2. 设计车速

自行车的速度可以达到接近 30 英里/小时(48 千米/小时)或更高,但是一般均在 7～20 英里/小时(10～32 千米/小时)。因此,理想条件下自行车的设计车速定为 20 英里/小时(32 千米/小时)。在丘陵地带并且坡度普遍大于 4% 时,设计车速可为 30 英里/小时(48 千米/小时)。

3. 车道宽度

自行车道路面铺装的实际宽度取决于自行车的宽度、驾驶自由度、自行车之间的侧向净宽以及车道边缘条件。

双车道的路外自行车道路面最小宽度为 8 英尺(2.4 米),理想宽度为 12 英尺(3.6 米),每一侧还须增加 2 英尺(0.6 米)的坡面宽度。车道至少宽 10 英尺(3 米),以便维修车和应急车辆使用。

当自行车道与普通的人行道共用一个车道时,自行车与行人之间保证至少 2.5 英尺(0.75 米)的横向间隔(最好更大一些)。也就是说,车道必须有 11～15 英尺(3.3～4.5 米)的宽度才能同时容纳行人和骑车人。

处于路边的单向自行车道要求最小宽度为 4 英尺(1.2 米)(从路缘石的外表面算起)。单向自行车道与路边停车道相邻时,要求停车道与自行车道宽度之和为 13 英尺(3.9 米);路缘石与机动车道边缘之间最好是 15 英尺(4.5 米)。这一尺寸考虑了路边停靠车辆打开车门时延伸出的宽度 3.5 英尺(1.05 米)和自行车道的宽度。无路缘石和排水沟时,在机动车道外侧的自行车道最小宽度是 4 英尺(1.2 米)。

在桥上、隧道内或类似的结构设施上,出于经济原因,与机动车交通流分开的行人和自行车共用道路的宽度可以使用最小值。当行人与自行车交通量较低时,其混合道路宽度可为 8 英尺(2.4 米)。当存在中等到较大交通量时,应适当增加理想的额外道路宽度。

4. 坡度

由于骑车人对地势的变化很敏感,因此车道的坡度显得很重要。对骑车人来说可接受的坡度取决于一些可变条件,如骑车人特性(年龄、体重和个人条件)、自行车特性(型号、齿轮比、车胎)、路面平整度、风速和坡长。

骑车人在短距离内可以通过坡度为 10% 的道路,但合理的最大路面坡度为 4%～5%。

5. 交叉口的处理

事故统计资料表明,自行车或机动车碰撞事故中有三分之二都发生在交叉口。有两种情况对骑车人尤其危险:第一种是骑车人与右转机动车的冲突;第二种是左转自行车与直行机动车的冲突。应考虑尽量减少这两种冲突。

Reading Material

Levels of Service for Pedestrians

Many western societies are rediscovering walking. Until the 20th century, all cities were defined by their walkable scale. Nowadays, most aspects of our daily lives are not exclusively walkable. Walking is sometimes treated as a trivial case in transport studies, often dismissed as a 'soft mode'. However, as is increasingly evident from the media and professional discussions, in practice, it is the technological measures that need to be described as 'soft' while changing travel behavior is most definitely 'hard'.

A key determinant of the amount of travel by any mode is the utility or Levels of Service (LOS) offered by that mode. The concept of a traveler's LOS is defined in more detail in the *Highway Capacity Manual* (*HCM*), which remains a definitive work in the consideration of highway LOS, but covers pedestrian design capacities mainly where pedestrians interact with street traffic.

Unfortunately, externalities mean that many of the actions that have led to improved LOS and capacities for vehicles on highways have also affected land use patterns and have penalized non-motorized travel. This feature considers the other wider aspects of LOS for pedestrians.

1. Definition

The *HCM* used LOS based on a number of key definitions such as interrupted flow and capacities. The LOS concept is a qualitative measure describing operational conditions within a traffic stream, and their perception by motorists and/or passengers. The LOS definition generally describes this condition in terms of such factors as speed and travel time, freedom to maneuver, traffic interruptions, comfort and convenience, and safety. Six LOS's are defined for each type of facility for which analysis procedures are available. They are given letter designations, from A to F, with LOS F being the worst.

For each type of facility, LOS is defined based on one or more operational parameters that best describe operating quality for the subject facility type. While the concept of LOS attempts to address a wide range of operating conditions, limitations on data collection and availability make it impractical to treat the full range of operational parameters for every type of facility. The parameters selected to define LOS for each facility type are called 'measures of effectiveness' and represent those available measures that best describe the quality of operation on subject facility type.

2. Pedestrian characteristics

Traditional Pedestrian characteristics in *HCM* terms are: observed volumes and flow rates for different facilities; transport variation (seasonal, daily, hourly, sub-hourly); spatial distribution (directional split, composition, e.g., percentage of disabled or mobility impaired); speed (trends, variation by time and trip purpose, which might include 'just walking about'); density (relationships with speed, volume or both); spacing characteristics.

The principles of pedestrian flow analysis are similar but subtly different to those used for vehicular flow. The fundamental relationships among speed, volume and density are similar. As the volume and density of a pedestrian stream increases from free-flow to more crowded conditions, speed and ease of movement decrease. When the pedestrian density exceeds a critical level, volume and speed become erratic and rapidly decline.

The qualitative measures of pedestrian flow similar to those used for vehicular flow are the freedoms to choose desired speeds and to bypass others. Other measures more specially related to pedestrian flow include the abilities to cross a pedestrian traffic stream, to walk in the reverse direction of a major pedestrian flow, and to generally maneuver without conflicts and changes in walking speed or gait. Additional environmental factors that contribute to the walking experience and perceived LOS are:

(1) Comfort factors include weather protection, climate control, arcades, transit shelters and other pedestrian amenities.

(2) Convenience factors include walking distances, pathway directness, grades, sidewalk ramps, directional signing, directory maps and other features making pedestrian travel easy and uncomplicated.

(3) Safety is provided by separation of pedestrians from vehicular traffic, horizontally in malls and other vehicle-free areas, and vertically using overpasses and underpasses. Traffic control devices can provide for time separation of pedestrian and vehicular traffic.

(4) Security features include lighting, open lines of sight, and the degrees and types of street activity.

(5) Economy aspects relate to the user costs associated with travel delays and inconvenience, and to the rental value and retail development as influenced by pedestrian environment.

These supplemental factors can have an important effect on the pedestrian perception of the overall quality of the street environment. While auto users have reasonable control over most of these factors, the pedestrians have virtually no control over them. The *HCM* notes that although the *HCM* methods emphasize LOS analysis, which relates primarily to pedestrian flow measures, such as speed and space, these environmental factors should always be considered because they greatly influence pedestrian activities.

3. Conclusions

The *HCM* approach to estimating LOS based on densities and speeds remains a robust design tool and measure for areas where local capacity is the key design issue. However, the full consideration of all factors determining a LOS for pedestrians is far broader and includes consideration of at least five broad environmental factors: comfort, convenience, safety, security and economy. While measures of effectiveness can be developed for these, in many cases, the data collection, analysis and interpretation process would be too onerous for the designers or managers. On balance, the next best single measure for basing pedestrian LOS is considered to be average delay per pedestrian along a link or through a node. The quantitative relationship between delay and pedestrian LOS requires further research.

The community interest in walking is a wide one, if not universal. Even more so than driving vehicles, walking has a very broad range of participants, environments and behaviors.

Exercises

I True or false.

(　　)(1) Many actions, which led to improve LOS, also improved the land use patterns.

(　　)(2) The definitions such as capacities are used to define LOS in *HCM*.

(　　)(3) The volume and speed will decline gradually when the pedestrian density reaches some levels.

(　　)(4) The pedestrians virtually the same as drivers have no control over the factors that can have important influence over pedestrian perception of the quality of street environment.

(　　)(5) Further researchs will be needed for the study of quantitative relationship between postpone and pedestrian LOS.

II Complete the following sentences.

(1) _____ is sometimes treated as a trivial case in transport studies, often dismissed as a 'soft mode'.

(2) The LOS concept is a qualitative measure describing operational conditions within a _____, and their perception by motorists and/or passengers.

(3) Six LOS's are defined for each type of facility for which analysis procedures are available. They are given letter designations, from _____ to _____, with LOS _____ being the worst.

(4) The parameters selected to define LOS for each facility type are called '_____' and represent those available measures that best describe the quality of operation on subject facility type.

(5) The full consideration of all factors determining a LOS for pedestrians is far broader and includes consideration of at least five broad environmental factors: _____, _____, _____, _____ and _____.

III Answer the following questions.

(1) What is the most important determinant of the amount of travel?

(2) What is the basis on which LOS is defined?

(3) When will the speed and freedom of movement decline?

(4) Which category does open lines of sight belong to?

(5) How many additional environmental elements should be considered in deciding LOS for the walkers?

参 考 译 文

行人服务水平

许多西方国家开始重新重视步行交通。直到 20 世纪,所有城市还都是由它们的可步行程度来区分的。如今,我们日常生活的大多数方面并不是仅靠步行就能完成的。在交通领域,步行有时甚至被认为是一种微不足道的出行方式,经常被当作"软模式"而放弃。然而,通过媒体与专业人员的讨论,这个问题变得越来越明确,实际上,技术措施属于"软"的,而改变出行行为才是真正"硬"的手段。

决定某种模式出行量的关键因素在于该模式所能提供的效用或服务水平。关于出行者的服务水平,在《道路通行能力手册》里有更详细的定义,该书关于道路服务水平的定义是比较权威的,但它主要阐述的是行人与道路交通之间相互作用处的行人设计通行能力。

遗憾的是,人们采取的许多措施虽然提高了道路交通的服务水平与通行能力,但同时也影响了土地利用方式,并对非机动车交通产生了不利的影响。本文主要考虑了行人服务水平。

1. 定义

《道路通行能力手册》所采用的服务水平是以一些关键概念为基础的,如间断交通流、通行能力。它所指的服务水平是对一个交通流行驶条件的定性描述,以及这些条件给机动车驾驶人和(或)乘客的感觉。服务水平的定义通常根据诸如速度、行驶时间、行驶的自由度、交通间断、舒适便捷程度以及安全性等因素来描述运行条件。分析程序为所适用的每一种设施类型均定义了六级服务水平,分别用 A 到 F 六个字母表示,其中 F 级服务水平最低。

对于每种设施类型,服务水平一般以一个或多个运行参数为基础进行定义,这些参数能全面地描述各种目标设施类型的运行质量。尽管服务水平试图对运行条件设定一个较大的范围,但由于数据采集和有效性的限制,对每种设施类型运行参数在整个范围内进行数据处理还是不太现实的。为确定每种设施的服务水平而选择的参数,称为"效率度量",表示能够最恰当地描述该类设施运行质量的可用度量指标。

2. 行人的特征

在《道路通行能力手册》中,传统的行人特征包括不同设施的观测流量和流率、流量的变化(季节性变化、日变化、小时变化、间隔小于 1 小时的变化)、空间分布(流向分配、人员组成,例如残疾人或行动有障碍的人所占比例)、速度(不同方向、不同时间与不同出行目的,这里出行目的可能包括"闲逛")、密度(密度—速度关系、密度—流量关系或者密度—速度—流量关系)、空间特征等。

行人交通规律的分析与车辆交通规律分析相似但稍有不同。速度、流量和密度之间的基本关系是相似的。当行人交通流的流量和密度从自由流增加到更加拥挤时,速度的自由度就下降了。当行人的密度超过临界值时,流量与速度就会变得不稳定而且迅速下降。

与车辆交通流相似的行人交通流的定性指标是期望行进速度与超越他人速度的自由度。其他与行人流量相关的指标包括穿越行人交通流的能力、在较大的行人流量中逆向行走的能力以及在人流中行走时不与他人产生冲突、不改变步行速度或步态的能力。其他与行走经验相关的环境因素以及可以感受到的服务水平有:

(1)舒适因素,包括不良天气防护设施、气候调节设施、街道拱廊、公交换乘站以及其他行人便利设施。

(2)便利因素,包括行走间距、路径的直达性、坡度、人行匝道、路标、地图以及其他使行人行走简便、一目了然的特征、标志。

（3）安全性，横向采用隔离墩和设置无车行驶区域等，在竖向则通过人行天桥和地下通道将行人与车辆交通分离开。而交通控制设备则可提供行人和机动车在时间上的分隔。

（4）保障特征，包括照明、视距以及道路活动的等级和类型。

（5）经济因素，与出行延误和出行不便相关的用户成本、受行人环境影响的租费和零售业的发展有关。

这些补充因素对于行人对道路环境整体质量的感受有重要影响。汽车使用者对这些因素大都有合理的控制方法，然而行人实际上并没有任何办法。尽管《道路通行能力手册》中提出的方法强调服务水平分析（主要与行人交通流指标相关，如速度和空间），但对这些环境因素也应该经常加以考虑，因为它们对行人的活动产生很大影响。

3. 结论

美国《道路通行能力手册》评估服务水平的方法是建立在密度和速度基础上的，这对于局部通行能力为主要设计因素的地区仍不失为一种可靠的设计工具。然而，确定行人交通服务水平要考虑的因素非常广泛，至少应当包括以下五项环境因素：舒适性、便利性、安全性、保障性以及经济性。尽管可以提出一些评价指标来衡量这些因素，但在许多情况下数据采集、分析和解释过程无论对于设计者还是管理者来说都太繁重。总而言之，建立行人服务水平的下一个最好的衡量指标是通过路段或穿过交叉口时行人的平均延误时间。延误和行人服务水平之间的定量关系还需进一步研究。

公众对步行的兴趣即使不够普遍，也是非常广泛的。与驾驶汽车相比，步行的参与者、出行范围和环境更广泛。

Knowledge Link

Functional Classification of Bicycle Lanes

1. Recreational

Recreational bicycle lanes are designed for the leisure and sports of bicycles.

This kind of bicycle lanes are usually set up on bicycle-only roads, only bicycles can enter, and other motor vehicles are totally prohibited from entering.

2. Transportation

Transportation lanes can be divided into the following three categories according to the right-of-way.

（1）Bicycle-only roads

Bicycle-only roads refer to the right of a road, which belong entirely to bicycles (and pedestrians), and are separated from motor vehicle roads.

（2）Bicycle lanes

Bicycle lanes are usually set on the outside of the road, and the right to use the special lanes set on the outside belongs to the bicycles entirely. Other motor vehicles are prohibited from driving on the lanes. There are also sidewalks, which separate pedestrians from bicycles by separating islands.

(3) Bicycle shared lanes

The bicycle shared lanes are the common mixed traffic lanes, that is, the lanes are not only for motor vehicles, but also for bicycles. Only bicycles can usually use the outside lanes.

Unit 11

Freeways

Text

1. Introduction

The highest type of arterial highway is the freeway, which is defined as an expressway with fully controlled access.

Control of access is the condition where the right of owners or occupants of abutting land to access a highway is fully or partially controlled by public authorities. Full control of access means that the authorities to control access are exercised to give preference to through traffic by providing access connections with selected public roads only and by prohibiting crossings at grade or direct private driveway connections.

The principal advantages of control of access are the preservation of the as-built capacities of the highway, high speed, and improved safety to highway users. Highways with fully controlled access have separations at all roads, and grade separations or interchanges at selected public crossroads. The remaining crossroads are interconnected or terminated.

Essential freeway elements include medians, grade separations at cross streets, ramp connections for entrance to and exit from through pavements for interchange of traffic (see Figure 11-1), and (in some cases) frontage roads.

Freeways are selected for principal arterial corridors that are intended to provide for safe and efficient movement of high volumes of traffic at relatively high speeds.

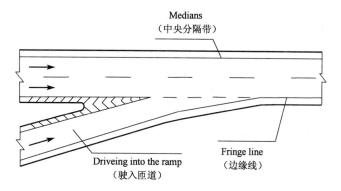

Figure 11-1   Essential freeway elements(高速公路的基本要素)

2. Design speeds

As a general consideration, the design speeds of urban freeways should reflect the desired safe operating speeds during nonpeak hours, but should not be so high that it exceeds the limits of prudent construction, right-of-way and socioeconomic costs. A large proportion of vehicles are detained during periods of peak flow. The design speeds should never be less than 50mph(80km/h). The important safety considerations are to have a properly posted speed limit and to enforce the speed limit during off-peak hours, wherever this minimum design speed is used. On many urban freeways, particularly in suburban areas, a design speed of 60mph(96km/h) or higher can be provided with little additional cost. The corridors of the main line may also be relatively straight, and the characters and locations of interchanges may permit high-speed design. Under these conditions, a design speed of 70mph(112km/h) is desirable because the high design speeds are closely related to the overall qualities and safety of the facilities. A design speed of 70mph should be used for rural freeways. Where terrain is mountainous, a design speed of 60mph or 50mph, which is consistent with driver expectancies, may be used.

3. Design traffic volumes

Both urban and rural freeways, especially on new locations, are normally designed to accommodate traffic projections for a 20-year period. Some elements of freeway reconstruction may be based on a lesser design period. Specific design requirements should be determined from Design Hourly Volume (DHV) for the appropriate design period. In large metropolitan areas, the selection of appropriate design traffic and design periods may be influenced by system planning. Segments of freeways may be constructed or reconstructed to be commensurate with either intermediate traffic demands or traffic based on the completed systems, whichever may be most appropriate.

4. Levels of service

Techniques and procedures for adjusting operational highway factors to compensate for conditions other than ideal are found in the *Highway Capacity Manual* (*HCM*). It also presents a thorough discussion of the level-of-service concept. Although choice of the design level of service is left to the user of the *HCM*, designers should strive to provide the highest level of service feasible and consistent with anticipated conditions. For acceptable degrees of congestion, freeways and their auxiliary facilities, i. e. ramps, main line weaving sections, and C-D roads in urban and suburban areas, should generally be designed for level-of-service C. In heavily developed sections of metropolitan areas, conditions may necessitate the use of level-of-service D. In rural areas, level-of-service B is desirable for through and auxiliary lanes, although level-of-service C may be acceptable on auxiliary facilities carrying unusually high volumes.

5. Pavement and shoulders

Freeways should have a minimum of two through-traffic lanes for each direction of travel. Through-traffic lanes should be 12ft(3.6m) wide. Pavements should have a high-type surface with adequate skid resistance and provide a high degree of structural adequacy. Cross slope should range between 1.5 and 2 percent on tangent sections consisting of two lanes in each direction with a crown at the centerline of the pavement. The high value is recommended for areas of moderate rainfall. For areas of heavy rainfall a cross slope of 2.5 percent may be necessary to provide adequate pavement drainage. For elevated freeways on viaducts, two-lane pavement usually is sloped to drain the full width of the roadway. On wider facilities, particularly in areas of heavy rainfall, surface drainage may be two ways on each traveled way, the crowns being located on the lane lines at one-third or one-half the total width from one edge. In snow areas, surface drainage should be two ways on each traveled ways so that snow stored in the median will not melt and drain across the traveled ways, or the median should be designed to prevent this occurrence.

There should be continuous paved shoulders on both the right and the left sides of all freeway facilities. The usable paved width of the right shoulder should be at least 10ft(3m). Ramp shoulder widths are usually constructed adjacent to acceleration and deceleration lanes with transitions to the freeway shoulder widths at the taper ends. Shoulder cross slope should range between 2 and 6 percent and should be at least 1 percent more than the pavement cross slope on tangent sections to facilitate drainage. It is desirable that the colours and texture of the shoulders be different from that on the through lanes. On viaducts, differentiation between traveled way and shoulders is sometimes effected by striping and pavement marking or corrugated depressions.

New Words and Expressions

freeway['friːweɪ]   *n.* 高速公路
arterial highway   干线公路
expressway[ɪk'spresweɪ]   *n.* 高速道路
driveway['draɪvweɪ]   *n.* 车道;马路
terminate['tɜːmɪneɪt]   *v.* 停止;结束;终止
socioeconomic[ˌsəʊsɪəʊˌekəˈnɒmɪk]   *adj.* 社会经济学的
location[ləʊ'keɪʃn]   *n.* 位置;场所;特定区域

expectancy [ɪkˈspektənsɪ]　　　　　　　　n. 期待;期望
metropolitan [ˌmetrəˈpɒlɪtən]　　　　　adj. 主要都市的;大城市的
auxiliary [ɔːgˈzɪlɪərɪ]　　　　　　　　adj. 辅助的;补充的
slope [sləʊp]　　　　　　　　　　　　n. 坡度;斜坡;斜率;倾斜　vt. (使)倾斜
crown [kraʊn]　　　　　　　　　　　　n. 路拱
drainage [ˈdreɪnɪdʒ]　　　　　　　　　n. 排水;排泄;排水装置
viaduct [ˈvaɪədʌkt]　　　　　　　　　n. 高架桥;高架铁(道)路
occurrence [əˈkʌrəns]　　　　　　　　n. 发生;出现;事件
corrugated [ˈkɒrəgeɪtɪd]　　　　　　　adj. 缩成皱纹的;使起波状的
rainfall [ˈreɪnfɔːl]　　　　　　　　　n. 降雨量;降雨
feasible [ˈfiːzəbl]　　　　　　　　　　adj. 可行的;行得通的
abut [əˈbʌt]　　　　　　　　　　　　vt. & vi. (与……)邻接;毗连;紧靠
preservation [ˌprezəˈveɪʃn]　　　　　n. 保护;维护;保存;维持
ramp [ræmp]　　　　　　　　　　　　n. 匝道;斜坡;坡道
intermediate [ˌɪntəˈmiːdɪət]　　　　　adj. 之间的;中间的;中级的;中等的
skid [skɪd]　　　　　　　　　　　　　vi. 侧滑;打滑;滑行　n. 侧滑;打滑;滑橇
adjacent [əˈdʒeɪsnt]　　　　　　　　　adj. 与……毗连的;邻近的;接近的

Exercises

Ⅰ True or false.

(　) (1) The highest type of arterial highway is grade-separated, which is defined as an expressway with fully controlled access.

(　) (2) Control of access is the condition where the right of owners or occupants of abutting land to access a highway is fully or partially controlled by local government.

(　) (3) Both urban and rural freeways, especially on new locations, are normally designed to accommodate traffic projections for a 20-year period.

(　) (4) Techniques and procedures for adjusting operational and highway factors to compensate for conditions other than ideal are found in the *Traffic Engineering Manual* (*TEM*), which also presents a thorough discussion of the level-of-service concept.

(　) (5) Freeways should have a minimum of one through-traffic lanes for each direction of travel. Through-traffic lanes should be 12ft(3.6m) wide.

Ⅱ Complete the following sentences.

(1) The principal advantages of control of access are _____.

(2) Essential freeway elements include _____.

(3) Wherever this minimum design speed is used, _____ are to have a properly posted speed limit and to enforce the speed limit during off-peak hours.

(4) Cross slope should range between _____ and _____ percent on tangent sec-

tions consisting of two lanes in each direction with a crown at the centerline of the pavement.

(5) The usable paved width of the right shoulder should be at least _____ ft.

III Answer the following questions.

(1) What is the definition of expressways?
(2) What are the essential elements of expressways?
(3) What is the control of access?
(4) What are the advantages of control of access?
(5) How to design the cross slope?

Topics for Discussion

(1) What do you think of expressways?
(2) What are the advantages of expressways?
(3) What are the requirements for expressway design?

参 考 译 文

高 速 公 路

1. 简介

高速公路是最高级别的干线公路,它被定义为出入口处于完全控制下的快速路。

出入口控制是指毗邻土地的业主或住户进出公路的权利完全或部分由公共部门控制的状态。出入口完全控制意味着有关部门行使控制通道的权力,只提供与选定公共道路连接的通道,禁止出现平交道口或与私人车道直接相连的情况,从而可以使车辆优先通过。

控制通行的主要优势是可以保持公路建成后的通行能力、高速通行、提高公路用户的安全性。出入口完全控制的高速公路在所有公路上都有分隔带,在选定的公共十字路口有立体交叉,剩余的十字路口则会被连接或作为终点站。

高速公路的基本要素包括中央分隔带、立体交叉、用于立体交叉的直通出入口的连接匝道(见图11-1)以及(在某些情况下的)临街道路。

选择高速公路作为主要干道走廊,旨在提供安全、高效、高速、高流量的运输。

2. 设计速度

作为一般考虑,市区高速公路的设计速度应反映在非高峰时段所需的安全运行速度上,但不应过高,不应超过安全施工、通行权和社会经济成本的限制。在高峰流量时段道路上会滞留大量的车辆。设计车速不应低于50英里/小时(80千米/小时)。在任何使用最低设计速度的地方,重要的安全注意事项都是在非高峰时段设置适当的限速标志。在许多市区高速公路上,特别是在郊区,60英里/小时(96千米/小时)或更高的设计速度只产生很少的额外费用。主路的通道可能比较直,立交的特征和所处位置可能允许较高的设计速度。在这种情况下,理想的设计速度可为70英里/小时(112千米/小时),因为高的设计速度与设施的整体质量和安全密切相关。乡村高速公路应采用70英里/小时的设计速度。在地形为多山的地方,可以使用与驾驶人期望一致的60英里/小时或50英里/小时的设计速度。

3. 设计交通量

城市和乡村高速公路,特别是新区的高速公路,通常都是为了适应未来20年的交通预测需求而设计的。高速公路改造的一些要素可能是基于较短的设计周期。在恰当的设计周期内,应根据设计小时交通量确定具体的设计要求。在大城市,设计交通量和设计周期的选择可能会受系统规划的影响。部分高速公路可以选择恰当的方式与中等交通需求相适应或基于已完成的交通系统来新建或重建。

4. 服务水平

在《道路通行能力手册》中,可以调整公路运行系数以补偿非理想状态的技术和程序。它还对服务水平的概念进行了深入的讨论。尽管设计服务水平的选择权留给《道路通行能力手册》的用户,但设计人员应努力提供可行的、可持续的、符合预期条件的最高服务水平。对于可接受的拥挤程度,高速公路及其辅助设施(市区和郊区的匝道、主线交织区和C-D等级路段)一般应按C级服务水平进行设计。在大都市的发达地区,可能需要使用D级服务水平。在乡村地区,B级服务水平是主要车道和辅助车道的理想选择,虽然在流量较大的辅助车道上,C级服务水平也是可以接受的。

5. 路面和路肩

高速公路的每个行驶方向应至少有两条直行车道,直行车道应为12英尺(3.6米)宽。路面应具有高等级的铺装,具有足够的防滑性,并提供较高的结构强度。在由两条车道组成的正切部分上,横坡坡度应在1.5%~2%之间,每个行车方向的路面中心线处应有一个路拱。建议中等降雨量的地区采用高值。对于暴雨地区,可能需要2.5%的横坡,以提供足够的路面排水能力。对于高架桥上的高速公路,双车道路面通常是倾斜的,从而可以排干整个路面的积水,特别是在强降雨地区更宽的高速公路上,每个行驶方向上的路面都是双向排水,路拱设置在距离一侧道路边缘总宽度三分之一或二分之一的地方。在积雪地区,在每个行车方向上路面排水都应采用双向排水,以防止残留在道路中央的积雪融化后形成的水横穿行车道,或者设计中央分隔带来防止这种情况发生。

所有高速公路的左右两侧都应该铺砌连续的路肩,右侧路肩的可用铺砌宽度应至少为10英尺(3米)。匝道路肩的建设通常与加速和减速车道相邻,从锥形端过渡到高速公路路肩宽度。路肩横坡应在2%~6%之间,并且在正切部分应至少比路段纵向的路面横坡高1%,以便于排水。路肩的颜色和纹理最好与直行车道的颜色和纹理不同。在高架桥上,行车道和路肩之间的区别有时会受条纹、路面标线或波纹状凹陷的影响。

Reading Material

Basic Freeway Segments

1. Introduction

A freeway may be defined as a divided highway facility having two or more lanes for the exclusive use of traffic in each direction and full control of access and egress.

The freeway is the only type of highway facility that provides completely 'uninterrupted' flow.

There are no external interruptions to traffic flow, such as signalized or STOP-controlled intersections. Access to and egress from the facility occurs only at ramps, which are generally designed to permit high-speed merging and diverging maneuvers to take place, thus minimizing disruptions to mainline traffic.

Because of these characteristics, operating conditions primarily result from interactions among vehicles in the traffic stream, and between vehicles and the geometric characteristics of the freeway. Operations are also affected by environmental conditions, such as weather, pavement conditions, and/or the occurrence of traffic incidents.

2. Components of a freeway

In general, a freeway is composed of three different types of component subsections:

(1) Basic freeway segments—sections of the freeway that are unaffected either by merging or diverging movements at nearby ramps or by weaving movements.

(2) Weaving areas—sections of the freeway where two or more vehicle flow must cross each other's path along a length of the freeway. Weaving areas are usually formed when merge areas are closely followed by diverge areas. They are also formed when a freeway on-ramp is followed by an off-ramp and the two are connected by a continuous auxiliary lane. There are three types of weaving areas, see in Figure 11-2.

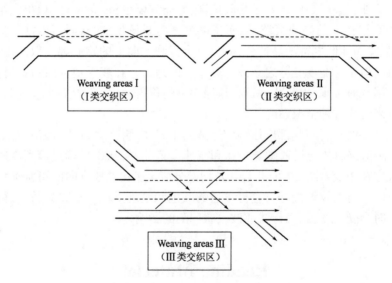

Figure 11-2　Types of weaving areas(交织区的分类)

(3) Ramp junctions—points at which on and off-ramps join the freeway. A junction formed at this point is an area of turbulence due to concentrations of merging or diverging vehicles.

Basic freeway segments are located outside of the influence area of any ramp or weaving area.

3. Overall considerations

The procedures treat only the isolated characteristics of the segment under consideration. The procedures assume:

(1) Good pavement conditions.
(2) No traffic incidents.
(3) Good weather conditions.

Should any of these conditions not exist, the users must use judgment to alter the results of the analysises, consider this when interpreting results, or both.

In practice, it is essential to analyze sections of freeway in an integrated manner to estimate overall capacities of the freeway system and to identify points of minimum capacities, which could become potential bottlenecks. The interaction between and among adjacent freewaysubsegments is of extreme importance, particularly when a breakdown in one causes queues to extend into upstream segments.

4. Definitions

The following terms and definitions are of specific interest to material in this paper.

(1) Freeway capacity is the maximum sustained (15min) rate of flow at which traffic can pass a point or uniform segment of freeway under prevailing roadway and traffic conditions. Capacity is defined for a single direction of flow, and is expressed in vehicles per hour (vph).

(2) Roadway characteristics are the geometric characteristics of the freeway segment under study, These include the numbers and widths of lanes, lateral clearances at the roadside and median, design speeds, grades and lane configurations.

(3) Traffic conditions refer to any characteristic of the traffic stream that affects capacities or operations. These include the percentage composition of the traffic stream by vehicle types, lane distribution characteristics and driver characteristics (such as the differences between weekday commuters and recreational drivers).

It should be noted that capacity analysis is based on point locations or freeway segments of uniform roadway and traffic conditions. If either of these prevailing conditions changes significantly, the capacities of the segment and its likely operating conditions change as well.

Such segments also should have reasonably uniform design speeds. Accordingly, all straight and level segments of freeway are considered to have a design speed of 70mph(112km/h). It may be necessary to consider isolated elements with lower design speeds separately, such as a curve with a design speed significantly lower than 70mph. On the other hand, a long segment of freeway dominated by many geometric elements with reduced design speeds could be analyzed as a single unit, based on the reduced design speeds.

5. Levels of service

Freeway operating characteristics include a wide range of rates of flow over which speeds are relatively constant. This means that speed alone is not adequate as a performance measure by which to define levels of service.

Although speed is a major concern of drivers with respect to service quality, freedom to maneuver and proximity to other vehicles are equally important parameters. These other qualities are directly related to the densities of the freeway traffic stream. Further, rates of flow increases with increasing densities throughout the full range of stable flow.

For these reasons, density is a parameter used to define levels of service for basic freeway segments. The densities used to define the various Levels of Service (LOS) are as Table 11-1.

Density of LOS　　　　　　　　　　　　　　　　　　　Table 11-1

Levels of Service	A	B	C	D	E
Densities (pc/mi/ln)	12	20	30	42	67

These values are boundary conditions representing the maximum allowable density for the associated level of service. The LOS—E boundary of 67pc/mi/ln has been generally found to be the critical density at which capacity most often occurs. This corresponds to an average travel speed of 30mph(48km/h) and a capacity of 2000pc/ph/pl for 60mph(96km/h) and 70mph design speeds. The exact speed and density, however, at which capacity occurs may vary somewhat from location to location.

Exercises

I True or false.

(　　)(1) The freeway is one type of highway facility that provides completely "uninterrupted" flow.

(　　)(2) The operations of vehicles are also affected by environmental conditions, such as weather, pavement conditions, and/or the occurrence of traffic incidents.

(　　)(3) The interaction between and among adjacent freeway subsegments is of extreme unimportance.

(　　)(4) If the traffic conditions change significantly, the capacities of the segment and its likely operating conditions change as well.

(　　)(5) Speed is the only concern of drivers with respect to service quality.

II Complete the following sentences.

(1) _____ may be defined as a divided highway facility having two or more lanes for the exclusive use of traffic in each direction and full control of access and egress.

(2) In general, a freeway is composed of three different types of component subsections: basic freeway segments, weaving areas and _____.

(3) _____ — sections of the freeway where two or more vehicle flow must cross each other's path along a length of the freeway.

(4) Basic freeway segments are sections of the freeway that are unaffected either by _____ or _____ movements at nearly ramps or by wearing movements.

(5) Traffic conditions refer to any _____ of the traffic stream that affects capacities or operations.

Ⅲ Answer the following questions.

(1) What are the roadway characteristics?
(2) What are the traffic conditions?
(3) What is the definition of expressway?
(4) What is the definition of weaving areas?
(5) What is the freeway capacity?

参 考 译 文

高速公路基本路段

1. 引言

高速公路可定义为每个方向具有两条或两条以上汽车专用车道,并且进出口完全控制的被分隔的公路设施。

高速公路是唯一一种提供完全"不间断"运行服务的公路设施。交通流没有外部干扰,如信号灯或由停止信号控制的交叉口。进出设施仅在匝道上设置,匝道的设计通常允许进行高速合流和分流操作,从而最大限度地减少对主线交通的干扰。

由于高速公路具有这些特点,因此车辆运行情况主要取决于交通流中车辆之间以及车辆与高速公路几何特性之间的相互作用。此外,车辆运行状况也受环境条件的影响,如气候条件、路面状况以及是否发生交通事故等。

2. 高速公路的组成

一般来说,高速公路是由三种不同类型的路段组成的:

(1) 高速公路基本路段——不受匝道附近车流的合流、分流及交织运行影响的高速公路路段。

(2) 交织区——沿着高速公路一定长度,两条或多条车流穿过彼此车行路线的高速公路路段。一般合流区和紧接着的分流区将形成交织路段。当驶出高速公路匝道以后紧接着驶入匝道,且两条匝道由一条连续的辅助车道相连接时,也会形成交织区。三种类型的交织区,如图11-2所示。

(3) 匝道连接点——驶入及驶出匝道与高速公路的连接点。由于汇集了合流或分流的车辆,因而形成的连接点是一个紊流区。

高速公路基本路段处于任何匝道或交织区的影响区域之外。

3. 总体考虑

研究过程仅讨论路段的各自特点。在讨论中假定:

(1) 有良好的路面条件。
(2) 没有交通事故。
(3) 有良好的气候条件。

如果这些条件不具备,使用者应对分析结果加以判断并进行修正,或者在说明结果时考虑这些因素,也可两法并用。

实际上,重要的是应将高速公路各路段作为一个整体进行分析,以确定整个高速公路系统的综合通行能力,并鉴别出那些可能成为潜在"瓶颈"的最低通行能力点。此外,高速公路相邻路段之间与路段内的相互影响也非常重要,特别是在某一段内因故障造成排队并延伸到其上游路段时,这种影响尤为显著。

4. 定义

下列术语和定义与本文内容有密切的联系。

(1)高速公路通行能力是指在当前正常的道路和交通条件下,高速公路某一点或某一均匀路段所容许通过的最大持续(15分钟)交通流。通行能力是针对单向车流而言的,并用辆/小时表示。

(2)道路特性是指高速公路路段几何线形特性,包括车道宽度、车道数、路边和中央分隔带的侧向净空、设计车速、坡度和车道配置等。

(3)交通条件是指任何影响通行能力或运行情况的交通流特性,包括交通流中各种车辆类型的占比组成、车道分布特点以及驾驶人特性(例如,每天上下班的通勤驾驶人与假期时驾驶人之间的差别)。

应当注意的是,通行能力分析是针对具有相同道路和交通条件的一些点位或高速公路路段的。如果这些主要条件之一发生了显著变化,则路段通行能力和运行条件也会随之变化。

这样的路段还应具有合理均衡的设计速度。因此,所有高速公路平直路段都按70英里/小时(112千米/小时)的设计速度来考虑。而对一些特殊情况,则有必要考虑分别采用较低的设计速度。例如,对于曲线段,采用明显低于70英里/小时的设计速度。另外,可以将设计速度降低,把带有多种几何要素的高速公路长路段作为一个单元进行分析。

5. 服务水平

高速公路运行特性中,在一个相当大的流率范围内,车速是相对不变的。这说明,仅以车速作衡量服务水平的标准是不够的。

对于服务质量来说,尽管驾驶人最关心的是速度,但行车自由度以及车辆间相互靠近的程度也同样是重要的参数。这些额外的特性与高速公路交通流的密度直接相关。此外,在整个稳定交通流范围内,流率是随密度的增加而增加的。

由于这些原因,可将密度作为确定高速公路基本路段服务水平的参数。用来确定各级服务水平(LOS)的密度值见表11-1。

服务水平密度值 表11-1

服务水平	A	B	C	D	E
密度(辆小客车/英里/车道)	12	20	30	42	67

这些密度值分别为相应服务水平所能容许的最大密度边界值。其中,E级服务水平的边界值67辆小客车/英里/车道一般是达到通行能力时的临界密度值。这相当于设计速度在60英里/小时(96千米/小时)和70英里/小时之间,平均行驶速度为30英里/小时(48千米/小时),通行能力为2000辆小客车/小时/车道。但是,当(交通量)达到通行能力时,具体的速度和密度值还是会因地而异。

Knowledge Link

Design Hourly Volume

Traffic volume has the characteristics of changing with times and peak hours, which must be taken into account when planning and designing road facilities. In order to ensure that the road can pass smoothly in most hours during the planning period without causing serious congestion, and avoid the low traffic volumes and low investment benefit after completion, it is stipulated that the appropriate hourly traffic volumes should be selected as the design hourly volume. According to American research, the 30th highest hourly traffic volume is the most appropriate. The so-called maximum hourly traffic volume (30HV) of the 30th place is the hourly traffic volume of 8760 hours measured in a year, arranged in order from the largest to the smallest, and ranked in the 30th place.

For multi-lane highways, the numbers and widths of lanes can be determined by using the designed hourly volume, and good economic benefits can be obtained by accurate calculation. For the two-lane highway, because the number of lanes has been determined, the designed hourly volume is mainly used to calculate the peak hourly traffic volumes in different periods, and to evaluate the levels of road service, quality of use, and so on.

Unit 12
Intersections

Text

1. General

An intersection is where two or more roads come together. Intersections are also known as junctions. There can be stop signs on one or both sides of the intersection. There can also be a stop light.

In rural areas there is often space to provide generous layouts for new junctions, and land cost is relatively low and it is usually possible to adjust the overall scheme layout to achieve full design standards. There are, of course, constraints such as the difficult terrains found in mountainous or hilly areas that physically restrict the freedom of the engineer to optimize designs. There are other constraints, which have increased in importance in recent years, such as Areas of Outstanding Natural Beauty (AONB), Site of Special Scientific Interest (SSSI), listed buildings and conservation areas; archaeological sites and high-quality farm land.

Even with these constraints, it is important and usually possible to achieve close adherence to design standards. Design speeds in rural areas are usually higher than in urban areas and the consequences of accidents and collisions at higher speeds are more severe.

Within urban areas the physical constraints are more related to the built environment. Property values are higher and opportunities to appropriate land for highway improvements are fewer. Even within the highway boundary the presence of underground services can impose conditions upon the layout. With some small traffic schemes, the cost of protecting or rerouting services can be 10 times (or more) than the cost of the highway and signing works.

With any urban scheme the most important consideration is the size, turning characteristics and space requirements of the design vehicles. In most instances this means the largest legally permitted road vehicles. In residential areas the predominate vehicles will be the private cars, but large vehicles regularly penetrate these areas for refuse collection, gulley cleaning, maintenance, household deliveries, school buses and public transport. In towncenters, department stores, supermarkets, public houses and fast food outlets receive regular deliveries by the largest heavy goods vehicles.

Occasionally, abnormal loads enter town and city centers. Major cities, such as London, have designated abnormal load routes that avoid weak or low bridges, difficult turning manoeuvres or overhead telephone and power lines. The engineers must be aware of these and ensure that provision is made, within new designs, for these eventualities. The additional cost of installing hardened overrun areas and demountable street furniture can sometimes be recovered from the operators of these outsized vehicles.

In very rare cases the design vehicles can be limited to less than the largest vehicles where there is a physical width or mass limit. Where general traffic volume and HGV (Heavy Goods Vehicle) movements are low, the occasional large vehicles can be allowed to dominate the full width of a road for the short timeit needs to complete its manoeuvres.

At urban road junctions it is often not possible to provide full standards for large vehicles. Where their numbers are small and speeds are low, they can be allowed to dominate two or more traffic lanes at urban roundabouts and traffic signals. Traffic islands, kerb lines and street furniture must, of course, be placed outside the vehicle swept paths. Standard vehicle swept path plots are available for checking layouts, but for more complex multiple turns the DOT computer program— TRACK is recommended.

Apart from abnormal load vehicles the longest vehicle in everyday use in the U.K. is the 18m drawbar trailer combination. When designing junctions at confined site, it is not enough to check that the layout is adequate for the largest vehicles. Swept path is dependent on a number of factors: rigid or articulated, wheelbases (or tractor wheelbases), front and rear overhang; widths and lengths of trailers.

In some instances, an articulated vehicle has a smaller turning circle and smaller swept area than a long rigid vehicle. Vehicles with long front or rear overhang, such as the 12m European low floor buses can pose particular problems. If such a vehicle is stationary and its steering wheels are on full lock the rear will tend to move outwards as it starts to move. If the vehicle is close to the kerb the bodywork might strike a pedestrian.

2. Selection of junction type

Selection of junction type can be very simple and obvious in some cases, for example:
(1) Two lightly trafficked residential roads—priority junction.
(2) The through carriageways of a motorway—grade separation.

(3) Heavily trafficked urban crossroads with heavy pedestrian volume—traffic signal.

(4) Suburban dual carriageways with substantial heavy goods traffic—conventional roundabout.

However, there are very many cases where the solution is anything but obvious and the engineers should resist making a decision until all the evidence has been examined and analyzed.

Frequently, when an existing junction is to be upgraded to handle more or different types of vehicles, the existing form or control method must be considered. The form of the other junctions on the main route might determine the form of the new or improved junction, for example, it might be inappropriate to construct a mini roundabout on a route that has a series of linked signaled junctions and pedestrian crossings. Similarly, a signaled junction on an otherwise free-flowing rural dual carriageway with generously designed priority junctions or roundabouts could prove to be hazardous.

3. Priority junctions

Priority junctions are the simplest and most common of intersections and range from single lane approach T-junctions to high-capacity channelised layouts. The control at priority junctions depends upon give-way road markings and post mounted signs.

Crossroad layouts should be avoided wherever possible because they concentrate a large number of vehicle movements and, therefore, conflicts within the junctions. On unlit rural roads at night, drivers on the side roads can be confused into thinking that they are on the major route, particularly when there is an approaching vehicle on the far side of the crossroads.

New Words and Expressions

rural [ˈruərl] adj. 乡村的
layout [ˈleɪaut] n. 布局;设计;安排
generous [ˈdʒenərəs] adj. 慷慨的,大方的;丰盛的;肥沃的;充足的
constraint [kənˈstreɪnt] n. 约束;强制;限制
Area of Outstanding Natural Beauty (AONB) (受到国家保护的)杰出自然风景区
conservation [kɒnsəˈveɪʃn] n. 保存;保持;保护
collision [kəˈlɪʒn] n. 碰撞;冲突
traffic schemes 交通方案,交通计划
rerouting [riːˈruːtɪŋ] v. 变更旅程
vehicle [ˈviːɪkəl] n. 交通工具;车辆
predominate [prɪˈdɒmɪneɪt] vt. 在……占优势;支配;统治 vi. 占支配地位;占优势 adj. 主要的;突出的;占优势的
grade separation 立体交叉口
manoeuvre [məˈnuːvə(r)] n. 策略;调动;操纵 vt. 策划;(敏捷地)操纵
demountable [dɪˈmauntəbl] adj. 可卸下的
drawbar [ˈdrɔːbɑː] n. 列车间的挂钩;牵引车的挂钩

wheelbase ['wiːlbeɪs] n. (车轮)轴距
crossroad ['krɒsˌrəʊd] n. 十字路口
optimize ['ɒptɪmaɪz] vt. 使最优化；充分利用
archaeological [ˌɑːkɪə'lɒdʒɪkl] adj. 考古的；考古学的；考古学上的
roundabout ['raʊndəbaʊt] n. (交通)环岛 adj. 迂回的，间接的，兜圈子的
dual ['djuːəl] adj. 两部分的；双重的；双的
rear [rɪə(r)] n. 后部 adj. 后面的；后部的

Exercises

I True or false.

(　　)(1) In urban areas there is often space to provide generous layouts for new junctions.

(　　)(2) Within rural areas the physical constraints are more related to the built environment.

(　　)(3) With any rural scheme the most important consideration is the size.

(　　)(4) In residential areas the predominated vehicle will be large vehicles.

(　　)(5) In very rare cases the design vehicle can be limited to less than the largest vehicles where there is a physical width or mass limit.

II Complete the following sentences.

(1) _____, _____ and _____ must, of course, be placed outside the vehicle swept paths.

(2) Apart from abnormal load vehicles the longest vehicle in everyday use in the U. K. is _____ m drawbar trailer combination.

(3) _____ are the simplest and most common of intersections and range from single lane approach T-junctions to high-capacity channelised layouts.

(4) Frequently, when an existing junction is to be upgraded to handle more or different types of vehicles, _____.

(5) The control at priority junctions depends upon _____ and _____.

III Answer the following questions.

(1) What is the most important consideration with any urban scheme?

(2) What is the purpose of designating abnormal load routes for London?

(3) What is the result when a vehicle with long front or rear overhang is stationary and its steering wheels are on full lock?

(4) Please take examples for selection of junction type.

(5) Why should crossroad layouts be avoided wherever possible?

Topics for Discussion

(1) Why is that at urban road junctions it often not possible to provide full standards for large vehicles?

(2) What does the control at priority junctions depend upon?

(3) Why must the existing form or control method be considered, when an existing junction is to be upgraded to handle more or different types of vehicle?

参 考 译 文

交 叉 口

1. 概述

交叉口是两条或多条道路交汇的地方,也称为交叉路口。可以在交叉口的一侧或两侧设置停车标志,也可以设置一个停车灯。

在乡村地区,通常有充足的空间布置规划新的交叉口,土地成本相对较低,通常可以调整总体方案布局以全面达到设计标准。当然,存在诸如山区或丘陵地区复杂地形的限制,从客观上约束了工程师优化设计的自由度。近年来,一些其他限制因素变得越来越重要,如著名的自然风景区、具特殊科学价值的地点、登记入册的建筑物和保护区、考古遗址和优质农田。

即使存在这些限制,仍然需要严格遵守设计标准。乡村的设计速度通常高于市区,因此乡村地区内发生事故和高速碰撞的后果更为严重。

在市区,客观限制与建筑环境更相关。物业价值越高,适合用于改建公路的土地越少。即使在公路边界内,地下设施的存在也会影响布局条件。对于一些小型交通方案,维持或重新设计服务的成本可能是建设公路和设置标志标线成本的10倍(或更多)。

对于任何城市方案,最需要考虑的是设计车辆的尺寸、转弯特性和空间需求。在大多数情况下,这意味着限定合法通过道路的最大型车辆尺寸。在住宅区,私家车占主导地位,但大型车辆经常穿过这些区域收集垃圾、清洁沟渠、检修、进行家庭运输、作为校车和公共交通工具。在市中心,百货商店、超市、公共建筑和快餐店等处还要定期接收重型货车的送货。

异常负载的车辆偶尔会进入城镇和市中心。伦敦等主要城市已经为异常负载的车辆指定了行车路线,规避了危桥或低桥、难以转弯的地方、架空的电话线或电线。工程师必须注意以上位置并确保在新的交通设计中为突发事件做出预防措施。有时可以从这些大型车辆的运营商处收取额外费用,用于设置加固的超限区域和可拆卸的街道家具。

在极少数情况下,在有物理宽度或质量限制的地方,设计车辆可以限制为小于所能通过的最大车辆。在一般交通流量和重型货车交通量较低的情况下,可以允许偶尔出现的大型车辆在其完成操作所需的短时间内占据整个道路的宽度。

在市区道路的交叉口,通常不可能达到大型车辆需要的全部标准。在车辆数量较小且速度较低的情况下,可以允许它们在市区环形交叉口和信号交叉口中占据两个或更多的车道。当然,交通岛、路缘线和街道家具必须放置在车辆扫掠路径之外。标准车辆扫掠路径图可用于检查其分布,但对于更复杂的多个转向,建议使用DOT计算机程序——TRACK。

除异常载重车辆外,英国日常使用的最长车辆是18米的牵引杆拖车。在有限的场地设计交叉口时,仅检查布局是否适合最大型车辆通过是不够的。车辆扫掠路径取决于许多因素,如刚接的或铰接的、轴距(包括拖拉机轴距)、前后悬挂、宽度和拖车长度。

在一些情况下,铰接式车辆的转向半径和扫掠面积比刚接车辆更小。具有长前悬或后悬的车辆可能会造成特定问题,例如欧洲 12 米的低底盘公交车。如果这样的车辆前半部分被固定住并且其方向盘处于锁死状态,则后半部分在开始移动时倾向向外侧移动。如果这时车辆离路边很近,车身可能会撞到行人。

2. 选择交叉口类型

在某些情况下,可以很容易地选择交叉口的类型,例如:
(1)两条交通量较小的住宅区道路——优先通行交叉口。
(2)高速公路的直行车道——立体交叉口。
(3)行人流量较大的大交通量城市十字路口——信号交叉口。
(4)有大量重型货物运输的郊区双车道——常规的环形交叉口。

然而,在很多情况下,解决方案不是显而易见的,工程师应在所有数据经过检查和分析之前拒绝做出决定。

通常,当要升级现有交叉口以容纳更多或不同类型的车辆时,必须考虑现有的交叉口形式或控制方法。主要路线上的其他交叉路口形式可能确定新建的或改善的交叉路口形式。例如,在有一系列连续信号交叉口和人行横道的路线上,修建微型环形交叉口可能是不适合的。同样地,对于一条通常设计优先通行交叉口或环形交叉口的乡村自由流双车道,要在上面设计信号交叉口可能是危险的。

3. 优先通行交叉口

优先通行交叉口是最简单和最常见的交叉口,从单车道 T 形交叉口到大容量渠化布局都属于其范围。优先通行交叉口的管控取决于让路标线和单柱式标志。

应尽可能避免十字形的交叉口布局,因为它们在交叉路口内集中了大量车辆和交通冲突。在夜间无灯光的乡村道路上,特别是在十字交叉口的远侧有一辆正在接近的车辆时,处于辅路的驾驶人可能会误认为自己行驶在主要路线上。

Reading Material

Grade-separated Junctions and Interchanges

Grade-separated junctions have been defined as ones which require use of an at-grade junction at the commencement or termination of the slip roads. These at-grade junctions, in the form of either major-minor priority junctions or roundabouts together with the slip roads, can produce diamond junctions, half-cloverleaf junctions or roundabout junctions.

In the United Kingdom, decisions, as to junction types are no longer made by the use of design standards, which relate choice to traffic forecasts. Decisions are made on the basis of relative economic and environmental advantages of competing junction types. The choice of junction type is particularly difficult because of the sensitivity of delay to the future traffic forecast. Below a volume in the region of 85 percent capacity, average vehicle delay is relatively uniform whilst above 85 percent of capacity, average delays increase rapidly. As a result, small differences in estimates of future demand flow or junction capacity can have a considerable effect on delay estimates. With grade-separated junctions in urban areas, environmental factors may have considerable influence on the choices of junction type.

1. Three-way junctions

At a three-way junction the usual layout adopted is the trumpet, illustrated in Figure 12-1. It allows a full range of turning movements but suffers from the disadvantage that there is a speed limitation on the minor road right turning flow due to radius size. Where topographical conditions make it necessary the junction can be designed to the opposite hand, but this layout has the disadvantage that vehicles leaving the major road have to turn through a small radius.

It may sometimes in the future become necessary to convert a three-way junction to a four-way junction, and the design should allow for this future conversion. A suitable form of junction is the partial bridged rotary shown in Figure 12-2. Alternatively the trumpet intersection shown in Figure 12-1 may be converted to a cloverleaf intersection (see Figure 12-3).

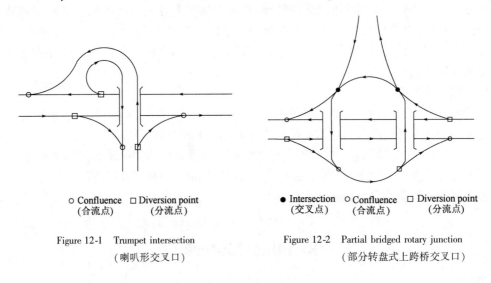

Figure 12-1 Trumpet intersection
（喇叭形交叉口）

Figure 12-2 Partial bridged rotary junction
（部分转盘式上跨桥交叉口）

2. Four-way junctions

Frequently four-way junctions are formed by the intersection of a major and a minor road. In such instances it is often possible to allow traffic conflicts to take place on the minor road. The simplest type of intersection where this occurs is the diamond. This is a suitable form of layout in which there are relatively few turning movements from the major road on to the minor road since the capacities of the two exit slip roads from the major road is limited by the capacity of the priority intersection with the minor road. Care needs to be taken with this and other designs by the use of channelisation, so that wrong-way movements on the slip roads are prevented.

In some circumstances site conditions may prevent the construction of slip roads in all of the four quadrants as required by the diamond. A solution in this case would be the construction of a half-cloverleaf interchange. Where site conditions make it necessary or where right-turning movements from the major road are heavy then the opposite hand arrangement may be used, with the disadvantage however of a more sudden speed reduction for traffic leaving the major road. As the traffic importance of the minor road and the magnitude of the turning movements increase, additional slip roads may be inserted into the partial cloverleaf design until the junction layout approaches the full cloverleaf design.

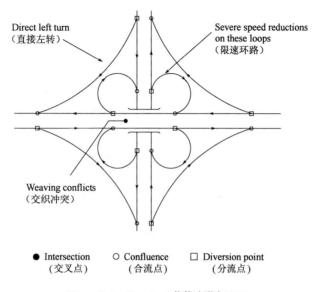

Figure 12-3　Cloverleaf(苜蓿叶形交叉口)

An advantage of both the diamond and the half-cloverleaf junctions is that only one bridge is required, but it is recommended that in its design provision should be made for the future likely construction of a safety island on the minor road.

Where major traffic routes intersect, it is no longer possible for the traffic conflicts to be resolved on the road of lesser traffic importance and the simpler junction type previously described are then likely to be unsatisfactory, both from the point of view of capacity and accident potential. The design of intersections of this type is always carried out after consideration of the individual directional traffic flow, having regard for the topographical features of the area. Nevertheless it is possible to discuss the general forms of these intersections and the traffic flow that are likely to warrant their construction.

The advantages of this type of junction are that it occupies a relatively small area of land and has less carriageway area than other junctions of this type. It also allows easy U-turns to be made, a factor of some importance in rural areas where intersections may be widely spaced or in urban areas where a number of slip roads may join the major route between interchanges.

As the traffic importance of the minor road increases then a disadvantage of this form of junction is the necessity for all vehicles on the road of lesser traffic importance to weave with the turning traffic from the other route. For this reason the capacities of the weaving sections limit the capacities of the intersection as a whole.

An alternative form of intersection, while popular in the United States, has found limited application in Great Britain is the cloverleaf, shown in Figure 12-3. With this form the straight ahead traffic on both routes is unimpeded and in addition, left-turning movements may be made directly from one route to the other. The cost of structural works is also less than with the grade separated roundabout because only one bridge is required although the bridge will normally be wider. On the other hand the carriageway area is greater for the cloverleaf.

Operationally the cloverleaf intersection has many disadvantages. Vehicles leaving both routes to make a right turn have to reduce speed considerably because of radius restrictions and there is also a weaving conflict between vehicles entering and leaving each route, which peak at the same time. This conflict can however be reduced by the provision of a separate weaving lane on either side of each carriageway but this will increase carriageway and bridge costs. There are also four traffic connections onto each route and U-turns may present some difficulty to drivers unfamiliar with the junction. Sign posting has also been stated to present some difficulties.

Where heavy right-turning movements in one direction are anticipated at a cloverleaf type intersection, this movements has frequently been given a direct connection by a single link, requiring extra bridgeworks but eliminating one loop with its small radius and restricted speed.

Exercises

I True or false.

(   )(1) In the United Kingdom, decisions, as to junction types are still made by the use of design standards, which relate choice to traffic forecasts.

(   )(2) At a three-way junction the usual layout adopted is the trumpet. It has a disadvantage that there is a speed limitation on the minor road right turning flow.

(   )(3) A disadvantage of the half-cloverleaf junction is that it requires building more bridge than the diamond junction.

(   )(4) When major traffic routes intersect, it is not impossible for the traffic conflicts to be resolved on the road of lesser traffic importance.

(   )(5) Operationally the cloverleaf intersection doesn't have any disadvantages.

II Complete the following sentences.

(1) The choice of junctiontype is particularly difficult because of the _____ of delay to the future traffic forecast.

(2) Alternatively the trumpet intersection shown in Figure 12-3 may be converted to a _____ intersection.

(3) An advantage of both the diamond and the half-cloverleaf junctions is that _____, but it is recommended that in its design provision should be made for the future likely _____.

(4) Frequently four-way junctions are formed by the intersection of _____.

(5) There are also four traffic connections onto each route and _____ may present some difficulty to drivers unfamiliar with the junction.

III Answer the following questions.

(1) What is the definition of grade-separated junctions?

(2) Why is four-way junction a suitable form of layout in which there are relatively few turning movements from the major road on to the minor road?

(3) For the diamond, as the traffic importance of the minor road and the magnitude of the turning movements increase, what can be done?

(4) What are the advantages of four-way junction?

(5) What are the advantages of cloverleaf?

参 考 译 文

立体交叉口和互通式立交

立体交叉口被定义为在支路开始或终止时需要使用平面交叉的交叉口。这些平面交叉口(主路优先通行交叉口或环形交叉口)连同匝道一起可以形成菱形、半苜蓿形或环形交叉口。

在英国,设计交叉口类型不再遵守根据交通预测制定的设计标准,而是比较交叉口类型在经济和环境上所具有的优点。由于车辆延误变化影响未来交通量预测,因此交叉口类型的选择特别困难。当一个地区的交通流量小于通行能力的85%时,车辆平均延误大致相同。但当交通流量大于通行能力的85%时,车辆平均延误急剧增加。因此,对未来交通流和交叉口通行能力预测的微小差异,都可能对延误估计产生很大的影响。对于市区立体交叉口,环境因素对交叉口类型的选择影响很大。

1. 三路相交的交叉口

三路相交交叉口的布置通常采用喇叭形,如图12-1所示。它保证了车辆的各种转向需要,但它的缺点是次要道路转弯半径过小,使右转车辆在速度上受到限制。在地形条件允许的情况下,交叉口可以设计成相反的方向,但这种布局的缺点是离开主要道路的车辆必须经过一个较小半径的弯道。

当一个三路交叉口将来有可能改建成为四路交叉口时,在交叉口设计上就要有相应的考虑。一种较适合的交叉口形式是设置成部分转盘式上跨桥,如图12-2所示。图12-1所示的喇叭形交叉口也可改建成为一个苜蓿叶形交叉口(图12-3)。

2. 四路相交的交叉口

四路相交的交叉口常常是由一条主要道路和一条次要道路相交形成的。在这种情况下,一般设法使车辆的冲突尽可能只发生在次要道路上。最简单的交叉口形式是菱形。当从主要道路转到次要道路上的车辆比较少时,菱形交叉口也比较合适。因为从主要道路上出来的两条出口道的通行能力,将被次要道路优先通行交叉口的通行能力所限制。对于这种或其他相似的设计,要妥善地运用交通渠化的方法,以防止在引道上出现行车方向错误等交通流动情况。

在有些情况下,现场可能不具备菱形交叉口所需要的在所有四个象限上修建引道的条件。

一个解决方法是修建半苜蓿叶形的立交。如果现场条件有必要，或主要道路的右转交通量较大，则可采用反向布置，但缺点是离开主要道路的车辆会突然减速。如果次要道路的交通重要性和转向运动的幅度增加，可将额外的支路插入部分苜蓿叶形设计中，直到交叉口布局形成完整的苜蓿叶形设计。

菱形立交和半苜蓿叶形立交一个共同的优点就是只需建造一座桥，但是建议在它们的设计中考虑将来可能在次要道路上修建一个安全岛的情况。

如果两条相交的道路都是主干道，那就不需要将交通冲突放在次要道路上来解决。

以上所述几种较简单的立交形式，无论从通行能力或从事故隐患方面来看，可能都不会使人满意。进行这种交叉口设计时，往往先要结合当地的地形特征来考虑各方向的车流情况。不过，还是可以根据来往的车流情况决定是否应该修建这些一般形式的立交。

这种类型交叉口的优点是，占用的土地面积相对较小，并且比这种类型的其他交叉口具有更少的车道面积。它还允许进行简单的调头，这在交叉口间距较大的乡村地区，或在一些匝道可能连接互通式立交之间主要路线的市区，具有一定的重要性。

当次要路线的交通重要性逐渐增大时，上述形式也有一个缺点，就是所有次要道路上的车辆都要与从另一条路上转出来的车辆相交织。因此，交织段的通行能力会限制整个立交的通行能力。

另一种替换形式是苜蓿叶形交叉口，如图 12-3 所示，这种形式在美国很普遍，在英国已部分应用。采用这种形式对在两条路线上的直行交通都不妨碍，而且左转车辆可直接从一条线路转到另一条线路。由于只需要修建一座跨线桥（虽然一般要宽一些），这种方式在修建费用上要低于立体式环形交叉。另外，苜蓿叶形立交所提供的车行道面积也要多一些。

从行车角度来看，苜蓿叶形立交也有许多缺点。因为受匝道转弯半径的限制，不论从哪一条路线上驶出并要右转的车辆，都要大大降低速度；在进入和离开各条路线的车辆之间也都有因交织而产生的冲突，而且又都集中在同一时间。虽然通过在每一条车行道的旁边设置专用交织车道可以减少这种冲突，但这也增加了修建车行道和桥梁的成本，而且在每条路线上各有四个车流交汇点，对于不熟悉该交叉口的驾驶人来说，调头可能比较困难。另外，其在交通标志设置方面也存在一些困难。

对于苜蓿叶形交叉口，如果估计未来某方向的右转车辆相当多，常常需要另建一条专用匝道，这样，虽然增加了修建立交桥的成本，但却减少了一个限制车速的小半径环形引道。

Knowledge Link

Roundabout Intersections

Roundabouts have been commonly used in central city areas where traditionally they were used to resolve traffic and pedestrian conflicts in the large open squares, which existed in the early part of the twentieth century. The central island frequently covered a large area of the square and was utilized for ornamental flower beds whilst traffic circulated around the surrounding carriageways. Increasing traffic demands and the pressure to allow pedestrians to cross the carriageways at surface level has resulted in many of these roundabouts being converted to signal control so that more positive control over traffic movements on an area wide basis may be exercised.

In suburban areas, roundabouts are frequently found at the intersections of radial and ring type roads where they are subjected to peak hour traffic demands due to commuter flow.

Roundabouts are also used on rural roads where traffic flow or the road types do not justify the provision of a grade-separated intersection. In these situations, speeds are high on the approaches to roundabouts and safety is an important consideration.

Unit 13

Geometric Design Controls and Criteria

Text

In geometric design, various controls and criteria are employed to ensure that the facility will accommodate the expected traffic requirements and to encourage consistency and uniformity in operation. To some degree, these controls and criteria are applicable to all streets and highways.

1. Control of access

(1) Definition

Control of access is the condition in which the right of owners or occupants of abutting land or other persons to access, light, air or view in connection with a highway is fully or partially controlled by public authorities. There are two degrees of access control:

①Full control of access, where the authorities to control access is exercised to give preference to through traffic by providing access connections only with selected public roads through the prohibition of crossings at grade or direct private driveway connections.

②Partial control of access, where the authorities to control access is exercised to give preference to through traffic to a degree, in addition to access connections with selected public roads, there may be some crossings at grade and some private driveway connections.

(2) Application

Access control is accomplished either by providing access rights or by using frontage roads. When a freeway is developed on new location, of course, adjoining property owners have no right to direct access to a highway.

Highway function should determine the degree of access control needed. Freeways whose main function is to provide mobility should have full control of access. Urban arterial streets and major rural highways should have as great a degree of access control as is feasible.

The principal operational difference between a highway with and without control of access is in the amount of interference with through traffic by other vehicles and pedestrians. With access control, entrances and exits can be located at points best suited to enable vehicles to enter and leave safely without interfering with through traffic. Vehicles are prevented from entering or leaving elsewhere so that regardless of the types or intensities of development of the roadside areas, the efficiencies and capacities of the highway are maintained at a high level and the accident hazard remains low.

When there is no control of access on some new or improved arterial streets, such as a bypass route, the concentrated flow of traffic can be expected to attract roadside businesses with resultant traffic interference, reduction in capacities of the highway, and increase in accident hazard. As traffic increases and roadside businesses multiply, the hazard increases and considerable congestion may develop. Any remedial treatment may be frustrated by the high value of the roadside properties. It is, therefore, desirable to obtain access control initially before land value has increased. In designing arterial streets and highways without access control, initial allowance, such as extra lanes or a two-way left-turn lane, should be made for potential roadside commercial development and their effects on the operation of the facilities.

In summary, points of access on streets and highways should be carefully planned to the extent possible. Access should not be allowed at locations where entering and leaving vehicles will create a hazard (such as at locations where sight distance is limited or at a point too close to another intersection).

2. Design speed

(1) Definition

A speed determined for design and correlation of the physical features of a highway that influences vehicle operation—the maximum safe speed maintainable over a specified section of highway when conditions permit design features to govern.

(2) Application

Some features, for example, curvature, superelevation, sight distance and gradient, are directly related to and vary appreciably with design speed. Pavement and shoulder widths and clearances to walls and rails are less directly related to design speed, but because they can affect vehicle speeds, higher standards for them should be used on highways with higher design speed. Thus, nearly all geometric design elements of the highway are affected by the selected design speed.

(3) Basis for selection

Design speed selection is influenced by the character of terrain, the density and character of the land use, the classification and function of the highway, the traffic volumes expected to use the highway, and by economic and environmental considerations. Usually, a highway in level terrain warrants a higher design speed than one in mountainous terrain; one in a rural area, a higher design speed than one in an urban area; an arterial highway, a higher design speed than a local road; and a high-volume highway, a higher design speed than one carrying low traffic volumes. Except for local roads and streets in urban areas, the design speed should be as high as possible commensurate with economic and environmental considerations.

3. Other speed to be considered

(1) Average running speed

For all traffic or component thereof, the summation of distance divided by the summation of running times.

(2) Operating speed

The highest overall speed at which a driver can travel on a given highway under favorable weather condition and under prevailing traffic condition without any time exceeding the safe speed as determined by the design speed on a section-by-section basis.

Operating speed is usually about 5mph (8km/h) higher than the average running speed for low-volume condition on free-flow facility. It is used as a measure of level of service for those highways that provide uninterrupted flow conditions (usually rural only) for vehicular travel and is therefore useful in determining the level of service provided by a specific traveled way.

(3) Average overall speed

The summation of distances is traveled by all vehicles over a given section of highway during a specified period of time, divided by the summation of overall travel times.

Average overall speed is used as a measure of level of service for interrupted flow conditions (urban arterial and downtown streets) and is therefore useful in determining the level of service of a specific traveled way in urban areas.

New Words and Expressions

abutting land	毗邻的土地
frontage road	沿街道路,临街道路
roadside [ˈrəudsaɪd]	n. 路边;路旁 adj. 路边的;路旁的
arterial street	城市干道,干线道路
curvature [ˈkɜːvətʃə(r)]	n. 弯曲;曲率;弯曲部分
superelevation [ˌsjuːpəˌelɪˈveɪʃən]	n. 超高;曲线超高;外轨超高
gradient [ˈgreɪdɪənt]	n. 梯度;倾斜度;坡度
commensurate [kəˈmenʃərət]	adj. 相称的;同量的;同样大小的
average running speed	平均行驶速度

operating speed	运行速度
average travel speed	平均行程速度
consistency [kənˈsɪstənsɪ]	n. 一致性；连贯性；前后一致
inherent [ɪnˈhɪərənt]	adj. 固有的；内在的
multiply [ˈmʌltɪplaɪ]	vt. & vi. 乘以；成倍增加；(使)繁殖
remedial [rɪˈmiːdɪəl]	adj. 补救的；纠正的
warrant [ˈwɒrənt]	n. 授权证；许可证 vt. 保证；授权；批准
thereof [ˌðeərˈɒv]	adv. 在其中；由此
give preference to	优先考虑
interference [ˌɪntəˈfɪərəns]	n. 干涉；干预；介入
intensity [ɪnˈtensətɪ]	n. 强烈；强度；剧烈；烈度
resultant [rɪˈzʌltənt]	adj. 因而发生的；结果必然发生的
be frustrated by	使……受挫；对……感到沮丧
summation [sʌˈmeɪʃn]	n. 和；总和；合计
shoulder [ˈʃəʊldə]	n. 路肩

Exercises

I True or false.

(   )(1) Geometric Design Controls and Criteria are applicable to all streets and highways.

(   )(2) Freeways should have full control of access, so should do urban arterial streets and major rural highways.

(   )(3) Points of access on streets and highways should be carefully planned to the extent possible.

(   )(4) Design speed is very important, so nearly all geometric design elements of highway are affected by the selected design speed.

(   )(5) Usually, a highway in level terrain warrants a lower design speed than one in mountainous terrain.

II Complete the following sentences.

(1) Control of access is the condition in which _____ of abutting land or other persons to access, light, air or view in connection with a highway is fully or partially controlled by public authorities.

(2) The principal operational difference between _____ is in the amount of interference with through traffic by other vehicles and pedestrians.

(3) The highest overall speed at which a driver can travel on a given highway under _____ and _____ without any time exceeding the safe speed as determined by _____.

(4) When a freeway is developed on new location, of course, adjoining property owners have

_____ to direct access to a highway.

(5)_____ is used as a measure of level of service for interrupted flow condition and is therefore useful in determining the level of service of a specific traveled way in urban areas.

Ⅲ Answer the following questions.

(1) What is the definition of control of access?

(2) How is access control accomplished?

(3) What is the principal operational difference between a highway with and without control of access?

(4) What is the definition of design speed?

(5) What is the definition of operating speed?

Topics for Discussion

(1) What is the difference between full control of access and partial control of access?

(2) What is the difference between average running speed and average overall speed?

(3) What is design speed selection influenced by?

参 考 译 文

几何设计控制与标准

在几何设计中,为了确保交通设施能适应预估的交通需求,并且保证交通运行的连续性和一致性,需要使用各种不同的控制方式和准则。这些控制方式和准则在一定程度上对所有城市道路和公路都是适用的。

1. 出入口控制

(1)定义

出入口控制是指邻近土地的业主、居民或其他人与公路有关的出入、采光、空气或景观方面的权利被公共交通部门完全或部分地控制。出入口控制方式主要分为两种:

①出入口完全控制。公共交通部门优先为过境交通提供与选定公共道路相连的出入口,并在平面交叉或直接私人车道连接处禁止出入。

②出入口部分控制。公共交通部门除了选定公共道路相连接的出入口外,还可以在一些平面交叉和私人车道连接处为过境交通提供一定程度的出入优先。

(2)应用

出入口控制通过提供出入权或者利用临街道路来实现。当高速公路在一个新的位置建成时,邻近的业主没有直接进出的公路权利。

公路的功能决定了所需要出入控制的程度。以提供流动性为主要功能的高速公路应实施出入口完全控制。城市主干道和主要乡村公路应尽可能在一定程度上控制出入。

在运行方面公路有无出入口控制的主要区别在于其他车辆和行人对直行车流的干扰程度。针对控制出入的道路,应将其出口和入口设置在最适于车辆安全出入而又不影响直行车流的位置。避免车辆在其他地点进出,可以不必考虑沿途区域开发的类型或强度,并保持较高的公路运行效率和通行能力、较低的交通事故率。

当一些新建道路或改建的主干道(比如绕行道路)没有出入控制时,集中的交通流将促进路边商业的产生,从而产生交通干扰、降低道路通行能力并增加交通事故危险性。随着交通量的增长和路边商铺的激增,交通事故和拥挤也会增多。任何的补救措施都可能会因为路边昂贵的土地价格而受阻。因此希望在土地价值升值以前就尽早实行出入口控制。在设计无出入口控制的城市主干路和公路时,首先应考虑潜在的路边商业发展对交通设施运行的影响(例如附加车道和双向左转车道)。

总之,城市道路和公路的出入口处应尽可能细致地加以规划。出入口不应该设在会让进出车辆遭遇危险的地方(例如设在视距受限或距其他交叉口较近处)。

2. 设计速度

(1) 定义

设计速度是指确定公路设计指标并使其相协调的设计基准速度,这些指标影响车辆的运行,即在设计的几何指标条件允许的情况下,在特定路段上可维持的最大安全速度。

(2) 应用

例如,平曲线、超高、视距和纵坡等指标均与设计速度有直接关系,并随设计速度的改变而产生明显的变化。路面和路肩的宽度、护墙和铁道之间的净空与设计车速几乎没有什么直接关系,但由于它们会对车速产生影响,在设计速度较高的公路上,这些宽度指标也应采用较高的标准。因此,几乎所有公路几何设计要素都要受到所选择设计速度的影响。

(3) 选择的基础

设计速度的确定受地形特点、土地利用的性质和使用强度、公路的等级和功能、公路预测交通量及经济和环境等因素的影响。一般而言,位于平原区的公路比山岭区公路的设计速度高,乡村公路比城市道路设计速度高,干线公路的设计速度高于地方性道路,交通量大的公路设计速度高于交通量小的公路。除了地方性道路和城市道路外,设计速度应该尽可能地高一些,以适应经济和环境等方面的需要。

3. 其他速度

(1) 平均行驶速度

平均行驶速度是指交通流中全部车辆或部分车辆的行驶距离总和除以行驶时间总和。

(2) 运行速度

运行速度是驾驶人在良好的天气条件和普遍的交通条件下,在不超过由设计速度确定的安全速度的情况下,在给定的公路上逐段行驶的最高总速度。

通常在自由流设施和低流量的情况下,运行速度比平均行驶速度高5英里/小时(8千米/小时)。运行速度被用来作为衡量车辆出行的连续流公路(通常仅仅乡村公路)服务水平的一项技术指标,很适合用于确定特定车行道所提供的服务水平。

(3) 平均行程速度

平均行程速度是指在特定的时段内、在指定的公路路段上,所有车辆行驶距离的总和除以总的行驶时间。

平均行程速度作为确定间断交通流(城市主干道和中心区道路)服务水平的一项技术指标,对于确定城市区城市道路特定车行道的服务水平非常有用。

Reading Material

Horizontal and Vertical Alignment

1. Horizontal alignment

For balance in highway design all elements should, as far as economically feasible, be determined to provide safe, continuous operation at a speed likely under the general conditions for that highways or streets. For the most part, this is done through the use of design speed as the overall control. In the design of highway curves it is necessary to establish the proper relation between design speed and curvature and also their joint relations with superelevation and side friction. Although these relations stem from the laws of mechanics, the actual values for use in design depend on practical limits and factors determined more or less empirically over the range of variables involved. These limits and factors are explained below with determination of logical controls for highway curve design.

When a vehicle moves in a circular path, it is forced radially outward by centrifugal force. The centrifugal force is counterbalanced by the vehicle mass component related to the roadway superelevation or the side friction developed between tires and surface or by a combination of the two. From the laws of mechanics, the basic point mass (curve) formula for vehicle operation on a curve is the following.

$$\frac{e+f}{1-ef} = \frac{0.067V^2}{R} = \frac{V^2}{15R} \tag{13-1}$$

Where, e——rate of roadway superelevation;

f——side friction factor;

V——vehicle speed, km/h;

R——radius of curve, m.

The value of the product ef in this equation is always small. As a result, the $(1-ef)$ term is normally omitted in highway and street designs, thus providing slightly more conservative values.

When a vehicle travels at constant speed on a curve superelevated so that the f value is zero, the centrifugal force is balanced by the mass component of the vehicle and, theoretically, no steering force is required. A vehicle traveling faster or slower than the balance speed develops tire friction as steering effort is applied to prevent movement to the outside or to the inside of the curve. On nonsuperelevated curves, travel at different speeds is also possible by utilizing side friction in appropriate amounts to resist the varying centrifugal force.

2. Vertical alignment

(1) Terrain

The topography of the land traversed has an influence on the alignment of roads and streets. Topography does affect horizontal alignment, but it is more evident in the effect on vertical alignment.

To characterize variations, engineers generally separate topography into three classifications according to terrain.

①Level terrain is that condition where highway sight distances, as governed by both horizontal and vertical restrictions, are generally long or could be made to be so without construction difficulty or major expense.

②Rolling terrain is that condition where the natural slopes consistently rise above and fall below the road or street grade and where occasional steep slopes offer some restriction to normal horizontal and vertical roadway alignment.

③Mountainous terrain is that condition where longitudinal and transverse changes in the elevation of the ground with respect to the road or street are abrupt and where benching and side hill excavation are frequently required to obtain acceptable horizontal and vertical alignment.

Terrain classifications pertain to the general character of a specific route corridor. Routes in valleys or mountainous areas that have all the characteristics of roads or streets traversing level or rolling terrain should be classified as level or rolling terrain. In general, rolling terrain generates steeper grades, causing trucks to reduce speeds below those of passenger cars, and mountainous terrain aggravates the situation, resulting in some trucks operating at crawl speeds.

(2) Grades

Roads and streets should be designed to encourage uniform operation throughout. Use of a selected design speed as previously discussed is a means towards this end by correlation of various geometric features of the road or street. Design values have been determined and agreed upon for many highway features, but few conclusions have been reached on roadway grades in relation to design speed.

Exercises

I True or false.

(   )(1) For balance in highway design all elements should be determined to provide safe, continuous operation at a speed likely under the general conditions for highways or streets.

(   )(2) It is necessary to establish the proper relation not only between design speed and curvature but also their joint relations with superelevation and side friction.

(   )(3) The topography of the land traversed hasn't an influence on the alignment of roads and streets.

(   )(4) The topography is separated into three classifications according to terrain. They are Level terrain, Rolling terrain and Mountainous terrain.

(   )(5) In general, rolling terrain generates steeper grades, causing trucks to increase speeds at a high speed.

II Complete the following sentences.

(1) In the design of highway curves it is necessary to establish the proper relation between _____ and _____ and also their joint relations with _____ and _____.

(2) When a vehicle moves in a circular path, it is forced radially outward by _____ force.

(3) The _____ of the land traversed has an influence on the alignment of roads and streets.

(4) Roads and streets should be designed to encourage _____ operation throughout.

(5) On nonsuperelevated curves, travel at different speeds is also possible by _____ in appropriate amounts to resist _____.

Ⅲ Answer the following questions.

(1) What is necessary to establish in the design of highway curves?

(2) How can the varying centrifugal force be resisted on nonsuperelevated curves?

(3) To characterize variations, which three classifications are generally devided according to terrain?

(4) How does rolling terrain influence a road?

(5) Please take examples for that terrain classifications pertain to the general character of a specific route corridor.

参 考 译 文

平面与纵断面线形

1. 平面线形

为了使设计道路各个部分协调,应在经济可行的情况下,确定道路的所有要素,使得在该公路或城市道路行驶的车辆能够以一般情况下的速度安全、连续地运行。在大多数情况下,这是通过使用设计速度作为总体控制来完成的。在公路曲线设计中,必须建立设计速度和曲率之间的恰当关系以及它们与超高和侧向摩擦力之间的相关关系。虽然这些关系来自力学定律,但是设计中采用的实际数值,除了取决于实际情况的限制和公式中的变量以外,或多或少也有凭经验确定的因素。这些限制和因素,以及它们对公路曲线设计的合理控制将在下面进行讨论。

汽车在圆形轨迹中运行时,由于离心力的作用受到了径向的力;这一离心力与车行道超高有关的车辆质量分力、轮胎与路面之间的侧向摩擦力或两者的合力相平衡。根据力学定律,汽车在曲线上运行的质点(曲线)基本公式为:

$$\frac{e+f}{1-ef} = \frac{0.067V^2}{R} = \frac{V^2}{15R} \tag{13-1}$$

式中:e——车行道超高率;

f——侧向摩擦因数;

V——行车速度,千米/小时;

R——曲线半径,米。

公式中 ef 乘积的数值一般很小,因而在公路和城市道路设计中 $(1-ef)$ 项通常忽略不计,因为这样得出的值略偏保守。

当车辆以恒定速度在超高曲线上行驶时,f值为零,离心力由车辆的质量分量平衡,理论上不需要转向力。当施加转向力以防止车辆向曲线外侧或内侧移动时,比平衡速度更快或更慢的车辆会产生轮胎摩擦。在不设超高的曲线上,车辆通过适当的侧摩擦力来抵抗不同的离心力,也能以不同的速度行驶。

2. 纵断面线形

(1)地形

地形对公路与城市道路的定线是有影响的。地形对平面线形有较大的影响,但对纵断面线形的影响更为明显。为了表现地形的变化特征,工程师们一般都根据地形条件将其划分成以下三种类型:

① 平原区,公路视距(受平、纵面限制)一般都很长,或可以修建得较长而无施工困难或费用增大问题。

② 丘陵区,自然坡度一般在公路或城市道路要求的坡度范围内起伏,并且偶尔出现陡坡,给正常的平、纵面道路线形造成某些限制。

③ 山岭区,相对公路或城市道路来说,地面标高的纵向和横向变化急剧;为了得到容许的平、纵面线形,经常需要半挖半填。

地形分类与特定路线走廊的一般特征有关。沿山谷或山区垭口的路线,如具有平原区或丘陵区的公路或城市道路的特征,则应归类为平原区或丘陵区。一般情况下,在丘陵区出现较陡的纵坡,会使载重汽车减速到小客车速度以下;而在山岭区则会加重这种情况,导致有些载重汽车只能以爬行速度运行。

(2)纵坡

公路和城市道路设计应鼓励全线运营的统一。如前所述,根据公路和城市道路的各项几何特征的相互关系选定一个设计速度,就是达到这一目的的手段。针对大部分公路特征已定出设计值,并且取得了一致认可,但在与设计速度有关的道路纵坡方面却很少有定论。

Knowledge Link

The *Highway Capacity Manual*

The *Highway Capacity Manual* (*HCM*) is a publication of the Transportation Research Board of the National Academy of Sciences. It includes concepts, guidelines and computational procedures for calculating the capacities and service qualities of various highway facilities (including expressways, highways, trunk roads, circular intersections, signalized and unsignalized intersections and rural highways), as well as the impacts of public transport, pedestrians and bicycles on the performance of these facilities.

From 1950 to 2016, six versions of the program were improved and updated, and the 1985 version of *HCM* was significantly updated in 1994, 1997 and 2015. *HCM* has become the reference material for global traffic engineers and practitioners, and is also the basis of specific capacity manuals for several countries. The current version of the sixth edition of the *Highway Capacity Manual—Multimodal Transport Analysis Guide*, or *HCM 2016*, or *HCM 6*, was released in October 2016. The sixth edition included the latest research on road capacity, quality of service, active traffic and demand management, and travel time reliability.

There were more than six decades of researches behind the *HCM*. The first edition of the *Highway Capacity Manual* was released in 1950 and contained 147 pages broken apart into eight parts. It was the result of a collaborative effort between the Transportation Research Board (TRB) and the Bureau of Public Roads, predecessor to the Federal Highway Administration.

In 2013 the Transportation Research Board contracted the development of a major update to the *2010 Highway Capacity Manual*. The new and revised material was scheduled to be published as a 2015 interim update of the *HCM 2010*, known as the *HCM 2015 Update*. The final version, published as *the Highway Capacity Manual*, Sixth Edition: *A Guide for Multimodal Mobility Analysis*, or *HCM 2016*, or *HCM 6*, was released in October 2016 and is available from TRB. The sixth edition incorporates the latest researchs on highway capacity, quality of service, active traffic and demand management, and travel time reliability.

Unit 14
Sight Distance

Text

The ability to see ahead is of the utmost important in the safe and efficient operation of a vehicle on a highway. On a railroad, trains are confined to a fixed path, yet a block signal system and trained operators are necessary for safe operation. In addition, the paths and speeds of motor vehicles on highways and streets are subject to the control of drivers whose abilities, training, and experience are quite varied. For safety on highways the designers must provide sight distance of sufficient length that drivers can control the operation of their vehicles to avoid striking an unexpected object on the traveled way. Certain two-lane highways should also have sufficient sight distance to enable drivers to occupy the opposing traffic lane without hazard. Two-lane rural highways should generally provide such passing sight distance at frequent intervals and for substantial portions of their length. Conversely, it normally is of little practical value to provide passing sight distance on two-lane urban streets or arterials. The lengths and intervals of passing sight distance should compatible with the criteria established pertaining to that specific highway or street classification.

Sight distance is discussed in four steps: stopping sight distance—the distance required for stopping, applicable on all highways; decision sight distance—the distances needed for decisions at complex locations; passing sight distance for two-lane highways—the distances required for the passing of overtaken vehicles, applicable only on two-lane highways; sight distance for multilane highways—the criteria for measuring these distances for use in design.

1. Stopping sight distance

Sight distance is the length of roadway ahead visible to the drivers. The minimum sight distance available on a roadway should be sufficiently long to enable a vehicle traveling at or near the design speed to stop before reaching a stationary object in its path. Although greater length is desirable, sight distance at every point along the highway should be at least that required for a below average operator or vehicle to stop in this distance.

Stopping sight distance (S) is the sum of two distances: the distance traversed by the vehicle from the instant the driver sights an object necessitating a stop to the instant the brakes are applied, and the distance required to stop the vehicle from the brake application begins. These are referred to as brakes reaction distance (l_1) and braking distance (l_2), respectively, shown in Figure 14-1.

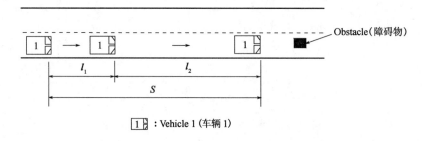

Figure 14-1　Stopping sight distance(停车视距示意图)

2. Decision sight distance

Stopping sight distances are usually sufficient to allow reasonably competent and alert drivers to come to a hurried stop under ordinary circumstances. However, these distances are often inadequate when drivers must make complex or instantaneous decisions, when information is difficult to perceive, or when unexpected or unusual maneuvers are required. Limiting sight distance to those provided for stopping may also preclude drivers from performing evasive maneuver, which are often less hazardous and otherwise preferable to stopping. Stopping sight distance may not provide sufficient visibility distances for drivers to corroborate advance warnings and to perform the necessary maneuvers. It is evident that there are many locations where it would be prudent to provide longer sight distance. In these circumstances, decision sight distance provides the greater length that drivers need.

Decision sight distance is the distance required for a driver to detect an unexpected or otherwise difficult-to-perceive information source or hazard in a roadway environment that may be visually cluttered, recognize the hazard or its threat potential, select an appropriate speed and path, and initiate and complete the required maneuver safely and efficiently. Because decision sight distance gives drivers additional margin for error and affords them sufficient length to maneuver their vehicles at the same or reduced speed rather than to just stop, its values are substantially greater than stopping sight distance.

3. Passing sight distance for two-lane highways

Most roads and numerous streets are considered to qualify as two-lane two-way highways on which vehicles frequently overtake slower moving vehicles, the passing of which must be accomplished on lanes regularly used by opposing traffic. If passing was to be accomplished with safety, the driver should be able to see a sufficient distance ahead, clear of traffic, to complete the passing maneuver without cutting off the passed vehicle in advance of meeting an opposing vehicle appearing during the maneuver, shown in Figure 14-2. When required, a driver can return to the right lane without passing if he sees opposing traffic is too close when the maneuver is only partially completed. Many passings are accomplished without the driver seeing a safe passing section ahead, but design based such maneuver does not have the desired factor of safety. Because many cautious drivers would not attempt to pass under such conditions, design on this basis would reduce the usefulness of the highway.

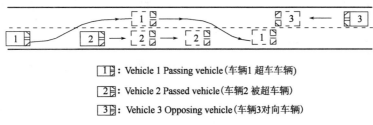

① : Vehicle 1 Passing vehicle(车辆1 超车车辆)
② : Vehicle 2 Passed vehicle(车辆2 被超车辆)
③ : Vehicle 3 Opposing vehicle(车辆3对向车辆)

Figure 14-2　Overtaking sight distance(超车视距示意图)

Passing sight distance for use in design should be determined on the basis of the length needed to safely complete normal passing maneuvers. While there may be occasions to consider multiplepassings, where two or more vehicles pass or are passed, it is not practical to assume such conditions in developing minimum design criteria. Instead, sight distance is determined for a single vehicle passing a single vehicle. Longer sight distance occurs in design and these locations can accommodate an occasional multiple passing.

4. Sight distance for multilane highways

It is not necessary to consider passing sight distance on highways or streets that have two or more traffic lanes in each direction of travel. Passing maneuvers on multilane roadways are expected to occur within the limits of each one-way traveled way. Thus passing maneuvers that require crossing the centerline of four-lane undivided roadways or crossing the median of four-lane divided roadways are reckless and should be prohibited.

New Words and Expressions

sight distance　　　　　　　　　视距
passing sight distance　　　　　　超车视距
hazard[ˈhæzəd]　　　　　　　　 n. 冒险;危险;冒险的事　vt. 冒险

applicable [ə'plɪkəbl]	adj.	适当的;可应用的
compatible [kəm'pætəbl]	adj.	谐调的;一致的;兼容的
necessitate [nɪ'sesɪteɪt]	vt.	使……成为必要
circumstance ['sɜːkəmstəns]	n.	环境;详情;境况
perceive [pə'siːv]	v.	察觉;感知;感到;认识到
pertaining [pə(ː)'teɪnɪŋ]	n.	与……有关系的;附属……的 v. 关于;有关
stopping sight distance		停车视距
traverse [trə'vɜːs]	vt.	横过;穿过;经过
decision sight distance		决策视距
instantaneous [ˌɪnstən'teɪnɪəs]	adj.	瞬间的;即刻的;即时的
visibility [ˌvɪzə'bɪlətɪ]	n.	可见度;能见度
corroborate [kə'rɒbəreɪt]	vt.	证实
prudent ['pruːdnt]	adj.	谨慎的;精明的
potential [pə'tenʃl]	adj.	潜在的;可能的;势的;位的 n. 潜能;潜力;势能;电位
initiate [ɪ'nɪʃɪeɪt]	vt.	开始;发动;传授;发起
multiple ['mʌltɪpl]	adj.	多样的;多重的 n. 倍数,若干 v. 成倍增加
median ['miːdɪən]	adj.	中央的;[数]中值的 n. 中部;中值;中位数
evasive [ɪ'veɪsɪv]	adj.	逃避的;推托的
reckless ['rekləs]	adj.	不计后果的
utmost ['ʌtməust]	adj.	极度的;最远的;最大的 n. 极限;最大限度
confine [kən'faɪn]	n.	界限;边界;限制 vt. 限制
sufficient [sə'fɪʃnt]	adj.	足够的;充分的
strike [straɪk]	vt.	撞击 n. 袭击
conversely [kɒn'vɜːslɪ]	adv.	相反地;反之
decision sight distance		决策视距

Exercises

I True or false.

(   )(1) The paths and speeds of motor vehicles on highways and streets are subject to the control of drivers whose abilities, training, and experience are quite varied.

(   )(2) Design sight distances are usually sufficient to allow reasonably competent and alert drivers to come to a hurried stop under ordinary circumstances.

(   )(3) When required, a driver can return to the right lane without passing if he sees opposing traffic is too close when the maneuver is only partially completed.

(   )(4) Passing sight distance for use in design should be determined on the basis of the length needed to safely complete normal passing maneuvers.

(   )(5) It is necessary to consider passing sight distance on highways or streets that have two or more traffic lanes in each direction of travel.

II Complete the following sentences.

(1) For safety on highways the designers must provide _____ of sufficient length that drivers can control the operation of their vehicles to avoid striking an unexpected object on the traveled way.

(2) _____ is the sum of two distances: the distance traversed by the vehicle from the instant the driver sights an object necessitating a stop to the instant the brakes are applied, and the distance required to stop the vehicle from the brake application begins.

(3) Stopping sight distance may not provide _____ for drivers to corroborate advance warnings and to perform the necessary maneuvers.

(4) Many passings are accomplished without the driver seeing _____ ahead, but design based such maneuver does not have the desired factor of safety.

(5) _____ occurs in design and these locations can accommodate an occasional multiple passing.

III Answer the following questions.

(1) What is the definition of stopping sight distance?
(2) What may stopping sight distance not do?
(3) What is the definition of decision sight distance?
(4) What should passing sight distance be determined on for use in design?
(5) What circumstances can ignore considering passing sight distance on highways or streets?

Topics for Discussion

(1) What are the paths and speeds of motor vehicles on highways and streets subject to?
(2) What is the difference between stopping sight distance and decision sight distance?
(3) How many distances are involved in stopping sight distance? And what are they?

参 考 译 文

视 距

在高速公路上安全高效地操作车辆时，看向前方是最重要的。在铁路上，列车被限制在固定轨道上，但是为了安全运行，仍需要一个区间信号系统和训练有素的驾驶人。另外，公路和城市道路上的机动车行驶路径和速度在不同程度上受驾驶人能力、受训程度和经验多少的影响。为了保证公路安全，设计者必须提供足够长的视距，以便驾驶人能够控制车辆的运行，避免在行车道上意外地撞到物体。某些双车道公路也应该有足够的视距，以使驾驶人能够在没有危险的情况下进入对向车道。双车道乡村公路通常应该以频繁的间隔在公路的大部分长度中提供超车视距；相反，在双车道城市道路或主干道上提供超车视距通常没有什么实际价值。

超车视距的长度和间隔应符合该特定公路或城市道路等级规定的标准。

从四个方面对视距进行讨论：停车视距——适用于所有公路停车所需的距离；决策视距——在情况复杂地点进行决策所需的距离；双车道公路的超车视距——仅适用于双车道公路超车车辆所需的超车距离；多车道公路的视距——设计中多车道公路超车车辆所需的超车距离标准。

1. 停车视距

视距是驾驶人员可见的前方道路长度。道路上可用的最小视距应该足够长，以使得在路径上以设计速度或近似设计速度行驶的车辆能够在撞到静止物体之前停车。尽管视距越长越好，但道路沿线各点的视距至少应为平均水平以下的驾驶人或车辆停车所需的距离。

停车视距（S）是两个距离的总和——驾驶人从看到需要停车的物体到踩制动踏板过程中车辆所经过的距离以及从踩制动踏板到车辆停止所需的距离，分别称为反应距离（l_1）和制动距离（l_2），如图 14-1 所示。

2. 决策视距

在正常情况下，停车视距通常足以让合格的和谨慎的驾驶人迅速停车。然而，当驾驶人必须做出复杂或瞬时的决定时，当获取信息发生困难时，或者需要进行突发的或非常规的操作时，这些距离通常是不充足的。将视距限制在停车视距范围内，可能会妨碍驾驶人进行规避操作。规避操作通常危险性更低，并且比停车操作更可取。停车视距可能无法为驾驶人提供足够的可见距离用以确认预警并执行必要的操作。很明显，在许多地方提供更长的视距是明智的。在这些情况下，决策视距给驾驶人提供了所需的更长距离。

决策视距是指驾驶人在视觉混乱的道路环境中发现意外或难以察觉的信息源或危险，识别危险或其潜在威胁，选择适当的速度和路径，开始操作和安全高效地完成操作所需的距离。由于决策视距为驾驶人提供了额外的误差裕度，并为驾驶人提供了足够的长度，使其能够以不变或降低过的车速驾驶车辆，而不是仅仅停车，因此其价值远大于停车视距。

3. 双车道公路的超车视距

大多数公路和城市道路都被认为是双车道双向公路，在这种公路上，车辆经常超过行驶速度较慢的车辆，这必须在对向车辆经常使用的车道上完成。如果要安全地完成超车，驾驶人应能看到前方足够远的地方清晰的交通情况，以便在完成超车操作前不会因为遇到对向车辆而被打断，如图 14-2 所示。如果驾驶人在仅完成部分操作时看到对向车辆距离过近，则驾驶人可以取消超车行为并返回右侧车道。大部分超车行为是在驾驶人未看到前方安全超车区的情况下完成的，但是基于这种操作的设计中不存在期望的安全系数。由于许多谨慎的驾驶人不会尝试在这种情况下超车，因此在此基础上进行设计会降低公路的实用性。

在设计中使用的超车视距应根据安全完成正常超车操作所需的距离来确定。虽然有时可能会考虑多次超车的情况，包括两辆或更多车辆超车或被超车，但在制定最低设计标准时，不可能考虑这些条件；相反，视距是由单个车辆超过单个车辆来决定的。在设计中一些位置的视距较长，可以允许偶然性的多次超车。

4. 多车道公路的视距

在每个行驶方向上有两条或两条以上车道的公路或城市道路上无须考虑超车视距。预计在多车道道路上进行的操作将在每个单向行驶的道路内发生。因此，穿过未分隔道路中心线或有中央分隔带的四车道道路的超车操作是鲁莽的，应予以禁止。

Reading Material

Capacity of Signalized Intersections

Capacity at intersections is defined for each lane group. The lane group capacity is the maximum rate of flow for the subject lane group that may pass through the intersection under prevailing traffic, roadway and signalization conditions. The rate of flow is generally measured or projected for a 15min period, and capacity is stated in vehicles per hour (vph).

Traffic conditions include volumes on each approach, the distribution of vehicles by movements (left, through and right), the vehicle type distribution within each movement, the locations of and use of bus stops within an intersection area, pedestrian crossing flow, and parking numbers within an intersection area.

Roadway conditions include the basic geometrics of the intersection, including the numbers and widths of lanes, grades, and lane use allocations (including parking lanes).

Signalization conditions include a full definition of the signal phasing, timing, and type of control, and an evaluation of signal progression for each lane group.

The capacity of designated lane groups within an approach is evaluated and determined using the procedures. This may be done to isolate lanes serving a particular movement or movements, such as an exclusive right-turn or left-turn lane. Lanes so designated for separate analysis were defined earlier as lane groups. The procedure contains guidelines for when and how separate lane groups should be designated on an approach.

Capacity at signalized intersection is based upon the concept of saturation flow and saturation flow rate. Satuation flow rate is defined as the maximum rate of flow that can pass through a given lane group under prevailing traffic and roadway conditions, assuming that the lane group has 100 percent of real time available as effective green time. Saturation flow rate is given the symbol s and is expressed in units of vehicles per hour of effective green time (vphg) for a given lane group.

The flow ratio for a given lane group is defined as the ratio of the actual or projected demand flow rate for the lane group (v_i) to the saturation now rate (s_i). The flow ratio is given the symbol $(v/s)_i$ (for lane group i).

The capacity of a given lane group may be stated as

$$c_i = s_i(g_i/C) \tag{14-1}$$

where, c_i——capacity of lane group i, vph;

s_i——saturation flow rate for lane group i, vphg;

g_i/C——effective green ratio for ratio group i.

The ratio of flow rate to capacity (v/c), often called the volume-to-capacity ratio, is given the symbol X in intersection analysis. This new symbol is introduced to emphasize the strong relationship of capacity to signalization conditions and for consistency with the literature, which also refers to this variable as the degree of saturation.

For a given lane group i:

$$X_i = (v/c)_i = v_i/(s_i g_i/C) = v_i C/(s_i g_i) \tag{14-2}$$

Where, X_i——$(v/c)_i$ = ratio for lane group i;

v_i——actual or projected demand flow rate for lane group i, vph;

s_i——saturation flow rate for lane group i, vphg;

g_i——effective green time for lane group i, s.

Sustainable values of X_i range from 1.0 (when the flow rate equals capacity) to zero (when the flow rate is zero). Values above 1.0 indicate a temporary excess of demand over capacity.

Another capacity concept of utility in the analysis of signalized intersections, however, is the critical v/c ratio, X_c, which is the v/c ratio for the intersection as a whole, considering only the lane groups that have the highest flow ratio (v/s) for a given signal phase.

For example, in a two-phase signal opposing lane groups move during the same green time. Generally, one of these two lane groups will require more green time than the other (i.e., it will have a higher flow ratio). This would be the "critical" lane group for the subject signal phase. Each signal phase will have a critical lane group that determines the green-time requirements for the phase. When signal phases overlap, the identification of these critical lane groups becomes somewhat complex.

The critical v/c ratio for the intersection is defined in terms of critical lane groups or approaches:

$$X_c = \sum_i (v/s)_{ci} \times [C/(C-L)] \tag{14-3}$$

Where, X_c——critical v/c ratio for the intersection;

$\sum_i (v/s)_{ci}$——summation of flow ratios for all critical lane groups, i;

C——cycle length;

L——total lost time per cycle, computed as the sum of 'start-up' lost time and change interval minus the portion of the change interval used by vehicles on the critical lane group for each signal phase.

Equation (14-3) is useful in evaluating the overall intersection with respect to the geometrics and total cycle length provided and also in estimating signal timings when they are unknown or not specified by local policies or procedures. It gives the v/c ratio for all critical movements, assuming that green time has been appropriately or proportionally allocated. It is therefore possible to have a critical v/c ratio of less than 1.0 and still have individual movements oversaturated within the signal cycle. A critical v/c ratio less than 1.0, however, does indicate that all movements in the intersection can be accommodated within the defined cycle length and phase sequence by proportionally allocating green time. In essence, the total available green time in the phase sequence is adequate to handle all movements if properly allocated.

Exercises

I True or false.

(　　)(1) Roadway conditions consist of basic geometrics of the intersection, numbers and lengths of lanes, grades and lane use allocations.

(　　)(2) The capacity of a given lane group can be computed as the capacity of lane-saturation flow rate for lane effective green ratio for lane group.

(　　)(3) The unit of S_i is vphg.

(　　)(4) When the critical v/c ratio is less than 1.0, that doesn't mean all the movements are under saturated level.

(　　)(5) We can use the summation of green time to deal with all the movements if we could allocate the green time appropriately.

II Complete the following sentences.

(1) The lane group capacity is _____ that may pass through the intersection under prevailing traffic, roadway and signalization conditions.

(2) Capacity at signalized intersection is based upon the concept of _____.

(3) The capacity of designated lane groups within _____.

(4) It gives the v/c ratio for all critical movements, assuming that _____.

(5) A critical v/c ratio less than 1.0, however, does indicate that all movements in the intersection can be accommodated within _____.

III Answer the following questions.

(1) What is the definition of the lane group capacity?

(2) What do roadway conditions include?

(3) The capacity of designated lane groups within an approach is evaluated and determined using the procedures, what is the purpose of this?

(4) What is the definition of saturation flow rate?

(5) What is the definition of the flow ratio for a given lane group?

参 考 译 文

信号交叉口的通行能力

交叉口的通行能力是对每个车道组定义的。车道组的通行能力是指在普通的交通流、道路和信号条件下,某一指定车道组能通过交叉口的最大流率。通常测量或预测流率的时间长度为15分钟。而通行能力则以辆/小时表示。

交通条件包括每条进口道的交通量、车辆的流向(左转、直行交右转)分布、每个流向的车型分布、在交叉口区域内公交站的位置和使用情况、行人过街流量和交叉口范围内的停车数量。

道路条件包括交叉口的基本几何形状、车道的数量和宽度、坡度和车道的利用分配情况（包括停车车道）。

信号条件包括对信号相位、配时和控制类型的完整定义，以及对每个车道组信号序列的评估。

我们可以使用程序评估和确定引道内指定车道组的通行能力。这样做是为了区别服务于一个特定流向或多个特定流向的车道，例如专用右转车道或左转车道。指定为单独分析的一些车道，在前面定义为车道组。这一程序还可用以指导在一个进口道内什么情况下设置及如何确定单独的车道组。

信号交叉口的通行能力以饱和流和饱和流率为基础。饱和流率是指在通常的道路和交通条件下，能通过交叉口指定车道组的最大流率（假定车道组有 100% 的实时有效绿灯时间可以利用）。饱和流率的符号为 s，其单位用有效绿灯小时内通过指定车道组的车辆数表示（辆/绿灯小时）。

指定车道组的流率定义为：车道组的实际流率或预测流率 v_i 与其饱和流率 s_i 之比。对于车道组 i，流率的符号为 $(v/s)_i$。

指定车道组的通行能力可表示为：

$$c_i = s_i(g_i/C) \tag{14-1}$$

式中：c_i——车道组 i 的通行能力，辆/小时；

s_i——车道组 i 的饱和流率，辆/绿灯小时；

(g_i/C)——车道组 i 的绿信比。

在交叉口分析中，定义交通流率与通行能力之比 (v/c)（常称作流量与通行能力之比）为 X。引用这一新符号以强调通行能力与信号条件之间的密切关系，这样便于与称该值为"饱和度"的相关文献保持一致。

对指定的车道组 i，有：

$$X_i = (v/c)_i = v_i/(s_i g_i/C) = v_i C/(s_i g_i) \tag{14-2}$$

式中：X_i——车道组 i 的饱和度；

v_i——车道组 i 的实际流率或预测流率，辆/小时；

s_i——车道组 i 的饱和流率，辆/绿灯小时；

g_i——车道组 i 的有效绿灯时间，秒。

车流可持续通行的条件下 X_i 值的范围是 1.0（当流率等于通行能力）到 0（当流率等于零）。X_i 大于 1.0 时表明交通率暂时超过通行能力。

信号交叉口分析中使用的另一个通行能力的概念是临界 v/c 比——X_c，它是指整个交叉口的 v/c 比，只考虑在指定信号相位中具有最高流量比 (v/s) 的车道组。

例如，一个二相位信号中，在同一绿灯时间内对向各车道组都有车辆流动。一般来说，这两个车道组中的一个比其中另一个需要更多的绿灯时间（具有较高的流率）。这个车道组即是该相位的"临界"车道组。每个相位都有一个确定该相位所需绿灯时间的临界车道组。在相位重叠时，鉴别这些临界车道组就变得有些复杂。

交叉口的临界 v/c 比根据临界车道组或引道来确定：

$$X_c = \sum_i (v/s)_{ci} \times [C/(C-L)] \tag{14-3}$$

式中： X_c——交叉口临界 v/c 比；

$\sum_i (v/s)_{ci}$——所有临界车道组 i 流量比的总和；

C——周期长度，秒；

L——每个的周期总损失时间，由每个相位变换间隔与"起动"损失时间之和，减去每个信号相位中被每个临界车道组上的车辆使用的部分变换间隔时间计算得出。

公式(14-3)可用于评估整个交叉口的几何线形和周期总长度，也可用于估计未知的或当地规范(或程序)未规定的信号配时。对所有关键流向，其流量比 v/c 是在假定绿灯时间适当地或按比例地被分配的情况下给出的。因此，临界 v/c 比可能小于1.0，并且在信号周期内仍有个别流向过于饱和。然而，小于1.0的临界 v/c 比确实表明，通过按比例分配绿灯时间，交叉口中的所有交通流都可以适应规定的周期长度和相序。实质上，如果分配得当，相序中的总可用绿灯时间足以处理所有交通流。

Knowledge Link

Delay in Signalized Intersections

Quality of service in intersection is anindicator, which is measured by several criteria such as delay, capacity, speed, number of stops, queue length and saturation degree. Among these, delay is the most important criterion due to displaying wasted travel time and the spent fuel. However, measuring the delay is not easy due to uncertainty in the nature of vehicles' entering and exiting models from the intersection. So, one of the important elements affecting the delay is the randomness of the number of vehicles entering to the intersection. If vehicles enter to the intersection randomly, the number of coming vehicles will constantly change and this leads to delay variation imposed on vehicles in intersection at different time intervals. So it is necessary that the delay to be calculated with considering the distribution of different number of vehicles entering to the intersection so that we can achieve more real estimation of the delay imposed on the vehicles with the help of this method.

Unit 15

Highway Capacity

Text

1. Capacity and levels of services

A principal objective of capacity analysis is the estimation of the maximum number of people or vehicles that can be accommodated by a given facility in reasonable safety within a specified time period. However, because facilities generally operate poorly at or near capacity, they are rarely planned to operate in this range. Accordingly, capacity analysis also provides a means of estimating the maximum amount of traffic that can be accommodated by a facility while maintaining prescribed operational qualities.

Capacity analysis is, therefore, a set of procedures for estimating the traffic-carrying ability of facilities over a range of defined operational conditions. It provides tools for the analysis of existing facilities and for the planning and design of improved on future facilities.

The definition of operational criteria is accomplished by introducing the concept of levels of service. Ranges of operating conditions are defined for each type of facility and are related to amounts of traffic that can be accommodated at each level.

2. Ideal conditions

In principle, an ideal condition is one for which further improvement will not achieve any increase in capacity. Ideal conditions assume good weather, good pavement conditions, users being familiar with the facility, and no incidents impeding traffic flow. Examples of ideal conditions are given below for uninterrupted flow facilities and for intersection approaches.

Ideal conditions for uninterrupted flow facilities include the following: lane widths of 12ft (3.6m), clearances of 6ft (1.8m) between the edges of the travel lanes and the nearest obstructions or objects at the roadside and in the median, design speeds of 70mph (113km/h) for multi-lane highways, 60mph (97km/h) for two-lane highways; only passenger cars in the traffic stream, level terrain.

Ideal conditions for intersection approaches include the following: lane widths of 12ft, level grade, no curb parking on the intersection approaches, only passenger cars in the traffic stream and no local transit buses stopping in the travel lanes, all vehicles traveling straight through the intersections, intersections located in non-central business district areas, no pedestrians, at signalized intersection approaches, green signal available at all times.

In most capacity analyses, prevailing conditions are not ideal, and computations of capacity, service flow rate, or levels of service must include predictive adjustments to reflect this absence of ideal conditions. Prevailing conditions are generally categorized as roadway, traffic, or control conditions. Vehicle control and technology represents conditions that change in the long term.

3. Roadway conditions

Roadway factors include geometric conditions and design elements. In some cases, these factors influence the capacity of a road, whereas in others, the factors may affect a measure of effectiveness, such as speed, while not affecting the capacity or maximum flow rate that can be carried by the facility.

Roadway factors include the following:
(1) The type of facility and its development.
(2) Lane widths.
(3) Shoulder widths and lateral clearances.
(4) Design speed.
(5) Horizontal and vertical alignments.
(6) Availability of queuing space at intersections.

The type of facility is critical. The existence of uninterrupted flow, the presence of medians, and other major facility type factors significantly affect flow characteristics and capacity. The development environment has also been found to affect the performance of two-lane roadways, multilane highways and signalized intersections.

Lane and shoulder widths can have a significant impact on traffic flow. Narrow lanes cause vehicles to travel closer to each other laterally than most drivers would prefer. Motorists compensate by slowing down or observing larger longitudinal spacing for a given speed, which effectively reduces capacity, service flow rate, or both.

Narrow shoulders and lateral obstructions have two important impacts. Many drivers will steer away from roadsides or median objects they perceive to pose a hazard. This action brings them laterally closer to vehicles in adjacent lanes and causes the same reactions as those exhibited in narrow lanes.

Restricted design speed affect operations and levels of service; drivers are forced to travel at somewhat reduced speeds and to be more vigilant in reacting to the harsher horizontal and vertical alignments resulting from a reduced design speed. In extreme cases, the capacity of multilane facilities has been found to be affected by low design speed.

The horizontal and vertical alignments of a highway depend greatly on the design speed used and the topography through which the roadway must be constructed. Procedure for uninterrupted flow facilities categorizes the general terrains of a highway as follows:

(1) Level terrain. Any combination of grades and horizontal and vertical alignments that allows heavy vehicles to maintain approximately the same speed as passenger cars; this terrain generally includes short grades of no more than 1 to 2 percent.

(2) Rolling terrain. Any combination of grades and horizontal or vertical alignments that causes drivers of heavy vehicles to reduce speeds to substantially below those of passenger cars, but does not require operation at crawl speeds for any significant length of time.

(3) Mountainous terrain. Any combination of grades and horizontal and vertical alignments that causes drivers of heavy vehicles to operate at crawl speeds for significant distances or at frequent intervals.

Crawl speed is the maximum sustained speed that heavy vehicles can maintain on an extended upgrade of a given percent.

These definitions are general and depend on the particular mix of heavy vehicles in the traffic stream. In general, as terrain becomes more severe, capacity and service flow rate is reduced. This impact is significant for two-lane rural highways, where the severity of terrain not only affects the operating capabilities of individual vehicles in the traffic stream, but also restricts the opportunities to pass slow-moving vehicles in the traffic stream.

In addition to the general impacts of terrain, isolated upgrades of significant length may have a substantial effect on operations. Heavy vehicles slow significantly on such upgrades, creating operational difficulties in the traffic stream and inefficient use of the roadway.

Grades also may have a major impact on the operation of intersection approaches. Vehicles must overcome both the grades and the inertia of starting from a stopped position at the same time.

4. Control conditions

Interrupt flow facilities and the controls of specific traffic flow time are the key factors affecting their capacity, service flow rate and service level. Traffic signals are the main control facilities for such facilities. The control mode, signal phase, green light time allocation, signal cycle length and the relationship with adjacent control measures all affects vehicle operation.

Parking signs and letting signs also affect traffic capacity, but they do not play a decisive role. Traffic signals are allotted a certain amount of time for each release. However, the parking signs at bi-directional parking control intersections only assign priority to the main road. Drivers on branch roads must stop and then find clearances in the main road traffic flow. Therefore, the capacity of the branch depends on the traffic condition of the main road. Omnidirectional stop-and-let control forces drivers to stop and then pass through intersections in turn. The traffic capacity and operation characteristics of intersections vary greatly with the traffic demand of each approach.

There are other types of regulations and rules that can also significantly affect capacity, service flow rate and service levels. Restricting roadside parking can increase the number of effective lanes in streets and highways; restricting turning can eliminate the conflict of traffic flow at intersections and improve traffic capacity; the function of controlling lanes can allocate road space to each flow direction and open up diversion lanes; and one-way lanes can eliminate the conflict between left-turn traffic flow and opposite traffic flow.

New Words and Expressions

estimation [ˌestɪˈmeɪʃn]	n. 估计;评价;判断
multilane [ˈmʌltɪleɪn]	adj. 多车道的(亦作 multilaned)
impede [ɪmˈpiːd]	vt. 阻碍;妨碍;阻止
longitudinal spacing	纵距
roadway [ˈrəudweɪ]	n. 车道;路面;道路
horizontal alignment	平面线形
vertical alignment	纵断面线形
topography [təˈpɒgrəfɪ]	n. 地形学
upgrade [ʌpˈgreɪd]	n. 升级;上坡;向上的斜坡 vt. 使升级;提升
inertia [ɪˈnɜːʃə]	n. [物]惯性;惯量
prescribe [prɪˈskraɪb]	vt. 规定;指定
prevail [prɪˈveɪl]	vi. 盛行;流行;占优势
obstruction [əbˈstrʌkʃn]	n. 障碍;阻碍;妨碍
district [ˈdɪstrɪkt]	n. 区域;地方
absence [ˈæbs(ə)ns]	n. 没有;缺乏;缺席
geometric [ˌdʒiːəˈmetrɪk]	adj. 几何学的;[数]几何学图形的
lateral [ˈlætərəl]	adj. 侧面的;横向的
narrow [ˈnærəu]	adj. 狭窄的;勉强的 n. 海峡;狭窄部分;隘路 vt. (使)变狭窄 vi. 变窄
isolate [ˈaɪsəleɪt]	vt. (使)隔离;(使)孤立 vi. 隔离;孤立 n. 被隔离的人(或物) adj. 孤独的;隔离的
crawl [krɔːl]	vi. 爬行;匍匐行进 n. 爬行;缓慢地爬行
interval [ˈɪntəvl]	n. 间隔;间距
vigilant [ˈvɪdʒɪlənt]	adj. 警惕的;警醒的;警戒的
harsh [hɑːʃ]	adj. 粗糙的

Exercises

I True or false.

(　　)(1) Capacity analysis is a set of procedures for estimating the traffic-carrying ability of facilities over a range of defined operational conditions.

(　　)(2) Ideal conditions for uninterrupted flow facilities include: design speed of 60mph (97km/h) for multilane highways, and 70mph(113km/h) for two-lane highways.

(　　)(3) Narrow lanes cause vehicles to travel closer to each other laterally than most drivers would prefer.

(　　)(4) The horizontal and vertical alignments of a highway depend greatly on the cruise speed used.

(　　)(5) In general, as terrain becomes more severe, capacity and service flow rate is increased.

II Complete the following sentences.

(1) A principal objective of capacity analysis is the estimation of _____ of people or vehicles that can be accommodated by a given facility in reasonable safety within a specified time period.

(2) The definition of operational criteria is accomplished by introducing the concept of _____.

(3) _____ assume good weather, good pavement conditions, users being familiar with the facility, and no incidents impending traffic flow.

(4) Roadway factors include _____, _____, _____, _____, _____, _____.

(5) _____ is the maximum sustained speed that heavy vehicles can maintain on an extend upgrade of a given percent.

III Answer the following questions.

(1) What is the principal objective of capacity analysis?

(2) What are the ideal conditions for uninterrupted flow facilities?

(3) What are the ideal conditions for intersection approaches?

(4) What are the roadway factors that influence highway capacity?

(5) How does procedure for uninterrupted flow facilities classify the general terrains of a highway?

Topics for Discussion

(1) What are the ideal conditions for analyzing highway capacity?

(2) What are the factors influencing the capacity of a road?

(3) What is the relationship between capacity and levels of service?

参 考 译 文

道路通行能力

1. 通行能力和服务水平

通行能力分析的一个主要目标是估计特定设施在特定时间内、处于安全的情况下可容纳的最大人数或车辆数。然而,由于设施一般在全部工作或接近饱和的情况下运行不良,因此很少规划在这一范围内运行。通行能力分析也提供了一种方法,即在保持规定运行质量的同时,估计设施可容纳的最大交通量。

因此,通行能力分析是一套程序,用于估计设施在一个确定运行条件下承载交通流的能力。它为分析现有设施以及规划和改建未来的设施提供了方法。

运行标准通过引入服务水平的概念来完成其定义。每种类型的设施都定义了运行条件的范围,并与每个级别可以容纳的交通量有关。

2. 理想条件

原则上,理想条件是进一步改善不再会带来通行能力的提高。理想条件假设天气良好,路面条件良好,用户熟悉设施,没有阻碍交通流的事件。下面给出连续流设施和交叉口引道的理想条件示例。

连续流设施的理想条件包括:车道宽度为 12 英尺(3.6 米),行车道边缘与路边和中央分隔带最近的障碍物相距 6 英尺(1.8 米),多车道公路的设计速度为 70 英里/小时(113 千米/小时),双车道公路为 60 英里/小时(97 千米/小时),交通流中只有小客车,路面是水平地形。

交叉口引道的理想条件包括:车道宽 12 英尺,无坡度,交叉口引道上没有路边停车,交通流中只有小客车,行车道上没有当地公交车停放,所有车辆直行穿过交叉口,交叉口位于非中心商务区处,没有行人,在信号交叉口引道处一直是绿灯。

在大多数通行能力分析中,普遍条件并不理想,通行能力、服务流率或服务水平的计算必须有预测性调整,反映这种理想条件的缺失。主要条件通常分为道路、交通和控制条件。车辆控制和技术是处于长期变化的条件。

3. 道路条件

道路因素包括几何条件和设计要素。在某些情况下,这些因素影响道路的通行能力,而在另一些情况下,这些因素可能影响有效性的度量(如速度),而不会影响设施可以承载的通行能力或最大流率。

道路因素包括:

(1) 设施的类型及其改建情况。

(2) 车道宽度。

(3) 路肩宽度和横向净空。

(4) 设计车速。

(5) 平面和纵断面线形。

(6) 交叉口排队空间的利用率。

设施的类型至关重要。连续流的存在,中央分隔带的存在,以及其他主要设施类型的因素,对交通流特性和通行能力有显著影响。环境条件也会影响双车道公路、多车道公路和信号交叉口的性能。

车道和路肩宽度会对交通流产生重大影响。狭窄的车道使车辆间的横向行驶距离比大多数驾驶人所希望的更近。驾驶人通过减速或观察给定速度的较大纵向间距来进行补偿,从而有效地降低通行能力、服务流率或两者兼而有之。

狭窄的路肩和横向障碍物有两个重要影响。许多驾驶人会避开他们认为会造成危险的路边或路中间物体,这种作用使它们横向靠近相邻车道上的车辆,并作出与处于狭窄车道时相同的反应。

受限的设计速度会影响运行和服务水平,驾驶人被迫以稍微降低的速度行驶,并因设计速度降低而导致对更粗糙的水平和垂直线形作出更为警惕的反应。在极端情况下,多车道设施的通行能力受设计速度过低的影响。

公路的水平和垂直线形在很大程度上取决于所用的设计速度和必须通过的地形。公路路段设计过程中将地形分为以下几类:

(1)平坦地形。任何坡度和水平与垂直线形的组合,使重型车辆保持与客车大致相同的速度。这种地形坡度通常较小,不超过1% ~ 2%。

(2)起伏地形。任何坡度和水平或垂直线形的组合,使重型车辆驾驶人的速度大大低于客车的速度,但车辆不需要长时间地以爬坡速度运行。

(3)山地地形。任何坡度和水平及垂直线形的组合,使重型车辆驾驶人在相当长的距离或频繁的时间间隔内以爬坡速度行驶。

爬坡速度是重型车辆在给定坡度的道路上爬坡时可以保持的最大持续速度。

这些定义是通用的,取决于交通流中重型车辆的实际占比。一般来说,随着地形变得更加恶劣,通行能力和服务流量会降低。这对双车道乡村公路影响很大,因为地形的不佳不仅影响交通流中单个车辆的运行能力,而且限制了在交通流中超过慢速车辆的机会。

除了地形的一般影响外,长距离的持续爬坡可能对运行状态产生很大影响。重型车辆在这种爬坡过程中会明显减速,造成交通流运行困难,使道路使用效率低下。

坡度也可能对交叉口引道的运行产生重大影响,车辆必须同时克服坡度和从停车位置出发的惯性。

4. 管制条件

间断流设施对具体交通流通行时间的控制是影响其通行能力、服务流率和服务水平的关键因素,这类设施最主要的控制设备是交通信号。使用的控制方式、信号相位、绿灯时间分配和信号周期长度,以及与邻近控制措施的相互关系均影响车辆运行。

停车标志和让车标志也影响通行能力,但不起决定作用。在每次允许放行时,交通信号都会分配一定的时间。然而,在双向停车控制交叉口的停车标志只是将优先通行权分配给主路,支路的驾驶人必须停车,然后在主路交通流中寻找间隙通过。因此,支路的通行能力取决于主路的交通状况。全向停让控制则强制驾驶人停车,然后依次通过交叉口。交叉口的通行能力和运行特性会因各引道的交通需求不同而发生很大变化。

还有其他类型的管制和规则也能极大地影响通行能力、服务流率和服务水平。限制路边停车能增加城市道路和公路中的有效车道数;限制转向能消除交叉口车流的冲突,提高通行能力;控制车道的使用功能可给各流向分配道路空间,打开分流车道;单行道则能够消除左转车流与对向车流之间的冲突。

Reading Material

Level of Service

1. LOS for at-grade intersections

The *HCM* defines LOS for signalized and unsignalized intersections as a function of the average vehicle control delay. LOS may be calculated per movement or per approach for any intersection configuration, but LOS for the intersection as a whole is only defined for signalized and all-way stop configurations. The classification of LOS is shown in Table 15-1.

Classification of LOS Table 15-1

LOS	Signalized Intersections (s)	Unsignalized Intersections (s)
A	≤10	≤10
B	10 ~ 20	10 ~ 15
C	20 ~ 35	15 ~ 25
D	35 ~ 55	25 ~ 35
E	55 ~ 80	35 ~ 50
F	>80	>50

When analyzing unsignalized intersections that are not all-way stop-controlled, each possible movement is considered individually. The rank of each movement is as follows, with the major roads being the road whose through movement is free, the minor roads being controlled by stop signs. As for vehicular movements that conflict with pedestrian movements of the same rank, pedestrians have priority.

(1) Through movements on the major road, parallel pedestrian movements, and right turns from the major road. LOS for movements of this rank is trivial, because LOS is determined by control delay. These are "free" movements, and the control delay is always zero.

(2) Left turns from the major road.

(3) Through movements on the minor road, parallel pedestrian movements, and right turns from the minor road.

(4) Left turns from the minor road.

Movements are analyzed in order of rank, and any capacity that is left over from one rank devolves onto the next rank. Because of this pecking order, depending on intersection volumes there may be no capacity for lower-ranked movements.

2. Theoretical considerations

The LOS concept was first developed for highways in an era of rapid expansion in the use and availability of the private motor car. The primary concern was congestion, and it was commonly held that only the rapid expansion of the freeway network would have kept congestion in check.

Since then, some professors in urban planning schools have proposed measurements of LOS that take public transportation into account. Such systems would include wait time, frequency of service, time it takes to pay fares, quality of the ride, accessibility of depots, and perhaps other criteria.

LOS can also be applied to surface streets, to describe major signalized intersections. A crowded four-way intersection where the major traffic movements were conflicting turns might have an LOS D or E. At intersections, queuing time can be used as a rubric to measure LOS; computer models given the full movement data can spit out a good estimate of LOS.

While it may be tempting to aim for an LOS A, this is unrealistic in urban areas. Urban areas more typically adopt standards varying between C and E, depending on the area's size and characteristics, while F is sometimes allowed in areas with improved pedestrian, bicycle, or transit alternatives. More stringent LOS standards (particularly in urban areas) tend to necessitate the widening of roads to accommodate development, thus discouraging use by these alternatives. Because of this, some planners recommend increasing population density in towns, narrowing streets, managing car use in some areas, providing sidewalks and safe pedestrian and bicycle facilities, and making the scenery interesting for pedestrians.

The standard uses American units and applies to pedestrian queues, walkways and stairwells. This standard is not considered a good measure of pedestrian facilities by the planning or engineering professions, because it rates undesirable (unused) sidewalks with an LOS A, while pedestrians tend to prefer active, interesting sidewalks, where people prefer to walk (but rate a worse LOS on this scale). To rectify this and other issues, the National Cooperative Highway Research Program (NCHRP) is conducting a project to enhance methods to determine LOS for automobiles, transit, bicycles and pedestrians on urban streets, with particular consideration to intermodal interactions.

The A to F scale deals only with delays and service reliability. These delays are typically caused by congestion, breakdowns or infrequent service. It does not deal, for instance, with cases where there is no bridge across a river, no bus or train service, no sidewalks, or no bike-lanes. It assumes there is a service in place that people can use. It also implies that poor LOS can be solved by increased capacity such as additional lanes or overcoming bottlenecks, and in the case of transit, more buses or trains.

An expanded LOS might look like: 0—no service exists. Latent demand may exist. 1—service is poor, unsafe or discouraging. Demand is suppressed below socially desirable levels. A to F—as per existing LOS scale. G—further expansion of capacity is limited. H—no expansion is possible. Radical or innovative solutions are required.

Exercises

I True or false.

(　　)(1) Vehicular movements that conflict with pedestrian movements of the same rank, vehicular have priority.

(　　)(2)A crowded four-way intersection where the major traffic movements were conflicting turns might have an LOS D or E.

(　　)(3)Rural areas more typically adopt standards varying between C and E, depending on the area's size and characteristics, while F is sometimes allowed in areas with improved pedestrian, bicycle or transit alternatives.

(　　)(4)An LOS standard uses American units and applies to pedestrian queues, walkways and stairwells.

(　　)(5)It also implies that poor LOS can be solved by increased capacity such as additional lanes or overcoming bottlenecks, and in the case of transit, more buses or trains.

Ⅱ Complete the following sentences.

(1)The primary concern was congestion, and it was commonly held that only the rapid expansion of _____ would have kept congestion in check.

(2)At intersections, _____ can be used as a rubric to measure LOS; computer models given the full movement data can spit out a good estimate of LOS.

(3)More stringent LOS standards (particularly in urban areas) tend to _____ to accommodate development, thus discouraging use by these alternatives.

(4)The A to F scale deals only with _____. These delays are typically caused by congestion, breakdowns or _____.

(5)The *HCM* defines LOS for signalized and unsignalized intersections as _____.

Ⅲ Answer the following questions.

(1)How does the *HCM* define LOS for signalized and unsignalized intersections?

(2)What is the rank of each movement when analyzing unsignalized intersections that are not all-way stop-controlled?

(3)What might an expanded LOS look like?

(4)What factors influence the measurements of LOS that take public transportation into account consider?

(5)The A to F scale deals only with delays and service reliability. How do these delays result?

参 考 译 文

服 务 水 平

1. 交叉口的服务水平

《道路通行能力手册》将信号交叉口和无信号交叉口的服务水平定义为平均车辆控制延误的函数。对于任何交叉口的结构，可以按流向或车道计算服务水平，但是仅针对有信号的和全流向停车控制的情况定义交叉口的服务水平。服务水平的等级划分见表15-1。

服务水平等级划分　　　　　　　　　　表15-1

服务水平	信号交叉口(秒)	无信号交叉口(秒)
A	≤10	≤10
B	10~20	10~15
C	20~35	15~25
D	35~55	25~35
E	55~80	35~50
F	>80	>50

在分析非全流向停车控制的无信号交叉口时,每一个方向可能出现的交通流都会被单独考虑。每个交通流都有一个等级。其中,主要道路是交通流自由通过的道路,次要道路则由停车标志控制。对于同一等级下与行人活动相冲突的车辆运动,行人优先。

(1)主路直行、同向前进的行人、主路右转。由于服务水平是由控制延误决定的,因此对于这种交通流,服务水平等级是不重要的。这些是"自由"运动,控制延误的总是为零。

(2)主路左转。

(3)次路直行、同向前进的行人和次路右转。

(4)次路左转。

按照等级的顺序分析道路使用者的活动,并且从一个等级"溢出"的通行能力都会转移到下一个等级。由于这种排列顺序,考虑交叉口的交通量,可能出现交叉口通行能力不足不能容纳等级较低交通流的现象。

2. 理论思考

服务水平的概念最初是在私人汽车实用性迅速扩大的时代为了公路的发展而提出来的,主要关注点是交通拥堵。人们普遍认为,只有快速扩张高速公路网才能控制交通拥堵。

从那时起,一些城市规划学校的教授提出了考虑公共交通服务水平的测量方法。此类系统包括等待时间、服务频率、票价支付时间、乘坐质量、公共汽车站的可达性,以及其他标准。

服务水平也可用于地面道路以描述主要的信号交叉口。一个主要交通流向是相互冲突的四路交叉口,其服务水平可能为D级或E级。在交叉口,排队时间可作为衡量服务水平的标准;使用完整交通流向数据的计算模型可以较好地估计服务水平。

在市区出现A级服务水平是不现实的,市区通常采用C级到E级之内的标准,这取决于该地区的大小和特征,而F级有时允许用于有完善的步行、自行车或公共交通出行的地区。更严格的服务水平标准(尤其是市区)往往需要拓宽道路以适应服务水平的提升,因此不鼓励使用这些替代方案。于是,一些规划者建议增加城镇人口密度,缩小道路范围,管理一些地区汽车的使用,提供人行道和安全的自行车设施,并使行人对风景感兴趣。

行人设施的服务水平标准使用美国的计量单位,适用于行人排队、人行道和楼梯间。规划或工程专业不认为本标准是对行人设施的一个很好的度量,因为它将不需要的(未使用的)人行道评为A级服务水平,而人们更喜欢步行于行人更活跃的、具有吸引力的人行道(但在这个标准上被评为较低的服务水平)。为了纠正这一问题和其他的问题,国家公路合作研究计划(NCHRP)实施一个项目,以改进确定城市道路上汽车、公交、自行车和行人服务水平的方法,尤其要考虑多种出行方式的协调。

A～F等级只研究延误和服务可靠性。这些延误通常是由拥挤堵塞、故障或服务不完善造成的。例如，没有过河桥梁，没有公共汽车或火车服务，没有人行道，或没有自行车道。这也意味着，假设有其他服务可以供人们使用，通过增加通行能力，如增加车道或克服堵塞，以及增加公共汽车或有轨车辆，可以解决服务水平低下的问题。

服务水平的划分：0——不存在服务，但可能存在潜在需求；1——服务差、不安全或令人不满，需求被抑制在低于社会期望的水平以下；A～F——根据现有的服务水平制定的等级；G——通行能力的进一步提升是有限的；H——不可能提升，需要彻底的或创新性的解决方案。

Knowledge Link

National Cooperative Highway Research Program

The National Cooperative Highway Research Program (NCHRP) focuses on issues affecting the planning, design, construction, operation and maintenance of American highways. It is managed by the Transportation Research Board (TRB) and supported by federal agencies, the State Department of Transportation and other non-profit organizations. The National Cooperative Highway Research Program was established under TRB in 1962 to promote research on serious road-related problems. It is sponsored by the National Highway and Transportation Association and the Federal Highway Administration of the United States Department of Transportation. The Federal Highway Administration finances NCHRP through a partnership agreement with the National Academy of Sciences. The plan is funded by the highway and transportation departments of all States in the United States, and the U.S. government requires state transportation departments to pay 5.5% of the State Planning and Research (SP&R) fund each year. In recent years, NCHRP has spent about $37 million annually.

Unit 16

Reinforcement in Concrete Road Slabs

Text

  The previous discussion on stress considerations has dealt only with plain road slabs, and no mention has been made so far of the effect of the introduction of steel reinforcement. The reason for this omission is that at this time there is no fully acceptable theory on which such a discussion could be based.

  Reinforcing steel is, being for many years, used in concrete road construction. It should be clear, however, that the term 'reinforcing' is used very loosely indeed in reference to concrete road slabs, as both the amount of steel used and its function are very different from those utilized in normal reinforced concrete building construction. When a bridge, a building or some other such structure is being constructed, the concrete is normally expected to carry only the compressive stress that are produced, and reinforcing steel is incorporated in the structure to withstand the tensile stress. On the one hand, if the relatively low tensile strength of the concrete is exceeded, the result could well be the complete collapse of the structure, with perhaps the loss of many lives. With a concrete road, on the other hand, slab "failure" does not result in any such dramatic happenings since the slab will still be supported. Indeed, if the pavement is on a good foundation the riding quality of the road may be so little affected that the only obvious damage is the aesthetic one of unsightly cracks in the surface. As a result, the generally accepted design approach has been fristly to include only sufficient reinforcing steel to minimize the development of cracks; and secondly is to make the steel support any of the induced tensile stress. A practical by-product of this form of usage is that it allows a considerably greater spacing to be used between transverse joints.

Examination of the literature on concrete roads shows that in the past there have been considerable differences of opinion as to where and how much of the reinforcing steel should be placed in a concrete pavement. This was primarily due to a lack of understanding of its function in the slab. If tensile stress resistance was the principal criterion, then it was of course logical that two layers of steel should be used, so that one layer was at the top and the other at the bottom of the slab. The function of the top layer of steel was to resist the load and warping tensile stress at the edges and corners at the top surface, while the bottom layer resisted the tensile stress set up at the interior of the underside of the slab. If only one layer of reinforcemented used and the governing criterion was again resistance to tensile stress, then the layer should be placed near the top of the slab, since it was there that the more critical stress was induced. Even if it were possible to analyze these stress exactly, it was doubtful whether in normal road construction the inclusion of sufficient steel in a road slab to completely resist the stress would be justified; not only is it not necessary from a safety aspect, but it is probably not an economical proposition either, since with modern construction methods additional load-carrying capacity could probably be secured at less cost by using additional thickness of concrete than by using the relatively large amounts of steel needed to increase the pavement's flexural strength to the same extent. Hence the decision, as has been stated before, is to add only the relatively small amounts of steel, which are necessary to resist crack development at the top of the slab.

New Words and Expressions

concrete [ˈkɒŋkriːt]　　　　　　　*adj.* 混凝土制的　　*n.* 混凝土　　*vt.* 用混凝土修筑;使凝固

previous [ˈpriːvɪəs]　　　　　　　*adj.* 在前的;早先的

slab [slæb]　　　　　　　　　　　*n.* 厚平板;厚片;混凝土路面;板层

reinforcement [riːɪnˈfɔːsmənt]　　*n.* 配筋;加强;加固

omission [əˈmɪʃn]　　　　　　　*n.* 省略;删节;遗漏

compressive [kəmˈpresɪv]　　　　*adj.* 有压缩力的

withstand [wɪðˈstænd]　　　　　*vt.* 抵挡;经受住

transverse [ˈtrænzvɜːs]　　　　　*adj.* 横向的;横断的

warp [wɔːp]　　　　　　　　　　*vt. & vi.* 弄弯;使翘曲;扭曲;曲解

proposition [prɒpəˈzɪʃn]　　　　　*n.* 主张,建议,陈述,命题

tensile [ˈtensaɪl]　　　　　　　　*adj.* 张力的;拉力的

criterion [kraɪˈtɪərɪən]　　　　　　*n.* 标准;准则;原则

crack [kræk]　　　　　　　　　　*v.* 破裂;裂开　　*n.* 裂纹;裂缝;狭缝

aesthetic [iːsˈθetɪk]　　　　　　　*adj.* 审美的;美学的;艺术的;美的　　*n.* 美感;审美观;美学标准

layer ['leɪə(r)]　　　　　　　　n. 层;表层;层次
resistance [rɪ'zɪstəns]　　　　　n. 反对;抵制;抵抗;抵抗力
collapse [kə'læps]　　　　　　　vi. (突然)倒塌;坍塌　n. 倒闭;崩溃

Exercises

I True or false.

(　　)(1) When a bridge is being constructed, the concrete is normally expected to carry only the tensile stress.

(　　)(2) If tensile stress resistance was the principal criterion, it was of course logical that only one layer of steel should be used, in a road slab.

(　　)(3) The function of the top layer of steel was to resist the load and warping tensile stress at the edges and corners at the top surface of a slab.

(　　)(4) If only one layer of reinforcement was used and the governing criterion was again resistance to tensile stress, then the layer should be placed near the bottom of the slab.

(　　)(5) With modern construction methods additional load-carrying capacity could probably be secured at less cost by using the relatively large amounts of steel than by using additional thickness of concrete needed to increase the pavement's flexural strength to the same extent.

II Complete the following sentences.

(1) Reinforcing steel is, and has been for many years, used in _____ construction.

(2) If the relatively _____ tensile strength of the concrete is _____, the result could well be the complete collapse of the structure, with perhaps the loss of many lives.

(3) The generally accepted design approach has been primarily to include only sufficient _____ to minimize the development of cracks and only secondly to regard the steel as taking any of the induced tensile stress.

(4) The _____ layer resisted the tensile stress set up at the interior of the underside of the slab.

(5) To add only the relatively small amounts of steel, which are necessary to resist crack development at _____.

III Answer the following questions.

(1) When a bridge, a building or some other such structure is being constructed, what is the function of the concrete and reinforcing steel?

(2) What is the reason for using reinforcing steel to withstand the tensile stress?

(3) What is the result of using sufficient reinforcing steel in road?

(4) If tensile stress resistance was the principal criterion, how many layers should be used?

And where should they be used?

(5) If only one layer of reinforcement was used and the governing criterion was again resistance to tensile stress, how should the layer be placed?

Topics for Discussion

(1) What are the advantages and disadvantages of reinforcement in concrete road slabs?

(2) What are the differences of opinion as to where and how much of the reinforcing steel should be placed in concrete pavement?

(3) What is the difference between one layer of steel and two layers of steel in the slab?

参 考 译 文

混凝土路面配筋

以前重点讨论的仅仅是混凝土路面本身所承受的应力，至今也还没有人阐述有关混凝土路面中配筋对路面应力所产生的影响。避而不谈的主要原因是，目前还没有一种可以被完全接受的理论能够作为该研究的基础。

多年来，钢筋一直用于混凝土路面结构。但是，很明显"配筋"一词在混凝土路梁板中使用非常宽泛。而其中所用钢材的数量及其功能，与一般钢筋混凝土建筑结构中使用的钢筋数量及其功能迥异。当一座桥梁、一座建筑物或其他类似结构物处于施工中，混凝土一般只用于承担所产生的压应力，而配置于结构内的钢筋则用于抵抗拉应力。一方面，如果拉应力超过混凝土相对较低的抗拉强度，会导致建筑物完全坍塌，甚至可能会造成重大人员伤亡。另一方面，对于混凝土道路，梁板"破坏"不会导致任何此类突发事件，因为梁板仍有支撑。事实上，如果路面基础良好，道路上驾驶质量受到的影响很小，唯一明显的损害是路面上会产生不美观的裂缝。因此，普遍接受的设计方法首先是加入足够的钢筋，以尽量减少裂纹的蔓延；其次是让钢筋承受任何诱导性的拉应力。这种做法还有一个实用的附加作用，即它允许在横向接合处存在相当大的间隙。

研究关于混凝土路面的文献发现，过去人们对钢筋在混凝土路面中放置的位置和数量有很多不同的意见，这主要是由于人们对钢筋在梁板中的作用缺乏理解。如果抗拉应力是一个主要标准，那么在理论上应放置两层钢筋，一层放在板的顶部，一层放在板的底部。顶层钢筋的作用是抵抗顶部边角处的荷载和翘曲拉应力，而底层钢筋抵抗的是在底部产生的内部拉应力。如果只使用一层钢筋，并且控制标准又是抗拉应力，那么该层应放置在靠近混凝土梁板顶面的位置，因为在那里会产生更大的临界应力。即使能够准确地分析这些应力，在一般的道路结构中，使用大量钢筋来抵抗应力，其合理性也是值得怀疑的。这不仅对安全性的提升没有帮助，而且也不经济，因为根据现代施工法，在路面抗弯强度增加同等程度的情况下，增加混凝土厚度与使用大量的钢筋相比前者成本更低。因此，如前面所述，决定只添加相对少量的钢筋，用于抵抗梁板顶部裂纹的蔓延。

Reading Material

Flexible Pavement

A highway pavement is a structure consisting of superimposed layers of selected and processed materials whose primary function is to distribute the applied vehicle loads to the subgrade. The ultimate aim is to ensure that the transmitted stress are sufficiently reduced that they will not exceed the supporting capacity of the subgrade. Two types of pavement are generally recognized as serving this purpose—flexible pavement and rigid pavement.

The distinguishing feature of a flexible pavement lies in its structural mechanics and the fact that the pressure is transmitted to the subgrade through the lateral distribution of the applied load with depth, rather than by beam and slab action as with a concrete slab. Thus a flexible pavement can be most easily defined by contrasting it with a rigid Portland cement concrete pavement.

When the subgrade deflects beneath a rigid pavement, the concrete slab is able to bridge over localized failures and areas of inadequate support because of its structural capabilities. Thus its thickness is relatively little affected by the quality of the subgrade as long as it meets certain minimum criterion.

In direct contrast to this, the strength of the subgrade is the main factor controlling the design of a flexible pavement. When the subgrade deflects, the overlying flexible pavement is expected to deform to a similar shape and extent. Thus the basic design criterion is the depth of pavement required to distribute the applied surface load to the subgrade; the subgrade must not be overstressed and caused to deform to a greater extent than the pavement itself can deform without damaging its own structural integrity.

In its simplest form, a flexible pavement is generally considered to be any pavement other than a concrete one. It is the definition that is accepted by the great majority of practicing engineers and so it is the one that is utilized in this textbook. It should be clearly understood, however, that the term is simply one of convenience and does not truly reflect the characteristics of the many different and composite types of construction masquerading as "flexible" pavement.

Before discussing in detail the various features of a flexible road, it is necessary to mention briefly some terminologies.

The cross-section of a flexible road is composed of a pavement superimposed on the basement soil or subgrade. The intersection of the subgrade and the pavement is known as the formation.

The subgrade is normally considered to be the in-situ soil over which the highway is being constructed. It should be quite clear. However, that the term subgrade is also applied to all native soil materials exposed by excavation and to excavated soil that may be artificially deposited to form a compacted embankment. In the latter case, the added material is not considered to be part of the road structure itself but part of the foundation of the road.

Exercises

I True or false.

(　　)(1) The distinguishing feature of a rigid pavement lies in its structural mechanics.

(　　)(2) When the subgrade deflects beneath a flexible pavement, the concrete slab can bridge over localized failures and areas of inadequate support.

(　　)(3) In rigid pavements, the thickness of concrete slab is relatively little affected by the quality of the subgrade as long as it meets certain minimum criterion.

(　　)(4) In its simplest form, any pavement can be considered as a flexible road except concrete one.

(　　)(5) The subgrade is normally considered to be the in-situ soil over which the highway is being constructed.

II Complete the following sentences.

(1) A highway pavement is a structure consisting of superimposed layers of selected and processed materials whose primary function is _____.

(2) The distinguishing feature of a flexible pavement lies in _____.

(3) _____ is the main factor controlling the design of a flexible pavement.

(4) When the subgrade deflects, the overlying flexible pavement is expected to deform to _____.

(5) The cross-section of a flexible road is composed of _____.

III Answer the following questions.

(1) What is the definition of a highway pavement?

(2) What is the distinguishing feature of a flexible pavement?

(3) When the subgrade deflects beneath a rigid pavement, what will happen to the concrete slab?

(4) What will deform when the subgrade deflects?

(5) What is the cross-section of a flexible road composed of?

参 考 译 文

柔 性 路 面

道路路面是在路基表面上用各种不同材料分层铺筑而成的一种层状结构物,其主要作用是将所承受的车辆荷载均匀地分布到路基。其最终目的是尽量减少所传递的应力,使之不超过路基的承受能力。通常认为有两种路面可以达到这一目的——柔性路面和刚性路面。

柔性路面突出的特点在于其结构力学特性,即以一定的深度将施加的荷载横向分布开,将压力传到路基,而不须通过类似混凝土板的梁板作用。这样,通过与刚性水泥混凝土路面相比较,就能很容易地给柔性路面下定义了。

若刚性路面下的路基变位(弯沉),混凝土梁板由于其结构特性,必然会跨越局部损坏点以及无支撑部位。因此,只要混凝土梁板能达到最低标准,路基的质量对其厚度的影响相对很小。

与此相比,路基强度是影响柔性路面设计的主要因素。当路基变形时,铺在其上的柔性路面也将以相似的形状在一定范围内变形。因此,基本设计标准是将施加的表面荷载分布到路基上所需的路面深度,勿使路基受超限压力,并且在不破坏路面自身结构完整性的前提下,使其变形程度不超过路面本身的变形程度。

由于柔性路面形式最为简单,除混凝土路面外,其他路面均可认为是柔性路面。这一定义为绝大多数工程师所认可。因此,本书也采用了这一定义。但应明确,这只是一个一般的术语,并不能确切反映各种不同类型的道路都称为柔性路面的结构特点。

在详细探讨柔性路面的各种特点之前,有必要概括地解释一些专用名词。

一个柔性道路的横断面由叠加在地基土壤或路基上的路面组成。路基和路面的交接处称为地层。

路基一般被认为是在路面结构下的原土。当然,很明显,路基这一术语也适用经挖掘而暴露的土壤及挖掘的土壤,这些土壤可用人工堆积方法夯实筑成路堤。在后一种情况下增添的材料不能算作道路结构的一部分,而应算作路基的一部分。

Knowledge Link

Pavement Management

Pavement management is the process of planning the maintenance of road network or other pavement facilities to optimize the pavement conditions of the whole road network. It also applies to airport runways and sea terminals. In fact, every highway supervisor has to do road management. Pavement management incorporates life cycle costs into a more systematic approach to small and large road maintenance and reconstruction projects. Before implementing the project, the needs of the entire network and budget projections need to be taken into account. Pavement management includes many aspects and tasks needed to maintain high-quality pavement inventory, and to ensure that the overall conditions of the road network can be maintained at the desired level. Pavement management covers the entire pavement life cycle from planning to maintain any transport infrastructures and road asset management. The object of concrete and road maintenance planning is more specifically road infrastructures.

Unit 17

Road Traffic Safety

Text

Road traffic safety refers to the methods and measures used to prevent road users from being killed or seriously injured. Typical road users include pedestrians, cyclists, motorists, vehicle passengers and passengers of on-road public transport (mainly buses and trams).

Road traffic crashes are one of the world's largest public health and injury prevention problems. According to the World Health Organization (WHO), more than 1 million people are killed on the world's roads each year. A report published by the WHO in 2004 estimated that some 1.2 million people were killed and 50 million injured in traffic collisions on the roads around the world each year and was the leading cause of death among children 10 to 19 years of age. The report also noted that the problem was most severe in developing countries and that simple prevention measures could halve the number of deaths.

The standard measures used in assessing road safety interventions are fatalities and Killed or Seriously Injured (KSI) rate, usually per billion passenger kilometers. Countries caught in the old road safety paradigm, replaces KSI rate with crash rate—for example, crashes per million vehicle kilometers.

1. Vehicle safety

Safety can be improved in various simple ways to reduce the chance of an accident occurring. Avoiding rushing or standing in unsafe places of the bus or coach and following the rules of the bus or coach itself will greatly increase the safety of a person travelling by bus or coach. Various safety features can also be implemented into buses and coaches to improve safety, including safety bars for people to hold onto.

Safety can be improved by reducing the chances of a driver making an error, or by designing vehicles to reduce the severity of crashes that do occur. Most industrialized countries have comprehensive requirements and specifications for safety-related vehicle devices, systems, designs and construction. These may include:

(1) Passenger restraints such as seat belts and airbags.

(2) Crash avoidance equipment such as lights and reflectors.

(3) Driver assistance systems such as Electronic Stability Control.

U.S. road casualty statistics show that motorcycle riders are 9 times more likely to crash, and 17 times more likely to die in a crash, than car drivers. The higher fatality risk is due in part to the lack of crash protection (unlike in enclosed vehicles such as cars), combined with the high speeds motorcycles typically travel at. According to U.S. statistics, the percentage of intoxicated motorcyclists in fatal crashes is higher than other riders on roads. Helmets also play a major role in the safety of motorcyclists. In 2008, the National Highway Traffic Safety Administration (NHTSA) estimated the helmets are 37 percent effective in saving lives of motorcyclists involved in crashes.

2. Regulation of motor vehicle users

Dependent on jurisdiction, driver's age, road type and vehicle type, motor vehicle drivers may be required to pass a driving test (public transport and goods vehicle drivers may need additional training and licensing), conform to restrictions on driving after consuming alcohol or various drugs, comply with restrictions on use of mobile phones, be covered by compulsory insurance, wear seat belts and comply with certain speed limits. Motorcycle riders may additionally be compelled to wear a motorcycle helmet. Drivers of certain vehicle types may be subject to maximum driving hour regulations.

Some jurisdictions, such as the U.S. states Virginia and Maryland, have implemented specific regulations such as the prohibiting mobile phone use by, and limiting the number of passengers accompanying young and inexperienced drivers. The *State of Safety Report* from the National Safety Council released in 2017 ranked states on these road safety regulations. It has been noticed that more serious collisions occured at night, when vehicles were more likely to have multiple occupants, and when seat belts were less likely to be used.

The Insurance Institute for Highway Safety proposes restrictions for new drivers, including: a "curfew" imposed on young drivers to prevent them driving at night, an experienced supervisor to chaperone the less experienced driver; forbidding the carrying of passengers; zero alcohol tolerance; raising the standards required for driving instructors and improving the driving test; vehicle restrictions (e.g., restricting access to "high-performance" vehicles); a sign placed on the back of the vehicle to notify other novice drivers; and encouraging good behavior in the post-test period.

While government has primary responsibility for providing safe roads, the challenges of development and equity require that all segments of society engage and contribute, including the private sector. Private and public sector coalitions, like Together for Safer Roads (TSR) and the Road to Zero Coalition exist to work alongside government policies to advance the business case of having safer roads; they help companies meet their duty of care to employees and minimize fleet-related dangers to the wider community. Safe roads also benefit business by improving employees' health and safety, by protecting assets, reducing productivity losses and healthcare costs, and enhancing the efficiency and effectiveness of supply chains.

New Words and Expressions

traffic safety	交通安全
halve [hɑːv]	vt. 二等分;把……减半
fatality [fəˈtælɪtɪ]	n. 死亡;灾祸
coach [kəutʃ]	n. 旅客车厢;长途汽车
severity [sɪˈverɪtɪ]	n. 严重;严格;猛烈
Electronic Stability Control	电子稳定控制
restraint [rɪˈstreɪnt]	n. 抑制;克制;约束;限制
intoxicate [ɪnˈtɒksɪkeɪt]	vt. 使喝醉;使中毒
helmet [ˈhelmɪt]	n. 钢盔;头盔
coalition [ˌkəuəˈlɪʃn]	n. 联合;结合;同盟
paradigm [ˈpærədaɪm]	n. 范例;样式;模范
specification [ˌspesɪfɪˈkeɪʃn]	n. 规格;说明书;详述
reflector [rɪˈflektə(r)]	n. 反射器;反射光的物体
casualty [ˈkæʒjuəltɪ]	n. 意外事故;伤亡人员
fatal [ˈfeɪtl]	adj. 致命的;重大的;命中注定的
equity [ˈekwətɪ]	n. 公平;公正
engage [ɪnˈgeɪdʒ]	vt. 吸引;引起注意 vi. 从事;参与;参加
curfew [ˈkɜːfjuː]	n. 宵禁
chaperone [ˈʃæpərəun]	n. 女伴;行为监督人 v. 伴护,当行为监护人
notify [ˈnəutɪfaɪ]	vt. 通告;通知;公布
novice [ˈnɒvɪs]	n. 初学者;新手

Exercises

I True or false.

(　　)(1) Road traffic safety refers to the methods and measures used to prevent road users from being killed or seriously injured.

(　　)(2) Road traffic crashes are the world's largest public health and injury prevention problems.

(　　)(3) Safety can be improved by reducing the chances of a driver making an error, or by designing vehicles to reduce the severity of crashes that do occur.

(　　)(4) The higher fatality risk of motorcycle riders is entirely due to the lack of crash protection.

(　　)(5) The *State of Safety Report* from the National Safety Council has been noticed that more serious collisions occur at night.

II Complete the following sentences.

(1) Typical road users include _____, _____, _____, _____ and passengers of on-road public transport (mainly buses and trams).

(2) A report published by the WHO in 2004 estimated that some 1.2 million people were killed and 50 million injured in _____ around the world each year and was the leading cause of death among children 10 to 19 years of age.

(3) The standard measures used in assessing road safety interventions are _____, usually per billion passenger kilometers.

(4) In 2008, The National Highway Traffic Safety Administration (NHTSA) estimated the _____ are 37 percent effective in saving lives of motorcyclists involved in crashes.

(5) NHTSA is the abbreviation of _____.

III Answer the following questions.

(1) What is the definition of road traffic safety?

(2) What do typical road users include?

(3) Why are motorcycle riders more likely to crash?

(4) What are the measures to improve safety on vehicle design?

(5) Who is responsible for the construction of road safety?

Topics for Discussion

(1) What are the standard measures used in assessing road safety interventions in different countries?

(2) How to reduce the chance of an accident occurring on the road?

(3) What is the regulation of motor vehicle users put forward by the Insurance Institute for Highway Safety?

参 考 译 文

道路交通安全

道路交通安全,是指防止道路使用者死亡或重伤的方法和措施。典型的道路使用者包括行人、骑车人、驾驶人、汽车乘客和道路公共交通(主要是公交车和有轨电车)乘客。

道路交通事故是世界上最大的公共健康和伤害预防问题之一。据世界卫生组织称,在世界各地,每年有100多万人因道路交通事故而丧生。世界卫生组织2004年发布的一份报告估计，在世界各地，每年发生的道路交通事故造成约120万人死亡，5000万人受伤，并且道路交通事故是10~19岁儿童死亡的主要原因。报告还指出，这一问题在发展中国家最为严重，采用简单的预防措施即可使死亡人数减少一半。

用于评估道路安全干预措施的标准是死亡数和死亡或重伤率，单位通常为每十亿乘客千米。那些使用旧道路安全模式的国家，用事故率取代了重伤率，例如每百万车英里的事故率。

1. 车辆安全

通过各种简单方法提高安全性，可以降低事故发生的可能性。避免在公交车和长途汽车上奔跑或站在不安全的地方，遵守乘坐公交车和长途汽车的规定，都将大大提高乘客的安全性。在公交车和长途汽车上还可以安装各种安全设施，以提高安全性，包括供人们抓握的安全杆。

通过降低驾驶人失误的可能性，或者通过车辆设计来降低事故的严重性，可以提高安全性。大多数工业化国家对安全相关的车辆装置、系统、设计和安装都有全面的要求和规范。这些包括：

（1）乘客约束装置，如安全带和安全气囊。

（2）避免碰撞的设备，如灯和反光镜。

（3）驾驶人辅助系统，如电子稳定控制系统。

英国道路交通事故统计数据显示，摩托车驾驶人发生车祸的可能性是汽车驾驶人的9倍，车祸中死亡的可能性是汽车驾驶人的17倍。其死亡风险更高的部分原因是其缺乏碰撞保护（不同于汽车等封闭式车辆），并且摩托车通常以高速行驶。根据美国的统计数据，道路上的致命车祸中醉酒的摩托车驾驶人比例高于其他类驾驶人。头盔对摩托车驾驶人的安全也起着重要作用。2008年，美国国家公路交通安全管理局估计，头盔在事故中挽救了37%摩托车驾驶员的生命。

2. 机动车驾驶人的管理

根据辖区、驾驶人年龄、道路类型和车辆类型的不同，机动车驾驶人需要通过驾驶考试（公共交通的车辆和货车驾驶人需要额外的培训和执照），遵守饮酒或服用各种药物后的驾驶限制，遵守手机使用限制，以及投保强制保险，系好安全带，遵守一定的限速规定。摩托车驾驶人还必须戴上摩托车头盔。某些车型的驾驶人需要遵守持续驾驶时间上限的规定。

一些辖区，如美国弗吉尼亚州和马里兰州，已经实施了一些特定的规定，例如禁止使用手机，并限制年轻和缺乏经验的驾驶人随行乘客的数量。2017年国家安全委员会发布《安全状况报告》，根据这些道路安全条例对各州进行了排名。人们已经注意到，在夜间，当车辆上乘客较多且安全带使用较少时，发生的碰撞会更严重。

公路安全保险协会提出了对新手驾驶人的限制，包括对新手驾驶人实行"宵禁"，以防止他们在夜间驾驶，并让有经验的监督者陪同经验不足的驾驶人。禁止载客，禁止饮酒，提高驾驶教练的任职标准以及改善驾驶考试，限制驾驶车辆（例如限制使用"高性能"车辆），在车的背面贴上一个标志，以告知其他驾驶人该车驾驶者是新手，以及鼓励驾驶人在考试后要表现良好。

虽然政府对道路安全的建设负有主要责任，但发展的挑战和公平要求社会上包括私营部门在内的各阶层参与并做出贡献。私营和公共部门建立联盟，如"携手创建更安全道路"的国际联盟（TSR）和民间道路联盟与政府政策合作，推进建设安全道路，帮助企业履行其照顾员工的义务,并将与车队有关的危险降到最低。更安全的道路亦会使企业受益,通过提高员工的身体健康和个人安全,可以保护资产,减少生产力损失和医疗保健成本,提高供应链的效率和效益。

Reading Material

Roadside Safety

1. History of roadside safety

Roadside safety design, as one component of total highway design, is a relatively recent concept. Most of the highway design fundamentals were established by the late 1940s. Additional refinements were made in the 1950s and 1960s with the development of the Interstate system. These components included horizontal alignment, vertical alignment, hydraulic design and sight distance to name some of the more common highway design elements. These elements have been revised and refined over the years through experience and research. However, the highway design components themselves have remained about the same for several decades.

Roadside safety design did not become a much discussed aspect of highway design until the late 1960s, and it was the decade of the 1970s before this type of design was regularly incorporated into highway projects.

2. The benefits of roadside safety

Roadside design might be defined as the design of the area outside the traveled way. Some have referred to this aspect of highway design as off-pavement design. A question commonly asked revolves around whether spending resources off the pavement is really beneficial given the limited nature of infrastructure funds. Perhaps some statistics can bring the potential of crash reduction and roadside safety into focus.

In 2009, 33808 people died in motor vehicle traffic crashes in the United States—the lowest number of deaths since 1950. During the same time period, the number of vehicle-kilometers of travel each year has increased by approximately six and one half times from 0.7 billion to 4.8 billion. Consequently, the traffic fatality rate per 100 million vehicle-kilometers of travel has decreased approximately 85 percent from 4.58 in 1950 to 0.71 in 2009.

This significant reduction is due to several factors. Motor vehicles are much safer today than they have been in the past. Protected passenger compartments, padded interiors, occupant restraints, and airbags are some features that have added to passenger safety during impact situations. Roadways have been made safer through improvements in features such as horizontal and vertical alignments, intersection geometry, traversable roadsides, roadside barrier performances, and grade separations and interchanges. Drivers are more educated about safe vehicle drivers' operation as evidenced by the increased use of occupant restraints and a decrease in driving under the influence of alcohol or drugs. All these contributing factors have reduced the motor vehicle drivers' fatality rate.

Unfortunately, roadside crashes still account for far too great a portion of the total fatal highway crashes. In 2008, 23.1 percent of the fatal crashes were single-vehicle, run-off-the-road crashes. This figure means that the roadside environment comes into play in a very significant percentage of fatal and serious-injury crashes.

3. Strategic plan for improving roadside safety

According to the Insurance Institute for Highway Safety (IIHS) and Highway Loss Data Institute (HLDI), the proportion of motor vehicle deaths involving collisions with fixed objects has fluctuated between 19 and 23 percent since 1979. Almost all fixed-object crashes involve only one vehicle and occur in both urban and rural areas. Trees were by far the most common objects struck, accounting for approximately half of all fixed-object fatal crashes. Utility poles were the second most common objects struck, accounting for 12 percent of all fixed object crashes, followed by traffic barriers with 8 percent. Furthermore, for 2008, 18 percent of fixed-object crashes involved vehicles that rolled over, while 18 percent involved occupant ejection.

In 1967, the American Association for State Highway Officials (AASHO; currently the American Association for State Highway and Transportation Officials, AASHTO) released its Highway Design and Operational Practices Related to Highway Safety, the first official report that focused attention on hazardous roadside elements and suggested appropriate treatment for many of them. This guide, also known as the AASHTO "Yellow Book" was revised and updated in 1974 with the introduction of the forgiving roadside concept. In 1989, AASHTO published the first edition of the *Roadside Design Guide*.

In 1998, AASHTO approved their Strategic Highway Safety Plan, which provided objectives and strategies for keeping vehicles on the roadway and for minimizing the consequence when a vehicle did encroach on the roadside. The National Cooperative Highway Research Program (NCHRP) also has published a series of guides, called the *NCHRP Report*, to assist states and local agencies in their efforts to reduce injuries and fatalities in targeted emphasis areas. These guides correspond to the emphasis areas outlined in AASHTO's Strategic Highway Safety Plan.

A vehicle will leave the roadway and encroach on the roadside for many reasons, including the following:

(1) Driver fatigues.

(2) Driver distraction or inattention.

(3) Excessive speed.

(4) Driving under the influence of drugs or alcohols.

(5) Crash avoidance.

(6) Adverse roadway conditions, such as ice, snow or rain.

(7) Vehicle component failure.

(8) Poor visibility.

Regardless of the reason for a vehicle leaving the roadway, a roadside environment free of fixed objects and with stable, flattened slopes enhances the opportunity for motorist to regain control of his vehicle and reduce crash severity. The forgiving roadside concept allows for errant vehicle leaving the roadway and supports a roadside design in which the serious consequences of incidents are reduced.

Through decades of experience and research, the application of the forgiving roadside concept has been refined to the point where roadside design is an integral part of the transportation design process. Design options for reducing roadside obstacles, in order of preference, are as follows:

(1) Remove the obstacles.

(2) Redesign the obstacles so they can be safely traversed.

(3) Relocate the obstacles to points where they are less likely to be struck.

(4) Reduce impact severity by using an appropriate breakaway device.

(5) Shield the obstacles with longitudinal traffic barriers designed for redirection or use crash cushions.

(6) Delineate the obstacles if the previous alternatives are not appropriate.

Experiencing a significant number of run-off-the-road crashes, one on-roadway safety feature that is becoming more prevalent nationwide is the use of rumble strips to supplement pavement edge lines. These indentations in the roadway shoulders alert motorists through noise and vibration that their vehicles have departed the traveled way and afford them an opportunity to return to and remain on the roadway safely. Several transportation agencies have reported significant reductions in single-vehicle crashes after installing shoulder rumble strips.

Exercises

I True or false.

(　　)(1) Roadside safety design did not become a much discussed aspect of highway design until the late 1960s, and it was the decade of the 1970s before this type of design was regularly incorporated into highway projects.

(　　)(2) Utility poles were by far the most common objects struck, accounting for approximately half of all fixed-object fatal crashes.

(　　)(3) Drivers are more educated about safe vehicle drivers' operation as evidenced by the increased use of occupant restraints and a decrease in driving under the influence of alcohol or drugs.

(　　)(4) Several transportation agencies have reported significant increases in single-vehicle crashes after installing shoulder rumble strips.

(　　)(5) Experiencing a significant number of run-off-the-road crashes, one on-roadway safety feature that is becoming more prevalent nationwide is the use of rumble strips to supplement pavement edge lines.

Ⅱ Complete the following sentences.

(1) Protected passenger compartments, padded interiors, _____, and airbags are some features that have added to passenger safety during impact situations.

(2) Roadways have been made safer through improvements in features such as _____, intersection geometry, traversable roadsides, _____, and grade separations and interchanges.

(3) Roadside design might be defined as _____. Some have referred to this aspect of highway design as off-pavement design.

(4) The National Cooperative Highway Research Program (NCHRP) also has published a series of guides, called _____, to assist states and local agencies in their efforts to reduce injuries and fatalities in targeted emphasis areas.

(5) _____ allows for errant vehicle leaving the roadway and supports a roadside design in which the serious consequences of incidents are reduced.

Ⅲ Answer the following questions.

(1) What did the highway design include in the 1950s and 1960s?

(2) When was the roadside safety design incorporated into highway projects regularly?

(3) How to define roadside design?

(4) Why does the motor vehicle fatality rate reduce?

(5) What are the reasons that a vehicle will leave the roadway and encroach on the roadside?

参 考 译 文

路 侧 安 全

1. 路侧安全发展史

路侧安全设计作为公路总体设计的组成部分,是一个相对新颖的概念。大多数公路设计基础知识都是在20世纪40年代末建立的。随着美国州际公路系统的发展,在20世纪50年代和60年代,公路设计得到了更大的提高。其组成部分包括平面线形、纵断面线形、给排水设计和视距等,被用于命名一些常见的公路设计要素。这些要素经过多年的经验和研究已经被修改和完善。然而,公路设计的组成部分本身在几十年内一直保持不变。

路侧安全设计直到20世纪60年代末才成为公路设计中一个被广泛讨论的方面,直到20世纪70年代,这种设计才被正式纳入公路项目中。

2. 路侧安全的价值

路侧设计可以定义为行车道以外区域的设计。有些人将道路设计的这个方面称为路面外设计。一个经常被提出的问题是,在基础设施资金有限的情况下,将资源花费在路面以外的地方是否真的有益。也许一些统计数据可以使减少车祸可能性和路侧安全成为焦点。

2009年,美国有33808人死于机动车交通事故,这是自1950年以来死亡人数最低的一年。在同一时期,车辆行驶的千米数从7亿增加到48亿,增长了约6.5倍。结果,每1亿车千米的交通死亡率从1950年的4.58降至2009年的0.71,下降了约85%。

这一大幅减少是由几个因素造成的。今天的机动车比过去更加安全,在碰撞情况下有乘客车厢、软垫内饰、乘员约束和安全气囊保护乘客安全。通过改善平面和纵断面线形、交叉口几何结构、路侧穿越条件、路侧护栏性能以及设置立体交叉和互通式立交等,可使道路变得更加安全。驾驶员受到了更多安全操作车辆的培训,表现为乘员更多地使用约束装置,以及饮酒或服用药物情况下驾驶行为的减少。所有这些因素都降低了机动车驾驶员的死亡率。

不幸的是,路侧交通事故仍然占致命道路交通事故总数的很大一部分。2008 年,23.1%的致命车祸是由车冲出道路产生的。这一数字意味着,在致命和严重伤害事故中,路侧环境发挥了非常重要的作用。

3. 改善路侧安全的战略计划

根据美国公路安全保险协会和公路损失数据研究所的数据,自 1979 年以来,涉及与固定物体碰撞的机动车乘员死亡比例一直在 19% ~23%之间波动。几乎所有与固定物体碰撞的事故只涉及一辆车,且在市区和乡区均有发生。目前为止,树木是事故中最常见的固定物体,约占所有致命撞车事故中固定物体的一半。电线杆是碰撞的第二大常见物体,占所有致命碰撞事故中固定物体的 12%。然后是护栏,占 8%。此外,2008 年,与固定物体碰撞的事故中有 18%出现翻车现象,有 18%出现乘员被抛出的现象。

1967 年,美国国家公路工作者协会(现为美国国家公路和运输工作者协会)发布了与公路安全有关的公路设计和运营条例。这是第一份官方报告。报告将注意力集中在危险的路侧元素上,并建议对其中许多元素进行适当处理。本指南,也被称为 AASHTO "小黄书",在 1974 年进行了修订和更新,引入了路侧安全的概念。1989 年,AASHTO 出版了《路侧设计指南》第一版。

1998 年,AASHTO 批准了其公路安全战略计划,该计划规定了将车辆维持在公路上的目标和策略,并将车辆侵入路侧的危害降至最低。国家公路合作研究计划还发布了一系列指南,称为《国家公路合作研究报告》,以协助国家和地方机构在重点地区有针对性地减少伤亡,这些指南与 AASHTO 战略公路安全计划中概述的重点地区相对应。

一辆汽车离开公路冲向路边,原因有很多,包括:

(1)驾驶人疲劳。

(2)驾驶人分心或注意力不集中。

(3)超速。

(4)驾驶中受到药物或酒精的影响。

(5)避免碰撞。

(6)不利的道路条件,如冰、雪或雨。

(7)车辆部件故障。

(8)能见度差。

无论车辆离开公路的原因是什么,没有固定物体和稳定、平坦的斜坡的路侧环境都能增加驾驶人重新控制车辆的机会,并降低事故的严重程度。路侧安全允许失控的车辆冲出道路,并支持减少事故严重后果的路侧设计。

经过几十年的经验积累和研究,路侧安全概念的应用已经完善到路侧设计中,并成为交通设计过程中不可或缺的一部分。减少路侧障碍物的设计方案按优先顺序排列如下:

(1)清除障碍物。

(2)重新设计障碍物,使车辆可以安全通过。

(3)将障碍物移到不太可能受到碰撞的地方。

(4)采用合适的脱离装置,降低冲击强度。

(5)使用装有防撞垫的纵向路障遮挡障碍物,或使用被设计成可以使车辆改变方向的障碍物。

(6)如果前面的备选方案不合适,则对障碍物进行标注。

一种在全国(美国)范围内越来越普遍的道路安全设施,是路面边缘能发出隆隆声的振荡标线,它的使用避免了许多车辆冲出道路的碰撞。路肩的这些振荡标线的凹痕通过噪声和振动提醒驾驶人他们的车辆已经离开了行车道,并为他们提供了返回并安全留在道路上的机会。一些运输机构的报告中谈到,在安装路肩的振荡标线后,产生的撞车事故大幅减少。

Knowledge Link

Together for Safer Roads

Together for Safer Roads (TSR) is a non-profit public welfare alliance that brings together leading global companies. It was formally established at the United Nations in November 2014. This cross-industry coalition supports the United Nations decade of road safety, supports road traffic safety education, and contributes to data analysis and sharing in order to improve road safety and reduce casualties caused by road traffic accidents. The Alliance hopes to work together with enterprises, the public and relevant agencies and departments to improve road safety through cooperation, and to achieve "a world with safe roads".

In 2015, the International Alliance for Building Safer Roads Together was launched in China. The members of the TSR Alliance and the Joint Laboratory of International Cooperation on Traffic Safety of Tongji University have carried out research and promotion on road traffic safety improvement in two aspects: accident-prone road safety improvement and operational driver safety education based on behavioral analysis in a scientific way and in a professional way. Exhibition of a number of research and development projects to promote the orderly development of TSR pilot projects.

Unit 18

The Environmental Effects of Highway Traffic Noise

Text

In our industrial society, the number of sources of sound is steadily increasing and when these sounds become unwanted they may be classed as noises. Sound is propagated as a pressure wave and so an obvious measure of sound levels is the pressure fluctuation imposed above the ambient pressure.

If the graph of pressure against time for a single frequency is examined, it is found to have a maximum amplitude (PM), and in sound pressure measurements it is the root-mean-square pressure that is recorded. Some sounds are a combination of many frequencies while others are composed of a continuous distribution of frequencies. When this occurs, the root-mean-square pressure values of all the individual frequencies are added together.

Using pressure units to describe sound levels requires a considerable range of numbers. It is frequently stated that the quietest sound that most people can hear has a sound pressure level of approximately 20μPa while at 100m away from a Saturn rocket on take-off, the sound pressure level is approximately 200kPa. Rather than use a measurement system with this range, the ratio of a sound pressure to a reference pressure is used so that the sound pressure level is given in decibels by the ratio.

$$20 \log_{10} \frac{\text{pressure measured}}{\text{reference pressure}} \text{decibel(dB)} \qquad (18\text{-}1)$$

The reference pressure is taken as $20\mu\text{Pa}$.

When sound pressure levels are measured adjacent to a highway, a meter measuring in dB might indicate the same value when a fast moving motor cycle with a high-pitched or high-frequency engine note passes and when a slow moving goods vehicle passes with a lower frequency note. The reason why the high-pitched note is usually found more annoying than the lower one from the goods vehicle is that the human ear is more sensitive to sounds with higher frequencies than it is to sounds with lower frequencies.

If a sound level scale is going to be useful for measuring annoyance to human beings, it must take this effect into account. Such a scale is measured in dB (A), the sound level measurements then being obtained by an instrument that weights the differing frequency components. This results in those frequencies that are relatively high or low receiving less weighting than those in the range 1 to 4kHz. With a sound level meter reading in dB (A), it would therefore be found that the higher frequency note of the fast motor cycle would give a higher reading in dB (A) than the goods vehicle, although both produce the same sound pressure level measured in dB.

Sometimes it is necessary to know not only the sound level in dB or dB (A) but also the contribution that differing frequencies make to the overall sounds. To obtain this information the sound is analyzed by an instrument that passes it through a system of filters and allows the relative proportions to be determined.

Road traffic noise differs from most other sources of noise in that the level of noise varies both considerably and rapidly. At low sound-pressure levels the noise emitted from vehicles does not cause a great deal of annoyance, but at higher levels the annoyance is considerable. For this reason many measures of noise nuisance specify a sound pressure level that is exceeded for 10, 20, 30 percent, etc. of the time.

When considering a scale that can be used to express a level of noise that should not be exceeded, it should be noted that this scale should be capable of expressing the relative effect on people of the noise being measured. Scholes and Sargent have stated that the unit selected should meet at least the following requirements. Firstly, the unit should correlate reasonably well with the criterion of dissatisfaction chosen so that noise levels measured using the unit will represent subjective reactions. Secondly, a reasonably accurate set of design rules should be available, covering the estimation of noise exposure from traffic data and the estimation of the performance of noise control techniques, in terms of the chosen unit.

The London Noise Survey measured noise levels at 540 sites and the subjective reactions of 1300 residents. During this survey, particular values noted were the L_{10} level (the sound pressure level in dB (A) exceeded for 10 percent of the time) and the L_{90} level (the sound pressure level in dB (A) exceeded for 90 percent of the time). These levels represent the extremes of the range that were recorded for 80 percent of the time. These values are referred to as the "noise climate" and, together with the L_{10} value, are often quoted in the Wilson Committee Report.

Using data from interviews with 1200 residents at 14 sites in the London area where the roads were all straight, level and carrying free-flowing traffic, Langdon and Scholes developed the "Traffic Noise Index" (TNI). They found this index correlated well with dissatisfaction with noise conditions when the TNI was given by.

$$4(L_{10} - L_{90}) + L_{90} - 30 \tag{18-2}$$

A study carried out in Sweden showed a good correlation between noise disturbance and three measures of noise, L_{10}, L_{50} and a noise exposure index based on the energy mean of the noise level, and given by the expression.

$$L_{eq} = K\log \frac{1}{100} \sum 10^{L_i/Kf_i} \tag{18-3}$$

Where, K——an empirically determined constant;

L_i——the median sound level for the 5dB (A) interval;

f_i——the percentage time that a sound level is in the i th interval.

This unit has not however been found to correlate well with experience in the U.K. The difference in performance between the two countries is considered to be caused by the lower noise levels and the greater variability experienced in Swedish traffic conditions.

Another unit has been proposed to cover a range of noise sources, whether highway traffic noise, aircraft noise or laboratory noise. It is referred to as the "Noise Pollution Level (LNP)" and is given by the following expression.

$$LNP = L_{eq} + 2.56\sigma \tag{18-4}$$

Where, L_{eq}——the energy mean noise level of a specified period;

σ——the standard deviation of the instantaneous sound level considered as a statistical time series over the same specified period.

It has been found that the "Noise Pollution Level" can express annoyance with traffic noise as well as the "Traffic Noise Index" but both of these units suffer from the fact that their prediction under a wide range of circumstances is still uncertain. For this reason the Building Research Station has proposed that, as an interim measure until further investigations are completed, the average L_{10} taken over the period 6 a.m. to 12 midnight on a weekday would provide a suitable standard for measuring traffic noise nuisance in dwellings. In a few years time however it is expected that sufficient experience will have been gained to use a unit incorporating the variability of traffic noise.

New Words and Expressions

propagate ['prɒpəgeɪt]　　　　　vt. 繁殖;传播;宣传
fluctuation [ˌflʌktʃu'eɪʃn]　　　n. 波动;起伏
ambient ['æmbɪənt]　　　　　　adj. 周围的　n. 周围环境
amplitude ['æmplɪtjuːd]　　　　n. 振幅
root-mean-square　　　　　　　均方根
frequency ['friːkwənsɪ]　　　　n. 频率;发生次数
Saturn ['sætɜːn]　　　　　　　　n. [天]土星;土星火箭

take-off	n.	起飞
decibel ['desɪbel]	n.	分贝
high-pitched	adj.	高音的
note [nəut]	n.	记录
annoyance [ə'nɜːɪəns]	n.	烦恼；可厌之事
reading ['riːdɪŋ]	n.	读数；仪表的指示数
filter ['fɪltə(r)]	n.	滤波器；过滤器；滤光器
nuisance ['njuːsns]	n.	讨厌的人或东西；麻烦事；损害
correlate ['kɔrəleɪt]	v.	使相互关联；和……相关
incorporate [ɪn'kɔːpəreɪt]	adj.	合并的；结社的；一体化的 vi. 合并，使组成公司 vt. 合并，混合，组成公司
industrial [ɪn'dʌstrɪəl]	adj.	工业的；产业的；从事工业的
ratio ['reɪʃɪəu]	n.	比率；比例
reference ['refrəns]	n.	参考；参考书目 v. 引用

Exercises

I True or false.

(　　)(1) Sound is propagated as a pressure wave and so an obvious measure of sound levels is the pressure fluctuation imposed above the ambient pressure.

(　　)(2) With a sound level meter reading in dB, it would be found that the higher frequency note of the goods vehicle would give a higher reading in dB than the fast motor cycle.

(　　)(3) At low sound-pressure levels the noise emitted from vehicles does not cause a great deal of annoyance, but at higher levels the annoyance is considerable.

(　　)(4) During the London Noise Survey, particular values noted were the L_{10} level (the sound pressure level in dB exceeded for 10 per cent of the time) and the L_{90} level (the sound pressure level in dB exceeded for 90 percent of the time).

(　　)(5) The Building Research Station has proposed that the average L_{10} taken over the period 6 a.m. to 12 midnight on a weekday would provide a suitable standard for measuring traffic noise nuisance in dwellings.

II Complete the following sentences.

(1) Some sounds are a combination of many frequencies while others are composed of _____.

(2) The reason why the high-pitched note is usually found more annoying than the lower one from the goods vehicle is that _____.

(3) Road traffic noise differs from most other sources of noise in that _____.

(4) Langdon and Scholes found the Traffic Noise Index (TNI) correlated well with dissatisfaction with noise conditions when the TNI was given by _____.

(5) The difference in performance between the Sweden and the U. K. is considered to be caused by _____ .

Ⅲ Answer the following questions.

(1) Why is the high-pitched note usually found more annoying than the lower one from the goods vehicle?

(2) Why does road traffic noise differ from most other sources of noise?

(3) How to calculate Noise Pollution Level (LNP)?

(4) What was the correlation between noise disturbance and three measures of noise, L_{10}, L_{50} according the study carried out in Sweden?

(5) What are the requests of a scale that can be used to express a level of noise?

Topics for Discussion

(1) What are the indicators of measuring sound levels?

(2) What is the measure of sound levels?

(3) What are the measures to reduce highway traffic noise?

参 考 译 文

公路交通噪声的环境影响

在我们的工业社会中,声源的数量在稳步增加,当这些声音变得不受欢迎时,它们会被归为噪声。声音以压力波的形式传播,因此衡量声级的一个明显指标是施加在环境压力以上的压力波动。

检查单个频率的压力与时间关系图会发现,其具有最大振幅(PM),并且在声压测量中记录的是均方根压力。有些声音是许多频率的组合,而有些则是由频率的连续分布组成的。当这种情况发生时,所有单独频率的压力值均方根会叠加起来。

使用压力单位来描述声级需要相当大的数字范围。通常,大多数人能听到的最安静的声音的声压级约为 20 微帕,而在距火箭起飞 100 米处,声压级约为 200 千帕。使用声压与参考压力之比,而不是使用具有此范围的测量系统,以便用分贝为单位表示声压级。

$$20 \log_{10} \frac{测得压力}{参考压力} 分贝(dB) \qquad (18\text{-}1)$$

参考压力取 20 微帕。

当在道路附近测量声压级时,以分贝为单位的仪表在高速行驶的摩托车通过发出尖厉的或高频的引擎音时,以及慢速行驶的货车通过发出低频音时,可能指示相同的值。高频音通常比货车发出的低频音更令人烦扰的原因是,人的耳朵对频率较高的声音比对频率较低的声音更敏感。

如果一个声级计想要用于测量声音令人烦扰的程度,则必须考虑这个影响。这样的声级是以分贝(A)为单位测量的,然后由一个对不同频率分量进行加权的仪器得到。这会导致相对较高或较低的频率比 1 到 4000 赫兹范围内的频率得到的权重更小。因此,如果声级计的读数以分贝（A）为单位，则会发现频率较高的高速摩托车声音的读数会高于货车，尽管两者产生的声压级是相同的。

有时不仅需要知道以分贝和分贝（A）测量的声级，还需要知道不同频率对整体声音的影响。为了获得这一信息，可以使用一个具有过滤系统的仪器来分析声音，并确定其相对比例。

道路交通噪声不同于大多数其他噪声源，因为其噪声水平变化很大且很快。在较低的声压级下，车辆发出的噪声不会引起很大的烦扰，但在较高的声压级下，引起的烦扰程度相当大。因此，许多噪声干扰措施都规定了超过10%、20%、30%的声压级。

在考虑可用于表示不应超过的噪声水平的标度时应注意，该标度应能够表示被测噪声对人的相对影响。斯科尔斯和萨金特表示，选定的指标至少应满足以下要求：首先，该指标应与选择的不满意标准合理关联，以便使用该指标测量的噪声水平能代表主观反应。其次，应提供一套合理准确的设计规则，包括根据所选的指标从交通数据中估计噪声暴露量和噪声控制技术的性能。

伦敦噪声调查测量了540个地点的噪声水平和1300名居民的主观反应。在本次调查中，受关注的特定数值为L_{10}级[10%的时间超过了分贝（A）的声压级]和L_{90}级[90%的时间超过了分贝（A）的声压级]。这些等级代表记录的80%时间范围内的极限值。这些值被称为"噪声气候"，威尔逊委员会的报告中经常引用这些数值以及L_{10}值。

利用对伦敦地区14个地点1200名居民的采访数据，兰登和斯科尔斯提出了"交通噪声指数"（TNI）。他们发现，这个指数与对噪声状况的不满密切相关。

$$4(L_{10} - L_{90}) + L_{90} - 30 \tag{18-2}$$

瑞典进行的一项研究表明，噪声干扰与L_{10}、L_{50}和基于噪声水平能量均值的噪声暴露量这三种噪声度量值之间存在良好的相关性，并通过表达式给出。

$$L_{eq} = K\log \frac{1}{100} \sum 10^{L_i/Kf_i} \tag{18-3}$$

式中：K——根据经验确定的常数；

L_i——5分贝间隔i的声级中值；

f_i——声级处于第i个间隔所占时间的百分比。

然而，该指标并没有与英国的经验很好地关联。两国表现的差异被认为是由于瑞典交通的噪声水平较低和状况变化较大造成的。

另一个指标已被建议涵盖包括公路交通噪声、飞机噪声和实验室噪声在内的一系列噪声源，其被称为"噪声污染水平（LNP）"，并由下式给出。

$$\text{LNP} = L_{eq} + 2.56\sigma \tag{18-4}$$

式中：L_{eq}——规定周期内的能量平均噪声水平；

σ——被视为同一规定周期内统计时间序列中瞬时声级的标准偏差。

研究发现，"噪声污染水平"和"交通噪声指数"都能表示交通噪声造成的烦扰，但这两个指标都面临在很多情况下预测仍不准确的事实。因此，建筑研究站建议，作为一项临时测量标准，在进一步调查完成之前，工作日上午6点至午夜12点期间的L_{10}平均值将为测量住宅中的交通噪声引起的烦扰程度提供合适的标准。不管怎样，几年后，预计将获得足够的经验来使用一个结合交通噪声可变性的指标。

Reading Material

The Environmental Effects of Highway Traffic Pollution

During recent years, there has been a widespread attempt to reduce air pollution from all sources. In the United Kingdom the *Clean Air Act* of 1956 has resulted in a noticeable decrease in coal consumption and a reduction in air pollution from domestic and industrial sources. During this same period there has been a marked increase in the volume of road traffic and consequently an increase in pollution from this source. The National Society for Clean Air estimated that, during 1956 in the United Kingdom, the total coal and oil consumed was equivalent to 276 million tons (coal equivalent) and only 26 million tons of this were used for road or rail transport. It is however an increasing source of pollution, which is emitted in situations close to human activity. Approximately one-third of the carbon monoxide in the atmosphere is produced from vehicle exhausts.

On occasions these components of the exhaust may react with each other to produce unpleasant secondary products. The most well-known effect of this type is the Los Angeles "smog", which, because of the bright sunlight and the topography of the region, is formed by the reaction of the oxides of nitrogen and some of the hydrocarbons.

Both petrol and diesel engines give rise to similar products in their exhausts but the relative proportions differ. Diesel engine exhaust gases contain significantly lower proportions of pollutants than do those produced by petrol engines. Unfortunately, an incorrectly operated or maintained diesel engine is liable to emit smoke and produce an offensive smell, but even then, apart from carbon particles, the degree of pollution is less than that produced by petrol engines.

It is generally accepted that the assessment of the air pollution due to a highway scheme may be made in terms of estimated levels of carbon monoxide. Where it is desired to consider other pollutants this may be achieved by relationships between the levels of carbon monoxide and the concentrations of hydrocarbons, lead and oxides of nitrogen.

In the initial stages of road design it is usual for several alternative route proposals to be considered but only outline details of road centre lines and estimates of speed and flow are available. A screening method for estimating air pollution has been developed to predict the annual maximum 8-hour concentration of carbon monoxide arising from traffic at a location near to a road network which consists of straight roads, junctions and roundabouts. This method uses either a series of graphs or mathematical relationships obtained from a computer model which considers vehicle flow, vehicle speed and the distance of the point being considered from the roads. Meteorological and other variables have a large effect on the concentrations of pollutants but they are not considered in this screening process because the method provides an estimate of the maximum concentration likely to occur. The resultant chosen is the highest probable value from a distribution of 8-hour concentrations which is based on the average hourly value.

The method makes use of four relationships. Firstly, for long straight roads the concentrations of carbon monoxide as a function of the distance D (m) are linked to the road and the receptor, for long straight roads. The relationship is

$$C = 1.5e^{-0.025D} \tag{18-5}$$

This relationship was derived for A and B roads, a four-lane dual carriageway and a six-lane motorway. The fall of concentration with increasing distance from the road was found to be represented by this relationship when distance was measured from the centre line of each road type. The relationship was derived for a flow of 1000 vehicles per hour and for other flow the concentration should be multiplied by the expected peak hour flow in thousands of vehicles.

The relationship was derived for input weather and traffic conditions and gives the 1-hour average concentration expected for vehicles travelling at 100km/h. A correction factor for different vehicle speeds can be made from the relationship

$$F = 38.9S^{-0.795} \tag{18-6}$$

Where, S—— the vehicle speed, km/h;

F——the ratio of the emission rate at speed S to the emission rate at 100km/h.

A similar relationship was derived for roundabouts with a range of diameters, and a common relationship for all diameters was found when distances D (m) were measured from the centre line of the circulating carriageway. As roundabouts have a wide range of diameters, it is suggested that where the central island diameter is 10m or less then the roundabout should be considered as a straight stretch of road. The relationship is

$$C = 1.55e^{-0.033D} \tag{18-7}$$

There are no United Kingdom recommendations on exposure limits for ambient carbon monoxide and as a consequence *United States Federal Air Quality Standards* have been suggested as suitable for interpretation of the results of this predictive method. They specify carbon monoxide concentrations of 35ppm and 9ppm which should not be exceeded more than once a year for exposure periods of one hour and eight hours respectively. The Transport and Road Research Laboratory have noted from air pollution survey data that the 8-hour standard is more difficult to meet than the 1-hour standard and for this reason the 8-hour standard of 9ppm was selected to indicate if a more detailed air quality survey was required. The previous relationships gave a 1-hour average value and so it is necessary to estimate the 8-hour average value from the previously derived 1-hour average from

$$C_8 = 1.19 + 1.85C_1 \tag{18-8}$$

Where, C_8——the 8-hour concentration exceeded once a year;

C_1——the peak 1-hour concentration.

As this method was derived for very long straight roads, it is necessary to divide the road network into a few continuous roads as possible to prevent over-estimation of air pollution; only those sections nearest to the reception point should be considered. For example, a four-arm roundabout is divided into three sections, one for each of the two intersecting roads, and the third section is the circulating carriageway of the roundabout. A five-arm in roundabout would have one additional section caused by the fifth leg and in all cases the distance would be the shortest distance (not necessarily perpendicular) to the section.

If this preliminary procedure indicates that concentration of carbon monoxide give rise to concern, then the Department of Transport advises that detailed air quality investigations should be carried out using a suite of computer programs developed by the Transport and Road Research Laboratory.

This suite of programs base three major parts. The first and fundamental part predicts the hourly average concentration of carbon monoxide likely at a particular location for given weather and traffic conditions. This result may be used in the remaining two parts for estimating the range of concentration of carbon monoxide likely for a variety of averaging periods or it may be used to give an indication of likely levels of oxides of nitrogen, hydrocarbons or lead at the site being considered.

Exercises

I True or false.

(　　)(1) Los Angeles "smog" is the direct result of air pollution.

(　　)(2) The pollution of diesel engine is less than that of petrol, but the diesel engine is noiser.

(　　)(3) The varieties of weather and other situations lay a large effect on the concentration of pollutants, so they are thoroughly considered.

(　　)(4) If the diameter is beyond 10m, we can't look the roundabout as a straight stretch of road.

(　　)(5) A five-arm roundabout should be divided into 5 parts due to its 5 "legs".

II Complete the following sentences.

(1) In the United Kingdom the *Clean Air Act* of 1956 has resulted in a noticeable decrease in coal consumption and _____ from domestic and industrial sources.

(2) Approximately one-third of the carbon monoxide in the atmosphere is produced from _____.

(3) Both petrol and diesel engines give rise to similar products in their exhausts but _____ differ.

(4) It is generally accepted that the assessment of the air pollution due to a highway scheme may be made in terms of _____.

(5) In the initial stages of road design it is usual for several alternative route proposals to be considered but only _____ and _____ are available.

III Answer the following questions.

(1) What was the result of the *Clean Air Act* of 1956 of the U.K.?

(2) What was the percentage of the consumption of coal and oil for traffic in the U.K., 1956?

(3) How to estimate the air pollution caused by traffic?

(4) Why are the variables of weather and others not considered, though they are very important for the concentration of air pollutants?

(5) If the peak 1-hour concentration is 65%, then what's the 8-hour concentration exceeding once a year?

参 考 译 文

道路交通污染的环境影响

近年来,为了减少空气污染,人们从各方面都做出了很大的努力。在英国,1956 年颁布的《净化空气法》已经使煤的使用量锐减,来自民用与工业的空气污染也大幅度降低。但与此同时,道路交通量显著增加,道路交通污染也随之增多。据英国净化空气委员会估计,1965 年全国煤和石油的总消耗量相当于 2.76 亿吨煤,而其中只有 0.26 亿吨用于公路与铁路运输。但它却是一种呈上升趋势的污染源,而且该污染源与人类活动极为密切。大气中有将近三分之一的一氧化碳来自车辆的尾气排放。

有时,这些尾气的组成成分会相互反应而生成有害的副产物。其中最为著名的一种危害便是洛杉矶"烟雾"。强烈的阳光与该地区的地形情况,致使氮的氧化物与一些碳氢化合物相互反应,从而形成了这种现象。

汽油机与柴油机所排放的尾气中含有相似的产物,但是其相对比例却有所不同。柴油机排放的尾气中污染物所占的比例明显比汽油机的小。不幸的是,由于不正确的操作和保养,柴油机容易释放出浓烟和难闻的气味。即便如此,除了碳颗粒以外,柴油机尾气的污染程度仍然小于汽油机。

关于如何评估因道路交通而引起的空气污染,一种被普遍认同的做法是根据空气中一氧化碳的含量标准进行评估。对于其他的污染物,可以通过一氧化碳的含量水平与碳氢化合物、铅以及氮的氧化物等浓度之间的关系来进行分析评价。

在道路设计的初始阶段,通常有多种备选的路线方案可以考虑,但前提是必须获得道路中线的大概位置以及预估的车速和流量的详细资料。道路网包括路段、交叉口以及环形交叉,为了预测道路网附近交通流产生的一氧化碳的年最大 8 小时浓度,有人提出了一种估计空气污染的筛除法。该方法利用一系列图表或数学关系式来进行预测,其中数学关系式是利用计算机模型获得的,而计算机模型将车流、车速以及所预测地点与道路的距离都考虑在内。天气和其他条件的变化会对污染物的浓度产生很大的影响,但该方法并未将其考虑在内,因为这个方法是对可能发生的最大浓度的估计。根据小时平均浓度可得 8 小时浓度的分布,我们所选择的结果便是该分布中的最大可能值。

该方法利用了四个关系式。第一个是长直道路上一氧化碳浓度与道路和接收器之间距离 D 之间的关系,一氧化碳的浓度为距离 D 的函数,具体关系式为:

$$C = 1.5e^{-0.025D} \tag{18-5}$$

该关系式针对道路 A 与道路 B,道路 A 为双向四车道,道路 B 为双向六车道。从该关系式中可以看出,当距离 D 从两条道路的中线开始计算时,随着距离 D 的增加,一氧化碳的浓度随之降低。该关系式对应的流量为 1000 辆车/小时。对于其他流量,浓度值应该乘以预计的以千辆车为单位的高峰小时流量。

另外,该关系式需要知道天气以及交通条件,它是车速为 100 千米/小时对应的 1 小时平均浓度。对于不同的车速,可以通过下式算得一个修正系数:

$$F = 38.9S^{-0.795} \tag{18-6}$$

式中：S——车速，千米/小时；

F——速度 S 的排放速率与 100 千米/小时的排放速率之比。

对于直径在一定范围内的环岛，可以推导出一个相似的关系式；而且当距离 D(米) 是从环路的中心线开始计算时，还有一个通用公式。由于环岛直径的范围较广，故建议如果中心岛的直径小于或等于 10 米时，环岛可以被当作道路的直线段延伸。该关系式为：

$$C = 1.55e^{-0.033D} \tag{18-7}$$

英国没有关于一氧化碳排放限值的建议，因而认为《美国联邦空气质量标准》适合阐明该种预测方法的结果。该标准规定，一氧化碳的浓度标准分别为百万分之三十五和百万分之九，排放期分别为 1 小时和 8 小时，一年之中不允许超过 1 次。交通与道路研究实验室根据空气污染的调查数据指出，8 小时浓度标准比 1 小时的浓度标准更加难以达到，因此要选择百万分之九的 8 小时浓度标准，以表明是否需要进行更为详细的空气质量调查。之前的关系式给出了 1 小时平均浓度值的计算方法，所以有必要依据 1 小时的平均浓度值来估算 8 小时的平均浓度，其计算公式如下：

$$C_8 = 1.19 + 1.85C_1 \tag{18-8}$$

式中：C_8——1 年超过 1 次的 8 小时浓度；

C_1——1 小时浓度峰值。

由于该方法适用于长直道路，故有必要将路网尽可能划分为几段连续的道路，以防止过高估计空气污染。划分时应只考虑那些距离接收点最近的部分。例如，一个四路环岛应该分为三部分，第一、二部分为相交的两条道路，第三部分为环绕环岛的车行道。一个五路环岛因有第五条"车道"，则应该增加一部分；而且在所有的情况中，距离必须是与所研究部分的最短距离(不一定必须垂直于该部分)。

如果最初的计算显示一氧化碳的浓度已达到应引起注意的程度时，交通部门会建议使用交通与道路研究实验室开发的一套计算机程序进行详细的空气质量调查。

该套程序以三个主要部分为根据。第一部分，也是最基本的部分，用来预测在给定的天气及交通条件下，某一特定地点可能出现的一氧化碳小时平均浓度。其他两部分将利用第一部分所得到的结果来估计不同时期可能出现的一氧化碳平均浓度范围，或者用来确定被研究地点的氮的氧化物、碳氢化合物以及铅可能出现的含量。

Knowledge Link

Classification of Air Pollution Index

Air pollution index is divided into 0~50, 51~100, 101~150, 151~200, 201~250, 251~300 and more than 300 seven levels, corresponding to seven levels of air quality. The larger the index is, the higher the level is, indicating that the more serious the pollution, the more obvious the impact on human health.

Air pollution index is 0~50, air quality level is I, and air quality is excellent. At this time, there is no air pollution problem, and there is no harm to public health.

Air pollution index is 51~100, air quality level is II, and air quality is good. At this time, air quality is considered acceptable. Except for a few people who are particularly sensitive to certain pollutants, it is not harmful to public health.

The air pollution index is 101 ~ 150, the air quality level is Ⅲ (1), and the air quality is slightly polluted. At this time, it will have an impact on health of the people who are more sensitive to pollutants, such as children and the elderly, patients with respiratory diseases or heart diseases, and the people who like outdoor activities, but having little impact on the healthy population.

The air pollution index is 151 ~ 200, the air quality level is Ⅲ (2), and the air quality condition belongs to mild pollution. At this time, almost everyone's health will be affected, especially for sensitive people.

The air pollution index is 201 ~ 250, 251 ~ 300, and the air quality level is Ⅳ (1) and Ⅳ (2). The air quality status is moderate to severe pollution. At this time, everyone's health will be seriously affected.

The air pollution index is more than 300, the air quality level is Ⅴ, and the air quality condition belongs to serious pollution. At this time, everyone's health will be seriously affected.

Unit 19
Economics and Transportation Engineering

Text

An economic analysis should not be carried out as an afterthought. It should be used as part of a continuous process, starting with the objectives of the proposed transportation project (Can these objectives be satisfied in any other way?), running through the entire planning and design process, and only ending, as a final summing up, with the overall evaluation. It should consider the following questions:

(1) Project identification. Which projects or policies should be considered as possible solutions to a particular transport need?

(2) Establishing rough priorities. Which projects and policies should be considered in detail?

(3) Detailed evaluation. Which costs and benefits are relevant to the evaluation, how should they be measured, and how can they best be presented as an index of priority?

(4) Project selection. Should this project be selected, should it be rejected, or should it be postponed?

Economics is often overlooked as an aid to transportation planning and design. Yet any traffic engineering problem involves a whole series of essentially economic decisions. In the area of design, for example, the transportation engineers must choose materials, select an overall design concept, and then combine the component parts of the scheme into an effective and economical whole. A river crossing could thus be by ferry boat, causeway or bridge. In the latter case, it could be in steel, concrete or timber. It could be suspended, arched, or simply supported. What should the engineers choose?

The range of choice is not usually as large as this. Some solutions will be physically infeasible (e.g., by lack of suitable foundations for an arched bridge), but important choices will remain. In the absence of a rigorous economic analysis, the designers may make these choices on the basis of:

(1) Experience, which may or may not cover an adequate range of options.

(2) Preconceptions as to what is desirable (e.g., one solution uses less material).

(3) An innate view of mathematical or structural elegance (e.g., an arch is a more elegant structural form).

Economics avoids the need for these arbitrary rules by providing a tangible criterion-cost for choosing between alternative solutions. In many cases this can be done quite simply by drawing envelope of cost curves of, for example, steel girder bridges versus reinforced concrete bridges versus prestressed concrete bridges. By plotting cost (y) against span length (x) the engineers can choose which type is most economic over a given range of span lengths.

In practice, the engineers do not usually carry the economic analysis to this level of detail, although curves like this commonly form part of the standard highway design repertoire. It is more a question of the economic attitude of mind that asks: Is this the only possible solution, and if not, is there a better one? It is this general principle which eventually ensures that the final design is the most economical and the one which, if justified in aggregate terms, offers best value for money.

Economic efficiency and distribution

Economics is not concerned solely with the optimum allocation of resources, but with wider questions of equity and the distribution of costs and benefits among individuals, regions, etc. It is thus concerned with the questions: who does what, to whom, and at whose expense? In a sense, this concern complements the intertemporal considerations noted above. A dollar to one person is not necessarily worth the same amount to another. Since economics assumes that marginal values decline as income increases, interpersonal differences in income may thus affect any overall measure of consumer benefit.

Questions of distribution nevertheless go beyond mere differences in income. Institutional constraints usually prevent beneficiaries, defined in the broadest sense, from compensating people who are adversely affected. It is therefore often appropriate to separate the impact of a transport improvement into its effect on different interest groups, in addition to its effect on different income groups.

New Words and Expressions

identification [aɪˌdentɪfɪˈkeɪʃn] n. 鉴别；识别；认同
causeway [ˈkɔːzweɪ] n. 堤道；公路
preconception [priːkənˈsepʃn] n. 预想；预见
prestressed [priːˈstrest] adj. 预应力的（混凝土）

priority [prɑɪˈɒrətɪ]		n. 优先;优先权;[数]优先次序;优先考虑的事
ferry [ˈferɪ]		n. 渡船;摆渡;渡口 vi. 摆渡;来往行驶;用渡船运送;(乘渡船)渡过
suspend [səˈspend]		vt. 延缓,推迟;使暂停;使悬浮 vi. 悬浮;禁赛
plotting [ˈplɒtɪŋ]		n. 测绘;标图
curve [kɜːv]		n. 曲线;弯曲物 vt. 使弯曲 vi. 弯曲
principle [ˈprɪnsəpl]		n. 原则;原理;准则
rigorous [ˈrɪɡərəs]		adj. 严格的;严厉的;严酷的;严峻的
elegance [ˈelɪɡəns]		n. 高雅;典雅;优雅;雅致
arbitrary [ˈɑːbɪtrərɪ]		adj. 任意的,随意的;武断的;独裁的;专断的
versus [ˈvɜːsəs]		prep. 对(指诉讼、比赛中);与……相对
repertoire [ˈrepətwɑː(r)]		n. 全部节目;全部剧目
afterthought [ˈɑːftəθɔːt]		n. 事后的想法;后来添加的东西
postpone [pəˈspəʊn]		vt. 使……延期;把……放在次要地位 vi. 延缓;延迟
timber [ˈtɪmbə(r)]		n. (建筑等用的)木材,木料
infeasible [ɪnˈfiːzəbl]		adj. 不能实行的
innate [ɪˈneɪt]		adj. 固有的;天生的;天然的;内在的
marginal [ˈmɑːdʒɪnl]		adj. 小的,微不足道的;边的,边缘的;临界的
aggregate [ˈæɡrɪɡət]		n. 合计集料 adj. 总数的;总计的
allocation [ˌæləˈkeɪʃn]		n. 分配;配给
region [ˈriːdʒən]		n. 地区;区域;地方;行政区
intertemporal [ɪnˈtɜːtempərəl]		adj. 跨时期的
appropriate [əˈprəʊprɪət]		adj. 适当的;恰当的;合适的
beneficiary [ˌbenɪˈfɪʃərɪ]		n. [金融]受益人;受惠者;封臣 adj. 拥有封地的;受圣俸的

Exercises

I True or false.

(   )(1) Questions of distribution go beyond mere differences in income.

(   )(2) In the absence of a rigorous economic analysis, the designers may make their choices.

(   )(3) All solutions will be physically infeasible.

(   )(4) The engineers usually carry the economic analysis to this level of detail.

(   )(5) In many cases this can be done quite simply by drawing envelope of cost curves of, for example, steel girder bridges versus reinforced concrete bridges versus prestressed concrete bridges.

Ⅱ Complete the following sentences.

(1) Economics is often overlooked as an aid to _____ planning and design.

(2) Economics avoids the need for these arbitrary rules by providing a tangible criterion-cost-for choosing _____ alternative solutions.

(3) Institutional constraints usually prevent _____, defined in the broadest sense, from compensating people who are adversely affected.

(4) Some solutions will be physically infeasible, _____ important choices will remain.

(5) _____ usually prevent beneficiaries, defined in the broadest sense, from compensating people who are adversely affected.

Ⅲ Answer the following questions.

(1) Why economics should not be overlooked as an aid to transportation planning and design?

(2) In the absence of a rigorous economic analysis, how do the designers make choices?

(3) How does economics avoid the need for arbitrary rules?

(4) What should be considered in an economic analysis?

(5) How to choose the most economic type over a given range of span lengths?

Topics for Discussion

(1) Why is it often appropriate to separate the impact of a transport improvement into its effect on different interest groups?

(2) What should an economic analysis consider?

(3) What is the role of traffic engineering in economic development in your opinion?

参 考 译 文

经济学和交通工程

经济分析应该作为一个连续过程的一部分,不应该在事后进行。它应从提出交通工程项目的目标开始(这些目标是否能以其他方式来满足?),贯穿整个规划设计过程,并且仅在结束时对整体进行评估,作为最终的总结。进行经济分析时应考虑以下问题:

(1) 项目鉴别。哪些项目或政策应该被视为特定交通需求的可行性解决方案?

(2) 确定大致的优先顺序。应详细考虑哪些项目和政策?

(3) 详细评估。哪些成本和收益与评估相关?如何衡量它们?如何以最好的方式将它们作为优先指标来提出?

(4) 项目选择。该项目是应该被选择,被拒绝,还是应该被推迟?

经济学作为交通规划和设计的辅助手段常常被忽视。然而,任何交通工程问题都涉及一系列基本经济决策。例如,在设计方面,交通工程师必须选择设计材料,选择整体设计概念,然后将方案的组成部分组合成一个有效的、经济的整体。渡江可以通过渡船、堤道和桥。后面两例可以使用钢、混凝土或木材,可以被悬挂,成拱形,或被简单地支撑起来。对此工程师应该如何选择?

工程师选择的范围通常没有那么大。因外界条件限制,一些解决方案是不可行的(例如,缺乏建造拱桥的基础条件),但仍将保留重要的选择。在缺乏严格经济分析的情况下,设计师可以根据以下条件做出选择:

(1)经验(是否涵盖足够的选择范围)。
(2)对于什么是可取的有先入为主的想法(例如,某一种解决方案中使用的材料更少)。
(3)对数学或结构的美观有固有观点(例如,拱门是一种更精致的结构形式)。

经济学通过提供在备选方案之间进行选择的具体标准成本,避免了对这些专制的、规则的需要。很多情况下,这可以很简单地通过绘制"成本曲线"来完成,例如钢梁桥、钢筋混凝土桥与预应力混凝土桥的对比。通过绘制成本(y)与跨度长度(x)关系图,工程师可以在给定的跨度长度范围内选择最经济的类型。

在实践中,工程师通常不会进行如此详细的经济分析,尽管这样的曲线通常是标准公路设计的一部分。这更像是一个思维方法的问题:这是唯一可行的解决方案吗?如果不是,还有更好的吗?正是这一普遍原则,最后确保了最终设计是最经济的,并且如果总的来说是合理的,就能提供最佳的性价比。

经济效益与分配

经济学不仅涉及资源的最佳分配,而且涉及更广泛的公平问题以及个人、区域等之间的成本和利益的分配。因此,它涉及的问题是:谁做什么,对谁做什么,以什么为代价。从某种意义上说,这一问题是对上述跨时期考量的补充。一美元对不同人来说不一定具有相同的价值。由于经济学假设边际价值随着收入的增加而下降,因此收入的人际差异可能会影响对消费者利益的总体度量。

然而,分配问题不仅仅局限于收入差异。从广义上说,制度约束通常会阻止受益人补偿受到损害的人。因此通常情况下,除了考虑对不同收入群体的影响外,必须同时考虑交通改善对不同利益群体的影响。

Reading Material

Problems of Benefit-cost Analysis

In a great many countries benefit-cost analysis is the preferred, and in some cases the required, method of project or plan evaluation. Occasionally the more extended and more complex form of social benefit-cost analysis is used in which monetary estimates are made of the costs and benefits of social consequences which cannot be priced directly. In all these analyses the discounted stream of money costs are compared with the discounted streams of benefits converted into monetary terms. Where benefit-cost ratios in excess of unity are obtained, the project or plan is considered worthwhile and where a number of options are to be evaluated, that with the highest marginal benefit-cost ratio is considered preferable. Extended social benefit-cost analysis in the past has led to calculations of great complexity, but of course the value of the calculations is limited by the accuracy with which the numerous factors being considered can be quantified. Because so very few of these factors currently are described in any detail, it is scarcely surprising that the results of social benefit-cost analysis often have appeared to be regarded with suspicion by some nontechnical decision makers and the public at large. A case in point was the political selection of another site for the third London airport, though in the face of strong benefit-cost arguments for all the other evaluated site. The work of the Royal Commission on the third London airport must rank as one of the most extensive and costly benefit analyses ever carried out. The findings of the commission were based on benefit-cost analysis, but they were overturned by the British government because it was apparent to an "intelligent layman" that the findings were obviously wrong. This was largely due to the fact that the terms of reference of the committee were interpreted too narrowly and the technique of economic evaluation was applied in an incomplete manner. The exclusion of unquantifiable amenity considerations may render a whole social benefit-cost exercise unreliable.

First it must be recognized that the treatment of externalities and some other quantifiable impacts in terms of additional monetary costs and benefits to be added into the direct cash flow is likely to be a process of great uncertainty which may lead to disagreement with other planners and confusion for decision makers. For example, there seems to be little community-wide agreement of the true costs of noise disturbance. This in the past has been related both to the amount an individual was willing to pay to avoid noise and to the amount that he was willing to receive as compensation for enduring it. Similarly there is sharp disagreement on the true value of travel time savings and much debate about the question of whether very small savings have any value at all. Often called notional values, indirect costs and benefits of this nature account for a large proportion of the total costs and benefits that are involved in the most sophisticated extended social benefit cost analyses. Even more debatable is the question of the stability of these notional values over the very long periods of time involved in strategic plans. A number of writers indicate that even basic social values may change as developed nations enter the postindustrial phase. Certainly some changes are discernable between the early 1960s and the 1980s.

The question of the discount rate itself posed severe philosophical questions when examined in the context of long-term planning. In many countries (e. g., the United States and Western Europe countries), it has been required for years that public investment should bring rates of return that reflect the opportunity cost of capital invested in the private sector. Under current conditions, the use of high discount rates might therefore appear rational in long-term planning. However, high discount rates tend to militate against the long term in favor of the short term and results in effectively nullifying the effect of long-term impacts due to the combined effects of the high rates and the very long-term planning periods. Some analysts have therefore argued that this type of analysis, which heavily discounts future states and gives preference to the short term, is most unsuitable for long-term planning. They claim that it is irrational to act on decisions made largely on the type of economic justification where the future is heavily discounted by the application of high current discount rates to notional values determined by current thinking.

Further fundamental difficulties arise from the recognized fact that society is pluralistic. While a single-benefit-cost ratio can indicate that as a whole society will gain a net benefit from a certain course of action, the single-benefit-cost ratio cannot indicate who is gaining the benefits and who is paying the cost. It is entirely possible that in the case of the location of an airport or the choice of the alignment of a freeway the costs incurred to the affected parts of the community may be much larger than the concomitant benefits to them.

These three basic problems all point out that while benefit-cost analysis may be very suitable for comparing two similar schemes (e. g., alternative freeway alignments), it is less suitable for providing a comprehensive evaluation of the multiplicity of factors that are implied by a long-term transportation plan. Planners too frequently make the mistake of striving for mathematical rather than philosophical rigor.

Exercises

I True or false.

(　　)(1) Where benefit-cost ratios in excess of unity are obtained, the project is considered worthwhile and beneficial.

(　　)(2) The results of social benefit-cost analysis was not suspected by some nontechnical decision makers and the public.

(　　)(3) Many writers think that the basic social values can not change as developed nations enter the postindustrial phase.

(　　)(4) Under current conditions, the use of high discount rates might therefore appear rational in long-term planning.

(　　)(5) Planners too frequently make the mistake of striving for philosophical rather than mathematical rigor.

II Complete the following sentences.

(1) Extended social benefit-cost analysis in the past has led to _____ of great complexity.

(2) A number of writers indicate that even basic social values may change as developed nations enter the _____ phase.

(3) Further fundamental difficulties arise from the recognized fact that society is _____.

(4) It is entirely possible that in the case of the location of an airport or the choice of the alignment of a freeway the costs incurred to _____ may be much larger than _____.

(5) Planners too frequently make the mistake of _____ rather than _____.

III Answer the following questions.

(1) When should we consider the project or plan is worthwhile?

(2) Why did British government overturn the work of the Royal Commission on the third London airport?

(3) What role do the indirect costs and benefits play in total costs and benefits?

(4) What should be firstly concerned in benefit-cost analysis?

(5) Why some analysts have argued that the type of analysis which heavily discounts future states and gives preference to the short term is most unsuitable for long-term planning?

参 考 译 文

效益-成本分析问题

效益-成本分析法在许多国家是优先选用的(在某些情况下则是规定的)项目或方案评估方法。有时人们会采用更详细、更复杂的社会效益-成本分析方式,这时货币预估由成本和不能直接计价的社会效益构成。在所有这些分析中,成本现值与效益现值在货币化之后进行比较。当效益成本比(BCR)大于1时,认为项目或方案是可行的,当有多个方案需要比选择优时,通常采用边际效益成本比最大的方案。在过去,广义的社会效益成本分析需要大量复杂的计算,但是分析的结果受很多因素及定量精度的限制,为此这些因素很少被人具体提到。因此,社会效益-成本分析的结果经常受到一些非专业决策者和一般公众的怀疑也是不足为怪的。伦敦第三机场的选址是个典型的案例。方案评估中,虽然其他可选地点已经进行了有力的效益-成本论证,却因为政治的原因,政府最后把机场位置选在另一个位置。皇家委员会对伦敦第三机场选址方案的评估是所做的最详细、最昂贵的效益分析之一。委员会的选址是建立在效益-成本分析的基础之上的,但是它们却被英国政府推翻。因为对于这些"聪明的外行"而言,选址显然是错误的。这主要是因为委员会对所依据的条款解释得过于勉强,而且使用的经济评估技术又不完善。由于缺乏对那些难以量化的环境舒适性的考虑,导致整个社会效益-成本分析不可信,而且,有很多基本问题应该在评估之前就得到解决。

首先人们必须认识到,如何确定项目的外部效果及其他可量化的间接费用和间接效益是一个大问题,这个问题将有可能导致规划者意见无法一致并给决策者造成困惑。例如,噪声的污染成本就没有得到过社会全体公众的认同。过去,这个成本是与个人为避免噪声污染所愿意付出的费用及能够接受噪声污染赔偿的费用相联系的。类似地,人们对行车节省的时间价值的认同也无法统一,并对这种少量节省是否真的具有价值有争论。所谓的抽象价值,即间接的成本和效益,通常占总成本和总效益的很大一部分,总成本和效益涉及内容最复杂、最广泛的社会效益—成本分析。然而,更具争议性的问题还在于这些抽象价值在战略计划所涉及的一段很长时间内的稳定性。很多学者指出,一旦发达国家进入后工业化时期,甚至其基本的社会价值标准也会改变。在20世纪60年代初到80年代,一些基本的价值标准的确已经发生了改变。

当对远期规划的内容进行检查时,贴现率自身的问题引出了严密的哲学问题。在很多国家(如美国和西欧国家),多年来公众投资是要求有回报率的,它反映了投在私营公司的资金所带来的机会成本。在当前情况下,使用高贴现率似乎对于远期规划是合理的。但是,实际上高贴现率不利于远期规划项目,而是有利于近期规划项目,并且由于高贴现率和规划的长期性的综合影响,远期规划的作用将会逐渐消失。因此,一些分析家认为这种远期采用高贴现率和近期给予优先权的分析方法,对于远期规划并不合适。他们认为:目前所确定的抽象价值的贴现率太高,如果使用该贴现率,项目的价值在远期将会大打折扣;如果实际操作中采用该贴现率,则得出的结论是很不合理的。

由于社会多元性这一公认事实,更多的基本难题将会出现。单一的效益—成本比可以表明整个社会从某一特定项目中能获得的纯利润,但却不能表明在这一过程中哪些人得到了利益,哪些人为此遭受了损失。在诸如飞机场选址或高速公路的线形选择这样的案例中,项目对社会产生的负面影响有可能远大于它们带来的正面作用。

这三点基本问题都表明,效益-成本分析方法适合比较两个类似的方案(例如对高速公路线形的选择),而不太适合对远期交通规划中所包含的多种因素进行综合评价。规划者也经常犯这样的错误:只为努力达到数学上的精确性而经常忽略哲学上的严密性。

Knowledge Link

Benefit-Cost Ratio

Benefit-Cost Ratio (BCR) is an index for cost-benefit analysis, which attempts to summarize the total monetary value of a project or proposal. BCR is the rate of return of a project or proposal, expressed in currency, as opposed to its cost. All earnings and costs shall be expressed in discounted present value. BCR can be a profitability index in a profitable environment. BCR takes into account the monetary gains achieved by executing the project and the costs required for executing the project. The higher the BCR is, the better the investment is. The general rule of thumb is that a project is a good investment if the return is higher than the cost.

In the absence of capital constraints, the best value of a monetary item is the item with the highest net present value. If budgetary constraints exist, the ratio of Net Present Value(NPV) to expenditure within limits should be used. In practice, the ratio of present value of future net income to expenditure is expressed by BCR. BCR has been widely used in the field of transportation cost-benefit(BCR) evaluation. NPV shall be evaluated within the life span of the project.

Long-term BCRs, such as those involving climate changes, are very sensitive to the discount rates used in net present value calculations, and there is usually no consensus on the appropriate discount rates.

There are also problems in dealing with non-monetary impacts. They are usually estimated in monetary form by using measures such as WTP (Willingness to Pay), although these are often difficult to assess.

Unit 20

Transport Telematic

Text

1. Introduction

Transport telematic, also known as Intelligent Transport Systems (ITS), is concerned with the application of electronic information and control to improve transport. Some new systems have already been implemented and the pace of implementation can be expected to quicken. We can foresee how a typical journey to work may look in 10 years time.

Before leaving home, you check your travel arrangements over the internet. Often you choose to travel by public transport and you can identify travel times and any interruptions affecting the service. On this occasion, you choose to travel by car as you have an appointment later in the day at one of those old-fashioned business parks that are inaccessible by public transport. There are no incidents recorded on your normal route to work so you do not bother to use your computer route model to select an optimum route for you.

Once in your car, you head for the motorway and select the cruise control, lane support and collision avoidance system, allowing yourself to concentrate on your favorite radio service. Suddenly, this is interrupted by the radio traffic-message channel service giving you information about an incident on your route. You are not surprised when, at the next junction, the roadside Variable Message Sign (VMS) confirms this—motorway messages really are believable now!

You feel pleased with yourself that you have preceded your in-car navigation system with the coordinate of your final destination, and soon you are obtaining instructions on your best route with information updated from the local travel control center.

2. Using transport telematic

All these information and control services, and many more besides, are discussed in the U. K. government's consultation document. One way of to classify these services is into the following application areas:

(1) Traffic management and control.
(2) Tolling and road pricing.
(3) Road safety and law enforcement.
(4) Public transport travel information and ticketing.
(5) Driver information and guidance.
(6) Freight and fleet management.
(7) Vehicle safety.
(8) System integration.

All these applications are being developed with assistance from research and pilot implementation programmes in Europe, U. S. A. and Japan.

3. Traffic management and control

Any traffic management and control system needs information on traffic flow, speeds, queues, incidents (accidents, vehicle breakdowns, obstructions) air quality and vehicle types, lengths and mass. This information will be collected using infrared, radio, loop, radar, and microwave or vision detectors. In addition, public and private organizations will provide information on planned events (roadworks, leisure events and exhibitions).

The use to which this information is put depends on the objectives set for management and control. Network management objectives set for urban areas include:

(1) Influencing traveller behavior, in particular modal choice, route choice and the times at which journeys are made.
(2) Reducing the impact of traffic on air quality.
(3) Improving priority for buses and LRT vehicles.
(4) Providing better and safer facilities for pedestrians, cyclists and other vulnerable road users.
(5) Restraining traffic in sensitive areas.
(6) Managing demand and congestion more efficiently.

The software systems used will include control application systems, such as SCOOT, SCATS, SPOT and MOTION. These are responsive systems, which control a network of traffic signals to meet these objectives. Automatic vehicle location and identification will provide information for giving priority or allowing access to certain vehicles only.

Interurban network management systems will have similar objectives but will make greater use of access control by ramp metering and other means, and of speed control and high-occupancy vehicle lane management. Regional traffic control centers will advise motorists of incidents and alternative routes by VMS and by RDS-TMC, a signal FM radio service broadcasting localized traffic messages and advice to drivers.

4. Tolling and road pricing

Interurban motorway tolling and urban road pricing provides another approach to meeting network management objectives while obtaining additional revenue that can be invested in transport. Singapore's electronic zone pricing, the TOLLSTAR electronic toll collection and ADEPT automatic debiting smart cards are examples of such application.

These systems rely on microwave or radio communication to an in-vehicle transponder in a smart card with detection of vehicle license plates using image processing.

5. Public transport travel information and ticketing

Travel information is needed by passengers at home or office and also during their journey. London Transport's ROUTES computer-based service offers routing, timetable and fare information on all public transport services in London through public inquiry terminals.

Real-time travel information is provided in London by the COUNTDOWN system which is being expanded to cover 4000 bus stops. A similar system called STOPWATCH is available in Southampton as part of the ROMANSE project and is based on Peek's Bus Tracker system which can detect buses using either radio beacons or GPS which uses satellites to identify locations.

ROMANSE also includesTRIP lanner interactive enquiry terminals with touch screens providing travel information.

New Words and Expressions

telematic [ˌtelɪˈmætɪk]	n. 信息通信业务;远程信息处理
Variable Message Sign (VMS)	可变信息标志
interruption [ˌɪntəˈrʌpʃn]	n. 中断;打断
inaccessible [ˌɪnəkˈsesəbl]	adj. 达不到的;难以见到的
optimum [ˈɒptɪməm]	adj. 最适宜的
motorway [ˈməutəweɪ]	n. (控制进出口的)高速公路
interurban [ˌɪntəˈrɜːbən]	adj. 都市间的
cruise [kruːz]	vi. 巡游;巡航 n. 巡游;巡航
roadwork [ˈrəudˌwɜːk]	n. 筑路工程
navigation [ˌnævɪˈgeɪʃn]	n. 航海;航空;导航;领航;航行
consultation [ˌkɒnsəlˈteɪʃn]	n. 请教;咨询;磋商
transponder [trænˈspɒndə(r)]	n. 异频雷达收发机
enforcement [ɪnˈfɔːsmənt]	n. 执行;强制;实施
inquiry [ɪnˈkwaɪərɪ]	n. 质询;调查

beacon ['biːkən]	n. 烟火;灯塔 vt. 照亮;指引
Light Rail Transit (LRT)	轻轨交通
Split-Cycle-Offset Optimization Technique(SCOOT)	绿信比—信号周期—时差优化技术
Sydney Co-ordinated Adaptive Traffic System(SCATS)	最优自动适应交通控制系统
Frequency Modulation (FM)	调频
confirm [kən'fɜːm]	vt. 确认;证实;批准;使巩固
instruction [ɪn'strʌkʃn]	n. 命令;指示;教导;用法说明
freight [freɪt]	n. 货运;运费;货物 vt. 运输

Exercises

I True or false.

(　　)(1) Automatic vehicle location and identification will provide information for giving priority or allowing access to certain vehicles only.

(　　)(2) Singapore's electronic zone pricing, the ADEPT electronic toll collection and TOLLSTAR automatic debiting smart cards are examples of such application.

(　　)(3) Real-time travel information is provided in London by the COUNTDOWN system which is being expanded to cover 4000 bus stops.

(　　)(4) ROMANSE also includes TRIP lanner interactive enquiry terminals with touch screens providing travel information.

(　　)(5) Real-time travel information is provided in London by the STOPWATCH system which is being expanded to cover 4000 bus stops.

II Complete the following sentences.

(1) _____, also known as ITS, is concerned with the application of electronic information and control to improve transport.

(2) Any traffic management and control system needs information on _____.

(3) Regional traffic control centers will advise motorists of incidents and alternative routes by _____ and by _____.

(4) London Transport's ROUTES computer-based service offers routing, timetable and fare information on all public transport services in London through _____.

(5) VMS is the abbreviation of _____.

III Answer the following questions.

(1) What is transport telematic?
(2) What will be a typical journey to work in 10 years?
(3) What are the application areas of transport telematic?
(4) How to collect the information on traffic flow, speeds, queues, incidents (accidents, vehicle breakdowns and obstructions), air quality and vehicle types, lengths and weights?

(5) What are the network management objectives for urban areas?

Topics for Discussion

(1) What areas do transport telematic apply to in the transportation?
(2) What are the objectives of traffic management and control in urban areas?
(3) What is the application prospect of transport telematic?

参 考 译 文

交通远程信息技术

1. 介绍

交通远程信息技术,又称智能交通系统(ITS),是应用电子信息和控制来改善交通的技术。一些新系统已经被应用,并且在未来的应用速度将加快。我们可以预见10年后普遍的工作出行会是怎样的。

在离开家之前,你可以通过互联网查看你的出行安排。通常,你选择乘坐公共交通工具出行,你可以确定出行时间和任何对公共交通服务的影响。若当天晚些时候要去那些公共交通不便的老式商业园区赴约,在这种情况下,你会选择乘坐客车出行。你的正常工作路线上没有记录任何事故,因此不必使用计算机路线模型来为你选择最佳路线。

一旦进入车内,你将前往高速公路并选择巡航控制、车道辅助和防撞系统,使自己能够专注于自己最喜欢的无线电频道。突然间,该频道被无线电交通信息服务频道中断了,这项服务向你提供有关路线上发生的事故信息。当在下一个交叉路口,从路边可变信息标志(VMS)确认这一点时,你并不感到惊讶——现在的高速公路信息真可靠!

你对自己先于车内导航系统得到了最终目的地的定位而感到满意,很快你就可以从当地的旅行控制中心获得关于最佳路线的最新指示信息。

2. 交通远程信息技术的应用

英国政府的咨询文件中讨论了这些信息和控制以及更多服务,并将这些服务分为以下应用领域:

(1) 交通管理与控制。
(2) 征税和道路收费。
(3) 道路安全与执法。
(4) 公共交通出行信息与票务。
(5) 驾驶人信息和指南。
(6) 货运和车队管理。
(7) 车辆安全。
(8) 系统集成。

所有这些应用程序都是在欧洲、美国及日本的研究和试点实施计划的支持下开发的。

3. 交通管理和控制

任何交通管理和控制系统都需要有关交通流、速度、排队、事件(事故、车辆故障、障碍物)、空气质量以及车辆类型、长度和重量的信息。利用红外线、无线电、线圈、雷达、微波或视频检测器可收集这些信息。此外,公共和私人组织将提供与计划好的活动(道路工程、休闲活动、展览)相关的信息。

这些信息的使用取决于管理和控制的目标。为市区设定的信号网络管理目标包括:
(1)影响乘客的行为,特别是方式选择、路线选择和出行时间。
(2)减少交通对空气质量的影响。
(3)提升公交车和轻轨的优先权。
(4)为行人、骑车人和其他易受伤害的道路使用者提供更好和更安全的设施。
(5)限制交通情况易变区域的交通量。
(6)更有效地管理交通需求和拥堵。

使用的软件系统将包括控制应用系统,如 SCOOT、SCATS、SPOT 和 MOTION。这些系统都是响应系统,它们通过控制交通信号网络来满足这些目标。车辆自动定位和识别将提供优先权信息或允许出入的某些车辆信息。

城际网络管理系统具有类似的目标,但会更多地利用匝道测量和其他方式进行出入口控制、速度控制和高利用车道的管理。区域交通控制中心将通过 VMS 和 RDS-TMC(一种传递本地交通信息并向驾驶人提供建议的信号调频无线电服务)向驾驶人提供事故信息和备用路线方面的建议。

4. 征税和道路收费

城际高速公路收费和城市道路收费为实现交通网络管理的目标提供了另一种方法,同时获得可投资于交通的额外收入。新加坡的电子区域定价、TOLLSTAR 电子收费和 ADEPT 自动借记智能卡就是这类应用的例子。

这些系统与嵌在一张智能卡上的车载应答器实现微波或无线电通信,它们利用图像处理技术检测车辆牌照实现管理目的。

5. 公共交通出行信息与票务

出行者在家或办公室以及出行过程中都需要出行信息。伦敦交通公司基于计算机 ROUTES 服务,通过公共查询终端机提供伦敦所有公共交通的路线、时间表和票价信息。

伦敦的 COUNTDOWN 系统提供实时出行信息,该系统的服务范围将扩展到 4000 个公交车站。作为 ROMANSE 项目的一部分,南安普敦也有一个类似的称为秒表的系统,该系统以 Peek 的公交线路跟踪器系统为基础,该系统可以使用无线电信标或利用卫星识别位置的全球定位系统来探测公交车。

ROMANSE 包括 TRIP Lanner 交互式查询终端,这种终端机带有提供出行信息的触摸屏。

Reading Material

Electronic Toll Collection

Electronic Toll Collection (ETC) is the use of various technologies to allow the manual in-lane toll collection process to be automated in such a way that customers do not have to stop and pay cash at a toll booth. With ETC, an actual toll plaza is not even a requirement to collect toll. The ETC equipment can be mounted on overhead gantries and/or in the pavement which allows vehicles to be charged while they proceed at highway speeds.

For an ETC implementation to be effective, reliable and achieve maximum throughput and customer acceptance, three major in-lane/roadway components are required: Automatic Vehicle Identification, Automatic Vehicle Classification, Video Enforcement Systems.

Automatic Vehicle Identification (AVI) uses a Radio Frequency (RF) device located in the vehicle to uniquely identify the vehicle to the toll equipment. Automatic Vehicle Classification (AVC) uses various sensors in and around the lanes to determine the type of vehicle so that the proper toll can be charged. Video Enforcement Systems (VES) capture images of the license plates of vehicles so that the owners can be identified and notified that a toll is due. All of these systems are tied together by what is commonly referred to as a "lane controller".

The lane controller is a computer that receives its inputs from the AVI, AVC and VES equipment. Usually, there is one lane controller per lane which coordinates the activities of all other lane equipment and creates the actual transactions which will be used to charge the customer's toll. The lane controller is also the device that maintains a list of valid tags which it uses to validate the information provided by AVI.

In addition to all this in-lane equipment, each toll plaza usually has a host computer which collects the transaction information from the lane controllers and is in communication with a central host computer which collects data from all plazas so that the data exists in one consolidated location. The plaza host computer is also used to transmit to each lane controller the list of valid tags which is used for AVI validation.

Finally, there is usually a Customer Service Center which enrolls customers, manages the customer's toll account, issues tags to customers, processes the violation images, and handles customer inquires. The Customer Service Center receives toll transactions from the in-lane/roadway equipment and posts these transactions against the appropriate customer account. The Customer Service Center also transmits to the plaza host computers the list of valid tags which will, in turn, be transmitted to the lane controllers for use in AVI validation.

Putting all this technology together can be a daunting task and most agencies hire a vendor to either integrate all this technology into their existing toll environment or to develop a whole new toll system which includes ETC. These vendors are often referred to as System Integrators or Integrators.

ETC allows the toll facility operators to improve customer service and satisfaction by speeding their trip through the toll plaza, removing the need for the customer to stop, fumble for change, or roll down their window. It also gives customers the flexibility of paying their toll with cash, cheque or even credit cards. Customers who use credit cards often have the option of having their credit card account automatically charged when their toll account dips below a predefined level thereby eliminating the customer's concern over funds for toll payment. In addition, customers can receive monthly statements detailing their toll usage and will not have to ask for receipts. Commercial customers have the added benefit of no longer being required to send drivers out with cash or some form of ticket which will get rid of the potential of being misused.

The toll facility operators also benefit from ETC. Facility throughput can be increased without the need to build additional infrastructure (such as more toll booths) and the amount of staff dedicated to the toll collection process can often be reduced.

Even the general public benefits from ETC since the fewer cars and trucks which idle at a toll plaza, the less exhaust is spewed into the air and the cleaner the air will be.

The Port Authority ETC System Architecture can be broken down into four main sub-components:

(1) Lane equipment. The Lane Equipment is comprised of all the hardware and software which detects vehicle presence, captures data regarding the vehicles, and creates the transactions for each vehicle. All the lane equipment is coordinated and the lane equipment can be broken down into five main sub-categories: Approach/Canopy Signage, AVI, AVC, VES, and DFS.

(2) Communication network. The Communication Network is the medium whereby the Lane Controller communicates with the ETC Central Host and the ETC Central Host communicates with the Customer Service Center. It is also the method whereby operation and management staff can interact with the ETC system.

(3) ETC central host. The ETC Central Host (ECH) consolidates data from all the Lane Controllers, provides the interface to the Customer Service Center and is the source of all ETC system reports.

(4) Customer central service. The Customer Service Center (CSC) refers to the collection of hardware, software, structures and staff resources which manage customer accounts.

Exercises

I True or false.

(　　)(1) Electronic Toll Collection equipment can be mounted on overhead gantries or in the pavement to charge their tolls while vehicles proceed at highway speed.

(　　)(2) The lane controller is also the device that maintains a list of valid tags which it uses to validate the information provided by AVC.

(　　)(3) Commercial customers have the added benefit. They send no longer drivers out with cash or some form of ticket, which will get rid of the potential of being misused.

(　　)(4) The toll facility operator benefits from ETC, the general public also benefits from ETC.

(　　)(5) The ETC Central Host (ECH) consolidates data from all the Lane Controllers, provides the interface to the Customer Service Center and is the source of all ETC system reports.

II Complete the following sentences.

(1) In order to be efficient, reliable and achieve maximum throughput and customer acceptance, ETC requires three major roadway components: _____, _____, _____.

(2) The lane controller is a computer: _____.

(3) In addition to all this in-lane equipment, each toll plaza usually has a host computer whose function is _____.

(4) There is usually a Customer Service Center which _____.

(5) The Port Authority ETC System Achitecture can be broken down into four main sub-components, they are _____, _____, _____ and _____.

Ⅲ Answer the following questions.

(1) What are the components of an ETC?
(2) What is the lane controller?
(3) What is the function of a host computer of each toll plaza?
(4) What are the benefits of ETC?
(5) What are the sub-components of the Port Authority ETC System Architecture?

参 考 译 文

电 子 收 费

电子收费(ETC)采用多种技术手段,使车道内的人工收费过程实现自动化,驾驶人不用在收费亭停车缴纳现金。有了电子收费,甚至已经不需要实际的收费场所。电子收费的设备被安装在空中的高架上,或者安装在路面上,对道路上高速行驶的车辆进行收费。

为了使电子收费有效、可靠实施,并获得最大的通过量和用户满意度,电子收费由三个主要的路上部分组成,即自动车辆识别系统、自动车型分类系统和录像执行系统。

自动车辆识别系统(AVI)利用设置在车辆中的射频(RF)装置,为收费设备提供唯一的车辆识别。自动车型分类系统(AVC)利用安装在车道内和道路周围的多个传感器来确定车辆类型,以确保收费的正确性。对于那些没有有效标识的车辆,录像执行系统(VES)可以捕捉到它们的牌照图像,因此车主就被识别并被告知该交费了。所有这些系统将被联系在一起,组成我们通常所说的车道控制器。

车道控制器是一台从自动车辆识别系统、自动车型分类系统和录像执行系统获得信息的计算机。通常来说,每条车道只安装一部车道控制器,它与其他车道的设备相配合,得到真实的处理结果,并按照该结果对车主进行收费。车道控制器也是一部记录着一系列有效标识清单的装置,用于确定由自动车辆识别系统提供的信息的有效性。

除了这些道路上的设备以外,每一个收费站通常有一部主机,它会从车道控制器那里收集经过处理的信息,并与从各个收费站收集数据的中央主机交换信息,从而使数据的存在并不是孤立的。收费站主机的另外一个作用是向每个车道控制器传送有效标识,以确定自动车辆识别系统识别的有效性。

最后,通常要设一处客户服务中心,为客户进行登记,管理客户的账目,向客户发送标识,加工处理违规的车辆图像,以及回答客户的咨询。客户服务中心从安装在道路上的设备得到收费的处理信息,然后将这些信息加入相应客户的账目中。客户服务中心还向收费站的主机发送有效标识的名单。该名单再被依次传达给车道控制器,从而确定自动车辆识别系统识别的有效性。

将所有这些技术合并统一是一项十分艰巨的任务,大多数机构都会雇请一名供应商来将这些技术合成到他们现有的收费系统中,或者开发一整套包括电子收费在内的新的收费系统。这些被雇请的人就是通常所说的集成商或系统集成商。

电子收费使客户不再需要停车、找零钱和开车窗,加快了客户通过收费站的速度,使收费系统操作者的服务质量和客户满意程度得以提高,同时,还为客户究竟是采用现金、支票还是信用卡的支付方式提供了灵活性。使用信用卡的客户常有这样的选择,即当他们的交费账目低于一个预先确定的数值时,信用卡就会自动交费,从而消除了客户对支付收费资金的忧虑。此外,客户可以得到每月的详细交费清单,没有必要再去要收据。对于商业用户还有另外一个好处,即不用再发给驾驶人现金或支票,从而消除了滥用公款的可能性。

收费系统的操作者也同样可以从电子收费中获益。收费系统不需要修建附加的基础设施(如收费亭)就可以增加其周转量,并且收费人员的数量也可以减少。

甚至连一般公众都会从电子收费当中获益,因为在收费站停留的汽车数量越少,向大气中排放的汽车尾气就越少,空气也会越洁净。

电子收费系统的机构可以分解为以下四个主要的组成部分:

(1)车道设备。车道设备由所有的硬件和用于检测车辆存在、获得车辆有关信息和生成每辆车处理信息的软件组成。所有车道设备相互协调。车道设备由五个部分组成,即引道/标志门架、自动车辆识别系统、自动车型分类系统、录像执行系统及驾驶人反馈系统。

(2)信息网。信息网是车道控制器与电子收费中心主机以及电子收费中心主机与客户服务中心之间进行信息交换的媒介,也是操作管理人员同电子收费系统互相作用的一种媒介。

(3)电子收费中心主机。电子收费中心主机(ECH)整合从车道控制器传来的数据,为客户服务中心提供接口,并且是所有电子收费系统报告的来源。

(4)客户服务中心。客户服务中心是硬件、软件、结构以及管理客户账目的集合。

Knowledge Link

Variable Message Sign

Variable Message Sign (VMS) is a kind of road traffic sign that uses remote control device to display the real-time driving environment of the road in front under weather, natural disasters, traffic accidents and other reasons. There are many kinds of information stored. According to the change of driving environment, the controller can make the sign display some corresponding information manually or automatically through remote control device, inform and warn the driver to take corresponding safe and reasonable driving measures. Generally, variable information signs are set in front of highway entrances and exits, long tunnel entrances and sections with other special requirements. Variable information signs should meet the following basic requirements:

(1) Variable information signs shall not display content unrelated to traffic, such as advertising information, etc.

(2) Variable information signs and static signs should be coordinated with each other, and the

contents should not be opposite or occluded from each other.

(3) Variable information signs should ensure sufficient front-end distance and give drivers sufficient recognition and reaction time.

(4) Animation effects such as simulation, dissolution and explosion should not be included in variable information signs.

Unit 21

ITS Offers A New Approach

Text

 A broad range of diverse technologies, known collectively as Intelligent Traffic Systems(ITS), hold the answer to many of our transportation problems. ITS is comprised of a number of technologies, including information processing, communications, control and electronics. Joining these technologies to our transportation system will save lives, save time, and save money.

 The future of ITS is promising. Yet, ITS itself is anything but futuristic. Already, real systems, products and services have been at work throughout the country. Still, the wide-scale development and deployment of these technologies represents a true revolution in the way we, as a nation, think about transportation. While many aspects of our lives have been made more pleasant and productive through the use of advanced technologies, we have somehow been content to endure a transportation system whose primary controlling technology is the four-way traffic signal—a technology that has changed little since it was first invented. It has taken transportation a long time to catch on, but now the industry is sprinting to catch up.

 Fulfilling the need for a national system that is both economically sound and environmentally efficient requires a new way of looking at and solving our transportation problems. The decades-old panacea of simply pouring more and more concrete neither solves our transportation problems, nor meets Congress' broad vision of an efficient transportation system.

 Traffic accidents and congestion take a heavy toll in lives, lost productivity, and wasted energy. ITS enables people and goods to move more safely and efficiently through a state-of-the-art, intermodal transportation system.

The revolutionary development of advanced systems demands an equally revolutionary plan for deployment. The use of ITS in Japan, Europe and Australia has been greatly accelerated through mutual cooperation of the public and private sectors. Similar cooperation is required in the United States. Yet, unlike the state-mandated cooperation found in many countries, the United States requires a voluntary commitment to cooperation that preserves the benefits of the free enterprise system while ensuring that the broad goals established by Congress are met. The model for this type of cooperation is the public/private partnership—a voluntary association of public and private interests committed to the successful development and deployment of ITS in the United States. It is the mandate of the Intelligent Transportation Society of America (ITS America) to coordinate that cooperative effort.

As mandated by Congress, ITS America is the only national public/private organization established to coordinate the development and deployment of ITS in the United States. People are talking about transportation. The public and their elected officials have begun to realize that transportation is one of the few elements of national infrastructure that is used by virtually every American, every day. Current transportation system is in need of improvement, and there is a rising concern over transportation-related problems.

The development and deployment of ITS have only increased the importance of the transportation issue. Until recently, surface transportation was largely the domain of construction companies and the large automobile manufacturers. The development of ITS, however, has turned the providers of advanced technologies, products and services into important players in the industry. The opportunities many of these non-traditional transportation companies have already realized will secure the continued contribution of both public-and private-sector investment in transportation and guarantee a steady flow of new developments to increase safety and efficiency.

ITS provides the intelligent link between travelers, vehicles and infrastructure. A projected \$209 billion has been invested in ITS over the past period of time—with 80% of that investment coming from the private sector in the form of consumer products and services. This is an enormous number, to be sure. Yet, when one examines the extensive range of technologies that fall under the ITS umbrella, it is possible to see how such a large investment is likely.

ITS technologies collect and transmit information on traffic conditions and transit schedules for travelers before and during their trips. Alerted to hazards and delays, travelers can change their plans to minimize inconvenience and additional strain on the system.

(1) Decrease congestion by reducing the number of traffic incidents, clearing them more quickly when they occur, rerouting traffic flow around them, and automatically collecting toll.

(2) Improve the productivity of commercial, transit and public safety fleets by using automated tracking, dispatch and mass-in-motion systems that speed vehicles through much of the red tape associated with interstate commerce.

(3) Assist drivers in reaching a desired destination with navigation systems enhanced with path finding, or route guidance.

These are just a few of the technologies being deployed. The complete list is lengthy and growing every day. The ITS industry in the United States is in the midst of a massive buildup.

Public agencies also stand to derive enormous benefits from the deployment of these technologies. For government agencies at all levels, the innovative application of advanced technologies means lower costs, enhanced services, and a healthier environment for the constituents these agencies serve.

New Words and Expressions

intelligent transportation systems (ITS)	智能交通运输系统
comprise [kəm'praɪz]	vt. 包含；由……组成
futuristic [fjuːtʃə'rɪstɪk]	adj. 未来的；未来派的，未来主义的
catch on	理解；明白
sprint [sprɪnt]	n. 冲刺；短跑 vi. 冲刺；全速短跑
panacea [ˌpænə'siːə]	n. 灵丹妙药；万能药
intermodal [ɪntə'məudl]	adj. 联合运输的
deployment [dɪ'plɔɪmənt]	n. 调度；部署
mutual ['mjuːtʃuəl]	adj. 共同的；相互的；彼此的
enterprise ['entəpraɪz]	n. 企业；事业；进取心；事业心
mandate ['mændeɪt]	n. 授权；命令；指令；委托管理；强制执行 vt. 授权；托管
domain [də'meɪn]	n. 领域；范围
manufacturer [ˌmænju'fæktʃərə(r)]	n. 制造商；[经]厂商
extensive [ɪk'stensɪv]	adj. 广泛的；大量的；广阔的
fleet [fliːt]	adj. 快速的；敏捷的 n. 舰队；港湾；小河 vi. 飞逝；疾驰；掠过
interstate [ɪntə'steɪt]	adj. 州际的；州与州之间的
diverse [daɪ'vɜːs]	adj. 不同的；相异的；多种多样的
productive [prə'dʌktɪv]	adj. 生产的；多产的
accelerate [æk'seləreɪt]	vt. 使……加快；使……增速 vi. 加速；促进；增加

Exercises

I True or false.

(　　)(1) The future of ITS is promising. Yet, ITS itself is nothing but futuristic.

(　　)(2) Traffic accidents and congestion take a heavy toll in lives, lost productivity, and wasted energy.

(　　)(3) The revolutionary development of advanced systems demands an equally revolutionary plan for deployment.

(　　)(4) A projected ＄209 billion will be invested in ITS from now to 2011 — with 85% of that investment coming from private sector.

(　　)(5) ITS technologies collect and transmit information on traffic conditions and transit schedules for travelers before and during their trips.

II Complete the following sentences.

(1) ITS includes a number of technologies, they are ＿＿＿＿, ＿＿＿＿, ＿＿＿＿ and ＿＿＿＿.

(2) The primary controlling technology of transportation system is ＿＿＿＿.

(3) A national system is both ＿＿＿＿ and ＿＿＿＿.

(4) ITS enables people and goods to move more safely and efficiently through ＿＿＿＿.

(5) As mandated by Congress, ITS America is ＿＿＿＿.

III Answer the following questions.

(1) What are the technologies that ITS is comprised of?

(2) How do advanced systems develop in the United States?

(3) What is the development direction of transportation system?

(4) Please list the application of ITS technology.

(5) Do public and government agencies support the development of ITS? Why?

Topics for Discussion

(1) What are the components of ITS?

(2) What is the development of ITS in different countries?

(3) What is the application prospect of ITS?

参 考 译 文

ITS——解决交通问题的新出路

ITS 包含多种多样的技术,这些技术为大部分交通问题提供了解决方案。ITS 由多项技术组成,包括信息处理、通信、控制和电子学。把这些技术与交通运输系统结合起来,将减少伤亡,节约资金,以及节省时间。

虽然 ITS 的未来充满希望,但 ITS 绝不是只在未来才投入使用。可以使用的系统、产品和服务已经在全美国范围内得到推广。这些技术的大规模发展和有效利用还说明美国对交通运输进行了真正的革命。当人们生活的许多方面已经通过使用高新技术变得更加舒适和高效时,却还要忍受这样一种交通运输系统:该系统最主要的控制技术是四路交通信号——一种自从其发明以后就没有什么改进的技术。交通运输已经在技术上停滞了很长时间,但是现在这个行业正在奋力追赶。

要实现一个既经济又环保的国家体系就需要一种新的方式来看待和解决美国的交通运输问题。过去几十年的"灵丹妙药"——浇筑越来越多的混凝土,这既不能解决交通运输问题,也不能达到国会提出的建立高效运输系统的要求。

交通事故和交通拥堵使人们在损失生命、降低生产率和浪费能源方面付出了沉重的代价。ITS通过一种联合运输系统的技术模式使人和物的移动更加安全、高效。

先进交通运输系统的革命性发展需要同样革命性的发展计划。在日本、欧洲和澳大利亚,ITS的应用通过政府部门和私人企业的相互合作得以加速发展。美国也需要类似的合作。然而,与许多国家建立的国家托管合作方式不一样的是,美国需要一个非官方的合作承诺,即在确保达到国会主要目标的同时,保护自由企业制度的利益。这种合作模式是公私伙伴关系——美国的一个代表公私双方利益并致力于发展ITS的自主联盟。美国智能交通协会的任务是协调这个合作成果。

受美国国会委托,美国ITS协会是在美国建立起来的协调发展和有效利用ITS技术的唯一公私合作机构。人们都在关注交通运输。公众及他们选出的官员们已经开始认识到交通运输实质上是国家每个人、每天都要使用的为数不多的基础设施要素之一。当前,需要改善交通运输系统,与交通运输有关的问题也越来越受到关注。

ITS的发展和有效利用恰好增加了交通运输问题的重要性。直到最近,地面交通在很大程度上还是属于工程建筑公司和大型汽车制造商的领域。然而,ITS的发展已经由先进技术、产品和服务的提供者转变为工业社会中的重要角色。许多新兴的运输公司已经意识到这种机遇将确保公、私两部门在交通运输上的投资能持续获利,并将保证有稳定的新发展,从而提升交通运输的安全和效率。

ITS在出行者、车辆和基础设施之间提供智能链接。在过去一段时间内,对ITS的投资已经达到2090亿美元。其中,80%是私人投资,投入消费者使用的产品和接受的服务上。的确,这是一笔巨大的数目。然而,当人们注意到ITS技术覆盖的广泛性时,就会明白这样一笔巨大的投入是值得的。

ITS技术为出行者在出行前和出行过程中采集和传送有关交通状况和公共交通时刻表信息,为出行者提醒危险和延误,使其能够调整计划,最大限度地减小不便,同时避免不必要的交通堵塞。

(1) 通过减少交通事故的数量来减少拥挤。当事故发生时,更快地将其处理好,为周围的车辆重新规划周边的交通流并自动收费。

(2) 通过使用自动跟踪、调度和自动称重系统提高商业、公共交通和公共安全部门的工作效率,可使车辆快速完成与州际商业相关的大量的复杂手续。

(3) 通过使用导航系统,加强路径选择和路线导航,帮助驾驶人到达预期的目的地。

这些仅仅是ITS技术有效应用的一小部分。ITS技术的全部清单是冗长的,而且每天都在增加。美国ITS产业正处于大规模的稳步发展中。

公众机构也认为从这些技术的有效应用中可以获得巨大的利益。对于所有的政府机构来说,先进技术的创新应用意味着较低的成本、优化的服务,以及给这些机构所服务的用户提供更优良的环境。

Reading Material

GIS and GPS in ITS

The growth of ITS has resulted in a significant improvement in road safety and monitoring, as it plays a key role in avoiding many transportation problems, such as road accidents and traffic congestion. ITS services include traffic management, electronic payment, route guidance, fleet management and emergency management vehicle services. These services are mainly supported by positioning and navigation capabilities, and most require real-time positioning data, which can be referred to as location-based ITS services.

Intelligent transportation systems vary in technologies applied, from basic management systems such as car navigation; traffic signal control systems; container management systems; variable message signs; automatic number plate recognition or speed cameras to monitor applications, such as security Closed-Circuit Television (CCTV) systems; and to more advanced applications that integrate live data and feedback from a number of other sources, such as parking guidance and information systems; weather information; bridge deicing (U.S. deicing) systems; and the like. Additionally, predictive techniques are being developed to allow advanced modelling and comparison with historical baseline data.

Two main components are found in any location-based ITS used in vehicle navigation systems and services, they are:

(1) A geometric positioning system, such as a Global Positioning System (GPS) or an integrated navigation system, such as Dead Reckoning (DR).

(2) A Geographic Information System (GIS) based on digital road maps.

Therefore, ITS services (e.g., route guidance) can affect the efficiency of the route guidance service and may confuse the driver depending primarily on the positioning data received from a positioning system (e.g., GPS). However, a stand-alone GPS cannot provide the high quality positioning data required by most ITS services. This is due to the various types of errors associated with the received positioning data such as signal outage, and errors due to atmospheric effects, receiver measurement errors, and multipath errors. Digital road maps are more reliablethan a stand-alone GPS, thus map matching algorithms can contribute to improving the accuracy of positioning data. This is because map matching algorithms consider different types of information including position, speed and direction in the matching process in order to identify the location of the vehicle on the road segment. However, map matching algorithms, may locate the vehicle on a wrong road segment due to the poor quality of input data which can lead to significant errors in ITS services. Therefore, it is important to check and monitor the quality of the positioning information obtained from the GPS sensor and other input data to the map matching algorithm in order to detect any misleading or faulty information and notify the user, thus increasing the integrity of the system. The integrity of a system refers to its ability to detect blunders in input data and faults in the map matching process.

At present, the developing GIS with GPS positioning as the main body will have great prospects. The combination of GPS and GIS system can establish the spatial information management and analysis system of comprehensive traffic planning, which not only greatly enhances the visualization and operability of traffic network processing, but also improves the efficiency of traffic planning. Traffic planning based on land use and travel attraction model still has its irreplaceable advantages, but its preparatory work is complex and costly, and its accuracy and uncertainty lead to unsatisfactory planning results. GPS system can observe and statistics traffic flow in full-time, all-weather, precise, timely and almost continuous way. This process is almost fully automated, and a lot of manpower is saved. The continuous and precise results are very important basic data for traffic planning. The combination of GPS monitoring data and GIS system can describe the traffic volume per hour on each road. If the traffic volume data of the road network for several consecutive days can be obtained, and the corresponding prediction models, such as the neural network model, can be used to predict the traffic flow and load of the road network for any hour of the next day. This short-term traffic prediction can help the management department to predict the traffic volume and load before the occurrence of traffic congestion and before the occurrence of traffic congestion. If accurate traffic flow data for several consecutive years can be obtained, long-term traffic flow forecasting can be made even if it is coordinated with urban land use planning and urban economic development.

Exercises

I True or false.

(　　)(1) The growth of intelligent transportation systems has resulted in a significant improvement in road safety and monitoring.

(　　)(2) ITS services are mainly supported by positioning and navigation capabilities, and all require real-time positioning data, which can be referred to as location-based ITS services.

(　　)(3) A stand-alone GPS can provide the high quality positioning data required by most ITS services.

(　　)(4) Intelligent transportation systems vary in technologies applied, from basic management systems to monitor applications, and to more advanced applications that integrate live data and feedback from a number of other sources.

(　　)(5) ITS services can affect the efficiency of the route guidance service and may confuse the driver depending primarily on the positioning data received from a positioning system.

II Complete the following sentences.

(1) ITS services include _____, electronic payment, _____, fleet management and emergency management vehicle services.

(2) Two main components are found in any location-based ITS used in vehicle navigation systems and services, they are _____ and _____.

(3) _____ are more reliable than a stand-alone GPS, thus map matching algorithms can

contribute to improving the accuracy of positioning data.

(4) Map matching algorithms, may locate the vehicle on a wrong road segment due to _____ which can lead to significant errors in ITS services.

(5) The integrity of a system refers to its ability to _____ in the map matching process.

Ⅲ Answer the following questions.

(1) What do ITS services include?

(2) What technologies are applied in ITS?

(3) What are the components of location-based ITS used in vehicle navigation systems and services?

(4) Can a stand-alone GPS provide the high quality positioning data required by most ITS services? Why?

(5) What does the integrity of a system refer to?

参 考 译 文

GIS 和 GPS 在 ITS 中的应用

ITS 的发展使道路安全和监控得到了显著改善,因为它在避免大部分交通问题(如道路交通事故和交通拥堵)方面发挥了重要作用。ITS 服务包括交通管理、电子支付、路线指导、车队管理和应急管理车辆。ITS 服务主要由定位和导航功能支持,并且大多数需要实时定位数据,也可以称为基于位置的 ITS 服务。

智能交通系统应用的技术各不相同,从汽车导航等基本管理系统、交通信号控制系统、集装箱管理系统、可变信息标志、自动车牌识别或速度摄像头到监控应用程序(如安全闭路电视系统),再到整合来自许多其他来源的实时数据和反馈,如停车引导和信息系统、天气信息、桥梁除冰(US 除冰)系统,等等。此外,正在开发预测技术,以便进行高级建模,并与历史基线数据进行比较。

基于位置的智能交通系统在车辆导航系统和服务中有两个主要组成部分:

(1) 几何定位系统,如全球定位系统(GPS)或综合导航系统,如航位推测(DR)。

(2) 基于数字路线图的地理信息系统(GIS)。

因此,ITS 服务(如路线引导)可能会影响路线导航服务的效率,并使主要使用定位系统(如 GPS)接收定位数据的驾驶人感到迷惑。但是,独立的 GPS 无法提供大多数 ITS 服务所需的高质量定位数据。这是由于接收的定位数据存在各种类型的误差,如信号中断,以及由于大气效应引起的误差、接收机的测量误差和多路径误差。数字道路地图比独立 GPS 更可靠,因此地图匹配算法有助于提高定位数据的准确性。这是因为地图匹配算法在匹配过程中考虑不同类型的信息,包括位置、速度和方向,以便识别车辆在路段上的位置。然而,由于输入数据质量差,地图匹配算法可能会将车辆定位在错误的路段上,从而导致其服务出现严重错误。因此,重要的是检查和监控从 GPS 传感器获取的定位信息和其他输入到地图匹配算法数据的质量,以检测任何存在误导性或错误的信息并通知用户,从而提高系统的完整性。系统的完整性是指能够检测出输入数据中的错误和地图匹配过程中的错误。

目前正在发展中的以 GPS 定位为主体的 GIS 大有前途。GPS 和 GIS 系统的结合,可以建立综合交通规划空间信息管理分析系统,这不仅极大地增强了交通网络处理的直观性和可操作性,而且提高了交通规划的工作效率。以土地利用和出行吸引模型为基础的交通规划目前仍有其不可替代的优点,但是其前期准备工作复杂且花费巨大。其在精度上的准确性和不确定性,导致了规划结果往往不尽如人意。GPS 系统可以全时、全天候、精密、适时、近乎连续不间断地对交通流进行观测与统计,这个过程几乎是完全自动化,省去了大量人力,得出的连续、精密的结果是交通规划极为重要的基础数据。GPS 监控数据与 GIS 系统的结合,可以给出每小时每条道路上的交通流量。如果能够取得连续若干天的路网流量数据,结合相应的预测模型,比如神经网络模型,就可以预测隔日任意小时的路网交通流和饱和度。这种短期交通预测有助于管理部门在交通拥挤发生前及时采取措施。如果能够获得连续数年的精确交通流资料,甚至可以配合城市的土地利用规划和城市经济发展,做长期的交通流预测。

Knowledge Link

Introduction to Map Matching

It is the basis of current vehicle navigation system to obtain vehicle trajectory in real-time by using vehicle GPS receiver and determine its position on the road of traffic vector map. To overcome GPS errors and map errors in independent vehicle-borne GPS navigation system, map matching algorithm is used to display the position of vehicles on the road network. That is to say, according to the data of GPS signals and the information of map road network, geometric method, probability statistics method, pattern recognition or artificial neural network technology are used to match the position of vehicles on the map road. Because most of the moving vehicles are on the road, the usual map algorithm has a default premise of vehicles on the road. The accuracy of map matching determines the accuracy, real-time and reliability of GPS vehicle navigation system. Specifically, it depends on two aspects: the accuracy of determining the current section of the vehicle is running and the accuracy of determining the location of the vehicle in the section. The former is the research focus of the existing algorithms, while the latter involves error correction along the road direction, which has not been effectively solved in the existing algorithms. The goal of map matching is to match the trajectory to the road. When the road is accurate, it becomes the accurate location of GPS. Then the vertical mapping method is used to complete the matching. To get the real-time road and location of the vehicle, map matching is a common and low-cost method. Generally speaking, the problem of map matching in vehicle navigation and positioning system is to match the position of GPS trajectory with errors obtained by vehicle GPS receivers to the corresponding position on the road of traffic vector map with errors.

Unit 22
Big Data in Traffic

Text

Big Data technology is attracting a great deal of attention, and many Research and Development (R&D) efforts related to it are under way around the world. These include R&D efforts on data warehouse products and large-scale distributed data processing platforms such as Hadoop, and those on data analytics technologies such as machine learning and data mining.

It is known that different types of cameras and sensors are the backbone of traffic monitoring today. How to collect data is no longer the topical issue of today. The question is how to store and handle increased amounts of data. Big Data technology gives the answer to this question. The term Big Data refers to an information resource that is characterized by large quantity, high-speed growth and a large variety of data that exceed capabilities of software that are commonly used for storage, processing and data management. It is the amount of data that can be measured inpetabytes(PB) and the speed of information inflow that is greater than the speed of processing.

1. Introduction

The term Big Data is often used when talking about the amount of data which exceed the commonly used software designed for storage, processing and data management. We could say that Big Data represents everything which does not fit into Microsoft Office Excel Workbook. An important feature of the data itself in the Big Data concept is the diversity of formats and data sources. The data generated by sensors and other intelligent devices in the field of transport contain all of these features.

2. Big Data in traffic-motivation

Observation of traffic includes the following activities: detecting the presence of vehicles, traffic counting, measuring length, categorization of the vehicles, and many more. In the current play of events, transportation industries cannot meet the rapid growth of data; also, the traditional data processing systems are facing the problem of inefficiency or even sometimes failure. As an important branch of economy, transportation and traffic confront the challenges and promises brought to us by Big Data. Currently, the most widely used data sources are traffic surveillance systems. Big Data systems are ideal for monitoring the behavior of the system, collecting and analyzing defects. These systems offer previously unimaginable possibilities for monitoring operation of the system in detail. The advantages of Big Data concepts are improving the safety of traffic and the efficiency of transportation industry in general. Traffic sensors for data collection are inductive-loop detectors, video image processing systems, pneumatic tubes, GPS, acoustic/ultrasonic sensors, aerial/satellite imaging, and RFID (Radio Frequency Identification) technology. They can be classified in many ways. The highly developed detection technologies can be classified into three categories: in-roadway detectors, over-roadway detectors and off-roadway technologies. Each of these sensors has their advantages that provide the real-time information for road users and transportation system operators to make better decisions. ITS use Big Data with the aim to increase energy efficiency, improve traffic safety, reduce air pollution, relieve traffic congestion, and improve homeland security. Every day, companies are investing more and more into this area. A railway operator invested in an automated system that uses Big Data to manage the rescheduling of more than 8000 trains. Likewise, the drivers in Boston can use an App known as "Street Bump" to detect the unmistakable jolt of a pothole. It captures bump data using GPS location. This data can be used to identify roads in greatest need of repair. Another purpose of using Big Data analytics is that transportation planners can allocate limited resources in the areas where they can boost the capacity of congested transportation networks. Obviously, there is a need to build an open platform allowing many departments of traffic, companies and individuals to collaborate and share the same data.

3. Big Data technology

The term Big Data was created in 2008. The very name "Big Data" clearly indicates that it is about a large amount of data. But how do we know whether, for example, a 10TB relational database is Big Data? The Big Data dimensions such as volume, variety and velocity, which were firstly defined by IBM, provide an answer to this question.

Volume—a high speed of growth of the amount of new data and keeping of the existing data leads to hundreds of terabytes(TB) of storage, and even much larger amounts of data. Variety—it is no longer enough to keep only the structured data, but also images, information from social networks, logs, sensor information, and so on. Velocity—the speed of the new incoming data is big and it is therefore higher than the speed of data processing. If some of the data we manage have these characteristics, then we could say that the system has/is Big Data.

4. A Big Data solution in traffic

We have recognized the sensory data, which is widely used in traffic, as a category of data that makes sense to cultivate using the Big Data technologies. The main indicator of the load of a certain section of the road is the Annual Average Daily Traffic (AADT). For sections where there are automatic traffic counters, AADT is calculated on the basis on data generated by the traffic counters on that particular section, throughout the year.

New Words and Expressions

Big Data	大数据
sensor [ˈsensə(r)]	n. 传感器
backbone [ˈbækbəun]	n. 脊柱；支柱；(计算机)主干网
characterize [ˈkærəktəraɪz]	vt. 描绘……的特性；具有……的特征 vi. 塑造人物
petabyte [ˈpetəbaɪt]	n. 千万亿字节或千T字节
device [dɪˈvaɪs]	n. 装置；策略；方法；手段；设备；终端
confront [kənˈfrʌnt]	vt. 面对；遭遇；碰到；比较
pneumatic [njuːˈmætɪk]	adj. 气动的；充气的；有气胎的 n. 气胎
acoustic [əˈkuːstɪk]	adj. 声学的；音响的；听觉的
ultrasonic [ʌltrəˈsɒnɪk]	adj. [声]超声的；超音速的；超音波的 n. 超声波
satellite [ˈsætəlaɪt]	n. 卫星；人造卫星
pothole [ˈpɒthəul]	n. 壶穴 vi. 探索洞穴
bump [bʌmp]	n. 肿块；撞击；隆起物 vt. & vi. 碰撞；冲撞颠簸 adv. 突然地；猛烈地
collaborate [kəˈlæbəreɪt]	vi. 合作；协作
velocity [vəˈlɒsəti]	n. [物]速度
indicator [ˈɪndɪkeɪtə]	n. 指标；迹象；指示器；[计]指示符
distribute [dɪˈstrɪbjuːt]	vt. 分配；散布；分开；把……分类
exceed [ɪkˈsiːd]	vt. 超过；胜过
format [ˈfɔːmæt]	n. 格式；版式 vt. 使格式化；规定……的格式 vi. 设计版式
surveillance [səˈveɪləns]	n. 监督；[法]监视
jolt [dʒəult]	vt. (使)颠簸；(使)震惊；(使)摇动 vi. 摇晃；颠簸而行 n. 颠簸；摇晃；震惊；严重挫折

Exercises

I True or false.

(   )(1) How to collect data is the topical issue of today.

(　　)(2) The term Big Data is often used when talking about the amount of data which exceed the commonly used software designed for storage, processing and data management.

(　　)(3) In the current play of events, transportation industries can meet the rapid growth of data.

(　　)(4) Transportation and traffic is an important branch of economy.

(　　)(5) There is no need to build an open platform allowing many departments of traffic, companies and individuals to collaborate and share the same data.

Ⅱ Complete the following sentences.

(1) The term Big Data refers to _____ that is characterized by large quantity, high-speed growth and a large variety of data that exceed capabilities of software that are commonly used for storage, processing and data management.

(2) An important feature of the data itself in the Big Data concept is _____.

(3) Observation of traffic includes the following activities: _____, traffic counting, measuring length, _____, and many more.

(4) Currently, the most widely used data sources are _____.

(5) RFID is the abbreviation of _____.

Ⅲ Answer the following questions.

(1) What are the traffic sensors used for data collection?

(2) What is definition of Big Data?

(3) What does observation of traffic include?

(4) How about the development of Big Data?

(5) What are the categories of highly developed detection technologies?

Topics for Discussion

(1) What is the purpose of using Big Data in ITS?

(2) How to define Big Data in traffic?

(3) How about the application of Big Data technology in traffic?

参 考 译 文

交通大数据

大数据技术正引起人们的广泛关注,世界各地都在进行着与之相关的大量研究与开发。其中包括数据储存产品和大型分布式数据处理平台(如 Hadoop),以及机器学习和数据挖掘等数据分析技术的研发工作。

众所周知,不同种类的摄像机和传感器是目前交通监控的基础。当今的热门话题已不是如何收集数据,而是如何存储和处理新增的大量数据。大数据技术给出了这个问题的答案。

大数据是指数据量大、增长速度快、数据种类多、超出常用软件的存储、处理和数据管理能力的信息资源。它是以千兆字节为单位的数据，其信息的流入速度远大于处理速度。

1. 介绍

大数据一词常用于数据量超过常用的存储、处理和数据管理软件的数据。我们可以说，大数据代表了所有不适合使用 Microsoft Office Excel 工作簿处理的数据。在大数据概念中，数据本身的一个重要特征是格式和数据源的多样性。交通领域的传感器和其他智能设备产生的数据包含所有这些特征。

2. 交通检测中的大数据

交通检测包括以下活动：车辆检测、交通计数、长度测量、车辆分类等。在当前情况下，交通运输业无法适应数据的快速增长，传统的数据处理系统也面临效率低下问题，甚至有时会出现故障问题。作为经济领域的一个重要分支，交通运输业面临大数据带来的挑战和希望。目前，最广泛使用的数据源是交通监测系统。大数据系统是监控系统行为、收集和分析缺陷的理想系统。这类系统使以前无法想象的详细监控系统运行成为可能。大数据概念的优势在于提升交通安全性和提高交通运输业的总体效率。用于数据采集的交通传感器包括感应线圈探测器、视频图像处理系统、气动导管、GPS、声学/超声波传感器、航空/卫星成像和 RFID（射频识别技术），可以用多种方式对它们进行分类。高度发展的检测技术可分为三类：路内检测技术、路面检测技术和路外检测技术。这些传感器都有各自的优点，可以为道路使用者和交通系统运营者提供实时信息，从而使他们能够做出更好的决策。ITS 使用大数据的目的是提高能源使用效率，提升交通安全，减少空气污染，缓解交通拥堵，提高国土安全。每天，许多公司都在向这个领域投入越来越多的资金。一家铁路运营商投资了一个自动化系统，该系统使用大数据来管理 8000 多辆列车的调度。同样，波士顿的驾驶人也使用一个叫作"道路颠簸"的应用程序来检测不平坦道路引起的颠簸，它使用 GPS 定位来获取颠簸数据，可用于识别最需要维修的道路。使用大数据分析的另一个目的是，交通规划者可以对有限的资源进行分配来提高拥挤地区的交通网络通行能力。显然，有必要构建一个开放的平台，使交通部门、企业和个人能够协作并共享数据。

3. 大数据技术

"大数据"一词被创建于 2008 年。"大数据"这个名称清楚地表明它的数据量特别大。但是举一个例子，我们如何判断一个 10TB 的相关数据库是否是大数据？IBM 首先定义了大数据的维度（如容量、多样性和速度），为这个问题提供了答案。

容量——新数据数量的高速增长和现有数据的保留导致数百兆字节的存储量，甚至出现更大的数据量。多样性——它不再满足于只保留结构化数据，还可以保存图像、社交网络的信息、日志、传感器信息等。速度——新数据输入的速度很大，并且会高于数据处理的速度。如果我们管理的一些数据具有这些特性，那么可以说这个系统有（是）大数据。

4. 交通中大数据的解决方案

我们已经认识到，在交通中广泛使用的感官数据应用了大数据技术，获取这类数据是很有意义的。某一路段荷载的主要指标是年平均日交通量（AADT）。对于有自动交通计数器的路段，AADT 是根据特定路段的交通计数器生成的全年数据计算的。

Reading Material

Application of Big Data

1. Introduction

While Big Data is seen as an emerging technology to both practitioners, researchers, academia, Federal and State agencies, industry, and other organizations. Discovering novel ways to manage and analyzing data to create value would increase the accuracy of predictions, improve the security of transportation infrastructure and enable informed decision-making.

Concepts and technologies related to transportation and traffic engineering covered various transportation applications from travel demand estimation to real-time traffic operations and safety monitoring. Broadly speaking, application can be categorized into three groups: transportation planning, traffic operations, safety.

The first category utilize mobile phone's call detail records, smart card systems, automatic passenger count systems, GPS, smart phone and vehicle location services, bike-sharing and social media data, and present Big Data applications, such as travel demand estimation, transit origi-destination estimation, daily travel pattern analysis, non-work destination choice, transit travel experience, origin-destination estimation by trip purpose and time of day, willingness to travel by activity types, and traffic zoning.

With respect to the second category dealing with traffic operations, researchers exploit Big Data sources from GPS, Bluetooth reader, loop detector, private sector travel time and floating cars for traffic flow prediction, travel time prediction, addressing GPS data requirements, and route travel time distribution.

Finally, the third category dealing with safety use Big Data sources come from video, microwave vehicle detection system, GPS and vehicle trajectory data. This group includes applications on proactive road safety analysis, traffic operation and safety monitoring, calibration of traffic simulation model for safety assessment, and instantaneous driving decisions modeling.

2. Application in transportation planning

The accelerating growth of cities has made the estimation of travel demand and the performance of transportation infrastructure a critical task for transportation and urban planners. To meet these challenges in the past, methods such as the widely used four-step model were developed to make use of available data computational resources. While the surveys that provide the empirical foundation for these models offer a combination of highly detailed travel logs for carefully selected representative population samples, they are expensive to administer and participate in. As a result, the time between surveys range from 5 to 10 years in even the most developed cities. The rise of ubiquitous mobile computing has led to a dramatic increase in new Big Data resources that capture the movement of vehicles and people in near real-time and promise solutions to some of these deficiencies. With these new opportunities, however, come new challenges of estimation, integration and validation with existing models. While these data are available nearly instantaneously and provide large, long running, samples at low cost, they often lack important contextual demographic information due to privacy reasons, lack resolution to infer choices of mode, and have their own noise and biases that must be accounted for. Despite these issues, their use for urban and transportation planning has the potential to radically decrease the time in-between updated surveys, increase survey coverage, and reduce data acquisition costs. In order to realize these benefits, a number of challenges must be overcome to integrate new data sources into traditional modeling and estimation tools.

3. Application in traffic operation

Actionable information is the lifeblood of effective transportation management. Traffic data can be used to estimate current traffic conditions so that travelers and agencies can make better decisions about how to use and manage the transportation network. As the challenges of traffic and congestion increase, particularly in urban areas and freight-heavy intercity corridors, real-time traffic information becomes steadily more important.

Currently, transportation agencies capture traffic data primarily from fixed sensors, such as loop detectors, that are relatively expensive to install and maintain. However with the recent growth of communication technologies, GPS and the mobile internet, an increasing amount of real-time location information is collected and distributed by private companies and even marketed for retail to public agencies such as state Departments of Transportation (DOT).

This body of data offers transportation agencies a potential opportunity to improve operation, but it also presents unique challenges such as a scarcity of precedent for its procurement and use, and loss of direct quality control. Further, the data collected from GPS devices is limited to position information (from which velocities can be computed), while typical system control strategies, such as ramp metering, normally require density or occupancy data. Thus, more work is needed to establish results for traffic management and operation.

4. Application in safety

Effective strategies to improve traffic operation and safety simultaneously require profound understanding about their features and relationships. In the age of information, these objectives could be efficiently realized through Big Data application. Traffic congestion can be viewed as a product of the interaction between demand and capacity. Periodic high demand at specific bottlenecks during peak hours can result in recurrent congestion while incidents reducing roadway capacity temporarily lead to non-recurrent congestion. To catch this dynamic process, Big Data generated from the ITS detection system could be leveraged to develop congestion measurement in real-time. In the meantime, crash occurrence is often regarded as random events affected by human behavior, roadway design, traffic flow and weather conditions. Big Data applications also introduce new perspectives in safety analysis. Thanks to the advantages brought by Big Data, researchers are able to restore the traffic conditions for each crash case and draw general conclusions using individual crash data. As a result, Big Data applications in the current work will focus on developing congestion measurement and uncovering the relationship between safety and congestion, both in real-time.

Exercises

I True or false.

(　　)(1) Concepts and technologies related to transportation and traffic engineering covered various transportation applications which can be categorized into transportation planning, traffic operations and safety.

(　　)(2) As the challenges of traffic and congestion increase, particularly in rural areas and freight-heavy intercity corridors, real-time traffic information becomes steadily more important.

(　　)(3) A number of challenges must be overcome to integrate new data sources into traditional modeling and estimation tools.

(　　)(4) Crash occurrence is regarded as certain events affected by human behavior, roadway design, traffic flow and weather conditions.

(　　)(5) Thanks to the advantages brought by Big Data, researchers are able to restore the traffic conditions for each crash case and draw general conclusions using individual crash data.

II Complete the following sentences.

(1) The accelerating growth of cities has made the estimation of ＿＿＿＿ a critical task for transportation and urban planners.

(2) Traffic data can be used to ＿＿＿＿ so that travelers and agencies can make better decisions about how to use and manage the transportation network.

(3) Currently, transportation agencies capture traffic data primarily from fixed sensors, such as ＿＿＿＿, that are relatively expensive to install and maintain.

(4) Traffic congestion can be viewed as a product of the interaction ＿＿＿＿.

(5) Big Data applications in the current work will focus on developing congestion measurement and uncovering ＿＿＿＿, both in real-time.

III Answer the following questions.

(1) What are Big Data applications?

(2) What are the advantages of Big Data resources in transportation planning?

(3) How does Big Data apply in transportation planning?

(4) How does Big Data apply in traffic operations?

(5) How does Big Data apply in safety?

参 考 译 文

大数据的应用

1. 引言

对于(美国)从业者、研究人员、学术界、联邦和州机构、其他行业和组织成员来说,大数据被视为一种新兴技术。研发新的方法来管理和分析数据以创造价值,将提高预测的准确性,改善运输基础设施的管理和安全性,并实现合理的决策。

与运输和交通工程相关的概念和技术涵盖了各种交通应用方面,从交通需求预测到实时交通运行和安全监控。从广义上讲,应用可分为三类:交通规划,交通运行,交通安全。

第一类应用是利用移动电话的详细通话记录、智能卡系统、自动乘客计数系统、GPS、智能手机和车辆定位服务、自行车共享和社交媒体数据,以及大数据应用,如出行需求预测、公交出发地和目的地预测、每日出行方式分析、休息日目的地选择、公交出行体验、出发地和目的地预测(根据出行目的和出行时间)、出行意愿(按活动类型分类)和交通分区。

第二类应用涉及交通运行的问题,研究人员利用来自 GPS、蓝牙读卡器、线圈检测器、私营部门出行时间和浮动车的大数据进行交通流预测、出行时间预测,解决 GPS 数据需求和得到路线出行时间分配等问题。

最后,第三类应用是用大数据处理安全问题,即应用来自视频、微波车辆检测系统、GPS 和车辆轨迹数据处理安全问题。这类数据的应用包括前瞻性道路安全分析、交通运行和安全监控、用于安全评估的交通仿真模型校准和即时驾驶决策建模。

2. 在交通规划中的应用

城市的快速发展使得对交通需求和交通基础设施性能的评估成为交通规划者和城市规划者的一项重要任务。利用现有计算数据资源,人们开发了被广泛使用的四阶段法等方法,以应对过去的这些挑战。虽然调查为模型提供了经验基础,并提出一种组合,该组合包含精心挑选的代表性人口样本高度详细的出行日志,但它们在管理和参与上费用很高。因此,即使是最发达的城市,调查的时间间隔也是从 5 年到 10 年不等。无处不在的动态计算兴起导致新的大数据资源的急剧增加。这些新的大数据资源几乎都能够实时地捕捉车辆和人员的移动,并能够克服其中的一些缺陷。然而,这些新的数据资源对现有模型的评估、集成和验证带来了新的挑战。虽然这些数据几乎是即时可用的,并且能够以低成本提供大量、长期运行的数据样本,但由于隐私的原因,它们往往缺乏重要的背景人口统计信息,缺乏推断方式选择的方法,并且数据本身具有缺陷和偏差。虽然存在这些问题,但它们在城市规划和交通规划中的应用有可能从根本上减少调查数据更新的时间间隔,增加调查覆盖率,并降低数据采集成本。为了实现这些有利结果,必须克服诸多挑战,将新的数据源集成到传统的建模和评估工具中。

3. 在交通运行中的应用

可操作信息是交通管理有效实施的生命线。交通数据可用于预测当前的交通状况,以便出行者和机构能够更好地决定如何使用和管理交通网络。随着交通拥堵情况的不断增强,城市地区和货运量大的城际走廊的实时交通信息变得越来越重要。

目前,交通运输机构主要从固定传感器(如线圈检测器)获取交通数据,这些传感器的安装和维护成本相对较高。然而,随着通信技术、GPS 和移动互联网的发展,越来越多的实时定位信息由私营公司收集和分发,甚至向国家交通运输部等公共机构进行出售。

这一数据体为运输机构提供了改进运营的潜在机会,但也带来了独特的挑战,如在采购和使用上先例不足,以及缺乏对数据质量的直接控制。此外,从 GPS 设备收集的数据仅限于位置信息(可用于计算速度),而典型的系统控制策略(如匝道测量),通常需要特定位置的密度或路面占用数据。因此,在交通管理和运营方面,还需要更多的工作来得到研究成果。

4. 在交通安全中的应用

同时改善交通运行和安全的有效策略需要深入了解其特点和关系。在信息时代,可以通过大数据应用程序有效实现这些目标。交通拥堵可以看作是交通需求和通行能力相互作用的产物。高峰时段,在特定瓶颈处周期性的高需求可能会导致经常性交通拥堵,同时,交通事故将降低道路通行能力,导致偶发性交通拥堵。为了捕捉这一动态过程,可以利用 ITS 检测系统生成的大数据进行实时拥堵评估。同时,事故的发生往往被认为是随机事件,其受人的行为、道路设计、交通流和天气条件的影响。大数据应用还引入安全分析这一新视角。由于大数据所带来的优势,研究人员能够恢复每个事故案例的交通状况,并利用单个事故数据得出初步结论。因此,当前工作中的大数据应用将重点放在拥堵评估的开发上,并同时揭示安全与拥堵之间的关系。

Knowledge Link

Radio Frequency Identification Technology

Radio Frequency Identification (RFID) technology is a communication technology, commonly known as electronic tags. Specific targets can be identified by radio signals and related data can be read and written without the need to establish mechanical or optical contact between the recognition system and specific targets. Radio frequency, usually microwave, $1 \sim 100 GHz$, is suitable for short-range identification communication.

Conceptually, RFID is similar to barcode scanning. For barcode technology, it attaches coded barcodes to the targets and uses special scanning reader to transmit information from barcode magnetism to scanning reader by optical signals. For RFID, it uses special RFID reader and special RFID tags which can be attached to the targets, and uses frequency signals to transfer information from the RFID tags. Transfer to the RFID reader. In terms of structure, RFID is a simple wireless system with only two basic components. The system is used to control, detect and track objects. The system consists of an interrogator (platform) and many transponders.

In recent years, because of the rapid development of radio frequency technology, transponder has a new meaning, also known as smart tag or tag. The reader of the RFID tag communicates with the RFID tag through the antenna. It can read or write the tag identification codes and memory data. RFID technology can identify high-speed moving objects and multiple tags at the same time, which is fast and convenient to operate. In the future, the rapid development of RFID technology is of great significance to the progress of the Internet of things.

Unit 23

Internet of Vehicles

Text

1. Concept of IoV

The Internet of Vehicles (IoV) is an integration of three networks: an inter-vehicle network, an intra-vehicle network and vehicular mobile Internet. Based on this concept of three networks integrated into one, we define an Internet of Vehicles as a large-scale distributed system for wireless communication and information exchange between vehicle, road, human and Internet according to agreed communication protocols and data interaction standards (examples include the IEEE 802.11p WAVE standard, and potentially cellular technologies). It is an integrated network for supporting intelligent traffic management, intelligent dynamic information service and intelligent vehicle control, representing a typical application of Internet of Things (IoT) technology in ITS.

2. IoV technology leads industrial revolution

The convergence of technology encompasses information communication, environmental protection, energy conservation and safety. To succeed in this emerging market, acquisition of core technologies and standards will becrucial to securing a strategic advantage. However, the integration of the IoV with other infrastructures should be as important as the building of the IoV technologies themselves. As a consequence of this, the IoV will become an integral part of IoT infrastructure by its completion. Here, it must be emphasized as primary, that collaboration and interconnection between the transportation sector and other sectors (such as energy, health-care, environment, manufacturing and agriculture, etc.) will be the next step in IoV development.

As human ability and experience evolve, future vehicles will have to be able to address a growing list of pertinent issues which affect an automotive society including road safety, energy consumption, environmental pollution, and traffic congestion. IoV technology is designed to address and solve many of these issues through promoting a goal of 'minimum accidents, low energy consumption, low emissions, and high-efficiency' through the development of automobiles and the transportation system. IoV technology will facilitate the concordant unification of humans, vehicles, roads and the environment. By promoting the integration of the IoV technologies with vehicles through manufacturing and industry, great contributions to economic growth and improving the global infrastructure will be made.

IoV technology is a driving force that will make major transformations to the automotive industry thanks to its role in expanding human ability, experience, safety, energy, environment, and efficiency issues inherent in living in an automotive society. There is a huge gap between the automotive and Information Technology(IT) industries in terms of culture, institutions and product development processes. The IoV technology in automobile factories is relatively under developed, far from the speed and experience requirements of innovative applications. However, the IT industry updates too quickly and is too open to ensure the reliability and safety when relevant products are used in vehicles. The collision and fusion of automobile industry and IT industry is an inevitable trend of IoV and even the whole automobile industry.

3. Opportunities and challenges of IoV

The research and development, as well as the industrial application of IoV technologies will promote the integration of automotive and information technology. The integrated information services of vehicle, vehicle safety and economic performance will contribute to a more intelligent urban transportation system and advance social and economic development. The IoV will have far reaching influence on the consumer vehicle market, consumer lifestyle, and even modes of behavior. The future IoV market will see rapid growth in the Asian-Pacific region. McKinsey Global Institute has reported by June 2013 that the IoT has the potential to launch around \$6.2 trillion in new global economic value annually by 2025. 80 to 100 percent of all manufacturers will apply IoT technology by then, leading to potential economic impact of \$2.3 trillion for the global manufacturing industry. According to the data on APEC website, the member countries share approximate 55 percent of world GDP. In other words, APEC members will be growing by \$3.41 trillion in GDP and manufacturers of the economies will embrace \$1.27 trillion growth in the meanwhile.

The application of IoV technology in providing information services, improving traffic efficiency, enhancing traffic safety, implementing supervision and control and other aspects will make millions of people enjoy more comfortable, convenient and safe traffic services. Large concentrations of vehicles, e.g., in city parking facilities during business hours, can also provide the ad-hoc computational resources which will be of interest to those in the IT fields. Complementary efforts should be made for developing and enhancing middle-ware platforms which will enable analytic and semantic processing of data coming from vehicles.

Lack of coordination and communication is the biggest challenge to IoV implementation. Lack of standards makes effective vehicle to vehicle (V2V) communication and connection difficult and prohibits ease in scaling. Only by adopting open standards can the current, closed and one-way systems, be integrated into an effective system for the smooth sharing of information. Dreams of intelligent transportation and even automatic drive systems can come true through an effective IoV. Both technological innovation and business model innovation in the Internet era depend on partnering across traditional boundaries. While maintaining a plan for improving products, services and experiences, we should make joint efforts to break barriers, stay open and inclusive, and to build a healthy and sustainable ecosystem. Therefore, the whole industrial chain can achieve joint development. One of the possible projects could be creating a trusted environment for cross-border document circulation. We see opportunities for cooperation in this area. Legally significant trust services could become one of the IoV services.

New Words and Expressions

Internet of Vehicles (IoV)	车联网
Internet of Things (IoT)	物联网
integration [ˌɪntɪˈgreɪʃn]	n. 结合;整合;一体化;混合;融合
convergence [kənˈvɜːdʒəns]	n. 趋同;融合
encompass [ɪnˈkʌmpəs]	vt. 包含;包括;涉及;包围;围绕
completion [kəmˈpliːʃn]	n. 完成;结束;完成交易;完成交割
collaboration [kəˌlæbəˈreɪʃn]	n. 合作;协作;合作成果(或作品)
crucial [ˈkruːʃl]	adj. 关键性的;至关重要的
automotive [ˌɔːtəˈməutɪv]	adj. 汽车的;机动车辆的
supervision [ˌsjuːpəˈvɪʒn]	n. 监督;监管
computational [ˌkɒmpjuˈteɪʃənl]	adj. 使用计算机的;计算的
semantic [sɪˈmæntɪk]	adj. 语义的
coordination [kəuˌɔːdɪˈneɪʃn]	n. 协作;和协调
protocol [ˈprəutəkɒl]	n. [计]协议;规程
integrated [ˈɪntɪgreɪtɪd]	adj. 集成的;综合的
ecosystem [ˈiːkəusɪstəm]	n. [生]生态系统
pertinent [ˈpɜːtɪnənt]	adj. 相关的;相干的
wireless [ˈwaɪələs]	adj. 无线的;无线电的 n. 无线电
dynamic [daɪˈnæmɪk]	adj. 动态的;动力的;动力学的
emerging market	新兴市场
acquisition [ˌækwɪˈzɪʃn]	n. 获得物;获得;收购
strategic [strəˈtiːdʒɪk]	adj. 战略上的;战略的
cellular [seljələ(r)]	adj. 细胞的

evolve [ɪˈvɒlv]　　　　　　　　　　　vt. 发展;进化;使逐步形成;推断出
　　　　　　　　　　　　　　　　　　vi. 发展;进展;进化;逐步形成
emission [ɪˈmɪʃn]　　　　　　　　　　n. (光、热、气等的)发出,射出,排放;发行;排放物;散发物
ad-hoc　　　　　　　　　　　　　　专门
complementary [ˌkɒmplɪˈmentrɪ]　　 adj. 互补的;补充的;补足的
inclusive [ɪnˈkluːsɪv]　　　　　　　 adj. 包含的,包括的;包含全部费用的;范围广泛的　adv. 包括一切费用在内地
cross-border [ˈkrɒsbɔːdə]　　　　　 adj. 跨国的;跨越边界的
integral [ˈɪntɪɡrəl]　　　　　　　　 adj. 积分的;完整的;整体的　n. 积分,部分,完整
trillion [ˈtrɪljən]　　　　　　　　　 n. [数]万亿　adj. 万亿的
embrace [ɪmˈbreɪs]　　　　　　　　 vt. & vi. 拥抱　vt. 包括,包含
prohibit [prəˈhɪbɪt]　　　　　　　　 vt. 阻止,禁止;防止;不准许
barrier [ˈbærɪə(r)]　　　　　　　　 n. 障碍;屏障;分界线
sustainable [səˈsteɪnəbl]　　　　　　adj. 可持续的

Exercises

I True or false.

(　　)(1) Compared with the IoV technologies, the integration of the IoV with other infrastructures are less important.

(　　)(2) The IT industry updates too quickly and is too open to ensure the reliability and safety when relevant products are used in vehicles.

(　　)(3) The collision and fusion of automobile industry and IT industry is an inevitable trend of IoV and even the whole automobile industry.

(　　)(4) Lack of standards is the biggest challenge to IoV implementation.

(　　)(5) None of the possible projects could be creating a trusted environment for cross-border document circulation.

II Complete the following sentences.

(1) IoV technology will _____ the concordant unification of humans, vehicles, roads and the environment.

(2) The IoV will have far reaching influence on the consumer vehicle market, _____, and even modes of behavior.

(3) There is a huge gap between the automotive and Information Technology industries _____ culture, institutions and product development processes.

(4) The research and development, as well as the industrial application of IoV technologies will _____ the integration of automotive and information technology.

(5) _____ makes effective vehicle to vehicle (V2V) communication and connection difficult and prohibits ease in scaling.

Ⅲ Answer the following questions.

(1) What does the IoV consist of?
(2) What is the definition of IoV?
(3) How to succeed in emerging market of IoV?
(4) What is the biggest challenge to IoV implementation?
(5) What do technological innovation and business model innovation in the Internet era depend on?

Topics for Discussion

(1) What can IoV technology be applied to?
(2) How to promote the integration of automotive and information technology?
(3) What are the applications of internet of vehicles in your life?

参 考 译 文

车 联 网

1. IoV 的概念

车联网(IoV)是三个网络的集成,即车间网络、车内网络和车辆移动网络。基于将这三个网络整合为一个网络的概念,我们将车联网定义为一个大型分布式系统,用于根据确定的通信协议和数据交互标准(协议包括 IEEE 802.11p Wave 标准和潜在的蜂窝技术)在车辆、道路、人和互联网之间进行无线通信和信息交换。它是一个支持智能交通管理、智能动态信息服务和智能车辆控制的综合网络,是物联网技术在 ITS 中的普遍应用。

2. IoV 技术引领产业革命

技术融合包括信息交流、环境保护、节能和安全。要在这个新兴市场取得成功,获得核心技术和标准将是确保战略优势的关键。然而,IoV 与其他基础设施的集成应该和 IoV 技术本身的构建一样重要。因此,IoV 将成为 IoT 基础设施的一个组成部分。在这里必须强调的是,运输部门与其他部门(如能源、卫生保健、环境、制造业和农业等)之间的合作与互联将是 IoV 发展的下一目标。

随着人类个人能力和经验的进步,未来的汽车必须能够解决一系列影响汽车行业的相关问题,包括道路安全、能源消耗、环境污染和交通拥堵。IoV 技术旨在通过汽车和运输系统的发展达到"少事故、低能耗、低排放和高效率"的目标,从而解决上述问题。IoV 技术将促进人、车、路、环境的和谐统一。通过制造业和工业促进 IoV 技术与汽车的融合,将为经济的增长和全球基础设施的改善作出巨大贡献。

IoV 技术是推动汽车行业发生重大变革的动力,因为它在提升人类个人能力和经验、提高道路安全、降低能源损耗、改善环境和提高汽车行业固有效率问题方面发挥着作用。汽车和信息技术产业在文化、制度和产品开发过程方面存在巨大的差距。汽车行业的 IoV 技术相对欠发达,远远没有达到创新应用发展的速度和经验要求。然而,IT 行业更新太快、太开放,从而无法确保相关产品在车辆上使用时的可靠性和安全性。汽车行业与信息技术行业的碰撞与融合是 IoV 乃至整个汽车行业发展的必然趋势。

3. IoV 的机遇和挑战

IoV 技术的研究与开发以及行业应用将促进汽车与信息技术的融合。车辆、车辆安全、经济效益的综合信息服务，将有助于城市交通系统的智能化，促进社会经济的发展。IoV 将对汽车消费市场、消费者生活方式甚至行为模式产生深远的影响。未来的 IoV 市场将在亚太地区快速增长。麦肯锡全球研究所在 2013 年 6 月发布报告称，到 2025 年，IoT 有望每年产生约 6.2 万亿美元的全球新增经济价值。到那时，80%～100% 的制造商将采用物联网技术，这将为全球制造业带来 2.3 万亿美元的潜在经济影响。根据亚太经合组织网站上的数据，亚太经合组织成员国的 GDP 约占世界的 55%。换言之，成员国的国内生产总值将增长 3.41 万亿美元，同时，各经济体的制造商将实现 1.27 万亿美元的经济增长。

IoV 技术在提供信息服务、提高交通效率、提高交通安全、实施监控等方面的应用，将使数百万人享受到更加舒适、便捷、安全的交通服务。例如在城市停车设施在营业时间内会有大量车辆集中在里面，可以将此提供给感兴趣的 IT 领域人员作为特定计算资源。它们应为开发和优化中间软件平台作出相应的努力，以便对来自车辆的数据进行分析和语义处理。

缺乏协调和沟通是阻碍 IoV 实施的最大问题。由于缺乏标准，车与车之间的有效通信和连接变得困难，并且不易扩展。只有采用开放标准，才能将现有的、封闭的、单向的系统集成到一个高效平稳的信息共享系统中。智能交通，甚至自动驾驶系统的愿望都可以通过高效的 IoV 实现。互联网时代的技术创新和商业模式创新都依赖跨越传统行业边界的合作。在不断提升产品、服务质量和体验的同时，我们应该共同努力冲破障碍，保持开放和包容的态度，建设一个健康和可持续的生态系统。因此，为了整个产业链可以实现共同发展，其中一个可行的项目是为跨境文件的流通创造一个可信任的环境。法律上重要的信托服务也可能成为 IoV 服务之一，这将会是一个 IoV 与信托领域合作的机会。

Reading Material

The IoV Technology

Technology has drastically transformed our lives by bringing in huge benefits that reflects the beginning of our associated future, such as vehicles associated with computers, onboard sensors, sensors in wearable devices, which notify the movements of objects and its current state of affairs. So, IoV is an inevitable juxtaposition of the mobility and the Internet of Things, in other words, it is the Internet of Things in the area of transport. The IoV aims at achieving an integrated smart transport system by improving traffic flow, preventing accidents, ensuring the road safety, and creating a comfortable driving experience. Mobility in transportation systems generates a huge amount of real data and it is a great challenge to deal with this data surge. So a multi-dimensional approach is required to handle and study the vast amount of generated data in structured as well as unstructured formats both from the independent and connected sensors of the Internet of Vehicle to obtain optimal results with safety measures. The Big Data technology provides a solution to this challenging problem to evolve such intelligent and smart vehicular system.

1. Hardware infrastructure

Convergenceof technologies in the design of vehicles is quickly making them as key devices in the IoT with the capabilities to accept data as well as send data to the cloud, to the traffic infrastructure, and to other vehicles. As a result, the IoV becomes an emerging technology in data communication with definite protocols that facilitates data transfer between cars, roadside equipment, wearable devices and traffic data management centers. So the IoV is the next technological revolution, which integrated with sensor networks, camera, mobile communication, real-time localization, ubiquitous computing and other technologies to realize the essential requirements for ITS applications.

2. Processing needs

Now, it is an era of smart objects with sensor inputs that are able to communicate via the Internet based on the protocols and/or prototype standards of ICT. Therefore, advanced techniques are necessary for effectively handling huge data generated from IoV and to perform efficient online analytical query processing.

The scalability and capability of Big Data analytics and predictions for IoV data management, exploration and exploitations lies in dynamic and scalable technological facts, which includes:

(1) It is vitally significant to identify and address IoV smart objects in order to interact query with various objects to realize each other's identity and address electively.

(2) Effective methods of data abstraction and compression should be developed for filtering out the redundant data. There are data indexing, archiving, access control and scalability for IoV data.

(3) Data warehouse and its query language for multi-dimensional analysis, semantic intelligibility and interoperability for diverse data of IoV.

(4) Time-series and even level data aggregation.

(5) It is essential for privacy and protection of data management of IoV.

3. Communication networks needs

Wireless networks can be organized into three major categories. An infrastructure wireless network is the first one. Second are ad-hoc network or non-structured network that gives equal roles to all stations in the network. Third, hybrid network which combines the first two categories. A case of hybrid network is hybrid vehicular ad-hoc network, which employ ad-hoc networks for communication among vehicles and infrastructure network, for example cellular systems for communication and Wireless Local Area Networks (WLAN) with a core network. Smart vehicles, through their finer communication potentiality, will be capable to work jointly not only with navigation and broadcast satellites, but also through passenger smart vehicles, smart phones and roadside units, making them an important component of IoT and the development of smart cities. Vehicular Ad-hoc Network(VANET) combines these with new applications and procedures to facilitate the intelligent communication among the connection to the Internet and the vehicles. VANET relies on On-board Units

(OBU) and Roadside Units (RSU) and to facilitate the connectivity. The RSU is communication infrastructure unit that is positioned next to road to communicate with vehicles and to a larger infrastructure or to a core network, depending upon metropolitan traffic topography. The OBU is a network device integrated with different sensors attached in vehicles that supports communication with different wireless networks, such as Dedicated Short-range Communication (DSRC) and WLAN. A VANET has a varied range of applications in road safety, traffic management by the detection and avoidance of traffic accidents, traffic flow, reduction of traffic congestion and infotainment to provide of driving comfort.

The progress and development of science and technology are constantly changing people's lives. In terms of travel, people can not do without cars. Nowadays, as the consumption demand grows, improving the level of automobile intelligence has become the focus of research and development of modern automobile enterprises, while the intelligent network and automatic driving are the key areas of technology research and development of automobile enterprises. Nowadays, in the new cars launched by automobile companies, the function of Intelligent Network Connection has been popularized, and facts have proved that a car with Intelligent Network Connection function is more acceptable to consumers.

4. Connected and autonomous vehicles

Intelligent network automobile is connected to the Internet to connect people and cars with home and life, providing more convenience and enjoyment for life. So, what is the relationship between intelligent networking and automatic driving? First of all, the Intelligent Network includes functions such as Internet access, listening to music, map navigation, car housekeeper, mobile phone remote control, and even playing games. These functions enable cars to participate in life more. Although the intelligent network alliance is closely related to the automatic driving vehicle, although not all the intelligent network will develop into an automatic driving vehicle, the automatic driving vehicle must have the function of intelligent network union.

The automatic driving vehicle requires intelligent and interconnected technology to carry out Big Data analysis on the road information collected by the sensors and the best route planning combined with the high-precision map, and realize the automatic driving through the intelligent assistant driving function. Let cars and cars, cars and roads, cars and people interconnect.

Generally speaking, the intelligent car is not exactly the same as the self driving vehicle. The intelligent network is the new stage of the intelligent vehicle, and the self driving is the highest stage of the intelligent vehicle.

Exercises

Ⅰ True or false.

(　　)(1)The IoV is an inevitable juxtaposition of the mobility and the Internet of Things.

(   )(2) The IoV becomes an emerging technology in data communication with indefinite protocols.

(   )(3) It is unessential for privacy and protection of data management of IoV.

(   )(4) Through their finer communication potentiality, smart vehicles will be capable to work jointly only with navigation and broadcast satellites.

(   )(5) VANET only relies on OBU to facilitate the connectivity.

Ⅱ Complete the following sentences.

(1) The Big Data technology provides a solution to this _____ problem to evolve such intelligent and smart vehicular system.

(2) _____ of technologies in the design of vehicles is quickly making them as key devices in the IoT.

(3) Advanced techniques are necessary for _____ handling huge data generated from IoV and to perform efficient online analytical query processing.

(4) Data indexing, archiving, access control and _____ for IoV data.

(5) Wireless networks can be organized into _____ major categories.

Ⅲ Answer the following questions.

(1) What is the aim of IoV?

(2) What provides a solution to evolve intelligent and smart vehicular system?

(3) How many kinds of wireless networks can be divided?

(4) What are the key devices in the IoT?

(5) What facilitates data transfer between cars, roadside equipment, wearable devices and traffic data management centers?

参 考 译 文

车联网技术

科技带来的巨大的好处反映在与我们相关的未来,从而彻底改变我们的生活,例如与计算机相关的车辆、车载传感器、可穿戴设备中的传感器,这些传感器可以传递物体的运动及事件的当前状况。因此,IoV 是车辆和物联网一次必然的结合,换句话说,它是交通领域的物联网。IoV 的目标是通过改善交通流、预防事故、确保道路安全和创造舒适的驾驶体验来实现一个集成的智能交通系统。交通系统中的车辆产生大量的实际数据,处理这种数量激增的数据是一个巨大的挑战。因此,需要一种多维的方法来处理和研究由车联网中独立的和相连接的传感器产生的、以结构化和非结构化格式生成的大量数据,使得安全措施获得最佳效果。大数据技术为这一具有挑战性的问题提供了解决方案,使这种智能化车辆系统得以发展。

1. 硬件基础设施

车辆设计中的技术融合使车联网迅速成为 IoT 中的关键设备,能够接收数据并向云端、交通基础设施和其他车辆发送数据。因此,IoV 成为一种新兴的数据通信技术,具有明确的协议,它有助于在车辆、路边设备、可穿戴设备和交通数据管理中心之间进行数据传输。因此,IoV 是实现 ITS 应用的基本要求,是集传感器网络、摄像机、移动通信、实时定位、泛用计算等其他技术于一体的技术革命。

2. 数据处理需求

现在是一个智能的时代,传感器输入的信息能够根据 ICT 协议和原型标准使用互联网进行交流。因此,先进的技术要求能够有效地处理 IoV 产生的大量数据和执行高效的在线查询分析。

大数据分析能力的提升以及对物联网数据管理、探索和开发的预测,在于动态的和可提升的技术因素,其中包括:

(1) 对 IoV 智能对象进行识别和寻址,以便与各种对象交互查询,实现彼此的身份认证和寻址选择,具有十分重要的意义。

(2) 开发有效的数据提取和压缩方法,以过滤掉多余数据,让 IoV 数据具有索引、存档、访问控制等功能和可扩展性。

(3) 数据仓库及其查询语言,用于 IoV 各种数据的多维分析、语义理解和相互操作。

(4) 时间序列和偶数级数据聚合。

(5) 对 IoV 数据管理的隐私保护至关重要。

3. 通信网络需求

无线网络可分为三大类;第一类是基础设施无线网络;第二类是临时网络或非结构化网络,它们为网络中的所有站点提供平等的位置;第三类是结合前两类的混合网络。混合网络的一个例子是混合车辆自组织网络。它使用自组织网络在车辆和基础设施网络之间进行通信,例如蜂窝通信系统和具有核心网络的无线局域网(WLAN)。智能车辆通过其良好的通信潜力,不仅能够与导航卫星和广播卫星共同工作,而且能够和客运智能车辆、智能手机和路边通信单元共同工作,使其成为物联网和智能城市发展的重要组成部分。车辆自组织网络结合这些新的应用和程序,以促进互联网和车辆之间的智能通信。车辆自组织网络依靠车载单元(OBU)和路边单元(RSU)连接而形成。RSU 是位于道路旁的通信基础设施单元,根据都市交通地形,与车辆大型基础设施以及核心网络进行通信。OBU 是一种集成了不同传感器的网络设备,例如专用短程通信(DSRC)和无线局域网,安装在支持与不同无线网络通信的车辆上。车辆自组织网络在交通安全、防范交通事故的交通管理、检测交通流、减少交通拥挤以及提供娱乐信息以提高驾驶舒适性等方面具有广泛的应用。

4. 智能网联车与自动驾驶

科技的进步与发展在不断改变人们的生活,在出行方面,人们已经离不开汽车。现如今,随着消费需求,提升汽车智能化水平成为现代车企的研发重点,而智能网联和自动驾驶,则是车企重点的技术研发领域。如今,在车企所推出的新车上,智能网联功能已经得到普及,而事实也证明,一台带智能网联功能的汽车,更容易被消费者接受。

智能网联汽车,是通过连接互联网将人和车,与家和生活相关联,以便为生活提供更多便利和享受。那么,智能网联和自动驾驶两者又是什么关系呢?首先,智能网联包含了上网、听音乐、地图导航、车管家、手机远程控制等功能,甚至还可以打游戏,这些功能让汽车能更多地参与生活。智能网联汽车和自动驾驶汽车关系紧密,虽然不是所有的智能网联汽车都会发展成为自动驾驶汽车,但自动驾驶汽车一定要有智能网联功能。

自动驾驶汽车,需要有智能和互联技术,将传感器收集反馈的路况信息进行大数据分析,结合高精地图给出最佳行驶路线规划,通过智能辅助驾驶功能实现自动驾驶,让车和车之间、车和路之间、车和人之间进行互联。

总体来说,智能汽车与自动驾驶汽车不完全等同,智能网联汽车是智能汽车新技术的阶段,无人驾驶是智能汽车最高阶段。

Knowledge Link

Internet of Things

The Internet of Things (IoT) is an important part of the new generation of information technology, and also an important stage of development in the era of 'informatization'. As the name implies, IoT is the Internet of Things. This has two meanings: first, the core and foundation of the Internet of Things is still the Internet, which is an extension and expansion of the network on the basis of the Internet; second, its user end extends and extends to any goods and objects to exchange and communicate information, that is, things interrelated. The IoT is widely used in the convergence of networks through intelligent sensing, identification and pervasive computing. It is also called the third wave of the development of information industry in the world after computers and the Internet. The IoT is an application expansion of the Internet. It is not so much a network as a business and application. Therefore, application innovation is the core of the development of the Internet of Things.

The definition of the IoT has developed due to the integration of various technologies, real-time analysis, machine learning, commodity sensors and embedded systems. Embedded systems, wireless sensor networks, control systems, automation (including home and building automation) and other traditional areas contribute to the realization of the Internet of Things. In the consumer market, Internet of Things technology is the most synonymous term for products related to the concept of 'smart home'. It includes devices and appliances that support one or more common ecosystems (such as lighting, thermostats, home security systems and cameras, and other household appliances) and can be controlled by ecosystem-related devices, such assmartphones and Intelligent Loudspeaker.

Unit 24

Unmanned Ground Vehicle

Text

1. Introduction

An Unmanned Ground Vehicle (UGV) is a piece of mechanized equipment that moves across the surface of the ground and serves as a means of carrying or transporting something. In the present day world, number of research activities are going on in the field of unmanned vehicles, which includes Unmanned Ground Vehicles (UGV), Unmanned Aerial Vehicles (UAV) and Unmanned Water Vehicles (UWV).

The UGV system generally consists of three main parts, such as vehicle control system, navigation system and obstacle detection system. UGV can be used for many applications where it may be inconvenient, dangerous, or impossible to have a human operator present. Space exploration, material handling, and transportation, medical transport of food and patients and future combat vehicles are areas that traditionally have been emphasized, and the laboratory results are beginning to find application in the real world.

UGV, in varying sizes to meet mission capability requirement, are today saving lives and providing critical supporting capabilities in current military operations worldwide.

The design of the UGV is 30cm timed 30cm size and 9cm height. The mass of the robot is approximately 5kg. It consists of two main tracks, 4 side arm tracks and a moving sensor panel at the top that consists of four ultrasound sensors.

The main intention of this design is to achieve the given goals below:
(1) Easy manoeuvrability in rough terrains.
(2) Detection and avoidance of obstacles in basic geometrical shapes.
(3) Adapting to sudden height changes.

The reason for using tracks instead of wheels was to achieve a bigger surface contact with the terrain. This, in turn, increases the efficiency of the UGV to travel in rough terrains. The maximum ground clearance is 21mm. Hence this can overcome on gravel terrains limited to this ground clearance. Another special feature is that the UGV was programmed to respond to specific height changes and climb inclined surfaces. Overall the UGV was designed and programmed in such a manner that it functions to the maximum efficiency.

2. Design and implementation

All the tracks of UGV in left and right are connected to each other hence when 120rpm DC motors rotated, it makes all the tracks rotate including the side arm tracks. Since left and right side 120rpm motors function independently, the robot can be controlled easily. During a requirement arises to deploy the side arms, the track attached to the arms rotate independently to the position it assumes. Rotary encoders are used for the four side arms to accurately determine the position it assumes. The left and right motor pairs are connected to motor shields that are connected to the microcontroller. The UGV base consists of two DC 120rpm motors, four 10rpm worm wheel motors connected.

The ability to detect obstacles autonomously is very crucial to the safety of UGV. Therefore, it has received a great deal of attention in recent years. According to the specific applications environment, the autonomous obstacle detection and navigation technology can be classified into the indoor environment and outdoor environment; and according to the topographical features, it can be classified into the structured environment and the unstructured environment. UGV navigation in the indoor and structured environments has achieved great progress and success. One of the most prominent pieces of work is the Navlab project, in which the UGV autonomously travelled across the American continent from the west coast to the east coast, where the UGV was navigated using neural network based vision system.

The goal of UGV research is to produce a machine capable of carrying out operation in the absence of, or with minimal, human intervention. In order to achieve the objective of operating autonomously in environments where direct human intervention is not feasible, self-diagnosis of faults and fault tolerance are the characteristics that UGV must have. As future works, using a camera attached to the UGV to receive a live feed and using more reliable sensors have been recognized as main improvements.

New Words and Expressions

autonomous [ɔːˈtɒnəməs]   *adj.* 自治的;自主的;自发的
terrain [təˈreɪn]   *n.* [地理]地形;地势;领域;地带

detection [dɪˈtekʃn]	n. 侦查;探测;发现;察觉
hence [hens]	adv. 因此;今后
rotate [rəʊˈteɪt]	vi. 旋转;循环 vt. 使旋转;使转动;使轮流
prominent [ˈprɒmɪnənt]	adj. 突出的;显著的;杰出的;卓越的
continent [ˈkɒntmənt]	n. 大陆;洲;陆地 adj. 自制的;克制的
neural [ˈnjʊərəl]	adj. 神经的;神经系统的
track [træk]	n. 轨道;足迹;小道 vt. 追踪;监测
ultrasound [ˈʌltrəsaʊnd]	n. 超声;超音波
manoeuvrability [məˌnuːvərəˈbɪləti]	n. 机动性;可移动
geometrical [dʒiːəˈmetrɪkl]	adj. 几何的;几何学的
gravel [ˈɡrævl]	n. 碎石;砂砾 vt. 用碎石铺;使困惑
deploy [dɪˈplɔɪ]	vt. 配置;展开 vi. 部署;展开 n. 部署
shield [ʃiːld]	n. 盾;防护物 vt. 遮蔽;庇护;保护;掩护 vi. 防御;起保护作用
worm [wɔːm]	n. 虫;蠕虫;螺纹 vt. 使蠕动;使缓慢前进
intervention [ˌɪntəˈvenʃn]	n. 介入;干涉;干预
Unmanned Ground Vehicle(UGV)	无人驾驶地面车辆
in the field of	在……方面;在……领域
panel [ˈpænl]	n. 嵌板;镶板;金属板
rough [rʌf]	adj. 高低不平的;粗糙的
inclined [ɪnˈklaɪnd]	adj. 倾斜的
obstacle [ˈɒbstəkl]	n. 障碍;障碍物;阻碍;绊脚石
microcontroller [ˌmaɪkrəʊkɒntˈrəʊlə(r)]	n. [自]微控制器
self-diagnosis	自我诊断

Exercises

I True or false.

(　　)(1) An Unmanned Ground Vehicle (UGV) is a piece of mechanized equipment that moves across the surface of the ground and serves as a means of carrying or transporting something.

(　　)(2) UGV can be used for many applications where it may be inconvenient, dangerous, or impossible to have a human operator present.

(　　)(3) Adapting to sudden height changes is one of main intention of UGV design.

(　　)(4) The reason for using tracks instead of wheels was to achieve a smaller surface contact with the terrain.

(　　)(5) Rotary encoders are used for the four side arms to accurately determine the position it assumes.

Ⅱ Complete the following sentences.

(1) Today, UGV are saving lives and providing _____ supporting capabilities in current military operations worldwide.

(2) _____ and avoidance of obstacles in basic geometrical shapes.

(3) Hence this can overcome on gravel terrains limited to this ground _____.

(4) Since left and right side 120rpm motors function _____, the robot can be controlled easily.

(5) The left and right motor pairs are connected to _____ that are connected to the microcontroller.

Ⅲ Answer the following questions.

(1) What is UGV?
(2) What does UGV system consist of?
(3) What kind of service does UGV provide?
(4) What is the goal of UGV research?
(5) What is the design of the UGV?

Topics for Discussion

(1) In your opinion, how does the application of UGV affect our life?

(2) Beside of a camera attached and more reliable sensors, what do you think the UGV can be improved in the future?

(3) What do you think are the disadvantages of UGV?

参 考 译 文

无人驾驶地面车辆

1. 引言

无人驾驶地面车辆(UGV)是一种自动化的运输设备,它可以在地面上移动,并作为装载或运输某物的工具。在当今世界,无人驾驶车辆领域的研究活动正在进行,包括无人驾驶地面车辆(UGV)、无人驾驶飞行器(UAV)和无人驾驶水上交通工具(UWV)。

UGV 系统一般由车辆控制系统、导航系统和障碍物检测系统三大部分组成。无人地面车辆可用于许多不方便的、危险的或无法人工操作等情况下的应用。太空探索、材料处理、交通运输、食品和患者的医疗运输以及未来的战斗车辆(一直被重视的领域),其实验成果开始在现实生活中得到应用。

为满足任务的需求,各种尺寸的无人驾驶地面车辆如今正在拯救生命,并在当前的全球军事行动中提供关键的支持能力。

UGV 的设计尺寸为 30 厘米×30 厘米,高度为 9 厘米。机器人的质量约为 5 千克。它由两条主履带、四条副履带和顶部的移动传感器面板组成,该面板由四个超声波传感器组成。

这种设计的主要目的是实现以下给定目标：
(1)在崎岖的地形中易于操纵。
(2)对基本几何形状障碍物进行检测和避让。
(3)适应突然的高度变化。

使用履带而不是车轮是为了实现与地形的更大表面接触，反过来又提高了无人地面车辆在崎岖地形中行驶的效率。最大离地间隙为 21 毫米，因此该离地间隙范围内可以克服在砾石地形上的行驶困难。另一个特点是，UGV 被编程为可以响应特定高度变化和爬升斜面。总体而言，UGV 的设计和编程方式使其功能效率最大化。

2. 设计和实施

UGV 左右两侧的所有履带相互连接，因此当 120 转/分钟的直流电机旋转时，所有履带都旋转（包括副履带）。由于左侧和右侧 120 转/分钟电机独立运行，因此可以轻松控制机器人。在要求展开侧臂的过程中，固定在侧臂上的履带独立地旋转到其设定的位置。旋转编码器用于四个侧臂，以精确确定其设定的位置。左右电机连接到电机护罩，电机护罩连接到微控制器。UGV 底座由两个 120 转/分钟直流电机和四个 10 转/分钟涡轮电机组成。

自主探测障碍物的能力对 UGV 的安全至关重要。因此，近年来受到广泛关注。根据特定的应用环境，自主障碍物检测和导航技术可分为室内检测导航和室外检测导航；根据地形特征，可分为结构化环境中的检测导航和非结构化环境中的检测导航。UGV 在室内和结构化环境中的导航取得了很大的进步和成功，其中最为成功的是 Navlab 项目。项目中的 UGV 使用基于神经网络的视觉系统导航，自主从西海岸到东海岸穿过美洲大陆。

UGV 研究的目标是生产一种能够在无人干预或干预最小的情况下进行操作的机器。为了实现在无法人工直接干预的环境下能够自主运行的目标，无人地面车辆必须具备故障自我诊断和容错的特点。在未来的工作中，使用连接到无人地面车辆上的摄像头接收实况转播和使用更可靠的传感器已经被认为是主要的发展方向。

Reading Material

The Technologies of Unmanned Driving

1. Introduction

The development of cars has experienced three different stages. The first stage relied totally on manual work without standardized parts and assembling process. The cars of this stage had high prices and their qualities were out of effective control. The second stage was characterized by standardized and streamlined production. Since the middle and later periods of the 1990s, the automobile industry has entered into the third stage. The technologies of comfort and intelligent safety have become the point of automobile industry. According to the statistics, from 1989 to 2010, the ratio of the costs of electronic equipment among the whole costs has increased from 16% to 23%. In some luxury vehicles, the cost of the electronic equipment has accounted for more than 50% of the total cost of the cars.

In recent years, the rapid development of artificial intelligence, cognitive science, automatic control, ground mapping, sensor technology and other fields promotes the essential change of automobile industry. The symbol of wheeled mobile robots in the subversive creation of cars is ready to go ahead. The wheeled mobile robots would rather realize the goal of intelligent driving and free human drivers from low-level, complicated and lasting driving activities and change the interactive mode between cars and drivers fundamentally not emphasize the change of vehicle dynamics properties. Thus, cars will become personal mobile sharing tools.

There are two main routes to realize wheeled mobile robots: the intelligent route and the Network route. The intelligent route considers cars as intelligent individuals with perception, cognition and decision-making abilities, which emphasizes autonomous driving while the network route considers cars as an adjustable node of the whole traffic system, which emphasizes overall coordination. The two routescross with each other and form the future intelligent traffic system together.

In 2013, Mckinsey Company listed twelve subversive technologies that can decide the future economy, among which advanced robot technologies and unmanned driving technologies are included. The research and development of unmanned cars rely on the newest research results of artificial intelligence, cognitive science, automatic control, sensor technology and other research fields, which is the best stage for tests. Unmanned driving technologies have become a research hotspot that attracts the attention of governments both at home and abroad, scientific research institutions and enterprises because of its great significance in civil use, military use and research fields.

2. The research status of unmanned driving

The U. S. National Highway Traffic Safety Administration released the *regulations of traffic policies of intelligent driving cars* in May, 2013. The regulations divided the automatic degree of cars into five levels: level zero was no autonomous control, level one was intelligent driving with independent functions, level two was intelligent driving with cooperative control, level three was autonomous driving with limits and level four was total autonomous driving.

The U. S. is the first one to study unmanned driving cars in the world. In the 1980s, DARPA established special funds to support the research of autonomous land vehicles and held three DARPA challenge matches in 2004, 2005 and 2007, which raised a great mass fervor of unmanned driving research.

Google began to research unmanned driving in 2009 and it has finished designing several kinds of sample cars and on-road test of nearly one million kilometers. *Under the promotion of Google, Nevada, Florida, California and Michigan allow unmanned driving cars to test on public highways one after another.*

Compared with the advanced development of unmanned driving technologies in foreign countries, China still has some deficiencies. First, these motor enterprises lack passion and commitment on unmanned driving technologies. The cooperation between the motor enterprises and scientific research institutions ends with providing cars platforms and cooperating mechanical reformation, which lacks deep involvement. Second, the unmanned driving tests to actual traffic flow are limited to normal highways and short of unmanned driving experimental verification under complicated situations.

Exercises

I True or false.

(　　)(1) The first stage of car development relied totally on manual work without standardized parts and assembling process.

(　　)(2) In some luxury vehicles, the cost of the electronic equipment has accounted for less than 50% of the total cost of the cars.

(　　)(3) In realize wheeled mobile robots, the intelligent route are more widespread than the network route.

(　　)(4) The England is the first one to study unmanned driving cars in the world.

(　　)(5) Under the promotion of Google, Nevada, Florida, California and Michigan allow unmanned driving cars to test on public highways one after another.

II Complete the following sentences.

(1) The symbol of wheeled mobile robots in the ＿＿＿＿＿ creation of cars is ready to go ahead.

(2) The two routes ＿＿＿＿＿ each other and form the future intelligent traffic system together.

(3) The U. S. National Highway Traffic Safety Administration ＿＿＿＿＿ the *regulations of traffic policies of intelligent driving cars* in May, 2013.

(4) ＿＿＿＿＿ the advanced development of unmanned driving technologies in foreign countries, China still has some deficiencies.

(5) The unmanned driving tests to actual traffic flow are limited to ＿＿＿＿＿ and short of unmanned driving experimental verification ＿＿＿＿＿.

III Answer the following questions.

(1) How many stages does the development of cars have been experienced?

(2) What are the two main routes to realize wheeled mobile robots?

(3) Which country is the first one to study unmanned driving cars in the world?

(4) What promotes the essential change of automobile industry in recent years?

(5) What has the Google done in unmaned driving?

参 考 译 文

无人驾驶技术

1. 引言

汽车的发展经历了三个不同的阶段。第一阶段完全依靠手工，没有标准化的零件和装配工艺。这个阶段的汽车价格很高,而且它们的质量不能得到有效保证。第二阶段的特点是生产标准化、流线化。自20世纪90年代中后期以来,汽车工业进入第三阶段,舒适性和智能安全技术已成为汽车工业的重点。据统计,从1989年到2010年,电子设备成本占汽车总成本的比例从16%上升到23%。在一些昂贵的汽车上,电子设备的成本已经占到汽车总成本的50%以上。

近年来,人工智能、认知科学、自动控制、地面测绘、传感器技术等领域的飞速发展,推动了汽车工业的根本性变革。在汽车颠覆性的创新中,轮式移动机器人的出现象征着无人驾驶技术已经准备就绪。轮式移动机器人偏向实现智能驾驶,将人类驾驶人从简单、烦琐、持续时间长的驾驶活动中解放出来,从根本上改变汽车与驾驶人之间的互动模式而不强调车辆动力学特性的变化。因此,汽车将成为个人移动共享工具。

制造轮式移动机器人的主要途径有两条:智能化和网络化。智能化路线将汽车视为具有感知、认知和决策能力的智能个体,重点在于自动驾驶;网络化路线将汽车视为整个交通系统的可调节点,重点在于整体协调。两条途径相互交叉,共同构成未来的智能交通系统。

2013年,麦肯锡公司列出了12项可以决定未来经济情况的颠覆性技术,其中包括先进的机器人技术和无人驾驶技术。无人驾驶汽车处于试验的最佳阶段,因其研究与开发依赖人工智能、认知科学、自动控制、传感器技术等研究领域的最新研究成果。无人驾驶技术在民用、军事、科研领域具有重要意义,已成为国内外政府、科研机构和企业关注的研究热点。

2. 无人驾驶的研究现状

美国国家公路交通安全管理局于2013年5月发布了《智能驾驶汽车交通政策条例》,该法规将汽车的自动化程度分为五个等级:零级为非自主控制,一级为独立的智能驾驶,二级为协同控制的智能驾驶,三级为有限程度的自动驾驶,四级为全自动驾驶。

美国是世界上第一个研究无人驾驶汽车的国家。20世纪80年代,国防高级研究计划局设立专项基金支持自主陆地车辆的研究,并于2004年、2005年和2007年举办了三次美国国防部高级研究计划局挑战赛,引起人们对无人驾驶研究的极大热情。

谷歌公司从2009年开始研究无人驾驶,并完成了几款样车的设计和近100万千米的驾驶测试。在谷歌的推动下,内华达州、佛罗里达州、加利福尼亚州和密歇根州允许无人驾驶汽车在公路上频繁地进行测试。

与国外无人驾驶技术的先进发展相比,我国仍然存在一些不足。一是这些汽车企业缺乏对无人驾驶技术的热情和投入。汽车企业与科研机构的合作仅达到提供使用汽车的平台和配合机械改造的程度,缺乏进一步参与。二是对实际交通流中的无人驾驶试验仅限于普通情况下的道路,缺乏复杂情况下的试验验证。

Knowledge Linkage

Unmanned Aerial Vehicle Express Delivery

Unmanned Aerial Vehicle express delivery (UAV express delivery) is a low-altitude vehicle operated by radio remote control equipment and self-contained program control device to deliver parcels to the destination automatically. Its advantages mainly lie in solving the distribution problems in remote areas, improving the efficiency of distribution, and reducing the cost of manpower. The disadvantage lies mainly in the inability of unmanned opportunity to deliver goods in bad weather and theunavoidability of man-made destruction during flight.

Automated UAV express delivery system uses UAV instead of manual delivery, aiming at realizing the automation, unmanned and informationization of express delivery, improving the delivery efficiency and service quality of express delivery, so as to alleviate the contradiction between express demand and express service capability. The realization of this system can effectively cope with the huge increase of orders, eliminate the danger of 'bursting warehouse' of express delivery, improve the service quality of express delivery industry, reduce the delay rate, damage rate, loss rate of express delivery and express complaint rate. At the same time, it can also reduce the operation cost, warehouse cost, human cost, and so on, enhance the competitiveness of the industry, and make the delivery of express delivery safer, more reliable and faster.

Key to Exercises

Unit 1

Text

Ⅰ (1) T   (2) F   (3) T   (4) T   (5) F   (6) T

Ⅱ (1) heavy motor vehicles   pedestrians

(2) interchanges of passengers and cargoes and for maintenance

(3) the way the vehicles are operated   the procedures set for this purpose

(4) air pollution   use large amounts of lands

(5) travel safety   efficiency

Ⅲ (1) Traffic laws are the laws which govern the traffic and regulate the vehicles, while rules of the road are both the laws and the informal rules that may develop over time to facilitate the orderly and timely flow of traffic.

(2) Organized traffic generally has well-established priorities, lanes, right-of-way, and the traffic control at intersections.

(3) Simulators of organized traffic frequently involve queuing theory, stochastic processes and equations of mathematical physics applied to traffic flow.

(4) Because transport enables trade between people, which is essential for the development of civilizations.

(5) In the transport industry, operation rights and ownership of infrastructures can be either public or private, depending on the country policies and manners in which the infrastructures are operated.

Reading material

Ⅰ (1) F   (2) F   (3) T   (4) F   (5) T

Ⅱ (1) the safe and efficient movement of people and goods on roadways

(2) dedicated transport facilities for cyclists   mixed-mode environments

(3) to reduce human error   increase productivities   enhance safety and comfort

(4) design and maintain flexible (asphalt) and rigid (concrete) pavements

(5) transportation engineering   concerning bicycles as a mode of transport

Ⅲ (1) Traffic engineering uses engineering techniques to achieve the safe and efficient movement of people and goods on roadways. It focuses mainly on research for safe and efficient traffic flow.

(2) The disciplines associated with traffic engineering are transport engineering, pavement engineering, bicycle transportation engineering, highway engineering, transportation planning, urban planning and human factors engineering.

(3) Highway engineers must take into account future traffic flow, design of highway intersections/interchanges, geometric alignment and design, highway pavement materials and design, structural design of pavement thickness, and pavement maintenance.

(4) Transportation planning is the process of defining future policies, goals, investments and designs to prepare for future needs to move people and goods to destinations.

(5) The goal of human factors is to reduce human error, increase productivities, and enhance safety and comfort with a specific focus on the interaction between the humans and the things of interest.

Unit 2

Text

Ⅰ (1) F   (2) T   (3) F   (4) F   (5) T

Ⅱ (1) provide an objective measure of an existing situation

(2) the summer period when schools are closed and workers tend to take annual holidays

(3) ensure that the survey provides a fair measure of the traffic conditions that are being studied

(4) decide what question has to be answered and choose the type of survey accordingly

(5) number plate survey   origin and destination survey   roadside interview survey

Ⅲ (1) Traffic engineering is used to either improve an existing situation or, in the case of a new facility, to ensure that the facility is correctly and safely designed and adequate for the demands that will be placed on it.

(2) If the facility is completely new, for example a road in a new development, then the expected traffic and the scale of construction needed has to be estimated in another way. This is usually done by a transport impact analysis, which will seek to assess the likely level of traffic by refer to the traffic generated by similar developments elsewhere.

(3) Traffic flow tends to vary by day of the week. On a typical urban road, traffic flow tends to build during the weekends and to a peak on Friday. Flow is lower at the weekend when fewer people works and lowest on Sunday; although the introduction of Sunday trading has affected the balance of traveling at the weekend.

(4) It is important to ensure that the survey provides a fair measure of the traffic conditions that are being studied.

(5) The starting point in defining a traffic survey is to decide what question has to be answered and choose the type of survey accordingly.

Reading material

Ⅰ (1) F   (2) T   (3) F   (4) T   (5) F

Ⅱ (1) speed　　flow　　density

(2) $\overline{V}_s = \overline{V}_f - \left(\dfrac{\overline{V}_f}{D_j}\right) D$

(3) $\dfrac{d\overline{V}_s}{dT} = -\dfrac{C^2}{D} \times \dfrac{\partial D}{\partial L}$

(4) $V_w = \dfrac{dQ}{dD}$

(5) the quality of service experienced by the stream

Ⅲ (1) The speed is the space mean speed; the density or concentration is the number of vehicles per unit length of highway and the flow is the number of vehicles passing a given point on the highway per unit time.

(2) Because they desire to estimate the optimum speed for maximum flow.

(3) Greenshields found a linear relationship between speed and density of the form in a study of rural roads in Ohio.

(4) Greenberg assumed that high density traffic behaved in a similar manner to a continuous fluid.

(5) Lighthill and Whitham using a fluid-flow analogy had shown that the speed of waves causing continuous changes of volume through vehicular flow is given by dQ/dD.

Unit 3

Text

Ⅰ (1) F　　(2) T　　(3) F　　(4) T　　(5) T

Ⅱ (1) trip generation　　trip distribution　　modal split　　traffic assignment

(2) a tabulation of trip origins or trip attractions by small areas

(3) the Fratar method　　the intervening opportunities model　　the gravity model

(4) converting person-trips into automobile trips or transit passenger trips

(5) the outputs from preceding tasks to a coded transportation network

Ⅲ (1) The urban transportation planning involves the planning of transportation facilities or operations responsive to the goals of the community being served.

(2) One way to bridge gaps between community viewpoints and the planner's technical processes is to set up an interlocking set of guiders that proceed from the general to the particular.

(3) Where mode choice is essential, several procedures are available to determine the split either before or after the trip-distribution step. Trip diversion based on travel-time differences between modes is the basis for some methods, but it is being supplanted by techniques relying heavily on trip-maker or household characteristics.

(4) The model's performance is first verified by using the network and traffic assignment techniques to see if model-produced OD patterns and network loadings are comparable to those obtained from trip surveys and their assignment to the network.

(5) The trip-generation and trip-distribution steps may be concerned with the problem of converting person-trips into automobile trips or transit passenger trips.

Reading material

Ⅰ (1) T　　(2) T　　(3) F　　(4) T　　(5) T

Ⅱ (1) Traffic assignment

(2) deal with highway traffic

(3) vary

(4) end at a zone centriod

(5) to introduce the traffic assignment methods

Ⅲ (1) The number of trips and their origins and destinations are known but the actual routes through the transportation system is unknown.

(2) Because it is usually not difficult to estimate the routes taken by public transport users and also because the loading trips on the public transport network does not materially affect the journey time.

(3) In assignment it is first necessary to describe the transport network to which trips are being assigned.

(4) For each zone centriod selected as origin, a set of shortest routes from the origin to all the other zone centroids are referred to as a minimum tree.

(5) Because of its simplicity, travel times are usually employed as a measure of link impedance, but travel times may not be precisely estimated by a traveler.

Unit 4

Text

Ⅰ (1) F　　(2) F　　(3) T　　(4) F　　(5) T

Ⅱ (1) one-way regulation

(2) capacity　　safety　　traffic flow　　economic conditions

(3) one-way traffic

(4) conflicts　　delays

(5) clear markings　　signal indications

Ⅲ (1) ① A street on which traffic moves in one direction at all times.

② A street that is normally one-way but at certain times may be operated in the reverse direction to provide additional capacity in the predominant direction of flow.

③ A street that normally carries two-way traffic but which during peak traffic hours may be operated as a one-way traffic. Such a street may be operated in one direction during the morning peak hours and in the opposite direction during the evening peak hours, with two-way traffic during all other hours.

(2) One-way regulation is generally used to reduce congestion and to increase the capacity of a

street network. Improved traffic movement and increased safety, generally produce broad economic benefits both to adjacent land users and to the general public.

(3) A primary reason for use of one-way traffic is to improve traffic operations and to reduce congestion.

(4) Traffic conflicts and delays at intersections are a principal cause of congestion and reduced travel time on two-way urban streets.

(5) Improved traffic movement and increased safety generally produce broad economic benefits both to adjacent land users and to the general public.

Reading material

Ⅰ (1) T   (2) T   (3) T   (4) F   (5) T
Ⅱ (1) pre-haul   long-haul   end-haul
(2) containerized
(3) multimodal   intermodal   co-modal   synchro modal
(4) Multimodal freight transportation
(5) Synchro modal freight transportation
Ⅲ (1) Demand for freight transportation results from producers and consumers who are geographically apart from each other.

(2) A transportation chain is basically partitioned in three segments: pre-haul (first mile for the pickup process), long-haul (door-to-door transit of containers), and end-haul (last mile for the delivery process).

(3) Key reasons for containerization are an increase in the safety of cargo, reduction of handling costs, standardization, and accessibility to multiple modes of transportation.

(4) Intermodal freight transportation is defined as a particular type of multimodal transportation where the load is transported from an origin to a destination in one and the same intermodal transportation unit without handling of the goods themselves when changing modes.

(5) Synchro modal freight transportation is positioned as the next step after intermodal and co-modal transportation, and involves a structured, efficient and synchronized combination of two or more transportation modes.

Unit 5

Text

Ⅰ (1) F   (2) T   (3) F   (4) T   (5) T
Ⅱ (1) road junctions
(2) In urban areas
(3) warning signs   regulatory signs   directional informatory signs   other informatory signs
(4) hazards
Ⅲ (1) Traffic management arose from the need to maximize the capacity of existing highway

networks within finite budget with a minimum of new construction.

(2) Accident reduction, demand restraint, public transport priority, environmental improvement, and restoring the ability to move around safely and freely on foot and by pedal cycle.

(3) New technologies in the form of smart cards and vehicle identification are needed to ensure that the congestion charging system is practical and fair.

(4) Capacity enhancements, accident reduction, environmental protection and enhancement, servicing of premises and providing access, providing assistance to pedestrians and cyclists, assisting bus or tram operators, providing facilities for persons with disabilities, regulating on-street and off-street parking.

Reading material

Ⅰ (1) F　　(2) F　　(3) T　　(4) T　　(5) F

Ⅱ (1) freeway traffic management systems

(2) the detection and servicing of incidents

(3) surveillance

(4) field observations　periodic studies　police reports　citizen calls

(5) Electronic surveillance

Ⅲ (1) Surveillance entails the status monitoring of traffic conditions and of control system operation as well as the collecting of information for implementing controls and for incident detection.

(2) For freeways, the most important aspect of surveillance is the detection and servicing of incidents.

(3) The earliest traffic surveillance techniques used for incident detection were field observations, periodic studies, police reports and citizen calls.

(4) Electronic surveillance for incident detection is accomplished by the real-time computer monitoring of traffic data.

(5) Most freeway incident detection algorithms involve the determination of changes in certain traffic-flow variables.

Unit 6

Text

Ⅰ (1) T　　(2) F　　(3) T　　(4) T　　(5) F

Ⅱ (1) inductive detectors

(2) real-time systems　controllers　internal logic

(3) safety time

(4) parameters　internal logic

(5) SCATS　SCOOTS

Ⅲ (1) Fixed-time or pre-timed controllers applied historical data to determine appropriate time for traffic signals.

(2) A fixed amount of time is required for clearing the intersections and starting the next phase after each phase, called the safety time.

(3) Longer waiting times and longer queues are the consequences of longer cycle times.

(4) Parameters like time, day, season, weather, and some unpredictable situations such as accidents and special events are highly influential on traffic load.

(5) The use of artificial intelligence methods to control traffic signals started in 1990s.

Reading material

I (1) T   (2) F   (3) F   (4) F   (5) T

II (1) 50%

(2) Through-band

(3) simultaneous   alternate   limited(simple) progressive   flexible progressive

(4) single alternate system

(5) double alternate system

III (1) When the red interval takes as much as less than 50% of the cycle length.

(2) The width of the through-band expressed in seconds, indicating the period of time available for traffic to flow within the band.

(3) When the vehicular travel time between signals are a multiple of one-half the common cycle length.

(4) All signals along a given street operate with the same cycle length and display the green indication at the same time. Under this system, all traffic moves at one time, and a short time later all traffic stops at the nearest signalized intersections to allow cross-street traffic to move.

(5) Use a longer cycle length during the morning and evening peak hours.

Unit 7

Text

I (1) T   (2) F   (3) F   (4) T   (5) T   (6) F

II (1) population densities are higher   pedestrian access is good

(2) employment   residences dispersed   sidewalks or direct access to transit stops

(3) few vehicles, each carrying a large number of passengers

(4) follow fixed routes   schedules along roadways

(5) on-line stops may help reduce overall person delay

III (1) These riders choose transit to avoid congestion, save money on fuel and parking, use their travel time productively for other activities, and reduce the impact of automobile driving on the environment.

(2) First, transit accommodates choice riders. Second transit is to provide basic mobility for segments of the population that are unable to drive for age, physical, mental, or financial reasons.

(3) Typical transit users do not have transit service available at the door and must walk, bicy-

cle, or drive to transit stops and walk or bicycle from the transit discharge points to their destinations.

(4) The frequency and reliability of service are important quality-of-service factors for transit users. Travel speed and comfort while making a trip are also important to transit users.

(5) The bus mode service can range from local buses stopping every two to three blocks along a street, to limited-stop service stopping every 1/2 to 1mi, to express service that travels along a roadway without stopping.

Reading material

Ⅰ (1) T　　(2) F　　(3) T　　(4) F　　(5) T

Ⅱ (1) sections of shared, semi-exclusive, and exclusive facilities

(2) in the median strip of wide arterials routes with crossings at grade

(3) This technology　　available funds　　serve the rail routes

(4) very detailed studies of demand, station locations and relative costs

(5) the location of the central terminals

Ⅲ (1) On-street track alignment is primarily determined by the geometry of the streets available for the routes.

(2) Semi-exclusive route sections can be placed in the median strip of wide arterial routes with crossings at grade.

(3) More direct service with branch or parallel lines can often be provided: stops may be located more accessible and spaced more closely to reduce walking distances.

(4) The network extent is necessarily limited by available funds, and feeder services are required to serve the rail routes.

(5) Heavy rail transit alignments are based on very detailed studies of demand, station locations and relative costs.

Unit 8

Text

Ⅰ (1) T　　(2) T　　(3) F　　(4) F　　(5) T

Ⅱ (1) kerb parking

(2) Parking surveys

(3) supply and demand　　supply　　demand

(4) parking supply　　parking demand

(5) duration survey

Ⅲ (1) Good parking management and control can lead to some or all of the following: higher car occupancies, decreasing person-trips, faster travel times and less travel delays, greater public transport usage, decreasing congestion, and reduced air and noise pollution.

(2) The objective of parking study is to determine facts, which will provide the logical points of

departure in relation to indicating parking needs.

(3) Parking supply survey is concerned with obtaining detailed information regarding those on-street and off-street features, the existing situation with regard to parking space, and how it is controlled.

(4) The purpose of a concentration survey is to determine not only where vehicles do park, but also the actual number parked at any given instant at all locations (on-street and off-street) within the survey area.

(5) The parker interview survey normally involves interviewing motorists at their places of parking and questioning them regarding the origins of the trips just completed, the primary destinations, and the purposes of the trip.

Reading material

Ⅰ (1) F   (2) F   (3) T   (4) F   (5) T

Ⅱ (1) public

(2) microprocessor-based systems

(3) 1.8   2.7   2.7~3.6

(4) 20~25

(5) 3.3   15.5

Ⅲ (1) Because most of the users are familiar with the geometry of the car park.

(2) The current regulations specify a standard bay width, of between 1.8 and 2.7m, although a bay width of 2.7~3.6m is specified for parking bays for the disabled.

(3) Parking facilities designed specifically for disabled drivers should be fully accessible throughout for wheelchair users. Parking bays should be 1.5 times the width of a normal bay with access by ramps with a maximum gradient of 7%. Where lifts are provided they should have controls at wheelchair level, that is at about 1.2~1.4m.

(4) Because drivers tend to have difficulty manoeuvring in and, particularly, out of the space.

(5) As a rule of thumb, to estimate the number of cars that can be accommodated on a site, each car space requires about 20~25m^2 of space.

Unit 9

Text

Ⅰ (1) T   (2) F   (3) T   (4) T   (5) F

Ⅱ (1) Park and ride

(2) suburbs of metropolitan areas   outer edges

(3) public transport

(4) Sweden

(5) congestion tax

Ⅲ (1) Park and ride facilities are parking lot with public transport connections that allow com-

263

muters and other people heading to city centers to leave their vehicles and transfer to a bus, rail system (rapid transit, light rail or commuter rail), or carpool for the remainder of the journey.

(2) Many park and rides have passenger waiting areas and/or toilets. Travel information, such as leaflets and posters, may be provided. At larger facilities, extra services such as a travel office, food shop, car wash or cafeteria may be provided.

(3) Park and ride facilities help commuters who live beyond practical walking distance from the railway station or bus stop.

(4) Park and ride facilities allow commuters to avoid a stressful drive along congested roads and a search for scarce, expensive city-center parking. They may well reduce congestion by assisting the use of public transport in congested urban areas.

(5) In Sweden, a tax has been introduced on the benefit of free or cheap parking paid by an employer, if workers would otherwise have to pay.

Reading material

Ⅰ (1) T (2) T (3) F (4) T (5) T

Ⅱ (1) Transit-oriented development (TOD)

(2) 1/4   1/2

(3) half-mile-radius

(4) reduced amounts of parking for personal vehicles

(5) Opponents of compact   TOD typically

Ⅲ (1) TOD is a type of urban development that maximizes the amount of residential, business and leisure space within walking distance of public transport.

(2) The densest areas of a TOD are normally located within a radius of 1/4 to 1/2 mile (400 to 800m) around the central transit stop, as this is considered to be an appropriate scale for pedestrians, thus solving the last mile problem.

(3) Many of the new towns created after World War II in Japan, Sweden, and France have many of the characteristics of TOD communities.

(4) Opponents of compact or transit-oriented development typically argue that Americans, and persons throughout the world, prefer low-density living, and that any policies that encourage compact development will result in substantial utility decreases and large social welfare costs.

Unit 10

Text

Ⅰ (1) T (2) F (3) T (4) T (5) T

Ⅱ (1) proper curb   gutters   sewer grates

(2) unusual circumstances   a selected portion of the sidewalk for bicycles

(3) signs   pavement markings

(4) 8ft (2.4m)   12ft (3.6m)   2ft (0.6m)   10ft (3m)

(5) bicycle width   maneuvering allowance   clearance between oncoming and passing bicycles   edge conditions

III (1) The actual bikeway pavement width depends on bicycle width, maneuvering allowance, clearance between oncoming and passing bicycles, and edge conditions.

(2) Two ways: ① let the bicycles share the sidewalk with pedestrians; ② save a portion of sidewalk for bicycles.

(3) When the rolling terrain and significant downgrades greater than 4% are prevalent.

(4) When a bikeway is shared with normal pedestrian traffic, there must be at least a 2.5ft (0.75m) horizontal separation between bicycles and pedestrians (preferably more). This means the sidewalk must be 11 to 15 ft (3.3 to 4.5m) wide to accommodate both pedestrians and bicyclists.

(5) Accident statistics indicate that about two-thirds of bicycle/motor vehicle accidents occur at intersections.

Reading material

I (1) F   (2) T   (3) F   (4) F   (5) T

II (1) Walking

(2) traffic stream

(3) A   F   F

(4) measures of effectiveness

(5) comfort   convenience   safety   security   economy

III (1) A key determinant of the amount of travel by any mode is the utility or LOS offered by that mode.

(2) For each type of facility, LOS is defined based on one or more operational parameters that best describe operating quality for the subject facility type.

(3) As the volume and density of a pedestrian stream increases from free-flow to more crowded conditions, speed and ease of movement decrease.

(4) Security features include lighting, open lines of sight, and the degrees and types of street activity.

(5) comfort   convenience   safety   security   economy

Unit 11

Text

I (1) F   (2) F   (3) T   (4) F   (5) F

II (1) the preservation of the as-built capacities of the highway, high speed, and improved safety to highway users

(2) medians, grade separations at cross streets, ramp connections for entrance to and exit from through pavements for interchange of traffic, and (in some cases) frontage roads

(3) the important safety considerations

(4) 1.5   2

(5) 10

Ⅲ (1) The highest type of arterial highway is the freeway, which is defined as an expressway with fully controlled access.

(2) Essential freeway elements include medians, grade separations at cross streets, ramp connections for entrance to and exit from through pavements for interchange of traffic, and frontage roads.

(3) Control of access is the condition where the right of owners or occupants of abutting land to access a highway is fully or partially controlled by public authorities.

(4) The principal advantages of control of access are the preservation of the as-built capacities of the highway, high speed, and improved safety to highway users.

(5) Cross slope should range between 1.5 and 2 percent on tangent sections consisting of two lanes in each direction with a crown at the centerline of the pavement. The high value is recommended for areas of moderate rainfall. For areas of heavy rainfall a cross slope of 2.5 percent may be necessary to provide adequate pavement drainage.

Reading material

Ⅰ (1) T   (2) T   (3) F   (4) T   (5) F

Ⅱ (1) A freeway

(2) ramp junctions

(3) Weaving areas

(4) merging   diverging

(5) characteristic

Ⅲ (1) Roadway characteristics are the geometric characteristics of the freeway segment under study. Those include the numbers and widths of lanes, lateral clearances at the roadside and median, design speeds, grades and lane configurations.

(2) Traffic conditions refer to any characteristic of the traffic flow that affects capacities or operations. These include the percentage composition of the traffic flow by vehicle types, lane distribution characteristics and diver characteristics.

(3) A freeway may be defined as a divided highway facility having two or more lanes for the exclusive use of traffic in each direction and full control of access and egress.

(4) Sections of the freeway where two or more vehicle flow must cross each other's path along a length of the freeway. Weaving areas are usually formed when merge areas are closely followed by diverge areas. They are also formed when a freeway on-ramp is followed by an off-ramp and the two are connected by a continuous auxiliary lane.

(5) Freeway capacity is the maximum sustained (15min) rate of flow at which traffic can pass a point or uniform segment of freeway under prevailing roadway and traffic conditions. Capacity is defined for a single direction of flow, and is expressed in vehicles per hour (vph).

Unit 12

Text

I (1) F (2) F (3) F (4) F (5) T

II (1) Traffic islands   kerb lines   street furniture

(2) the 18

(3) Priority junctions

(4) the existing form or control method must be considered

(5) give-way road markings   post mounted signs

III (1) With any urban scheme the most important consideration is the size, turning characteristics and space requirements of the design vehicles.

(2) London have designated abnormal load routes that avoid weak or low bridges, difficult turning manoeuvres or overhead telephone and power lines.

(3) If vehicles with long front or rear overhang are stationary and its steering wheels are on full lock the rear will tend to move outwards as it starts to move. If the vehicle is close to the kerb the bodywork might strike a pedestrian.

(4) ① Two lightly trafficked residential roads—priority junction;

② The through carriageways of a motorway—grade separation;

③ Heavily trafficked urban crossroads with heavy pedestrian flows—traffic signals;

④ Suburban dual carriageways with substantial heavy goods traffic—conventional roundabout.

(5) Crossroad layouts should be avoided wherever possible because they concentrate a large number of vehicle movements and, therefore, conflicts within the junctions.

Reading material

I (1) F (2) T (3) F (4) F (5) F

II (1) sensitivity

(2) cloverleaf

(3) only one bridge is required   construction of a safety island on the minor road

(4) a major and a minor road

(5) U-turns

III (1) Grade-separated junctions have been defined as ones which require use of an at-grade junction at the commencement or termination of the slip roads.

(2) Because the capacities of the two exit slip roads from the major road is limited by the capacity of the priority intersection with the minor road.

(3) For the diamond, the traffic importance of the minor road and the magnitude of the turning movements increase additional slip roads may be inserted into the partial cloverleaf design until the junction layout approaches the full cloverleaf design.

(4) The advantages of four-way junction are that it occupies a relatively small area of land and

has less carriageway area than other junctions of this type. It also allows easy U-turns to be made.

(5) The straight ahead traffic on both routes is unimpeded and in addition left-turning movements may be made directly from one route to the other. The cost of structural works is also less than with the grade separated roundabout because only one bridge is required although the bridge will normally be wider. On the other hand the carriageway area is greater for the cloverleaf.

Unit 13

Text

Ⅰ (1) T   (2) F   (3) T   (4) T   (5) F

Ⅱ (1) the right of owners or occupants

(2) a highway with and without control of access

(3) favorable weather condition   under prevailing traffic condition   the design speed on a section-by-section basis

(4) no right

(5) Average overall speed

Ⅲ (1) Control of access is the condition in which the right of owners or occupants of abutting land or other persons to access, light, air or view in connection with a highway is fully or partially controlled by public authorities.

(2) Access control is accomplished either by providing access rights or by using frontage roads.

(3) The principal operational difference between a highway with and without control of access is in the amount of interference with through traffic by other vehicles and pedestrians.

(4) A speed determined for design and correlation of the physical features of a highway that influences vehicle operation—the maximum safe speed maintainable over a specified section of highway when conditions permit design features to govern.

(5) The highest overall speed at which a driver can travel on a given highway under favorable weather condition and under prevailing traffic condition without any time exceeding the safe speed as determined by the design speed on a section-by-section basis.

Reading material

Ⅰ (1) T   (2) T   (3) F   (4) T   (5) F

Ⅱ (1) design speed   curvature   superelevation   side friction

(2) centrifugal

(3) topography

(4) uniform

(5) utilizing side friction   the varying centrifugal force

Ⅲ (1) In the design of highway curves it is necessary to establish the proper relation between design speed and curvature and also their joint relations with superelevation and side friction.

(2) On nonsuperelevated curves, travel at different speeds is also possible by utilizing side friction in appropriate amounts to resist the varying centrifugal force.

(3) Level terrain, rolling terrain and mountainous terrain.

(4) Rolling terrain is that condition where the natural slopes consistently rise above and fall below the road or street grade and where occasional steep slopes offer some restriction to normal horizontal and vertical roadway alinement.

(5) Routes in valleys or mountainous areas that have all the characteristics of roads or streets traversing level or rolling terrain should be classified as level or rolling terrain.

Unit 14

Text

I (1) T (2) F (3) T (4) T (5) F

II (1) sight distance

(2) Stopping sight distance

(3) sufficient visibility distances

(4) a safe passing section

(5) Longer sight distance

III (1) Stopping sight distance(S) is the sum of two distances: the distance traversed by the vehicle from the instant the driver sights an object necessitating a stop to the instant the brakes are applied, and the distance required to stop the vehicle from the brake application begins. These are referred to as brakes reaction distance(l_1) and braking distance(l_2), respectively.

(2) Stopping sight distance may not provide sufficient visibility distances for drivers to corroborate advance warnings and to perform the necessary maneuvers.

(3) Decision sight distance is the distance required for a driver to detect an unexpected or otherwise difficult-to-perceive information source or hazard in a roadway environment that may be visually cluttered, recognize the hazard or its threat potential, select an appropriate speed and path, and initiate and complete the required maneuver safely and efficiently.

(4) Passing sight distance for use in design should be determined on the basis of the length needed to safely complete normal passing maneuvers.

(5) It is not necessary to consider passing sight distance on highways or streets that have two or more traffic lanes in each direction of travel.

Reading material

I (1) F (2) F (3) T (4) T (5) T

II (1) the maximum rate of flow for the subject lane group

(2) saturation flow and saturation flow rate

(3) an approach is evaluated and determined using the procedures

(4) green time has been appropriately or proportionally allocated

(5) the defined cycle length and phase sequence by proportionally allocating green time

Ⅲ (1) The lane group capacity is the maximum rate of flow for the subject lane group that may pass through the intersection under prevailing traffic, roadway and signalization conditions.

(2) Roadway conditions include the basic geometrics of the intersection, including the numbers and widths of lanes, grades, and lane use allocations (including parking lanes).

(3) This may be done to isolate lanes serving a particular movement or movements.

(4) Saturation flow rate is defined as the maximum rate of flow that can pass through a given lane group under prevailing traffic and roadway conditions.

(5) The flow ratio for a given lane group is defined as the ratio of the actual or projected demand flow rate for the lane group (v_i) to the saturation now rate (s_i). The flow ratio is given the symbol $(v/s)_i$ (for lane group i).

Unit 15

Text

Ⅰ (1) T (2) F (3) T (4) F (5) F

Ⅱ (1) the maximum number

(2) levels of service

(3) Ideal conditions

(4) the type of facility and its development   lane widths   shoulder widths and lateral clearances   design speed   horizontal and vertical alignments   availability of queuing space at intersections

(5) Crawl speed

Ⅲ (1) A principal objective of capacity analysis is the estimation of the maximum number of people or vehicles that can be accommodated by a given facility in reasonable safety within a specified time period.

(2) Ideal conditions for uninterrupted flow facilities include the following: lane widths of 12ft; clearances of 6ft between the edges of the travel lanes and the nearest obstructions or objects at the roadside and in the median; design speeds of 70mph for multilane highways, 60mph for two-lane highways; only passenger cars in the traffic flow; level terrain.

(3) Ideal conditions for intersection approaches include the following: lane widths 12ft; level grade; no curb parking on the intersection approaches; only passenger cars in the traffic flow and no local transit buses stopping in the travel lanes; all vehicles traveling straight through the intersections; intersections located in non-central business district areas; no pedestrians; at signalized intersection approaches, green signal available at all times.

(4) ① The type of facility and its development.

② Lane widths.

③ Shoulder widths and lateral clearances.

④ Design speed.

⑤ Horizontal and vertical alignments.

⑥ Availability of queuing space at intersections.

(5) Procedure for uninterrupted flow facilities categorizes the general terrains of a highway as follows:

① Level terrain. Any combination of grades and horizontal and vertical alignments that allows heavy vehicles to maintain approximately the same speed as passenger cars; this terrain generally includes short grades of no more than 1 to 2 percent.

② Rolling terrain. Any combination of grades and horizontal or vertical alignments that causes drivers of heavy vehicles to reduce speeds to substantially below those of passenger cars, but does not require operation at crawl speeds for any significant length of time.

③ Mountainous terrain. Any combination of grades and horizontal and vertical alignments that causes drivers of heavy vehicles to operate at crawl speeds for significant distances or at frequent intervals.

Reading material

Ⅰ (1) F (2) T (3) F (4) T (5) T

Ⅱ (1) the freeway network

(2) queuing time

(3) necessitate the widening of roads

(4) delays and service reliability   infrequent service

(5) a function of the average vehicle control delay

Ⅲ (1) The *HCM* defines LOS for signalized and unsignalized intersections as a function of the average vehicle control delay.

(2) ① Through movements on the major road, parallel pedestrian movements, and right turns from the major road.

② Left turns from the major road.

③ Through movements on the minor road, parallel pedestrian movements, and right turns from the minor road.

④ Left turns from the minor road.

(3) 0—no service exists. Latent demand may exist.

1—service is poor, unsafe or discouraging. Demand is suppressed below socially desirable levels.

A ~ F—as per existing LOS scale.

G—further expansion of capacity is limited.

H—no expansion is possible. Radical or innovative solutions are required.

(4) Wait time, frequency of service, time it takes to pay fares, quality of the ride, accessibility of depots and so on.

(5) These delays are typically caused by congestion, breakdowns or infrequent service. It does not deal, for instance, with cases where there is no bridge across a river, no bus or train service, no

sidewalks, or no bike-lanes.

Unit 16

Text

Ⅰ (1) F　　(2) F　　(3) T　　(4) F　　(5) F

Ⅱ (1) concrete road

(2) low　　exceeded

(3) reinforcing steel

(4) bottom

(5) the top of the slab

Ⅲ (1) When a bridge, a building or an other such structure is being constructed, the concrete is normally expected to carry only the compressive stress that are produced, and reinforcing steel is incorporated in the structure to withstand the tensile stress.

(2) The reason for this is that if the relatively low tensile strength of the concrete is exceeded, the result could well be the complete collapse of the structure, with perhaps the loss of many lives.

(3) As a result, sufficient reinforcing steel in road can minimize the development of cracks and support any of the induced tensile stress. A practical by-product of this form of usage is that it allows a considerably greater spacing to be used between transverse joints.

(4) If tensile stress resistance was the principal criterion, then it was of course logical that two layers of steel should be used, so that one layer was at the top and the other at the bottom of the slab.

(5) If only one layer of reinforcement was used and the governing criterion was again resistance to tensile stress, then the layer should be placed near the top of the slab, since it was there that the more critical stress was induced.

Reading material

Ⅰ (1) F　　(2) F　　(3) T　　(4) T　　(5) T

Ⅱ (1) to distribute the applied vehicle loads to the subgrade

(2) its structural mechanics and the fact that the pressure is transmitted to the subgrade through the lateral distribution of the applied load with depth, rather than by beam and slab action as with a concrete slab

(3) The strength of the subgrade

(4) a similar shape and extent

(5) a pavement superimposed on the basement soil or subgrade

Ⅲ (1) A highway pavement is a structure consisting of superimposed layers of selected and processed materials whose primary function is to distribute the applied vehicle loads to the subgrade.

(2) The distinguishing feature of a flexible pavement lies in its structural mechanics and the fact that the pressure is transmitted to the subgrade through the lateral distribution of the applied load

with depth, rather than by beam and slab action as with a concrete slab.

(3) When the subgrade deflects beneath a rigid pavement, the concrete slab is able to bridge over localized failures and areas of inadequate support because of its structural capabilities.

(4) When the subgrade deflects, the overlying flexible pavement is expected to deform to a similar shape and extent.

(5) The cross-section of a flexible road is composed of a pavement superimposed on the basement soil or subgrade.

Unit 17

Text

Ⅰ (1) T　　(2) F　　(3) T　　(4) F　　(5) T

Ⅱ (1) pedestrians　　cyclists　　motorists　　vehicle passengers

(2) traffic collisions on the roads

(3) fatalities and Killed or Seriously Injured (KSI) rate

(4) helmets

(5) the National Highway Traffic Safety Administration

Ⅲ (1) Road traffic safety refers to the methods and measures used to prevent road users from being killed or seriously injured.

(2) Typical road users include pedestrians, cyclists, motorists, vehicle passengers and passengers of on-road public transport (mainly buses and trams).

(3) It is due in part to the lack of crash protection (unlike in enclosed vehicles such as cars), combined with the high speeds motorcycles typically travel at.

(4) ① Passenger restraints such as seat belts and airbags.

② Crash avoidance equipment such as lights and reflectors.

③ Driver assistance systems such as Electronic Stability Control.

(5) Government and all segments of society engage and contribute, while the private sectors have responsibility for providing safe roads.

Reading material

Ⅰ (1) T　　(2) F　　(3) T　　(4) F　　(5) T

Ⅱ (1) occupant restraints

(2) horizontal and vertical alignments　　roadside barrier performances

(3) the design of the area outside the traveled way

(4) the *NCHRP Report*

(5) The forgiving roadside concept

Ⅲ (1) These components included horizontal alignment, vertical alignment, hydraulic design and sight distance.

(2) It was the decade of the 1970s before this type of design was regularly incorporated into

highway projects.

(3) Roadside design might be defined as the design of the area outside the traveled way.

(4) This significant reduction is due to several factors. Motor vehicles are much safer today than they have been in the past. Protected passenger compartments, padded interiors, occupant restraints, and airbags are some features that have added to passenger safety during impact situations. Roadways have been made safer through improvements in features such as horizontal and vertical alignments, intersection geometry, traversable roadsides, roadside barrier performances, and grade separations and interchanges. Drivers are more educated about safe vehicle drivers' operation as evidenced by the increased use of occupant restraints and a decrease in driving under the influence of alcohol or drugs. All these contributing factors have reduced the motor vehicle drivers' fatality rate.

(5) ① Driver fatigue.

② Driver distractions or inattention.

③ Excessive speed.

④ Driving under the influence of drugs or alcohol.

⑤ Crash avoidance.

⑥ Adverse roadway conditions, such as ice, snow or rain.

⑦ Vehicle component failure.

⑧ Poor visibility.

Unit 18

Text

Ⅰ (1) T   (2) F   (3) T   (4) T   (5) T

Ⅱ (1) a continuous distribution of frequencies

(2) the human ear is more sensitive to sounds with higher frequencies than it is to sounds with lower frequencies

(3) the level of noise varies both considerably and rapidly

(4) $4(L_{10} - L_{90}) + L_{90} - 30$

(5) the lower noise levels and the greater variability experienced in Swedish traffic conditions

Ⅲ (1) It is because that the human ear is more sensitive to sounds with higher frequencies than it is to sounds with lower frequencies.

(2) Road traffic noise differs from most other sources of noise in that the level of noise varies both considerably and rapidly. At low sound-pressure levels the noise emitted from vehicles does not cause a great deal of annoyance, but at higher levels the annoyance is considerable. For this reason many measures of noise nuisance specify a sound pressure level that is exceeded for 10, 20, 30 percent, etc. of the time.

(3) $LNP = L_{eq} + 2.56\sigma$

(4) $L_{eq} = K\log \dfrac{1}{100} \sum 10^{L_i/Kf_i}$

(5) This scale should be capable of expressing the relative effect on people of the noise being measured. Firstly the unit should correlate reasonably well with the criterion of dissatisfaction chosen so that noise levels measured using the unit will represent subjective reactions. Secondly a reasonably accurate set of design rules should be available, covering the estimation of noise exposure from traffic data and the estimation of the performance of noise control techniques, in terms of the chosen unit.

Reading material

Ⅰ (1) F   (2) T   (3) F   (4) T   (5) F

Ⅱ (1) a reduction in air pollution
(2) vehicle exhausts
(3) the relative proportions
(4) estimated levels of carbon monoxide
(5) outline details of road centre lines   estimates of speed and flow

Ⅲ (1) The reduction of coal consumption and air pollution from domestic and industrial sources, also the increase in the volume of road traffic and the pollution from it.

(2) $\frac{26}{276} \times 100\% = 9.42\%$

(3) We use a standard of carbon monoxide concentration in the atmosphere.
(4) Because the method provides an estimation of the maximum concentration likely to occur.
(5) $C_8 = 1.91 - 1.85 \times 0.065 = 1.79$

Unit 19

Text

Ⅰ (1) T   (2) T   (3) F   (4) F   (5) T

Ⅱ (1) transportation
(2) between
(3) beneficiaries
(4) but
(5) Institutional constraints

Ⅲ (1) Because any transportation engineering problem involves a whole series of essentially economic decisions.

(2) The designer may make these choices on the basis of experience, preconceptions and an innate view of mathematical or structural elegance.

(3) By providing a tangible criterion-cost for choosing between alternative solutions, economics can avoid the need for arbitrary rules.

(4) Project identification, establishing rough priorities, detailed evaluation, project selection should be considered in an economic analysis.

(5) By plotting cost (y) against span length (x), we can choose the most economic type over a given range of span lengths.

Reading material

Ⅰ (1) T　(2) F　(3) F　(4) T　(5) F

Ⅱ (1) calculations

(2) postindustrial

(3) pluralistic

(4) the affected parts of the community　the concomitant benefits to them

(5) striving for mathematical　philosophical rigor

Ⅲ (1) When benefit-cost ratios in excess of unity, we should consider the project or plan is worthwhile.

(2) Because the fact that the terms of reference of the committee were interpreted too narrowly and the technique of economic evaluation was applied in an incomplete manner.

(3) Indirect costs and benefits account for a large proportion of the total costs and benefits.

(4) First it must be recognized that the treatment of externalities and some other quantifiable impacts in terms of additional monetary costs and benefits to be added into the direct cash flow is likely to be a process of great uncertainty which maylead to disagreement with other planners and confusion for decision makers.

(5) Because high discount rates tend to militate against the long term in favor of the short term and results in effectively nullifying the effect of long-term impacts.

Unit 20

Text

Ⅰ (1) T　(2) F　(3) T　(4) T　(5) F

Ⅱ (1) Transport telematics

(2) traffic flow, speeds, queues, incidents air quality and vehicle types, lengths and mass

(3) VMS　RDS-TMC

(4) public inquiry terminals

(5) Variable Message Sign

Ⅲ (1) Transport telematic, also known as Intelligent Transport Systems (ITS), is concerned with the application of electronic information and control to improve transport.

(2) ① Before leaving home, you check your travel arrangements over the internet. Often you choose to travel by public transport and you can identify travel times and any interruptions affecting the service. On this occasion, you choose to travel by car as you have an appointment later in the day at one of those old-fashioned business parks that are inaccessible by public transport. There are no incidents recorded on your normal route to work so you do not bother to use your computer route model to select an optimum route for you.

② Once in your car, you head for the motorway and select the cruise control, lane support and collision avoidance system, allowing yourself to concentrate on your favorite radio service. Suddenly, this is interrupted by the radio traffic-message channel service giving you information about an incident on your route. You are not surprised when, at the next junction, the roadside Variable Message Sign (VMS) confirms this—motorway messages really are believable now!

③ You feel pleased with yourself that you have preceded your in-car navigation system with the coordinate of your final destination, and soon you are obtaining instructions on your best route with information updated from the local travel control center.

(3) ① Traffic management and control.

② Tolling and road pricing.

③ Road safety and law enforcement.

④ Public transport travel information and ticketing.

⑤ Driver information and guidance.

⑥ Freight and fleet management.

⑦ Vehicle safety.

⑧ System integration.

(4) The information will be collected using infrared, radio, loop, radar, and microwave or vision detectors.

(5) ① Influencing traveller behavior, in particular modal choice, route choice and the times at which journeys are made.

② Reducing the impact of traffic on air quality.

③ Improving priority for buses and LRT vehicles.

④ Providing better and safer facilities for pedestrians, cyclists and other vulnerable road users.

⑤ Restraining traffic in sensitive areas.

⑥ Managing demand and congestion more efficiently.

Reading material

Ⅰ (1) T (2) F (3) T (4) T (5) T

Ⅱ (1) Automatic Vehicle Identification   Automatic Vehicle Classification   Video Enforcement System

(2) that receives its inputs from the AVI, AVC and VES equipment

(3) collecting the transaction information from the lane controllers and being in communication with a central host computer

(4) enrolls customers, manages the customer's toll account, issues tags to customers, processes the violation images, and handles customer inquires

(5) lane equipment   communication network   ETC central host   customer central service

Ⅲ (1) Automatic Vehicle Identification, Automatic Vehicle Classification, Video Enforcement Systems.

(2) The lane controller is a computer that receives its inputs from the AVI, AVC and VES

equipment. It is also the device that maintains a list of valid tags which it uses to validate the information provided by AVI.

(3) The plaza host computer is used to collect the transaction information from the lane controllers and it is in communication with a central host computer which collects data from all plazas so that the data exists in one consolidated location. It is also used to transmit to each lane controller the list of valid tags which is used for AVI validation.

(4) ① ETC allows the toll facility operators to improve customer service and satisfaction by speeding their trip through the toll plaza, removing the need for the customer to stop, fumble for change, or roll down their window. It also gives customers the flexibility of paying their toll with cash, cheque or even credit cards. In addition, customers can receive monthly statements detailing their toll usage and will not have to ask for receipts. Commercial customers have the added benefit of no longer being required to send drivers out with cash or some form of ticket which will get rid of the potential of being misused.

② The toll facility operator also benefits from ETC. Facility throughput can be increased without the need to build additional infrastructure (such as more toll booths) and the amount of staff dedicated to the toll collection process can often be reduced.

③ Even the general public benefits from ETC since the fewer cars and trucks which idle at a toll plaza, the less exhaust is spewed into the air and the cleaner the air will be.

(5) ① Lane equipment.

② Communication network.

③ ETC central host.

④ Customer central service.

Unit 21

Text

Ⅰ (1) F   (2) T   (3) T   (4) F   (5) T

Ⅱ (1) information processing   communications   control   eletronics

(2) the four-way traffic signal

(3) economically sound   environmentally efficient

(4) a state-of-the-art, intermodal transportation system

(5) the only nation private/public organization established to coordinate the development and deployment of ITS in the United States

Ⅲ (1) ITS is comprised of a number of technologies, including information processing, communications, control and electronics.

(2) It needs mutual cooperation of the public and private sectors. The United States requires a voluntary commitment to cooperation that preserves the benefits of the free enterprise system while ensuring that the broad goals established by Congress are met. The model for this type of cooperation is the public/private partnership — a voluntary association of public and private interests committed

to the successful development and deployment of ITS in the United States. It is the mandate of the Intelligent Transportation Society of America (ITS America) to coordinate that cooperative effort.

(3) Fulfilling the need for a national system that is both economically sound and environmentally efficient requires a new way of looking at and solving our transportation problems.

(4) ① Decrease congestion by reducing the number of traffic incidents, clearing them more quickly when they occur, rerouting traffic flow around them, and automatically collecting toll.

② Improve the productivity of commercial, transit and public safety fleets by using automated tracking, dispatch and mass-in-motion systems that speed vehicles through much of the red tape associated with interstate commerce.

③ Assist drivers in reaching a desired destination with navigation systems enhanced with path finding, or route guidance.

(5) They all support the development of ITS. Public agencies stand to derive enormous benefits from the deployment of these technologies. For government agencies at all levels, the innovative application of advanced technologies means lower costs, enhanced services, and a healthier environment for the constituents these agencies serve.

Reading material

Ⅰ (1) T　　(2) F　　(3) F　　(4) T　　(5) T

Ⅱ (1) traffic management　　route guidance

(2) a geometric positioning system　　a geographic information system based on digital road maps

(3) Digital road maps

(4) the poor quality of input data

(5) detect blunders in input data and faults

Ⅲ (1) ITS services include traffic management, electronic payment, route guidance, fleet management and emergency management vehicle services.

(2) There are basic management systems such as car navigation; traffic signal control systems; container management systems; variable message signs; automatic number plate recognition or speed cameras to monitor applications, such as security CCTV systems. And more advanced applications that integrate live data and feedback from a number of other sources, such as parking guidance and information systems; weather information; bridge deicing (U.S. deicing) systems. Additionally, predictive techniques are being developed to allow advanced modelling and comparison with historical baseline data.

(3) ① A geometric positioning system, such as a Global Positioning System (GPS) or an integrated navigation system, such as Dead Reckoning (DR).

② A Geographic Information System (GIS) based on digital road maps.

(4) No it can't. This is due to the various types of errors associated with the received positioning data such as signal outage, and errors due to atmospheric effects, receiver measurement errors, and multipath errors.

(5) The integrity of a system refers to its ability to detect blunders in input data and faults in the map matching process.

Unit 22

Text

I (1) F (2) T (3) F (4) T (5) F

II (1) an information resource

(2) the diversity of formats and data sources

(3) detecting the presence of vehicles   categorization of the vehicles

(4) traffic surveillance systems

(5) Radio Frequency Identification

III (1) These include R&D efforts on data warehouse products and large-scale distributed data processing platforms such as Hadoop, and those on data analytics technologies such as machine learning and data mining.

(2) The term Big Data refers to an information resource that is characterized by large quantity, high-speed growth and a large variety of data that exceed capabilities of software that are commonly used for storage, processing and data management. It is the amount of data that can be measured in petabytes and the speed of information inflow that is greater than the speed of processing.

(3) Observation of traffic includes the following activities: detecting the presence of vehicles, traffic counting, measuring length, categorization of the vehicles, and many more.

(4) Traffic sensors for data collection are inductive-loop detectors, video image processing systems, pneumatic tubes, Global Positioning System (GPS), acoustic/ultrasonic sensors, aerial/satellite imaging, and RFID (Radio Frequency Identification) technology.

(5) The highly developed detection technologies can be classified into three categories: in-roadway detectors, over-roadway detectors and off-roadway technologies.

Reading material

I (1) T (2) F (3) T (4) F (5) T

II (1) travel demand and the performance of transportation infrastructure

(2) estimate current traffic conditions

(3) loop detectors

(4) between demand and capacity

(5) the relationship between safety and congestion

III (1) Broadly speaking, application can be categorized into three groups: transportation planning, traffic operations and safety.

(2) They has the potential to radically decrease the time in-between updated surveys, increase survey coverage, and reduce data acquisition costs.

(3) Researchers exploit Big Data sources from mobile phone's call detail records, smart card

systems, automatic passenger count systems, GPS, smart phone and vehicle location services, bike-sharing and social media data, for travel demand estimation, transit origin-destination estimation, daily travel pattern analysis, non-work destination choice, transit travel experience, origin-destination estimation by trip purpose and time of day, willingness to travel by activity types, and traffic zoning.

(4) Researchers exploit Big Data sources from GPS, Bluetooth reader, loop detector, private sector travel time and floating cars for traffic flow prediction, travel time prediction, addressing GPS data requirements, and route travel time distribution.

(5) Researchers exploit Big Data sources from video, microwave vehicle detection system, GPS and vehicle trajectory data. It includes applications on proactive road safety analysis, traffic operation and safety monitoring, calibration of traffic simulation model for safety assessment, and instantaneous driving decisions modeling.

Unit 23

Text

I (1) F (2) T (3) T (4) T (5) F

II (1) facilitate
(2) consumer lifestyle
(3) in terms of
(4) promote
(5) Lack of standards

III (1) The IoV is an integration of three networks: an inter-vehicle network, an intra-vehicle network and vehicular mobile Internet.

(2) An Internet of Vehicles is a large-scale distributed system for wireless communication and information exchange between vehicle, road, human and internet.

(3) Acquisition of core technologies and standards will be crucial to securing a strategic advantage.

(4) Lack of coordination and communication is the biggest challenge to IoV implementation.

(5) Technological innovation and business model innovation in the Internet era depends on Partnering across traditional boundaries.

Reading material

I (1) T (2) F (3) F (4) T (5) F

II (1) challenging
(2) Convergence
(3) effectively
(4) scalability
(5) three

Ⅲ (1) The IoV aims at achieving an integrated smart transport system by improving traffic flow, preventing accidents, ensuring the road safety, and creating a comfortable driving experience.

(2) The Big Data technology provides a solution to evolve intelligent and smart vehicular system.

(3) Wireless networks can be divided into three major categories, including infrastructure wireless network, ad-hoc network or non-structured network and hybrid network.

(4) Convergence of technologies in the design of vehicles is the key device in the Internet of Things (IoT).

(5) The Internet of Vehicle transfers facilitates data between cars, roadside equipment, wearable devices and traffic data management centers.

Unit 24

Text

Ⅰ (1) T (2) T (3) T (4) F (5) T

Ⅱ (1) critical

(2) Detection

(3) clearance

(4) independently

(5) motor shields

Ⅲ (1) An Unmanned Ground Vehicle (UGV) is a piece of mechanized equipment that moves across the surface of the ground and serves as a means of carrying or transporting something.

(2) The UGV system generally consists of three main parts, such as vehicle control system, navigation system and obstacle detection system.

(3) UGV can be used for many applications where it may be inconvenient, dangerous, or impossible to have a human operator present.

(4) The goal of UGV research is to produce a machine capable of carrying out operation in the absence of, or with minimal, human intervention.

(5) The design of the UGV is 30cm × 30cm size and 9cm height. The mass of the robot is approximately 5kg. It consists of two main tracks, 4 side arm tracks and a moving sensor panel at the top that consists of four ultrasound sensors.

Reading material

Ⅰ (1) T (2) F (3) F (4) F (5) T

Ⅱ (1) subversive

(2) cross with

(3) released

(4) Compared with

(5) normal highways   under complicated situations

Ⅲ (1) The first stage relied totally on manual work without standardized parts and assembling process. The cars of this stage had high prices and their qualities were out of effective control. The second stage was characterized by standardized and streamlined production. Since the middle and later periods of the 1990s, the automobile industry has entered into the third stage.

(2) The intelligent route and the network route are the two main routes to realize wheeled mobile robots.

(3) The U.S. is the first one to study unmanned driving cars in the world.

(4) The rapid development of artificial intelligence, cognitive science, automatic control, ground mapping, sensor technology, and other fields.

(5) It has finished designing several kinds of sample cars and on-road test of nearly one million kilometers.

Vocabulary

A

abbreviate [əˈbriːvieɪt]	v. 缩略;把(词语、名称)缩写(成……)
absence [ˈæbsəns]	n. 没有;缺乏;缺席
abut [əˈbʌt]	vt. & vi. (与……)邻接;毗连;紧靠
abutting land	毗邻的土地
accelerate [ækˈseləreɪt]	vt. 使……加快;使……增速 vi. 加速;促进;增加
accident statistic	事故统计
accommodation [əˌkɒməˈdeɪʃn]	n. 住处;住宿
accordingly [əˈkɔːdɪŋli]	adv. 因此;于是;相应地
accumulative [əˈkjuːmjələtɪv]	adj. 积聚的;累积的
accuracy [ˈækjərəsi]	n. 准确(性);精确(性)
acoustic [əˈkuːstɪk]	adj. 声学的;音响的;听觉的
acquisition [ˌækwɪˈzɪʃn]	n. 获得物;获得;收购
actuate [ˈæktʃueɪt]	vt. 开动;激励;驱使
adaptive control	自适应控制
ad-hoc [ædˈhɑːk]	专门
adjacent [əˈdʒeɪsnt]	adj. 与……毗连的;邻近的;接近的
adverse [ˈædvɜːs]	adj. 不利的;有害的
aesthetic [iːsˈθetɪk]	adj. 审美的;美学的;艺术的;美的 n. 美感;审美观;美学标准
afford [əˈfɔːd]	vt. 提供;给予
afterthought [ˈɑːftəθɔːt]	n. 事后的想法;后来添加的东西
aggregate [ˈægrɪgət]	n. 合计集料 adj. 总数的;总计的
alleviate [əˈliːvieɪt]	vt. 减轻;缓和
alleyway [ˈæliweɪ]	n. 小巷;胡同;窄道;通道
allocation [ˌæləˈkeɪʃn]	n. 分配;配给
alternative [ɔːlˈtɜːnətɪv]	n. 可供选择的事物 adj. 可供替代的;备选的
ambient [ˈæmbiənt]	adj. 周围的 n. 周围环境
amplitude [ˈæmplɪtjuːd]	n. 振幅
annoyance [əˈnɔɪəns]	n. 烦恼;可厌之事
applicable [əˈplɪkəbl]	adj. 适当的;可应用的

appropriate [ə'prəʊprɪət]	adj. 适当的;恰当的;合适的
arbitrary ['ɑːbɪtrərɪ]	adj. 任意的,随意的;武断的,独裁的;专断的
archaeological [ˌɑːkɪə'lɒdʒɪkl]	adj. 考古的;考古学的;考古学上的
Area of Outstanding Natural Beauty (AONB)	<英>(受到国家保护的)杰出自然风景区
arterial highway	干线公路
arterial street	城市干道;干线道路
artificial intelligence	人工智能
assess [ə'ses]	vt. 估定;评定
assignment [ə'saɪnmənt]	n. 分配;委派;任务;(课外)作业
assume [ə'sjuːm]	v. 假定;认为
at all times	始终,一直
attainable [ə'teɪnəbl]	adj. 可到达的;可得到的
automobile ['ɔːtəməbiːl]	n. 小汽车
automotive [ˌɔːtə'məʊtɪv]	adj. 汽车的;机动车辆的
autonomous [ɔː'tɒnəməs]	adj. 自治的;自主的;自发的
auxiliary [ɔːg'zɪlɪərɪ]	adj. 辅助的;补充的
available [ə'veɪləbl]	adj. 可获得的;可找到的;有空的
average overall speed	平均行程速度
average running speed	平均行驶速度

B

backbone ['bækbəʊn]	n. 脊柱;支柱;(计算机)主干网
barrier ['bærɪə(r)]	n. 障碍,屏障;分界线
be frustrated by	使……受挫;对……感到沮丧
beacon ['biːkən]	n. 烟火;灯塔 vt. 照亮;指引
beneficiary [ˌbenɪ'fɪʃərɪ]	n. [金融]受益人,受惠者;封臣 adj. 拥有封地的;受圣俸的
bicycle lane	自行车道
Big Data	大数据
bikeway	自行车道,自行车专用道
block [blɒk]	n. 块;街区;大厦;障碍物
bottleneck ['bɒtlnek]	n. 瓶颈路段;瓶颈;阻碍;障碍
bump [bʌmp]	n. 肿块;撞击;隆起物 vt. & vi. 碰撞;冲撞颠簸 adv. 突然地;猛烈地
bypass ['baɪpɑːs]	n. 旁路;旁道;支路

C

cable ['keɪbl]	n. 缆绳;钢索;电缆

cafeteria [ˌkæfəˈtɪərɪə]	n. 自助餐厅；自助食堂
calibrate [ˈkælɪbreɪt]	v. 标定；校准(刻度；以使测量准确)
canal [kəˈnæl]	n. 运河；灌溉渠
capable of	可以……的；能……的；易……的；敢于……的
car wash	洗车处；洗车场
cargo [ˈkɑːgəʊ]	n. (船或飞机装载的)货物
carpool [ˈkɑːpuːl]	v. 合伙用车；拼车
carriageway [ˈkærɪdʒweɪ]	n. 车道；马路
casualty [ˈkæʒjuəltɪ]	n. 意外事故；伤亡人员
catch on	理解；明白
causeway [ˈkɔːzweɪ]	n. 堤道；公路
cellular [ˈseljələ(r)]	adj. 细胞的
census points	人口普查点
Central Business District (CBD)	中央商务区
centralized control	集中控制，中心控制
chaperone [ˈʃæpərəʊn]	n. 女伴；行为监督人 v. 伴护，当行为监护人
characterize [ˈkærəktəraɪz]	vt. 描绘……的特性；具有……的特征 vi. 塑造人物
circuitous [səˈkjuːɪtəs]	adj. 迂回的；绕道的；曲折的
circulation [ˌsɜːkjəˈleɪʃn]	n. 循环；运行；传播；流通(量)
circumstance [ˈsɜːkəmstəns]	n. 环境；详情；境况
clearance [ˈklɪərəns]	n. 清除；排除间隙；空隙
clear-cut [ˌklɪəˈkʌt]	adj. 明确的；明显的；鲜明
coach [kəʊtʃ]	n. 旅客车厢；长途汽车
coalition [ˌkəʊəˈlɪʃn]	n. 联合；结合；同盟
code [kəʊd]	n. 密码；暗码；电码；准则 v. 为……编码；编码
collaborate [kəˈlæbəreɪt]	vi. 合作；协作
collaboration [kəˌlæbəˈreɪʃn]	n. 合作；协作；合作成果(或作品)
collapse [kəˈlæps]	vi. (突然)倒塌；坍塌 n. 倒闭；崩溃
collision [kəˈlɪʒn]	n. 碰撞；冲突；(意见，看法)的抵触
commensurate [kəˈmenʃərət]	adj. 相称的；同量的；同样大小的
common sense	常识
community [kəˈmjuːnətɪ]	n. 社会；团体；社区；(政治)共同体
commuter [kəˈmjuːtə(r)]	n. (远距离)上下班往返的人
compatible [kəmˈpætəbl]	adj. 谐调的；一致的；兼容的
compensate [ˈkɒmpenseɪt]	vi. 补偿；赔偿；抵消 vt. 补偿；赔偿；付报酬
complementary [ˌkɒmplɪˈmentrɪ]	adj. 互补的；补充的；补足的
completion [kəmˈpliːʃn]	n. 完成；结束；完成交易；完成交割
comprehensive [ˌkɒmprɪˈhensɪv]	adj. 全面的；广泛的；综合的

compressive [kəmˈpresɪv]	*adj.* 有压缩力的	
comprise [kəmˈpraɪz]	*vt.* 包含；由……组成	
computational [ˌkɒmpjuˈteɪʃənl]	*adj.* 使用计算机的；计算的	
concentration [ˌkɒnsnˈtreɪʃn]	*n.* 集中；集合；专心；专注	
concrete [ˈkɒŋkriːt]	*adj.* 混凝土制的　*n.* 混凝土　*vt.* 用混凝土修筑；使凝固	
confine [kənˈfaɪn]	*n.* 界限；边界；限制　*vt.* 限制	
confirm [kənˈfɜːm]	*vt.* 确认；证实；批准；使巩固	
confront [kənˈfrʌnt]	*vt.* 面对；遭遇；碰到；比较	
congest [kənˈdʒest]	*vt.* 充满；拥挤	
congestion [kənˈdʒestʃən]	*n.* （交通）拥挤	
congestion charging	拥堵收费	
conjunction [kənˈdʒʌŋkʃn]	*n.* 联合；关联；连接	
conservation [ˌkɒnsəˈveɪʃn]	*n.* 保存；保持；保护	
consistency [kənˈsɪstənsɪ]	*n.* 一致性；连贯性；前后一致	
constraint [kənˈstreɪnt]	*n.* 约束；强制；限制	
consultation [ˌkɒnsəlˈteɪʃn]	*n.* 请教；咨询；磋商	
continent [ˈkɒntɪnənt]	*n.* 大陆；洲；陆地　*adj.* 自制的；克制的	
continuously [kənˈtɪnjuəslɪ]	*adv.* 连续不断地	
convergence [kənˈvɜːdʒəns]	*n.* 趋同；融合	
conversely [kɒnˈvɜːslɪ]	*adv.* 相反地；反之	
conversion [kənˈvɜːʃn]	*n.* 转变；转换；转化	
conveyance [kənˈveɪəns]	*n.* 运输；运输工具；财产让与	
coordination [kəʊˌɔːdɪˈneɪʃn]	*n.* 协作；协调	
copilot [ˈkəʊˌpaɪlət]	*n.* （飞机）副驾驶员	
correlate [ˈkɒrəleɪt]	*v.* 使相互关联；和……相关	
corridor [ˈkɒrɪdɔː(r)]	*n.* 通道；走廊	
corroborate [kəˈrɒbəreɪt]	*vt.* 证实	
corrugated [ˈkɒrəgeɪtɪd]	*adj.* 缩成皱纹的；使起波状的	
crack [kræk]	*v.* 破裂；裂开　*n.* 裂纹；裂缝；狭缝	
crawl [krɒːl]	*vi.* 爬行；匍匐行进　*n.* 爬行；缓慢地爬行	
criterion [kraɪˈtɪərɪən]	*n.* 标准；准则；原则	
cross-border [ˈkrɒsbɔːdə]	*adj.* 跨国的；跨越边界的	
crossroad [ˈkrɒsˌrəʊd]	*n.* 十字路口	
crown [kraʊn]	*n.* 路拱	
crucial [ˈkruːʃl]	*adj.* 关键性的；至关重要的	
cruise [kruːz]	*vi.* 巡游；巡航　*n.* 巡游；巡航	
curb [kɜːb]	*vt.* 控制；抑制；限定；约束（不好的事物）	
curfew [ˈkɜːfjuː]	*n.* 宵禁	

curvature [ˈkɜːvətʃə(r)]	n. 弯曲；曲率；弯曲部分
curve [kɜːv]	n. 曲线；弯曲物　vt. 使弯曲　vi. 弯曲
cycle track	自行车道

D

data base	数据库
debris [ˈdebriː]	n. 残骸；碎片；残渣；垃圾；废弃物
decibel [ˈdesɪbel]	n. 分贝
decline [dɪˈklaɪn]	vi. 下倾；下降　vi. 谢绝；婉拒　n. 下倾；下降；衰退
demand management	需求管理
demountable [dɪˈmaʊntəbl]	adj. 可卸下的
density [ˈdensɪti]	n. 密度
deploy [dɪˈplɔɪ]	vt. 配置；展开　vi. 部署；展开　n. 部署
deployment [diːˈplɔɪmənt]	n. 调度；部署
depot [ˈdepəʊ]	n. 仓库；停车场；航空站
decision sight distance	决策视距
design speed	设计速度
designate [ˈdezɪɡneɪt]	v. 指定；指明
desirable [dɪˈzaɪərəbl]	adj. 可取的；值得拥有的；值得拥有的
destination [ˌdestɪˈneɪʃn]	n. 目的地；终点
detection [dɪˈtekʃn]	n. 侦查；探测；发现；察觉
device [dɪˈvaɪs]	n. 装置；策略；方法；手段；设备；终端
dimension [daɪˈmenʃn]	n. 尺寸
diminish [dɪˈmɪnɪʃ]	vt. (使)减少；(使)变小
directional informatory sign	指示指路标志
disamenity [ˌdɪsəˈmiːnɪti]	n. 不舒适；不愉快
disprove [ˌdɪsˈpruːv]	vt. 反驳；驳斥；证明……是虚假的
dissatisfaction [ˌdɪsˌsætɪsˈfækʃn]	n. 不快；不悦；不满
distribute [dɪˈstrɪbjuːt]	vt. 分配；散布；分开；把……分类
district [ˈdɪstrɪkt]	n. 区域；地方
diverse [daɪˈvɜːs]	adj. 不同的；相异的；多种多样的
do nothing	无所作为
domain [dəˈmeɪn]	n. 领域；范围
drainage [ˈdreɪnɪdʒ]	n. 排水；排泄；排水装置
dramatically [drəˈmætɪkli]	adv. 戏剧性地；引人注目地
drawbar [ˈdrɔːbɑː]	n. 列车间的挂钩；牵引车的挂钩
driver's license	驾驶执照
driveway [ˈdraɪvweɪ]	n. 车道；马路

dual [ˈdjuːəl]	adj. 两部分的;双重的;双的
duration [djuˈreɪʃn]	n. 持续;持续时间
dwell time	停顿(留)时间
dynamic [daɪˈnæmɪk]	adj. 动态的;动力的;动力学的

E

easement [ˈiːzmənt]	n. 地役权;缓和;减轻
ecosystem [ˈiːkəʊsɪstəm]	n. [生]生态系统
edge condition	边界条件
Electronic Stability Control	电子稳定控制
elegance [ˈelɪɡəns]	n. 高雅;典雅;优雅;雅致
eliminate [ɪˈlɪmɪneɪt]	vt. 排除;消除;清除;淘汰
embrace [ɪmˈbreɪs]	vt. & vi. 拥抱 vt. 包括;包含
emerge [iˈmɜːdʒ]	v. 出现;浮现;显现;显露
emergency [ɪˈmɜːdʒənsɪ]	n. 紧急情况;突然事件;非常时刻
emerging market	新兴市场
emission [ɪˈmɪʃn]	n. (光、热、气等的)发出,射出,排放;发行;排放物;散发物
encompass [ɪnˈkʌmpəs]	vt. 包含;包括;涉及;包围;围绕
enforcement [ɪnˈfɔːsmənt]	n. 执行;实施;强制
engage [ɪnˈɡeɪdʒ]	vt. 吸引;引起注意 vi. 从事;参与;参加
enhancement [ɪnˈhɑːnsmənt]	n. 增进;增加
enterprise [ˈentəpraɪz]	n. 企业;事业;进取心;事业心
equilibrium [ˌiːkwɪˈlɪbrɪəm]	n. 平衡;平静;均衡
equity [ˈekwətɪ]	n. 公平;公正
estimation [ˌestɪˈmeɪʃn]	n. 估计;评价;判断
evasive [ɪˈveɪsɪv]	adj. 逃避的;推托的
evolve [ɪˈvɒlv]	vt. 发展;进化;使逐步形成;推断出 vi. 发展;进展;进化;逐步形成
exceed [ɪkˈsiːd]	vt. 超过;胜过
expectancy [ɪkˈspektənsɪ]	n. 期待;期望
expressway [ɪkˈspresweɪ]	n. 高速道路
extensive [ɪkˈstensɪv]	adj. 广泛的;大量的;广阔的

F

facilitate [fəˈsɪlɪteɪt]	vt. 促进;帮助;使容易
facility [fəˈsɪlətɪ]	n. 便利;条件;设备;设施工具
fare [feə]	n. 票价;费用;旅客

fatal ['feItl]	adj. 致命的;重大的;命中注定的
fatality [fə'tælItI]	n. 死亡;灾祸
favorable ['feIvərəbl]	adj. 赞成的;有利的;起促进作用的
ferry ['ferI]	n. 渡船;摆渡;渡口 vi. 摆渡;来往行驶
filter ['fIltə(r)]	n. 滤波器;过滤器;滤光器
financial [faI'nænʃl]	adj. 财政的;财务的;金融的
finite ['faInaIt]	adj. 有限的
fire truck	救火车;消防车
fixed amount	定额;固定金额
fixed-time	固定周期
fleet [fli:t]	adj. 快速的;敏捷的 n. 舰队;港湾;小河 vi. 飞逝;疾驰;掠过
flexibility [ˌfleksə'bIlətI]	n. 灵活性;弹性;适应性
fluctuation [ˌflʌktʃʊ'eIʃn]	n. 波动;起伏
footway ['futweI]	n. 人行道;小路
foregoing ['fɔ:gəʊIŋ]	adj. 在前的;前述的
format ['fɔ:mæt]	n. 格式;版式 vt. 使格式化;规定……的格式 vi. 设计版式
formerly ['fɔ:məlI]	adv. 以前;从前;原来;原先
freight [freIt]	n. 货运;运费;货物 vt. 运输
frequency ['fri:kwənsI]	n. 频率;发生次数
Frequency Modulation (FM)	调频
frontage road	沿街道路;临街道路
fuel [fjuəl]	vt. 供以燃料;给……加燃料 n. 燃料;刺激因素
futuristic [fju:tʃə'rIstIk]	adj. 未来的;未来派的,未来主义的

G

gap [gæp]	n. 间隙;差距,隔阂
gate-controlled	闸门控制的
gear ratio	齿轮比;传动比
generate ['dʒenəreIt]	vt. 产生;引起;造成
generous ['dʒenərəs]	adj. 慷慨的,大方的;丰盛的;肥沃的
geometric [ˌdʒi:ə'metrIk]	adj. 几何学的;[数]几何学图形的
geometrical [dʒi:ə'metrIkl]	adj. 几何的;几何学的
give preference to	优先考虑
globalization [ˌgləʊbəlaI'zeIʃn]	n. 全球化
grade separation	立体交叉口
gradient ['greIdIənt]	n. 梯度;倾斜度;坡度

gravel [ˈɡrævl]	n. 碎石;砂砾 vt. 用碎石铺;使困惑
gravity [ˈɡrævətɪ]	n. 地心引力;重力
gridlock [ˈɡrɪdlɒk]	n. 交通堵塞
gutter [ˈɡʌtə(r)]	n. 檐沟;天沟;路旁排水沟,阴沟 vi. 忽明忽暗;摇曳不定

H

halve [hɑːv]	vt. 二等分;把……减半
harsh [hɑːʃ]	adj. 粗糙的
hazard [ˈhæzəd]	n. 冒险;危险;冒险的事 vt. 冒险
hazardous [ˈhæzədəs]	adj. 危险的;冒险的
helicopter [ˈhelɪkɒptə(r)]	n. 直升机
helmet [ˈhelmɪt]	n. 钢盔;头盔
hence [ˈhens]	adv. 因此;今后
high-pitched	adj. 高音的
highway networks	公路网
home-based trip	基于家的出行
horizontal alignment	平面线形
household [ˈhaʊshəʊld]	n. 家庭 adj. 家庭的

I

identification [aɪˌdentɪfɪˈkeɪʃn]	n. 鉴别;识别;认同
identify [aɪˈdentɪfaɪ]	vt. 识别;认出
impede [ɪmˈpiːd]	vt. 阻碍;妨碍;阻止
implement [ˈɪmplɪment]	v. 贯彻;执行;实施
in contrast	相反
in response to	响应;回答;对……有反应
in terms of	根据;按照
intertemporal [ɪnˈtəːrtɪmpərəl]	adj. 跨时期的
in the case of	在……的情况下;假如;如果发生
in the field of	在……方面;在……领域
inaccessible [ɪnəkˈsesəbl]	adj. 达不到的;难以见到的
inclined [ɪnˈklaɪnd]	adj. 倾斜的
inclusive [ɪnˈkluːsɪv]	adj. 包含的,包括的;包含全部费用的;范围广泛
incorporate [ɪnˈkɔːpəreɪt]	adj. 合并的;结社的;一体化的 vi. 合并;使组成公司 vt. 合并;混合;组成公司
in-depth	彻底的;深入的
indication [ˌɪndɪˈkeɪʃn]	n. 指出;指示;迹象;暗示
indicator [ˈɪndɪkeɪtə]	n. 指标;迹象;指示器;[计]指示符

industrial [ɪnˈdʌstrɪəl]		adj. 工业的;产业的;从事工业的
inertia [ɪˈnɜːʃə]		n. [物]惯性;惯量
infeasible [ɪnˈfizəbl]		adj. 不能实行的
infrastructure [ˈɪnfrəstrʌktʃə(r)]		n. 基础建设;基础设施
inherent [ɪnˈhɪərənt]		adj. 固有的;内在的
initial [ɪˈnɪʃl]		adj. 最初的;开始的
initiate [ɪˈnɪʃɪeɪt]		vt. 开始;发动;传授;发起
innate [ɪˈneɪt]		adj. 固有的;天生的;天然的;内在的
inner city		内城区
innovation solutions		革新方案
inquiry [ɪnˈkwaɪərɪ]		n. 质询;调查
inspection [ɪnˈspekʃn]		n. 检查;视察;查看;审视
installation [ˌɪnstəˈleɪʃn]		n. 安装的设备;装置;安装
instantaneous [ˌɪnstənˈteɪnɪəs]		adj. 瞬间的;即刻的;即时的
instruction [ɪnˈstrʌkʃn]		n. 命令;指示;教导;用法说明
integral [ˈɪntɪɡrəl]		adj. 积分的;完整的;整体的 n. 积分;部分;完整
integrated [ˈɪntɪɡreɪtɪd]		adj. 集成的;综合的
integration [ˌɪntɪˈɡreɪʃn]		n. 结合;整合;一体化;混合;融合
intelligent transportation systems (ITS)		智能交通运输系统
intensity [ɪnˈtensətɪ]		n. 强烈;强度;剧烈;烈度
interference [ˌɪntəˈfɪərəns]		n. 干涉;干预;介入
interlocking [ˌɪntəˈlɒkɪŋ]		adj. 连锁的
intermediate [ˌɪntəˈmiːdɪət]		adj. 之间的;中间的;中级的;中等的
intermodal [ˌɪntəˈməʊdl]		adj. 联合运输的
Internet of Things (IoT)		物联网
Internet of Vehicles (IoV)		车联网
interruption [ˌɪntəˈrʌpʃn]		n. 中断;打断
intersection [ˌɪntəˈsekʃn]		n. 十字路口;交叉路口;交点;交叉;相交
interstate [ˌɪntəˈsteɪt]		adj. 州际的;州与州之间的
interurban [ˌɪntəˈrɜːbən]		adj. 都市间的
interval [ˈɪntəvl]		n. 间隔;间距
intervene [ˌɪntəˈviːn]		v. 干涉;干预;插入;介入
intervention [ˌɪntəˈvenʃn]		n. 介入;干涉;干预
intoxicate [ɪnˈtɒksɪkeɪt]		vt. 使喝醉;使中毒
inventory [ˈɪnvəntrɪ]		n. 详细目录;财产清册
inverse [ˌɪnˈvɜːs]		adj. 倒转的;反转的;逆向的
in-depth		彻底的;深入的
isolate [ˈaɪsəleɪt]		vt. (使)隔离;(使)孤立 vi. 隔离;孤立 n. 被隔离的人(或物) adj. 孤独的;隔离的

J

jolt [dʒəult]	vt. 使颠簸;使震惊 n. 颠簸;摇晃;震惊;严重挫折 vi. 摇晃;颠簸而行
junction [ˈdʒʌŋkʃn]	n. 交叉口
jurisdiction [ˌdʒuərɪsˈdɪkʃn]	n. 司法权;管辖权;管辖区域

K

kerb [kɜːb]	n. (由条石砌成的)路缘;道牙

L

lane [leɪn]	n. 小路;车道
lateral [ˈlætərəl]	adj. 侧面的;横向的
layer [ˈleɪə(r)]	n. 层;表层;层次
layout [ˈleɪaut]	n. 布局;设计;安排
leaflet [ˈliːflət]	n. 散页印刷品;传单;(宣传或广告)小册子 v. (向……)散发传单(或小册子)
legal [ˈliːgl]	adj. 法律的;法律允许的;合法的
Light Rail Transit (LRT)	轻轨交通
light rail	轻轨
location [ləuˈkeɪʃn]	n. 位置;场所;特定区域
longitudinal spacing	纵距

M

mandate [ˈmændeɪt]	n. 授权;命令;指令;委托管理;强制执行 vt. 授权;托管
maneuver [məˈnuːvə]	vi. 移动 vt. 操纵
manoeuvrability [məˌnuːvərəˈbɪlətɪ]	n. 机动性;可移动
manoeuvre [məˈnuːvə(r)]	n. 策略;调动;操纵 vt. 策划;(敏捷地)操纵
manufacturer [ˌmænjuˈfæktʃərə(r)]	n. 制造商;[经]厂商
marginal [ˈmɑːdʒɪnl]	adj. 小的,微不足道的;边的,边缘的;临界的
matrix [ˈmeɪtrɪks]	n. [数]矩阵
may be	多半
median [ˈmiːdiən]	adj. 中央的;[数]中值的 n. 中部;中值;中位数
meeting place	聚集的地方;会场
merchant [ˈmɜːtʃənt]	n. 商人;批发商;贸易商;店主 adj. 商业的;商人的

metropolitan [ˌmetrəˈpɒlɪtən]		adj. 主要都市的;大城市的
microcontroller [ˌmaɪkrəʊkɒntˈrəʊlə(r)]		n. [自]微控制器
mobility [məʊˈbɪlətɪ]		n. 移动性;机动性
monitor [ˈmɒnɪtə(r)]		n. 显示屏;监视器 vi. 监视 vt. 监听
moped [ˈməʊped]		n. 机器脚踏车;摩托自行车
motor vehicle		机动车
motorist [ˈməʊtərɪst]		n. 驾车旅行的人;开汽车的人
motorway [ˈməʊtəweɪ]		n. (控制进出口的)高速公路
multilane [ˈmʌltɪleɪn]		adj. 多车道的(亦作 multilaned)
multiple [ˈmʌltɪpl]		adj. 多样的 n. 倍数;若干 v. 成倍增加
multiply [ˈmʌltɪplaɪ]		vt. & vi. 乘以;成倍增加;(使)繁殖
mutual [ˈmjuːtʃʊəl]		adj. 共同的;相互的;彼此的

N

narrow [ˈnærəʊ]		adj. 狭窄的;勉强的 n. 海峡;狭窄部分;隘路 vt. (使)变狭窄 vi. 变窄
navigation [nævɪˈgeɪʃn]		n. 航海;航空;导航;领航;航行
necessitate [nɪˈsesɪteɪt]		vt. 使……成为必要
negative [ˈnegətɪv]		n. 否定;负数 adj. 否定的;消极的;负的 vt. 否定;拒绝(接受)
negotiate [nɪˈgəʊʃɪeɪt]		v. 谈判;达成(协议);通过
network [ˈnetwɜːk]		n. 网络;网状系统;路网 v. 将……连接成网络
nonhome-based trip		非基于家的出行
nonlocal [nɒnˈləʊkəl]		adj. 非局部的;非本地的
note [nəʊt]		n. 记录
notify [ˈnəʊtɪfaɪ]		vt. 通告;通知;公布
novice [ˈnɒvɪs]		n. 初学者;新手
nuisance [ˈnjuːsns]		n. 讨厌的人或东西;麻烦事;损害
number plate survey		车牌号调查
numerous [ˈnjuːmərəs]		adj. 很多的;许多的

O

obstacle [ˈɒbstəkl]		n. 障碍;障碍物;阻碍;绊脚石
obstruction [əbˈstrʌkʃn]		n. 障碍;阻碍;妨碍
occupant [ˈɒkjəpənt]		n. 占有者;居住者
occurrence [əˈkʌrəns]		n. 发生;出现;事件
offset [ˈɒfset]		n. 抵销 vt. 弥补;抵销;用平版印刷 vi. 偏移;形成分支

omission [əˈmɪʃn]	n. 省略；删节；遗漏
one-way traffic	单向交通
operating speed	运行速度
opposing traffic	对向交通；双向通行
optimal [ˈɒptɪməl]	adj. 最优的，最佳的
optimize [ˈɒptɪmaɪz]	vt. 使最优化；充分利用
optimum [ˈɒptɪməm]	adj. 最适宜的
organism [ˈɔːɡənɪzəm]	n. 有机体；生物体；有机体系
origin and destination survey	起讫点调查
original [əˈrɪdʒənl]	adj. 起初的；最早的；首创的；独创的 n. 原件；正本；原稿；原作
overestimate [ˌəʊvərˈestɪmeɪt]	n. 过高的评估 vt. 对……估计过高 vi. 高估

P

panacea [ˌpænəˈsiːə]	n. 灵丹妙药；万能药
panel [ˈpænl]	n. 嵌板；镶板；金属板
paradigm [ˈpærədaɪm]	n. 范例；样式；模范
parameter [pəˈræmɪtə(r)]	n. 限制因素；决定因素；参数
park and ride	停车换乘体系；转乘停车场
parking lot	停车场
passing sight distance	超车视距
pavement width	路面宽度
pedal [ˈpedl]	n. (自行车等的)脚蹬子；踏板 vt. 骑自行车
pedestrian [pɪˈdestrɪən]	n. 行人；步行者
pedestrian [pəˈdestrɪənz]	n. 步行者；行人 adj. 徒步的
pedestrian crossing	人行横道
perceive [pəˈsiːv]	v. 察觉；感知；感到；认识到
performance [pəˈfɔːməns]	n. 性能
perpendicular [ˌpɜːpənˈdɪkjələ(r)]	adj. 垂直的；成直角的；垂直式的 n. 垂直线
pertaining [pɜː(ː)ˈteɪnɪŋ]	n. 与……有关系的；附属……的 v. 关于；有关
pertinent [ˈpɜːtɪnənt]	adj. 相关的；相干的
petabyte [ˈpetəbaɪt]	n. 千万亿字节或千 T 字节
phenomenon [fəˈnɒmɪnən]	n. 现象
pipeline [ˈpaɪplaɪn]	n. 输油管道；输气管道；输送管线
platform [ˈplætfɔːm]	n. 平台；月台；站台
plot [plɒt]	n. (专用的)小块土地 v. 绘制(图表)
plotting [ˈplɒtɪŋ]	n. 测绘；标图
pneumatic [njuːˈmætɪk]	adj. 气动的；充气的；有气胎的 n. 气胎

poster [ˈpəʊstə(r)]	n. 招贴画;海报
postpone [pəˈspəʊn]	vt. 使……延期;把……放在次要地位 vi. 延缓;延迟
potential [pəˈtenʃl]	adj. 潜在的;可能的;势的;位的 n. 潜能;潜力;势能;电位
pothole [ˈpɒthəʊl]	n. 壶穴 vi. 探索洞穴
preconception [ˌpriːkənˈsepʃn]	n. 预想;预见
predetermine [ˌpriːdɪˈtɜːmɪn]	v. 预定,预先确定
predominant [prɪˈdɒmɪnənt]	adj. 有影响力的;卓越的;占主要地位的
predominate [prɪˈdɒmɪneɪt]	vt. 在……占优势;支配;统治 vi. 占支配地位;占优势 adj. 主要的;突出的;占优势的
preemption [prɪˈempʃən]	n. 优先权;先占
prescribe [prɪˈskraɪb]	vt. 规定;指定
preservation [ˌprezəˈveɪʃn]	n. 保护;维护;保存;维持
prestressed [priːˈstrest]	adj. 预应力的(混凝土)
pre-timed	预设周期
prevail [prɪˈveɪl]	vi. 盛行;流行;占优势
previous [ˈpriːvɪəs]	adj. 在前的;早先的
principle [ˈprɪnsəpl]	n. 原则;原理;准则
priority [praɪˈɒrəti]	n. 优先;优先权;[数]优先次序;优先考虑的事
productive [prəˈdʌktɪv]	adj. 生产的;多产的
prohibit [prəˈhɪbɪt]	vt. 阻止;禁止;防止;不准许
prominent [ˈprɒmɪnənt]	adj. 突出的;显著的;杰出的;卓越的
propagate [ˈprɒpəgeɪt]	vt. 繁殖;传播;宣传
property value	属性值;产权价值;物业价值
proportion [prəˈpɔːʃn]	n. 部分;份额;比例
proposition [ˌprɒpəˈzɪʃn]	n. 主张;建议;陈述;命题
prosperity [prɒˈsperəti]	n. 繁荣
protocol [ˈprəʊtəkɒl]	n. [计]协议;规程
prudent [ˈpruːdnt]	adj. 谨慎的;精明的
public transport	公共交通;公交车辆

Q

queue [kjuː]	n. (人、汽车等的)队;行列;队列 vt. (人、车等)排队等候 vi. (使)排队
queuing theory	排队论

R

railway station	火车站

rainfall [ˈreɪnfɔːl]	n. 降雨量;降雨
ramp [ræmp]	n. 匝道;斜坡;坡道
rapid transit	高速交通系统;地铁
ratio [ˈreɪʃɪəu]	n. 比率;比例
reading [ˈriːdɪŋ]	n. 读数;仪表的指示数
real time	实时
rear [rɪə(r)]	n. 后部　adj. 后面的;后部的
reckless [ˈrekləs]	adj. 不计后果的
reference [ˈrefrəns]	n. 参考;参考书目　v. 引用
reflector [rɪˈflektə(r)]	n. 反射器;反射光的物体
refueling depot	加油站
region [ˈriːdʒən]	n. 地区;区域;地方;行政区
registration [ˌredʒɪˈstreɪʃn]	n. 注册;登记
regulatory sign	禁令标志
reinforcement [riːɪnˈfɔːsmənt]	n. 配筋;加强;加固
relieve [rɪˈliːv]	vt. 减轻;解除;缓解
remedial [rɪˈmiːdɪəl]	adj. 补救的;纠正的
repertoire [ˈrepətwɑː(r)]	n. 全部节目;全部剧目
representative [ˌreprɪˈzentətɪv]	adj. 典型的;具有代表性的
rerouting [riːˈruːtɪŋ]	v. 变更旅程
residence [ˈrezɪdəns]	n. 住宅;住处
residential [ˌrezɪˈdenʃl]	adj. 适合居住的;住宅的
residential lot	居民区
resistance [rɪˈzɪstəns]	n. 反对;抵制;抵抗;抵抗力
responsive [rɪˈspɒnsɪv]	adj. 响应的;响应的
restraint [rɪˈstreɪnt]	n. 抑制;克制;约束;限制
resultant [rɪˈzʌltənt]	adj. 因而发生的;结果必然发生的
retrieve [rɪˈtriːv]	vt. 取回;索回
reverse [rɪˈvɜːs]	n. 相反;背面;反面;倒退　adj. 相反的;颠倒的　vt. (使)颠倒;(使)倒转
right-of-way	通行权;优先权;先行权;路权
right-of-way	通行权;优先权;先行权;路权
rigorous [ˈrɪɡərəs]	adj. 严格的;严厉的;严酷的;严峻的
roadside [ˈrəudsaɪd]	n. 路边;路旁　adj. 路边的;路旁的
roadside interview survey	路边访问调查
roadway [ˈrəudweɪ]	n. 车道;路面;道路
roadwork [ˈrəudˌwɜːk]	n. 筑路工程
rolling terrain	起伏地形
root-mean-square	均方根

rough [rʌf]	adj. 高低不平的;粗糙的
roundabout ['raundəbaut]	n. (交通)环岛　adj. 迂回的,间接的,兜圈子的
route [ruːt]	n. 路线;路途;常规路线　v. 按某路线发送;给……规定路线
rural ['ruərl]	adj. 乡村的

S

satellite ['sætəlaɪt]	n. 卫星;人造卫星
Saturn ['sætɜːn]	n. [天]土星;土星火箭
scale [skeɪl]	n. 规模;比例;数值范围;等级
scarce [skeəs]	adj. 缺乏的;不足的;稀少的;罕见的　adv. 勉强;仅仅;几乎不;简直不
schedule ['ʃedjuːl]	n. 工作计划;日程安排;清单　v. 安排;预定;将……列入计划表
scheme [skiːm]	n. 计划;方案　v. 计划;设计
screen line [skriːnlaɪn]	n. 核查线
seaport ['siːpɔːt]	n. 海港;港口都市
security [sɪ'kjuərətɪ]	n. 安全
seek [siːk]	vt. 寻找;探索;寻求
self-diagnosis	自我诊断
semantic [sɪ'mæntɪk]	adj. 语义的
sensor ['sensə(r)]	n. 传感器
sensory ['sensərɪ]	adj. 感觉的;感官的
severity [sɪ'verɪtɪ]	n. 严重;严格;猛烈
sewer ['suːə(r)]	n. 污水管,下水道,阴沟
shield [ʃiːld]	n. 盾;防护物　vt. 遮蔽;庇护;保护;掩护　vi. 防御;起保护作用
shoulder ['ʃəuldə]	n. 路肩
sidewalk ['saɪdwɔːk]	n. 人行道
sight distance	视距
signal-controlled	信号控制的
simulator ['sɪmjuleɪtə(r)]	n. 模拟器;仿真器
skid [skɪd]	vi. 侧滑;打滑;滑行　n. 侧滑;打滑;滑橇
slab [slæb]	n. 厚平板;厚片;混凝土路面;板层
slight [slaɪt]	adj. 轻微的;少量的;不重要的　vt. 轻视;忽略;怠慢　n. 轻蔑;忽视;冷落
slit [slɪt]	n. 狭长的切口;狭缝,裂缝　vt. 在……上开狭长口子;切开;划破
slope [sləup]	n. 坡度;斜坡;斜率;倾斜　vt. (使)倾斜

socioeconomic [ˌsəusɪəuˌekəˈnɒmɪk]		*adj.* 社会经济学的
somewhat [ˈsʌmwɒt]		*adv.* 有点；稍微
sparse traffic		稀疏的交通
specification [ˌspesɪfɪˈkeɪʃn]		*n.* 规格；说明书；详述
Split-Cycle-Offset Optimization Technique (SCOOT)		绿信比—信号周期—时差优化技术
sports arena		运动场；体育场
sprint [sprɪnt]		*n.* 冲刺；短跑 *vi.* 冲刺；全速短跑
statistical [stəˈtɪstɪkl]		*adj.* 统计的；统计学的
staunch [stɔːntʃ]		*adj.* 忠实的；坚定的
stochastic processes		随机过程
stopping sight distance		停车视距
strategic [strəˈtiːdʒɪk]		*adj.* 战略上的；战略的
stratify [ˈstrætɪfaɪ]		*v.* 分层；划分
streetcar [striːtkɑː(r)]		*n.* 有轨电车
strike [straɪk]		*vt.* 撞击 *n.* 袭击
subroutine [ˈsʌbruːtiːn]		*n.* 子程序
subsidize [ˈsʌbsɪdaɪz]		*vt.* 以津贴补助；资助
substantially [səbˈstænʃəlɪ]		*adv.* 充分地；本质上；实质上
suburban [səˈbɜːbən]		*adj.* 郊区的；城郊的 *n.* 郊区居民
sufficient [səˈfɪʃnt]		*adj.* 足够的；充分的
summation [sʌˈmeɪʃn]		*n.* 和；总和；合计
superelevation [ˌsjuːpəˌelɪˈveɪʃən]		*n.* 超高；曲线超高；外轨超高
supervision [ˌsjuːpəˈvɪʒn]		*n.* 监督；监管
suppress [səˈpres]		*v.* 镇压；压制；忍住；止住
surcharge [ˈsɜːtʃɑːdʒ]		*n.* 超载；追加罚款；额外费用 *vt.* 使装载过多；追加罚款
surveillance [səˈveɪləns]		*n.* 监督；[法]监视
survey [ˌsɜːveɪ]		*vt.* 调查；测量 *vi.* 测量土地 *n.* 测量；调查
suspend [səˈspend]		*vt.* 延缓，推迟；使暂停；使悬浮 *vi.* 悬浮；禁赛
sustainable [səˈsteɪnəbl]		*adj.* 可持续的
Sydney Co-ordinated Adaptive Traffic System (SCATS)		最优自动适应交通控制系统

T

tabulation [ˌtæbjuˈleɪʃn]	*n.* 作表；表格
take-off	*n.* 起飞
telematic [ˌtelɪˈmætɪk]	*n.* 信息通信业务；远程信息处理
tensile [ˈtensaɪl]	*adj.* 张力的；拉力的

terminal [ˈtɜːmɪnl]	n. 终点站;终端 adj. 末期;晚期的;定期的
terminate [ˈtɜːmɪneɪt]	v. 停止;结束;终止
terrain [təˈreɪn]	n. [地理]地形;地势;领域;地带
thereof [ˌðeərˈɒv]	adv. 在其中;由此
threshold [ˈθreʃhəʊld]	n. [物]阈值
timber [ˈtɪmbə(r)]	n. (建筑等用的)木材,木料
to an extent	在某种程度上
topographical [ˌtɒpəˈɡræfɪkl]	adj. 地形的,地貌的
topography [təˈpɒɡrəfɪ]	n. 地形学
tourism [ˈtʊərɪzəm]	n. 旅游业;观光业
track [træk]	n. 轨道;足迹;小道 vt. 追踪;监测
traffic capacity of road	道路通行能力
traffic flow	交通流
traffic management	交通管理
traffic safety	交通安全
traffic schemes	交通方案;交通计划
traffic sign	交通标志
transcribe [trænˈskraɪb]	v. 转录
transit [ˈtrænsɪt]	n. 轨道交通;经过;通行;搬动;运输
transponder [trænˈspɒndə(r)]	n. 异频雷达收发机
transport planning process	交通规划程序
transportation facility	运输设施
transverse [ˈtrænzvɜːs]	adj. 横向的;横断的
traverse [trəˈvɜːs]	vt. 横过;穿过;经过
trillion [ˈtrɪljən]	n. [数]万亿 adj. 万亿的
trolleybus [ˈtrɒlɪbʌs]	无轨电车
truck [trʌk]	n. (铁路上运送货物或动物的)敞篷车,无盖货车;卡车 v. 用载货汽车装运
trucking [ˈtrʌkɪŋ]	n. 货车运输;货车运输业
trunk road	干道

U

ultimate [ˈʌltɪmət]	adj. 最后的;最终的;终极的;极端的 n. 最好的事物,极品,精华
ultrasonic [ˌʌltrəˈsɒnɪk]	adj. [声]超声的;超音速的;超音波的 n. 超声波
ultrasound [ˈʌltrəsaʊnd]	n. 超声;超音波
unbiased [ʌnˈbaɪəst]	adj. 没有偏见的
undertake [ˌʌndəˈteɪk]	vt. 承担;许诺;保证

Unmanned Ground Vehicle(UGV)	无人驾驶地面车辆
upgrade [ʌpˈgreɪd]	n. 升级;向上的斜坡　vt. 使升级;提升
upstream [ˌʌpˈstriːm]	adv. 向(在)上游;逆流　n. 上游
urban sprawl	城市扩张
urban transportation planning	城市运输规划
usage [ˈjuːsɪdʒ]	n. 利用率
utmost [ˈʌtməʊst]	adj. 极度的;最远的;最大的　n. 极限;最大限度

V

variable [ˈveərɪəbl]	adj. 可变的;变化的;[生]变异的　n. 可变情况;变量;可变因素
Variable Message Sign (VMS)	可变信息标志
variation [ˌveərɪˈeɪʃn]	n. 变化;变动;变量;变异
vary from	不同于;不等于
vehicle [ˈviːɪkəl]	n. 交通工具;车辆
vehicular [vəˈhɪkjələ(r)]	adj. 车的;用车辆运载的
velocity [vəˈlɒsɪtɪ]	n. [物]速度
verify [ˈverɪfaɪ]	vt. 检验;核实;证明
versus [ˈvɜːsəs]	prep. 对(指诉讼、比赛中);与……相对
vertical alignment	纵断面线形
viaduct [ˈvaɪədʌkt]	n. 高架桥;高架铁(道)路
vigilant [ˈvɪdʒɪlənt]	adj. 警惕的;警醒的;警戒的
visibility [ˌvɪzəˈbɪlətɪ]	n. 可见度;能见度

W

walking distance	步行距离
warehouse [ˈweəhaʊs]	n. 仓库;货栈;货仓;大商店　vt. 存入仓库
warning sign	警告标志
warp [wɔːp]	vt. & vi. 弄弯;使翘曲;扭曲;曲解
warrant [ˈwɒrənt]	n. 授权证;许可证　vt. 保证;授权;批准
watercraft [ˈwɔːtəkrɑːft]	n. 船只;水运工具;驾船技术
well-established	既定的;固定下来的;久负盛名的
wheelbase [ˈwiːlbeɪs]	n. (车轮)轴距
wind velocity	风速
wireless [ˈwaɪələs]	adj. 无线的;无线电的　n. 无线电
withstand [wɪðˈstænd]	vt. 抵挡;经受住
worm [wɔːm]	n. 虫;蠕虫;螺纹　vt. 使蠕动;使缓慢前进

Z

zonal [ˈzəunl]   *adj.* 带状的

zone [zəun]   *n.* 地区;(规划的)区域   *v.* 将……划作特殊区域;将……分成区

Translation Skills

在学习和运用专业英文文献时,从英文到中文的翻译是一条必经之路。翻译包括两个过程——理解和表达,理解就是透彻掌握原文的内容和实质,表达就是运用各种不同的翻译技巧用规范的汉语呈现原文内容。

(1)理解过程
①通读全文,理解大意。
②明辨语法,理清关系。
③联系上下文,推敲词义。
(2)表达过程
①初译:忠实为主。
②核对:注重逻辑。
③敲定:润色文字以达到全文通顺。

1 词类的转译

在英译汉的过程中,有些句子可以逐词对译,有些句子则由于英汉两种语言的表达方式不同,需要转换词类,才能使译文通顺自然。常见的词类转译法有名词、形容词、动词、副词和介词的转译。

1.1 名词的词类转译

(1)名词译成动词

英语中具有动作意义的名词和由动词派生出来的名词以及某些表示身份特征或职业的名词(如 dancer、teacher 等),在句中含有较强的动作意味,英译汉时须译成动词。

【例】The last bulletin, shorter than usual, made no mention of the Marathon race.

【译】上一个节目比通常短,没有提到马拉松。

(2)名词译成形容词

从形容词中派生出来的名词,翻译时译成形容词。

【例】Accepting challenges is a necessity in growth process.

【译】接受挑战对成长来说是必要的。

(3)名词译成副词

表达心情、感觉的名词后接动词词组,翻译时将名词译成副词。

【例】It is our great fortune to see that China has made great progress in strength.

【译】我们很幸运地看到,我国的实力已经有了很大的进步。

1.2 动词的词类转译

动词译成名词(一般是名词派生的动词或名词转用的动词)

【例】To us, you personified absolute power.

【译】在我们看来,你就是绝对权威的化身。

【例】Neutrons act differently from protons.

【译】中子的作用不同于质子。

1.3 形容词的词类转译

(1)形容词译成名词

【例】He was humorous and elegant but soft.

【译】他很幽默、有风度,但很软弱。

(2)形容词译成动词

英语中表示知觉、欲望等心理状态的形容词,在系动词后作表语时,往往可译成动词。

【例】Uncle Liu is very fond of dogs.

【译】刘叔叔很喜欢小狗。

(3)形容词译成副词

当英语名词转译成动词时,修饰该名词的形容词往往转译成相应的副词。

【例】They regarded him as a potential adversary.

【译】他们认为他可能是他们的一个对头。

1.4 副词的词类转译

(1)副词译成名词

【例】They have not done so well organizationally, however, as ideologically.

【译】然而,他们的组织工作没有思想工作做得好。

(2)副词译成动词

【例】Now, I must be away, the time is up.

【译】现在时间已经到了,我该离开了。

(3)副词译成形容词

【例】The book impressed me deeply.

【译】这本书给我留下了很深的印象。

1.5 介词的词类转译

介词译成动词

【例】The teacher took the students around the science and technology museum.

【译】老师带着同学们参观科技馆。

2 被动句的译法

英语有别于汉语的一个特点就是被动语态的广泛应用,而汉语中却较少使用被动语态。

两者有别的另一个特点是被动语态的构成不同。英语是"形合"语言,其被动语态是通过改变动词的形式来实现的;汉语是"意合"语言,其被动语态则由有明显表示或暗含被动之意的字或词来实现。

英语被动语态在以下情况中使用：说不出主动者，或不愿意说出主动者；没有必要说出主动者，或为了突出被动者；为使上下文连贯衔接。被动语态应把要说明的问题放在句子的主语位置上，既要能唤起人们的注意又要简洁客观。汉语被动语态的使用范围较窄，因为汉语突出主题，而英语突出主语。汉语具有英语所没有的无主句，许多被动句可以用无主句来代替。

2.1 化"被动"为"主动"

由于英语被动语态结构用得多，英译汉时，变为主动语态的情形也就十分普遍了。

（1）译为有主句

这里，又有"反宾为主，变主为宾""增译主语，泛指'有人'""原文主语，'主'位坐稳"三种情形。

①反宾为主，变主为宾

翻译时，把原文的主语，即行为的客体，译成宾语，而把主体或相当于行为主体的介词宾语译成主语。

【例】The *Times* is read by the people who run the country; The *Guardian* is read by the people who would like to run the country; The *Financial Times* is read by the people who own the country; and The *Daily Telegraph* is read by the people who remember the country as it used to be.

这是一段说明报纸读者群体情况的英文原文。不同的报纸，拥有不同的读者，不同的读者追逐不同的消息。因此，就有了下文翻译中的四句意味深长的打油诗。

【译】在位掌权的人读《泰晤士报》，渴望掌权的人读《卫报》，大老板们读《金融时报》，怀念大英帝国曾经了不起的人读《每日电讯报》。

②增译主语，泛指"有人"

翻译时，把原文的主语译成宾语，增译"有人""人们""大家""我们"等泛指性的主语。

【例】With the rapid development of science and technology, news can be sent to every part of the world.

【译】随着科学技术的迅速发展，我们能把各种各样的新闻传到世界各地。

③原文主语、"主"位坐稳

翻译时，原文的主语地位不变，在译文中仍为主语。此时，汉语译文中虽无"被"字，但被动的意义已暗含在内。

【例】Over the last 20 years, the traffic theories have been developed to fit the characteristics of the times.

【译】在过去的20年中，交通理论已经发展到符合当前时代的特征。

在不知道或者不必说出行为主体时，常常可以发挥汉语译文的优势，把英语的被动语态译成汉语的无主句。这时，原文的主语译为动词的宾语。

【例】Before any road work is carried out, the traffic engineers should be informed so that a programme of work can be agreed.

【译】在任何道路开展工作之前，应该通知交通工程师，以便就工作程序达成一致。

（2）主语谓语合译

英语的一些动词短语含有名词，如 make use of, pay attention to, make reference to, take account of 等，变成被动语态时成为名词作主语的特殊被动语态。翻译时，可以把主语和谓语合起来译成汉语无主句的谓语。

【例】Care should be taken at all times to protect the computers and other instruments in the office from dust and damp.

【译】要一直注意保护办公室中的电脑和其他设备,不要使它们沾上灰尘,受潮。

2.2 以"主动"表"被动"

汉语有一种"是……的"结构,是一种形式主动,实际上是不用"被"字的被动句,着重说明一件事情是如何产生或在何时何地产生的。在翻译英语被动结构时,可以利用这种形式主动的"是……的"结构,表示被动的实际意义。

【例】The school is named after a man who made a contribution of 20 million dollars.

【译】这所学校是用一名出资2000万美元的人的名字命名的。

2.3 以"被动"译"被动"

虽然汉语被动语态使用的范围较窄,但并不是说汉语极少用被动句。汉语主要有四种表示被动的方式:

①在谓语前加上"被"字。
②在行为主体前加上"被""由""受""为……所"等字。
③谓语前省去"被"字且不出现行为主体的被动句。
④"是……的"的结构。前面已把第三种方式归入"化'被动'为'主动'",把第四种方式列为"以'主动'表'被动'",因此,这里只谈谈前面两种方式。

(1) 谓语之前加"被"字

当英语被动结构的句子中没有出现行为主体时,汉译句子可以在谓语的前面加上"被"字,表示原文的被动意义。

【例】Imagine that one or other continent is left out, forgotten, reduced to its poverty and its disorder. What will happen to the others?

【译】想象一下,如果这里或那里的大陆被遗弃或忘记,变得贫困混乱,那么其他大陆将会怎么样呢?

(2) 行为主体前加"把""被""由"等字

在英语被动结构的句子中出现行为主体时,译文可使用汉语中表示被动的一些语言手段,在其前面加上"把""被""由""受""遭""给""为……所"等字来突显原文句中的被动意义。

【例】I am now writing you, on behalf of the students, to express our appreciation for the hospitality, which was accorded to us during our visit to your museum.

【译】我现在代表我的学生给您写信,对我们在您博物馆参观期间受到的热情接待表示感谢。

2.4 打破原结构,译成新句型

英语被动结构句子的译法灵活多样,无一成不变的格式可套,甚至被动语态的原来结构也可以打破,译成新的其他句型。

【例】"Not to be served, but to serve."

这是香港中华基督教青年会郭琳褒纪念堂奠基石上的刻字。原文简洁典雅,石上的中文亦古朴简练,仅用八个汉字对译七个英文单词。

【译】"非以役人,乃役于人。"

2.5 常见形式主语被动句型的翻译

英语中有很多被动句,以 it 为形式主语、即"it + be + that"结构,汉译时通常使用主动语态,有时不加主语、有时加上泛指性主语,如"有人""大家""人们"等。

不加主语的:

It is found that… 据发现……
It is hoped that… 希望……
It is reported that… 据报道……
It may be safely said that… 可以有把握地说……
It has been illustrated that… 据(图示)所说……
It has been viewed that… 有人认为……
It was first intended that… 最初的想法是……
It is enumerated that… 列举如下……
It may be said without fear of exaggeration that… 可以毫不夸张地说……
It must be pointed out that… 必须承认……

可加主语的:

It is well known that… 众所周知……
It is taken that… 有人认为……
It is noted that… 人们注意到……

3 省译与增译

省译是指在翻译的过程中,原文中有的冠词、代词、介词等在译文中可以省略,即译文在没有这个词的情况下,已经能够完整地表达原文想要表达的意思,或者这个词在文中的意义是显而易见的,为了使译文读起来更加通顺流畅,符合中文的阅读习惯,需要在不影响原文思想的情况下进行一些删减。

增译是指在翻译英文文献时,按原文意义以及句法的要求,添加一些能够表示语义、逻辑关系和平衡结构的词。有些文献在翻译成汉语时,会出现意思不明确或表达不通顺的情况,因此,需要采用增译的技巧,完整流畅地表达原文的思想。

3.1 冠词的省译

(1) 不定冠词的省译

① 不定冠词表示类别时的省译

【例】An operational analysis determines the need for crossovers and storage tracks.

【译】运营分析将决定是否有必要修建天桥和备用轨道。

② 固定词组中不定冠词的省译

a body of 大量;in an attempt to 力图;as a result 因此。

307

③ 不定冠词表示单位之意时,则不能被省译,常被译为"每"或"一"

【例】A half mile corresponds to the distance someone can walk in 10 minutes at 3 miles an hour.

【译】半英里相当于一个人以每小时3英里的速度在10分钟内走完的距离。

(2)定冠词的省译

① 定冠词表示类别时的省译

【例】The traffic engineer has a vast array of measures, which can be applied to achieve his objectives.

【译】交通工程师有很多措施可以用来实现他的目标。

② 定冠词用于独一无二的对象时的省译

【例】The HCM used LOS based on a number of key definitions.

【译】《道路通行能力手册》所采用的服务水平以一些关键概念为基础。

③ 定冠词用于表示方位、左右等名词前的省译

【例】Greenberg observed traffic flow in the north tube of the Lincoln Tunnel, New York City.

【译】格林伯格对纽约市林肯隧道北段的交通流进行了观测。

④ 定冠词与形容词、分词连用时的省译

【例】The latter provide opportunity for turning trains back short of the end of the line, or for storing disabled vehicles.

【译】后者供车辆在路线终点倒车,或供不能行驶的车辆停放。

⑤ 专有名词前定冠词的省译

the People's Republic of China 中华人民共和国;the Indian Ocean 印度洋;the Alps 阿尔卑斯山。

⑥ 定冠词在形容词最高级前的省译

【例】The highest type of arterial highway is the freeway.

【译】高速公路是最高级的干线公路。

⑦ 定冠词在"the + 比较级……,the + 比较级……"结构中的省译

【例】The fewer cars, which idle at a toll plaza, the less exhaust is spewed into the air and the cleaner the air will be.

【译】在收费站停留的汽车数量越少,向大气中排放的汽车尾气就会越少,空气就会越洁净。

⑧ 定冠词在固定词组中的省译

in the depth of 在……深处;in the company of 陪同;on the instant 立即。

注:定冠词在某些情况下必须译出,即当定冠词起着指示代词(this,that,these,those)的作用时,被译为"这(该),那,这些或那些"。

【例】As this method was derived for very long straight roads, it is necessary to divide the road network into a few continuous roads as possible.

【译】由于该方法适用于长直道路,故有必要将路网尽可能划分为几段连续的道路。

3.2 代词的省译

(1)人称代词的省译

① 省译作主语和宾语的人称代词

【例】Are model-produced network loadings comparable to their assignment to the network?

【译】模型产生的路网荷载和实际分配到路网上的情况吻合吗？

② it 的省译

【例】It is never too late to mend.

【译】改过从不嫌迟。

(2) 自身代词的省译

【例】The subgrade must not be overstressed and caused to deform to a greater extent than the pavement itself can deform without damaging its own structural integrity.

【译】勿使路基受超限压力，以免引起路基变形的程度大于路面在不损害其结构完整的情况下可能出现的变形。

(3) 物主代词的省译

【例】Joining these technologies to our transportation system will save lives, save time, and save money.

【译】把这些技术同交通运输系统结合起来，将能减少伤亡，节省时间和资金。

3.3 介词的省译

(1) 表示时间的介词的省译

【例】How about the traffic condition on May Day?

【译】五一假期间的交通情况如何？

(2) 表示地点的介词的省译

【例】The percentage of intoxicated motorcyclists in fatal crashes is higher than other riders on roads.

【译】致命车祸中醉酒的摩托车驾驶人的比例高于道路上其他驾驶者。

(3) 用作补语的介词短语中的介词的省译

【例】John has got ahead with his work.

【译】约翰的工作取得了进展。

3.4 连词的省译

(1) 并列连词的省译

【例】The match has lasted for seven or eight hours.

【译】这场比赛持续了七八个小时了。

(2) 从属连词的省译

① 时间状语从句中某些从属连词的省译

【例】John rose as the train stopped.

【译】火车停了，约翰站了起来。

② 条件状语从句中某些从属连词的省译

【例】If the pressure gets low, the boiling-point becomes low.

【译】气压低，沸点就低。

③ 原因状语从句中某些从属连词的省译

【例】As the temperature increases, the vapor pressure of water increases.

【译】温度升高,水的蒸气压力也增高。

④ that 的省译

【例】The fact is that raw material prices have soare.

【译】事实上,原材料的价格已经大幅上涨。

3.5 增补语义上、修辞上需要的词

(1)在某些名词、动名词前后增补动词

【例】After the match, the chairman still has an important meeting.

【译】在观看完比赛后,主席还要参加一个重要会议。

(2)增补一些附加性的词

【例】After all preparation are made, we started making experiments.

【译】在一切准备工作就绪后,我们开始实验。

(3)增补某些联系性的词

【例】Doing our job, we must feel that we are making a difference.

【译】在工作时,我们一定要觉得自己在做一件有意义的事情。

(4)增补某些解释性的词

【例】According to reliable sources, China will build her own space shuttles.

【译】据可靠人士透露,中国也要研制自己的航天飞机。

(5)增补量词

【例】A car hit her on a crossing.

【译】一辆汽车在人行横道上撞了她。

(6)增补表示复数含义的词

【例】He looked the proposals through before approving them.

【译】他逐一审查了各项建议才予以批准。

(7)增补某些概括性的词

【例】This report summed up the new research achievements made by the institute in subway and light rail.

【译】这个报告总结了该研究在地铁和轻轨两方面的研究成果。

3.6 增补原文中的省略部分

(1)增补并列句中的省略成分

【例】The proportion of A is 10%, of B 20%.

【译】A 所占比例为 10%,而 B 所占比例为 20%。

(2)增补复合句中的省略成分

① 增补比较状语从句中的省略成分

【例】A is higher mass than B.

【译】A 的质量比 B 的大。

② 增补主语

【例】If being seen as an important role in urban transport strategy, traffic management can provide an enhanced transport environment for the city.

【译】如果交通管理成为整个城市交通战略重要部分,就可为该市提供更好的交通环境。

(3)增补回答部分的省略成分

【例】Is the vehicle's speed 80km/h? Yes, it is.

【译】这辆机动车的速度是80km/h吗? 是的,它的速度是80km/h。

3.7 增补原文的内容语意

(1)关于形容词最高级的增补

【例】He bragged that he was the highest player.

【译】他吹嘘自己是得分最高的选手。

(2)关于 could-with 结构的增补

【例】The bending rigidity of the structure could be sgnifcantly improved with setting transverse diaphragm.

【译】如果添加箱梁横隔板,结构的抗弯刚度就能显著提高。

(3)关于 with 引起的短语的增补

【例】With many his disappointment, he remains cheerful.

【译】尽管他经历了许多挫折,但他还是情绪高涨。

4 数字的翻译法

在专业英文文献的翻译过程中,常会遇上数字。数字的翻译既是难点,又是重点。英语和汉语在数字的增加和减少、倍增倍减等表达方式上有很大的不同,因此在翻译过程中须多加留意。

4.1 倍数增加或减少的翻译法

(1)"……系动词 + n times + 比较级形容词 + than …"

在表示倍数增加时,是净增的倍数,可照译为"……比……多 n 倍"。

【例】The turnover in 2000 is two times higher than that of last year.

【译】2000 年的营业额比上年高两倍。

在表示倍数减少时,是减少 n 倍,可译为"减少到 $1/(n+1)$"或"减少了 $n/(n+1)$"。

【例】The operation profit in 2005 is 3 times lower than that of last year.

【译】2005 年的运营利润减少到上年的 1/4。(或译为:2005 年的运营利润比上年减少了 3/4。)

(2)……系动词 + n times + as … as

表示是……的 n 倍,也可译为"多 $n-1$ 倍"。

【例】The profit obtained this year was twice as high as last year.

【译】今年获得的利润是去年的两倍。(或译为:今年获得的利润比去年多一倍。)

如果在 as…as 前不是倍数而是分数,翻译方法如下:

【例】Operation cost of A is one-tenth as high as B.

【译】A 的营运开支是 B 的 1/10。(或译为:A 的营运开支比 B 少 9/10。)

(3) 表示增加或减少意义的动词 + n times

表示倍数增加时,是"增加了 $n-1$ 倍"。

【例】The return of this year has increased 5 times as again 2000.

【译】今年的回报率比 2000 年增长了四倍。

表示倍数减少时,是"减少到 $1/n$"或"减少了 $(n-1)/n$"。

【例】Local demand in 2010 reduced 3 times.

【译】2003 年的本地需求减少到 1/3。(或译为:2003 年的本地需求减少了 2/3。)

(4) 表示增加意义的动词 + by n times

表示净增的数,可照译为"增加 n 倍"。

【例】The average interest of 2015 increased by twice.

【译】2015 年的平均利润提高了两倍。

4.2 数量增减的其他表示法的翻译法

(1) … as + many (high, long, low …) + as + n

表示多高、长、低……达……之意。

【例】The running speed of plane is as high as 900 千米/小时.

【译】飞机的飞行时速高达 900 千米/小时。

(2) …(by) n + 名词 + 比较级 + than …

表示净增减,数字 n 照译。

【例】Population of China is (by) 1.06 billion larger than that of America.

【译】中国的人口比美国多 10.6 亿(2018 年)。

(3) 表示增减意义的动词 + to + n

表示增加到 n 或减少到 n。

【例】Population of China has been increased to 1.39 billion.

【译】中国的人口已经增加到了 13.9 亿(2018 年)。

(4) too + 形容词

表示过于、差之意。

【例】The road is too short by 200 meters.

【译】这条路的长度还差 200 米。

(5) 减少一半的翻译法

英语中,有些短语是表示减半之意的,如 cut/break/spit … in half(into halves) 把……切成(分成)两半;decrease one-half 减去一半;one-half less 少一半;halve … 将……减半;not half 少于一半地;be less than half 比一半还少;shorten … two times 缩短一半。

【例】The work completed is less than half.

【译】所完成的工作还不到一半。

4.3 分数的翻译

分数由基数词 + 序数词构成,当分子大于一时,分母的序数词用复数,如 one third 三分之一;two thirds 三分之二;one(a) hunderdth 百分之一;three twentyfifths 二十五分之三;two and a half 二又二分之一;three and a third 三又三分之一;a few tenths of the given volume 给定体积的十分之几。

【例】We have finished two thirds of the project.

【译】我们已经完成了项目的 2/3。

5 长句的翻译

在交通工程专业英语中最常见也最难理解的组成部分就是长句,它们由短句复合而成,常常是一个主句带若干个从句,从句带短语,短语带从句,从句套从句,互相依附,相互制约,因而显得错综复杂。在翻译长句时,需要运用综合分析法,具体应用如下。

5.1 弄清关系,分清主次,化整为零

在翻译长复合句时,首先,要抓连接词(无连接词时抓谓语),将复合句划分为简单句;其次,分清主从关系;再次,确定各简单句内的次要成分与主要成分的关系;最后,将各简单句按逻辑进行串联,这样就有主有从,主次分明了。

【例】Although it may take some time to set up, we now have to install a communications infrastructure that will support computer-based wagon contol and other management information systems that are bound to be installed in the future.

【译】虽然建立通信网络需要时间,但是我们必须安装一套通信基础设施来支持以计算机为基础的车辆控制信息系统和其他将来必定要建立的管理信息系统的发展。

分析:这是一个比较简单的复合句,根据连接词 although 和两个 that,可知该句可分为 3 部分,每个部分都是简单句。

① Although it may take some time to set up, we now have to install a communications infrastructure

② that will support computer-based wagon contol and other management information systems

③ that are bound to be installed in the future

第一句为 Although 引导的让步状语从句,第二、三句为定语从句,分别修饰 a communications infrastructure 和 other management information systems。因此,按全句的语法关系,结合上下文的含义,把各个简单句的译文串起来,从而可得到忠实通顺的译文。

5.2 注意组合,看清前后搭配

出于修辞或句子结构安排的原因,英语中的固定词组在句子中有时会被隔开,这样给翻译带来了困难。因此,凡遇到有些词前后关系不清时,就得考虑是否是被某个词组或短语隔开了。

【例】One method, used in the United States, to trace through a junction the paths of vehicles approaching along one leg only is to ask the motorist, through prominently displayed signs, to switch on the vehicle's headlights while going through the junction.

【译】用在美国的一种跟踪车辆通过交叉口路径的方法是当车辆到达交叉口的一条道路上,只要请驾驶人在通过交叉口时,遇到突出显示的指示牌的地方打开车灯。

分析:固定词组 ask to 被插入语 through … signs 隔开了。

5.3 注意分裂结构,搞清内在联系

英语句子有各种分裂结构是地道的英语特点之一,造成这种结构的原因是出于对修辞及句子结构的合理安排的考虑。在翻译这类句子时应首先分析各成分之间的关系,搞清内在联系。

【例】The shield itself, slightly larger in diameter than he complete tunnel, encloses a circular steel cutting edge, which is forced slowly forward along the line of the tunnel.

【译】盾构本身直径略大于完工后的隧道直径(在盾构内有一个钢制环形切削刃),被推着沿隧道的走向缓缓前进。

分析:与主语关系密切的谓语 encloses 被 slightly larger … tunnel 这个独立结构隔开了。

Writing Skills

交通运输专业论文的写作要求是简洁(concise)、精确(precise)、清晰(clear)、通俗(familiar)、明快(forthright)、流畅(fluid)。

交通运输专业常见的英语论文写作类型有期刊论文、会议论文和学位论文等,现以最常见的期刊论文及会议论文为例进行分析。期刊论文及会议论文的体例一般由以下几部分组成:标题(Title)、摘要(Abstract)、关键词(Keywords)或主题词(Subjects)、引言(Introduction)、方法(Method)或过程(Procedure)、结果(Results)、讨论(Discussions)、总结(Summary)或结论(Conclusion)、致谢(Acknowledgements)、参考文献(Reference)或附录(Appendix)。

值得注意的是,对于生活和工作在中文环境中的英语应用者而言,运用英文进行写作不可避免地都有一个从"汉译英"到"用英语思考和写作"的过程,实现这个过程的转换正是中国读者撰写英语专业论文的难点。读者应在技巧及规范学习的基础上,按提示细心揣摩其应用,突破英语论文写作中一味地"汉译英",逐步过渡到"先有英文结构,再有字词翻译",最终实现"用英语思考和写作"。

1 语法技巧

1.1 多用被动结构

专业英语的文章中,经常会发现一句话中有多个被动结构。这与其他文体不一样,专业英语很多时候不出现具体的主动者。

【例】If the transport of dangerous goods cannot be efficiently *organized*, it might result in personal or facilities injury or in destruction of equipment. Therefore, great care should be *taken* in transporting dangerous goods.

上例由2个句子构成,其中出现了3个谓语动词,而运用被动结构(斜体部分)的就有2个。

1.2 多用动词非谓语结构

非谓语动词形式是指分词动词不定式和动名词,交通工程专业文献中常用非谓语动词形式有如下两个主要原因:

(1)非谓语动词形式能使语言结构紧凑,行文简练

【例】Traffic engineering is concerned with the use of the highway by the road user who deals with matters relating to the regulation and control of vehicle and pedestrian traffic on new and existing facilities.

【例】The scope of traffic engineering is wide, touching to some degree on each of the three Es—Engineering, Enforcement and Education.

上面两个例句中，relating to 后面的部分作 matters 的定语，touching to 后面作状语。这两个分词短语，如果不用非谓语形式，只能用 which are related to…和 it is touched to…等从句形式，那样会使语句冗长，不符合交通工程专业文献的行文要求，即无法以最少的篇幅表达最多的重要信息。

（2）非谓语动词形式能体现和区分出语句中信息的重要程度

【例】Selective-call telephone using open-wire pole lines were used for dispatching.

上例中谓语动词 were used 表达了主要信息，现在分词短语 using…提供细节，即非重要信息。这是现在分词和非谓语动词在表达信息功能上的主要分工和区别。

1.3 多用一般过去时

论文中不同的内容要考虑使用不同的时态，一般而言，交通工程专业文献主要反映与该领域有关的科学现象、规律、作业过程等，由于其客观性通常使用现在时态。而当论文叙述作者做了哪些研究工作，研究对象的情况，得出了什么结果，则主要用一般过去时。

【例】The LOS concept was first developed for highways in an era of rapid expansion in the use and availability of the private motor car. The primary concern was congestion, and it was commonly held that only the rapid expansion of the freeway network would have kept congestion in check.

1.4 名词化特点显著

名词化特点主要是指在交通工程文献中广泛使用能表示动作和状态的名词，或是起名词作用的非限定动词。

【例】In the initial stages of road design it is usual for several alternative route proposals to be considered but only outline details of road center lines and estimates of speeds and flows are available.

在交通工程专业文献中，名词一般由动词或形容词派生或转化而来，表示动作；名词一般以名词短语结构出现，典型结构为 $n. + of + n.$；而且名词还出现连用的情况，即中心词之前有一个以上其他名词，它们皆是中心名词的前置修饰语，以简化句子结构，便于理解。

1.5 多用语体正式的词汇

英语中有很多意义灵活的动词短语，而交通工程专业英语文献中则多用与之对应的意义明确的单个词构成的动词，这类动词除了意义明确、特点精练，还具有语体庄重、正式的特点。下面是一组对照，横线右边的词汇更适合交通工程专业英语文献。

to use up—to exhaust　　　　to take up, to take in—to absorb
to push into—to insert　　　　to speed up—to accelerate
to put in—to add to　　　　　carry out—to perform
to think about—to consider　　to breathe in—to inhale
to take away—to remove　　　to get together—to concentrate
to drive forward—to propel　　to fill up—to occupy
to keep up—to maintain　　　to find out—to discover

同时，单个的英语词汇也有正式和非正式之分，交通工程专业英语文献属于正式文体，因此多用正式词汇。下面是一组对照，横线左边为非正式用语，右边为正式用语。

finish—complete	oversee—supervise
underwater—submarine	hide—conceal
buy—purchase	enough—sufficient
similar—identical	inner—interior
handbook—manual	help—assist
careful—cautious	try—attempt
stop—cease	get—obtain
deep—profound	leave—depart
about—approximately	use—employ / utilize

2 格式与技巧

2.1 题目

题目写作的目的在于总结文章内容,吸引读者,便于检索。题目的撰写要求如下。

(1) 简要

论文标题一般不超过 20 个字,例如 The Architecture of Intelligent Transportation Systems。必要时可运用副标题,例如 Intelligent Transportation Systems— Vehicular Communication Options。同时写作时很少使用装饰形词组,如 on the…, reading…, investigation…, the method of…, some thoughts on…, a research of…, 以避免使标题显得冗长。

(2) 具体

论文标题应避免广泛抽象,例如 Safety and Productivity Improvement of Railroad Operations,根据内容建议改为 Safety and Productivity Improvement of Railroad Operations by Advanced Train Control System,这样文章的主要内容便会自然显现。必要时可使用副标题,例如 Scientific Analysis of the Circumstances and Causes of Traffic Accidents— Traffic Accident Characteristics from the Viewpoint of Driver Age。

(3) 避免问题标题

问题标题意味着一个疑问形式的完整句子,由于有一些多余的疑问词和符号(如 Is it…? Should be…? 等等),因而不利于检索。如果必须要用疑问含义,则可用不定词形式加问号形式,例如,a Dangerous Response to Traffic Analysis?

(4) 统一

标题的并行部分在语法上应该对称而不应混杂,例如名词对名词,动名词对动名词。例如:testing and adopting 或 test and adoption,而不能用 testing and adoption 或 test and adopting。

(5) 标准化

通常情况应避免使用不标准的缩写和符号或只有专家才能看懂的措辞术语,因为这样会给信息检索带来不便。至于主要单词的首字母是否大写,由所投杂志的具体要求决定。

2.2 作者

作者信息(姓名、联系方式等)写作的目的在于:担负法律责任,便于检索及联系,提升自己和所在单位在业界的声誉。

英语论文中,中国人的姓名按拼音书写。名字为两个字时,为区分姓和名,应与西方人的拼写习惯相协调,将姓和名第一个字的首个拼音字母大写,例如 Xin Weimin。

一般一篇文章的作者不要超过四人,当不得不超过时,建议使用"et al."(意为 and others)。同时,职业头衔(如 Chief Management, Doctor 等)应在姓名前省略。如必须附带此信息,可将其置于联系方式里,例如:

Xin Pengming

Professor, School of Traffic and Transportation, Southwest Jiaotong University

Chengdu, Sichuan, 610031, the People's Republic of China

至于多作者和多联系方式的书写格式根据所投杂志社的具体要求而定。另外,一些具体的内部小单位,特别是一些英语国家人无法理解的单位,如 Technical Innovation Group of…(……科技改革组),不宜写在联系方式中,必要时可写在脚注里。

2.3 关键词

关键词写作的目的在于便于检索,便于突出文章主题。

关键词写作时,常使用名词而不是动词,词数一般为 5~8 个。写作时,各关键词首字母大写,词间用","或";"隔开,最后一个关键词之后不用"."。同时,关键词必须是便于理解且富有专业性的,使用的缩写也必须是经过 International Standard Organization (ISO)认准的。

关键词多来源于标题和摘要,排序时应按照研究目的——研究类别—研究方法—研究结果的顺序;对于同序列的两个或多个关键词应按属种关系或由浅到深的顺序排列。

【例】GPS; ITS; Traffic safety; System design

2.4 摘要

摘要部分写作的目的在于浓缩全文内容以方便读者判断对该文感兴趣与否,帮助编辑判断对文章接受与否,通过信息检索帮助扩大文章流通。

各个杂志社对摘要字数的具体要求是不一样的,一般是文章字数的 3%~5%。一般来说摘要写作的字数限定为 200~500 词,短文章摘要为 50~100 词。

摘要部分形式较多,时态使用变化较大。通常认为用过去时描述作者的工作,用现在时描述得出的结论,少用现在完成时、过去完成时,基本不用进行时和其他复合时态。一篇好的摘要应具有如下特点。

(1)用第三人称

第一人称作主语往往带有强烈的个人感情色彩,因此摘要中尽可能少用或不用第一人称,多用第三人称被动语态,以示客观性。

(2)用专业术语

不熟悉的读者难以理解专门术语缩略语、简称及符号。为方便索引,摘要中应给出专业术语的缩写和全拼两种形式(通常第一次使用全拼形式)。不应使用非公认的符号,特殊字符(数学符号)及希腊字母尽量不用或少用。

(3)无非文字的内容

摘要一般尽可能采用文字形式,不使用图表和公式等非文字内容。当没有其他更好的表达形式时,为了简练清晰可使用少量短小的表格、方程结构式及图。摘要中的内容不加脚注。

(4) 逻辑连贯

如果不重视摘要的逻辑连贯只是逐句进行罗列,少有巧妙的连接,则摘要的可读性将大打折扣。

(5) 重点突出

① 着重反映创新点及取得的研究成果,取消或减少背景信息。

② 避免罗列一大堆数据,有几个关键的已足够了,因为读者阅读时关注的是:这是什么样的研究工作,为何要做这项研究,最终究竟得到了什么样的结果。

③ 去除本学科领域常识性内容。

④ 未来计划不列入摘要。

(6) 表达简洁、规范、确切

① 不要重复题目的内容,也不要重复论文中句子。写摘要时逐字照抄原文主要部分的句子为大忌。摘要中的句子功能和论文中的稍有不同,摘要力求以最简洁的语句概述尽可能多的信息,二者功能不同,因此原文的句式当然不可再用。

② 不应引用参考文献,即避免使用脚注、文献列表。若必须使用,则以( )标出,不使用上下标。

③ 不应有正文中未涉及的内容。

④ 不写无用的语句。摘要应客观、如实地反映所做的研究工作,作者不必进行自我评论,如"本文的研究工作是对过去工艺的一个极大的改进""本工作首次实现了……""经检索尚未发现与本文类似的文献""……待进一步研究提高""……效率得到很大提高""本文所描述的工作,属于……首创""本文所描述的工作,目前尚未见报道"等。

⑤ 取消不必要的句子,如 It is reported that…The author discusses…等。

⑥ 尽量不使用不必要的修饰词,如 in detail / briefly / here / new 等。

⑦ 简化某些表达,如将"not only…but also…"改为"and",将"From the results it can be concluded that…"改为"the results show…",等等。

⑧ 能用名词作定语就不用动名词,能用形容词就不用名词,可用动词的尽量避免用动词的名词形式。

⑨ 避免使用长的、连串的形容词、名词或形容词加名词来修饰名词,可以使用介词短语,或用连字符连接名词词组中的名词,形成修饰单元。

(7) 摘要的写作结构一般可化解为五部分:Abstract = A1 + A2 + A3 + A4 + A5

其中,A1 为一个句子,主要回答:文章主题涉及的知识领域是什么。

A2 为一个主题句,主要回答:文章研究主题是什么。

A3 为二到三个支持句子,主要回答:支持作者观点的方法或材料是什么。

A4 为一个句子,主要回答:文章得到的结论是什么。

A5 为一个句子,主要回答:文章的贡献是什么。

A2、A3、A4 常用的形式化结构如下:

① 主题句

主题句用来揭示文章的主题,常用的主题句如下:

The purpose of this paper is… 这篇论文的目的是……
The primary goal of this research is… 这项研究的主要目的是……
The intention of this paper is to survey… 这篇论文的目的是调查……
The overall objective of this study is… 这项研究的全部目的是……
In this paper, we aim at… 在这篇文章中,我们致力于……
The chief aim of the present work is to investigate the features of…
目前工作的主要目标是观察……的特性。
The authors are now initiating some experimental investigation to establish…
作者们现在开始进行实验观察以确立……
The wok presented in this paper focuses on several aspects of the following…
这篇论文陈述的工作集中在以下几个方面……
The problem we have outlined deals largely with the study of…
我们略述的难题主要涉及……的研究问题。
With his many years' research, the author's endeavor is to explain why…
通过多年的研究,作者致力于解释为什么……
The primary object of this fundamental research will be to reveal the cause of…
这项基础研究的主要目的是揭示……的原因。
The main objective of our investigation has been to obtain some knowledge of…
我们观察的主要目的是获得一些关于……的知识。

② 支持句

支持句一般来说紧随主题句之后,进一步具体化文章主题。在这部分里,研究方法、实验、程序、调查、计算、分析、结果及其他重要信息被提及,因此,这些支持句可被看作摘要的主体。常用的支持句如下:

The method used in our study is known as…
在我们的研究中使用的是……的方法。
The technique we applied is referred to as…
我们应用的技术作为……被提及。
The approach adopted extensively is called…
这个被广泛采用的方法被称为……
Detailed information has been acquired by the authors using…
通过作者运用……获得了详细的信息。
The research has recorded valuable data using the newly-developed method…
运用新发展的方法……这项研究记录了有价值的数据。
This is an operation theory, which is based on the idea that…
这是一个基于……观点的运营理论。
The fundamental feature of this theory is as follows.
这个理论的基础特征如下。
We have carried out several sets of experiments to test the validity of…
我们已经展开了一系列实验来测试……的有效性。

③ 结论句

作为文章的结尾部分,结论句通常分析结果、指出研究的重要性等。常用的结论句如下:

In conclusion, we state that...　总之,我们说……

In summing up it may be stated that...　总之,我们可以说……

It is concluded that...　总之……

The results of the experiment indicate that...　实验结果表明……

The studies we have performed showed that...　我们进行的研究表明……

The research we have done suggests that...　我们做过的实验表明……

The pioneer studies that the authors attempted have indicated in...
作者们尝试的前沿研究表明了……

We carried out several studies, which have demonstrated that...
我们展开了一些研究,这些研究表明……

The investigation carried out by...has revealed that...
由……进行的调查揭示了……

As a result of our experiments, we concluded that...
作为实验结果,我们推断出……

From the experiment, the authors came to realize that...
通过实验作者们开始意识到……

The author's pioneer work has contributed to our present understanding of...
我们目前对……的理解来源于作者的前沿工作的帮助。

The research work has brought about a discovery of...
这项研究工作带来了……的发现。

These findings of the research have led the author to the conclusion that...
这项研究的发现使作者推断……

The data obtained appear to be very similar to those reported earlier by...
得到的数据与先前由……报道的数据显得非常相似。

The author has satisfactorily come to the conclusion that...
作者得到了这个令人满意的结论,即……

2.5　引言

引言部分写作的目的在于,介绍主题,缩小研究范围,陈述文章写作目的,展示布局谋篇。写作时多用现在时(一般现在时,现在完成时),当在强调研究活动本身时可用一般过去时。引言写作一般可化解为三个部分:

(1)介绍研究背景

用来回答"做了什么",常用的介绍背景的句型有:

Over the past several decades...　在过去的几十年里……

Somebody reported...　有报道说……

The previous work on...has indicated that...　以前在……方面的工作表明……

Several researchers have theoretically investigated...

一些研究员已经对……进行了理论研究。

（2）展示现存难题

用来回答"什么还没做"，常用的介绍背景的句型有：

Great progress has been made in this field, but (however, nevertheless, etc.)...
这个领域虽然取得了很大进步，但是(尽管如此，然而等)……

Also, the consideration of… alone cannot explain the observed fact that...
同样，仅考虑……不能解释观察到的事实，即……

A part of the explanation could lie in…However...
……可以(对此)做一些解释、尽管如此，……

The kind of experiment we have in mind has not been carried out until now.
至今为止，我们想到的这类实验还没被实践过。

Until now no field experiments of… have been reported.
至今为止，……的现场实验还没有被报道过。

Not any experiment in this area has suggested that...
在这个领域还没有任何实验表明……

No clear advancement has so far been seen in...
至今为止，……中(我们)没有看到明显的进步。

（3）聚焦目前研究

用来回答"我要做什么"，常用的介绍研究工作的句型有：

This paper reportson... 本文报道了……

The primary goal of this research is…这项研究的主要目的是……

The present work deals mainly with…目前的工作主要解决……

In this paper… is investigated (studied, discussed, presented, etc.).
在本文中，……得以观察(研究、讨论、展现等)。

On the basis of existing literature data, we carried out studies in an effort to...
在现有文献数据的基础上，我们进行了致力于……的研究。

2.6 论文主体(方法、过程)

由于交通运输专业文献按内容可分为实验型(重点阐述实验)、理论型(重点阐述理论研究)和综述型(重点阐述某领域的历史、现状及发展方向)，因此论文主体也可相应分为这三大类。论文主体的逻辑展开可分为五种类型：按年代顺序展开，按研究进程展开，从抽象到具体展开，从具体到抽象展开，按其他逻辑顺序展开。论文主体常用的句型如下。

（1）描述实验方法(常采用一般过去时)

Five testers were selected at random and asked to...
随机选出五个接受实验者，并让他们……

...was measured (evaluated / weighed) through...
……通过……来进行测量(评估/称重)。

（2）理论分析(常用一般现在时)

Let us considerthe case... 让我们考虑这个情况，即……

Let d and v be… for… and…　记 d 和 v 分别为……和……
We now reduce Eq. (3) to a simpler form.　现在我们将公式(3)简化。
Substituting M in / into N, we obtain / have / get…　将 M 代入 N,我们得到……
The relationship between m and n is as follows …
m 和 n 的关系可表示为……
(3)图表文字说明(常用一般现在时)
As shown in Table / Figure 1…　如图1所示/见表1……
Table (Figure) 1 shows (provides / gives)…　表(图)1 显示(提供/给出)……
As can be seen from the data in Table (Figure) 1…　从表(图)1 中的数据可知……

2.7　结果、讨论和结论

(1)结果

写作目的:展示结果和数据并将其上升到理论高度。

写作要求:呈现的数据要有意义,揭示的结果要简短透明。

结果部分揭示研究或实验的结果,常用现在时(一般现在时,现在完成时),有时也用一般过去时。常用于结果的表达方式有:

The research we have done suggests an increase in…
我们所作的研究表明了……的增长。
This fruitful work gives an explanation of…
富有成效的工作解释了……
Our experimental data are briefly summarized as follows…
我们的实验数据可总结如下……
Figure 3 shows the results obtained from studies of…
图3 显示了从……研究中得出的结果。
Table 5 presents the data provided by the experiments on…
表5 列出了由……实验提供的数据。
This table summarized the data collected during the experiment of…
此表总结了在……实验过程中收集到的数据。
Some of the author's findings are listed in tables.
作者的一些发现列于各表中。

(2)讨论

写作目的(写作内容):分析数据,指出疑虑,解释观点,评述意义,指向结论。

写作要求:有效分析呈现的数据并指出其真实的关系,评价自己的工作成绩、坦率承认不足之处,表达要简短有力。

讨论部分陈述的是作者的见解和结论,因此常用一般现在时。常用于讨论的表达方式如下。

① 概述结果

These results provide substantial evidence for the original assumptions.
这些结果为最初的设想提供了实质性的证据。

These experimental results support the initial hypothesis that…
这些实验结果支持最初的假设,即……

The present results are consistent with those reported in our earlier work.
目前的结果和我们先前工作中报告的结果是一致的。

These results appear to refute the original assumptions.
这些结果似乎驳倒了最初的假设。

The results given in Figure 4 validate (support) the second hypothesis.
图4中给出的结果证实(支持)了第二个假设。

② 表示研究的局限性

The findings of this study are restricted to… 此项研究的发现受限于……

We should like to point out we have not… 我们应该指出我们还没有……

However, the findings do not imply… 可是,这些发现并不意味着……

Theanalysis has concerned on… 此分析聚焦于……

The findings of this study are restricted to…
此项研究的发现受限于……

This study has addressed only the question of…
这项研究仅解决了……的问题。

Unfortunately, we are unable to determine from this data…
不幸的是,从此数据,我们不能确定……

The result of the study cannot be taken as evidence for…
此研究结果不能作为……的证据。

It should be noted that this study has examined only…
值得一提的是,此研究仅调查了……

(3) 结论

写作目的:总结文章主体,综述文章结论,综述作者建议,优雅地结束全文。

写作要求:应针对引言中提到的要解决的问题及预期目标作出是非分明的回答,即与引言前后呼应;用语力求简洁明确,结论可以引用一些关键数字,但不宜过多;不要新增前文未涉及的新事实,但也不要简单重复摘要、引言结果或讨论中的内容,尤其不要重复其中的句子,应重新组织句子结构。

结论部分总结的是研究者到目前为止作了哪些工作,得出了什么结果,这些结果的意义,等等,常用现在时(一般现在时和现在完成时)。常用于结论的表达方式有:

We have demonstrated in this paper… 在这篇文章中,我们证实……

The results of the experiment indicate… 实验结果显示……

From…, we now conclude… 从……我们可以得出结论……

To sum up, we have revealed… 总之,我们揭示了……

In conclusion, the result shows… 总之,结果表明……

Wehave described…, we found… 我们记述了……,并发现……

On the basis of…, the following conclusion can be made…
基于……,(我们)可以得出如下结论……

2.8 参考文献/资料、附录

(1) 参考文献/资料

写作目的:尊重他人的劳动成果,便于文献检索。

写作要求:标注直接引用的及最主要的参考文献,注意标注标准化。标注的参考文献须是正式出版物。

参考文献写作按照编排顺序可分为两大类:一种是按参考文献作者姓名或发表年代为序;另一种是按参考文献在文中的引用先后为序。参考文献写作按照性质不同可分为六大类:专著(M)、科技期刊(J)、专利(P)、会议论文集(C)、学位论文(D)。

(2) 附录

附录部分展示的是论文需要的补充材料,但如果将其置于主体部分则会分散读者对主体的注意力。附录部分也有可能是专家需要而普通读者不需要的材料。

2.9 致谢

写作目的:表达作者(们)对资助对象的感谢。一般来说资助对象可分为两大类,一类是在经费上给予支持的,另一类是在技术、方法、条件、资料、信息等方面给予支持的。

写作要求:言辞恳切,实事求是;指出感谢的具体原因;征得被感谢人的同意。

致谢部分常用的时态为现在时(一般现在时,现在完成时)。常用的致谢表达方式有:

We wishto express our thanks to… 我们对……表示感谢。

Acknowledgments are made to…for… 感谢之情献给……,感谢他们……

Support for this program (project / study) is provided by…
此项计划(项目/研究)由……提供支持。

We thank the following people for their helpful comments on drafts of this paper:…
我们感谢以下人士……对本文草稿所提供的有益评论。

The anonymous reviewers have also contributed considerably to the publication of this paper.
匿名审稿人对本文的发表也帮助颇多。

This investigation received financial assistance from…
此项研究得到了……的经济援助。

References

[1] Baerwald, John Edward. *Transportation and Traffic Engineering Handbook*[M]. New Jersey: PrenticeHall, 1976.

[2] R. J. Salter. *Highway Traffic Analysis and Design*[M]. London: Macmillan, 1989.

[3] James L. Pline. *Traffic Engineering Handbook*[M]. Washington DC: Institute of Transportation Engineers, 1999.

[4] Mike Slinn, Arnold. *Traffic Engineering Design*[M]. Oxford: Elsevier Butterworth-Heinemann, 2005.

[5] AASHTO. *A Policy on Geometric Design of Highways and Streets*[M]. Washington DC: American Association of State Highway and Transportation Officials, 1995.

[6] National Research Council. *Highway Capacity Manual*[M]. Washington DC: Transportation Research Board, 1994.

[7] OFlaherty, Coleman Anthony. *Highways*[M]. London: Edward Arnold, 1974.

[8] Paul H. *Transportation Engineering, Planning and Design*[M]. New Jersey: Ronald Press, 1989.

[9] Steadieseifi M, Dellaert N P, Nuijten W, et al. *Multimodal freight transportation planning: A literature review*[J]. European Journal of Operational Research, 2014, 233(1):1-15.

[10] Binjammaz T A, Al-Bayatti A H, Al-Hargan A H. *Context-aware GPS integrity monitoring for intelligent transport systems*[J]. Journal of Traffic and Transportation Engineering(English Edition), 2016, 3(1):1-15.

[11] Manish Kumar Pandey, Karthikeyan Subbiah. *Social Networking and Big Data Analytics Assisted Reliable Recommendation System Model for Internet of Vehicles*[M]. Berlin: Springer International Publishing, 2016.

[12] Ekinhan Eriskin, Sebnem Karahancer, Serdal Terzi, Mehmet Saltan. *Optimization of Traffic Signal Timing at Oversaturated Intersections Using Elimination Pairing System*[J]. Procedia Engineering, 2017, 187:295-300.

[13] Anthony D. Patire, MatthewWright, BorisProdhomme, Alexandre M. Bayen. *How much GPS data do we need?*[J]. Transportation Research Part C: Emerging Technologies, 2015, 58: 325-342.

[14] QiShi, MohamedAbdel-Aty. *Big Data applications in real-time traffic operation and safety monitoring and improvement on urban expressways*[J]. Transportation Research Part C: Emerging Technologies, 2015, 58:380-394.

[15] Xinyu Zhang, Hongbo Gao, Mu Guo, Guopeng Li, Yuchao Liu, Deyi Li. *A study on key technologies of unmanned driving*[J]. CAAI Transactions on Intelligence Technology, 2016, 1(1).

[16] R. J. 索尔特. 道路交通分析与设计[M]. 张佐周,等,译. 北京:中国建筑工业出版社, 1992.

[17] AASHTO. 公路与城市道路几何设计[M]. 饶东平,译. 西安:西北工业大学出版

社,1992.

[18] 李棣荪. 土木英语[M]. 北京:中国建筑工业出版社,1995.
[19] 李嘉. 专业英语[M]. 北京:人民交通出版社,1996.
[20] 赵永平. 道路工程英语[M]. 北京:人民交通出版社,1999.
[21] 刘澜. 交通运输专业英语[M]. 成都:西南交通大学,2006.
[22] 美国交通研究委员会(TRB). 道路通行能力手册(*HCM* 2010)[M]. 任福田,等,译. 北京:人民交通出版社,2007.
[23] 邬岚. 交通工程专业英语[M]. 北京:人民交通出版社股份有限公司,2016.